MEDIA SYSTEMS
······· IN ·······
SOCIETY

MEDIA SYSTEMS
·······IN·······
SOCIETY

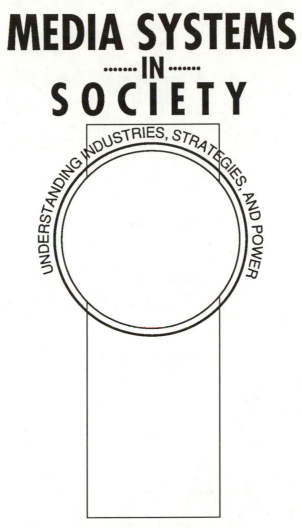

UNDERSTANDING INDUSTRIES, STRATEGIES, AND POWER

JOSEPH TUROW
The Annenberg School for Communication

University of Pennsylvania

Longman
New York & London

Media Systems in Society:
Understanding Industries, Strategies, and Power

Longman, 10 Bank Street, White Plains, N.Y. 10606

Associated companies:
Longman Group Ltd., London
Longman Cheshire Pty., Melbourne
Longman Paul Pty., Auckland
Copp Clark Pitman, Toronto

Executive editor: Kathleen Schurawich
Development editor: Virginia Blanford
Production editor: Dee Amir Josephson
Cover design: Kevin C. Kall
Cover illustration: Kevin C. Kall
Production supervisor: Joanne Jay

Library of Congress Cataloging-in-Publication Data

Turow, Joseph.
    Media systems in society : understanding industries, strategies,
and power / Joseph Turow.
        p.   cm.
    Includes index.
    ISBN 0-8013-0599-3
    1. Mass media—Economic aspects. 2. Mass media—Social aspects.
I. Title.
P96.E25T8   1991
302.23—dc20   91-24587
                                                        CIP

2 3 4 5 6 7 8 9 10-MA-959493

for my parents

Contents

List of Charts, Tables, and Talking Points

Preface

Ours is a world where traditional mass media categories sometimes get in the way of understanding. Consider the term *movie industry*. Not too many years ago, you could accurately describe a movie studio executive's job as helping to create audiovisual products for "movie theaters." Today, if a high-level Warner Brothers studio executive took to believing that he or she would probably not hold the job for long.

The reason is that nowadays "movie" executives have to calculate global production and distribution strategies with a wide variety of locations and techologies in mind. In addition to theater screens, they must think of pay per view cable, ordinary pay cable, basic cable, home video, broadcast network TV, and independent broadcasting stations. By the same token, "pay cable" firms such as Home Box Office (HBO) regularly release their productions to theaters, broadcast TV networks, and homevideo stores around the world. For people who work in Warner Bros. and HBO (both owned, incidentally, by Time Warner) the term *movie industry* begins to blur. Where does the movie industry end and the cable industry begin?

That is only one example of the category-shattering changes taking place. We live in a boundary-blurring world where executives of some of the largest corporations are involved daily in planning ways to create and distribute *stories*—news and entertainment stories—across a mind-spinning galaxy of locations, many of which they themselves own. Books are made into films, films into books. Newspaper comic characters get on greeting cards and get turned into TV shows and books. Newswork becomes the basis not only for articles in papers and magazines, but for information in lucrative data banks owned by the news firms. Entire cross-media industries get created around stars such as Michael Jackson, Madonna, and New Kids on the Block.

- How can we understand what goes on in the firms that carry out these activities?
- How can we think about the organizational, institutional, legal, political, economic, historical, and "cultural" considerations that shape the menus of choice that millions of people confront when they watch TV, read books, buy greeting cards, stare at billboards?
- What does the future hold for different mass media, why, and with what possible social consequences?

The questions raise issues that are fascinating, exciting, and important. This book addresses them and many others through a wide-ranging framework for understanding mass communication as a social and industrial process.

The ideas are a product of more than two decades of learning about, and teaching, mass communication while conducting research in many different sorts of media organizations. I was an undergraduate at the University of Pennsylvania, majoring in English and dabbling in American Studies, when I first started asking the questions listed here. I carried on the work during my graduate studies in communication at Penn, then at Purdue University for ten years, then back at Penn's Annenberg School for Communication, where I now work.

There have been many people to thank along the way—teachers, students, colleagues, and, not least, "subjects" of my research. For this book, I am particularly grateful to the late Tren Andersen, an editor at Longman and a friend, who asked me to write it. Elsa Van Bergen, Barry Cole, Dee Amir Josephson, Carolyn Marvin, Kathy Schurawich, Marsha Siefert, and Jean Ward all let me bounce ideas off them and came back with insightful comments and suggestions. Annenberg graduate students Lori Silbersweig, Nadine Cantor, Kelli D'Apice, Lynn Edwards, Maggie Williams and William Hoffman reviewed the manuscript as it evolved, offering help and frank critiques.

Judith Turow, my wife, has followed this book and many other projects from beginning to end. Her suggestions, patience, and understanding have been invaluable. As for my children, Jonathan, Marissa, and Rebecca, patience is not yet their strongest asset. Nevertheless, I thank them for distracting me from this project long enough to have other sorts of fun.

Joseph Turow

MEDIA SYSTEMS
······ IN ······
SOCIETY

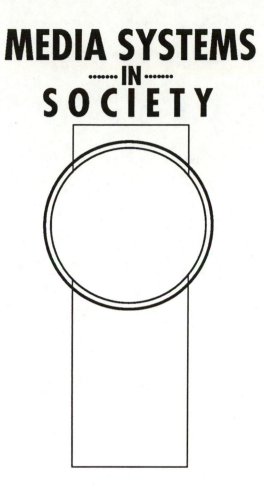

CHAPTER ONE

Mass Media Industries:
What Are They?
Why Study Them?

The 1990s are a challenging time for trying to understand American mass media. Consider some of the changes taking place:

- The three traditional television networks (ABC, CBS, and NBC) are nowhere near the powerhouse audience-grabbers they were a decade and a half ago. Whereas in the late 1970s, the networks could reliably reach nearly 90% of all Americans watching television during the evening, the early 1990s saw that figure dwindle to around 65%. Network executives are nervous that advertisers who have used network TV to reach huge segments of the population will desert them.

- Cable television, hardly a competitor to over-the-air TV in the early 1980s, has been an important factor in the broadcast networks' audience loss. While most cable channels still garner relatively small audiences according to industry surveys, services such as the ESPN sports network have been known to attract the numbers and kinds of viewers that bring in many advertising dollars and make them highly profitable.

- The Hollywood production industry (typically known as "the movie business") has been undergoing wrenching alterations and power struggles. During the late 1980s, Rupert Murdoch's Australian firm, News Corp, took over 20th Century Fox; Pathé, a French-Italian firm, bought MGM and United Artists; and Japanese electronics manufacturer Sony took over Columbia Pictures. The purchases reflect the increasing international competition for control of movies, television shows, books, and other media "products," as countries in Europe and elsewhere allow more private broadcast and cable operations—as homevideo markets surge around the world.

- Foreign incursions into U.S. media have been ringing alarm bells through the American media. Taking advantage of the low value of the dollar relative to their currencies, British, German, and French firms made substantial purchases

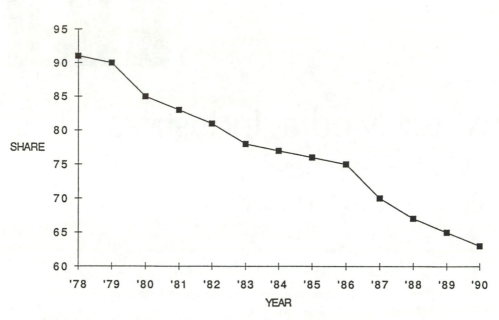

CHART 1.1   Combined Prime Time Share of ABC, CBS, and NBC 1978–1990

Since the 1970s, the Big Three networks' share of the TV viewing audience has dropped about 30%.

SOURCE: *Channels Magazine 1986 Field Guide*, p. 82; and Nielsen Media Research

in the U.S. advertising, magazine and book industries during the late 1980s. Observers worried about foreign control of American culture and the movement of corporate profits abroad. Warner Communications and Time Incorporated played on an emerging fear of these non-American international media conglomerates to stave off government attempts to stop their huge U.S.-based merger. Similarly, the American TV networks, long prevented from owning more than a small portion of the programming they air, pointed to the foreign purchases of American film studios as one reason to allow them to create as well as distribute entertainment beyond their airwaves.

• The newspaper industry has been trying to come to terms with the new electronic media environment. Major city newspapers, particularly, are seeing newspaper reading decline among younger segments of the population. New newspaper formats, and new systems of news delivery, are topics of major concern in an industry increasingly preoccupied with the need to attract a TV-oriented populace.

• The advertising and public relations industries have been affected drastically by the maelstrom of changes in the media they work with. The multiplication of cable channels, the decline of network TV audiences, the growth of specialty magazines, the growth of advertiser-supported media around the world, the explosive increase in the direct-selling business (what used to be called mail order)—these and other changes have forced advertising and PR executives to rethink the strategies they have used for decades. Their desire to use the new media to reach customers in innovative ways is sending huge tremors through media firms throughout the world.

- Adding to the brew of changes is a gamut of new technologies that confront mass media executives. Here are some:

  High-definition television (HDTV) can bring a finer and wider picture to viewing that makes today's sets seem Neanderthal by comparison.

  Liquid display tubes are being developed that can make possible wall-size images that far exceed the abilities of today's projection screen devices.

  New generations of **tape and laser disc player-recorders** can allow viewers to record and play noise-free music and video.

  Increased sophistication of **satellite technology** will soon allow international transmission of mass media materials to very small dishes on the roofs of houses.

  The spread of **fiber-optic cable** and new **signal compression technology** will expand the number of audio and visual channels that stream into the home and office. The two-way capability of the cable will allow the consumer to call up entertainment and information "banks" which access specific programs on demand.

The foregoing list of wrenching alterations and impressive possibilities could be a lot longer. Many people are involved in charting and implementing the directions of various media. Many careers hang on the success or failure of their work.

Millions and millions of people who have nothing directly to do with this work are also affected. That is because mass media industries create many of the materials people throughout society read, see, hear, touch, and even smell. Network TV comedies, newsmagazine feature stories, rock albums, comic books, scratch-and-sniff perfume ads, direct mail catalogs—these are only fragments of the environment of symbols that mass media industries release for popular consumption in the United States every day.

In fact, people's use of media materials is spectacularly common. Research on the way people spend their time reinforces the idea that a large portion of Americans' lives revolves around the mass media. In 1974, 71% of the responses a national sample of people gave when they noted a "favorite leisure activity" related directly to the media—TV watching, moviegoing, radio listening, and reading.[1] Moreover, that number is probably only the tip of a media use iceberg. It is nearly impossible to escape the output of media industries in contemporary society.

Consider "dancing," noted in 4% of the favorite leisure activities that people mentioned in 1974. Certainly, face-to-face dancing is not directly the product of a mass media industry. After all, what can be less "industrial" than two people danc-

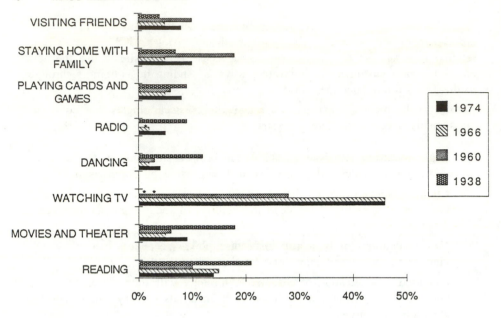

CHART 1.2   Favorite Leisure Activities Selected Years, 1938–1974

The use of various mass media has clearly been an important component of people's activities for decades. Watching television has a high place unto itself as the favorite pastime.

  * means radio received less than 1% of the responses
** indicates that television was not mentioned

SOURCE: *Social Indicators 1976* (Washington, D.C.: U.S. Government Printing Office, 1977), p. 492.

---

ing? Nevertheless, the music played during contemporary dancing is quite likely to be media-related. For one thing, it is typical for dance music (rock or otherwise) to be controlled by a music rights company, which acts as a publisher. For another, radio and records often take the place of a live band.

The aim of this book is to help you understand the way mass media industries make their way into our lives. In particular, the purpose is to give you the tools to understand the torrent of changes that are taking place—their implications for media industries themselves as well as for society at large.

The present chapter is designed to introduce various types of questions that can be asked around these concerns. Different kinds of questions encourage exploration of the workings of mass media industries in different ways. Looking at the industries from several viewpoints helps us better grasp the strategies behind their activities and the implications of the meaning of those strategies for society.

TWO PRINCIPLES

Our approach is guided by two basic principles. The first is that **mass media industries are increasingly interrelated.** Certainly, it will be useful to consider ways to understand individual mass media industries—the theatrical film and cable TV businesses, for example. For people who work with movies, however, it is often impossible to know where the movie industry ends and the cable and broadcast television industries begin. Movies that show up in theaters one month may appear on pay-per-view cable the next and on homevideo cassettes a few months after that.

To get a firm grip on how media develop and what they do in society, we must step back from a focus on one or another media industry alone. Instead, we must pay attention to the way media industries relate to one another. These interrelationships form what can be called the **media system** of a society.

The second principle that guides this book is that **in order to understand the mass media's present and future, we have to gain a broad understanding of the organizations, strategies, and power considerations that guide the creation of mass media materials.** Individual people may write particular news reports we read or direct specific movies we attend. It is of large importance, though, that those people must work with other people in their organizations to get their work completed and released to the public. Of equal importance, those organizations must interact with other organizations if the work is to be released successfully to its intended audiences. All these activities involve issues of strategy and power that go beyond the individual. They have to be understood if the process of creating and distributing materials across media industries is to make sense.

To understand the usefulness of this approach, we need only look at predictions from decades ago about what new media technologies would be like and do. In many cases the prognostications ignored the interrelationship of mass media and, especially, the organizations, strategies, and power considerations that guided the creation of media technologies and the content they released. The result was a naive approach to media policy, planning, and criticism.

PREDICTIONS, PAST AND PRESENT

Back in the mid-nineteenth century, for example, there was no shortage of discussion of how the telegraph and the railway, both startlingly new vehicles of communication, would improve society. One commentator, rapturous over the new possibilities for transmitting religious messages far and wide, proclaimed that the nation was "on the border of a spiritual harvest because thought now travels by steam and magnetic wires."[2] Another writer stated lyrically that in the future "a perfect network of electric filaments" would "consolidate and harmonize the social union of mankind" by connecting people to one another.[3]

Historians Charles and Mary Beard were among those who reflected this same **deterministic** attitude about media technology during the early twentieth century. They saw radio as one of the offsprings of electricity that would emancipate humankind, bringing education and cosmopolitanism to all.[4] They also seemed to feel that the materials carried on these channels would merely add to the glorious possibilities of the technology. They did not think it important to ask, for example, whether violent radio dramas and speeches by bigoted radio ministers could cancel out the impulses toward international interconnections and cooperation that they seemed to think were dictated by the radio technology itself.

Current Scenarios

It is easy to point out now, decades after the introduction of radio, that ignorance, wars, and parochialism still exist. Yet while we might chuckle condescendingly about the naiveté of decades past, we often do not realize that the same type of reasoning about media is taking place today. Many writings on the directions of the new technologies mentioned earlier practically glow with speculations about the great advances that can be realized when consumers begin to interconnect the new gadgets with traditional mass media and, especially, the computer.

A typical scenario might be of a college student—say, a French major—preparing for a summer trip to Europe. She might link her TV monitor via computer and cables to the public library's tape archive to view a HDTV video on the country, getting theaterlike effects at home. Or, the student might turn to the international satellite transmissions coming into her house to view the evening news on one of France's TV networks. Alternatively, a rented video disc of a recent French film (in stereo on a high-definition wall monitor) might be her choice to bone up on the language while being entertained.

To many observers such soon-to-be-commonplace experiences will be only the most obvious manifestation of deeper alterations in the way we think and relate to our environment. They foretell that the new media will inevitably bring with them sweeping economic, political, social, and cultural changes. One author predicts that the media will cause "the most total revolution that the human race has witnessed since the industrial revolution."[5]

Such writers argue that the consumer at the computer will become the ultimate programmer, creating a personal menu of choices from a huge array of entertainment and information possibilities. It is already beginning, they say. The large number of channels aimed at individuals and special interest groups available through cable television, video discs, and satellite broadcasting—a strategy called **narrowcasting**—is replacing the broadcasting of lowest-common-denominator entertainment. Years to come will see even more dramatic changes, these writers contend. The newspaper of tomorrow will consist of information selected by viewers to fit their needs and interests from data banks accessible via home computers.

In this view, social historian Daniel Pope points out, even advertising will change drastically. The new interactive media systems will encourage the use of video catalogs, allowing consumers to examine, order, and pay for products at home, thus bypassing established channels of distribution. This interactivity will place a priority on individual needs, to which marketers would have to respond as never before. Producers will allow more opportunities for communication by consumers as equals. Sellers and buyers will share the same information about needs and products and therefore share power. Advertising via the media will then be a genuinely democratic dialogue.[6]

But not all writers who spin tales about where the media will lead society are optimists. A strong contingent of pessimists has insistently voiced concerns that the hundreds of possibilities available through the onslaught of homevideo equipment, satellite dishes, cable channels, and their interaction through home computers must *diminish* the chances for organized democratic consciousness and actions. They worry that as the number of television stations and videotapes available increases, the chances for getting many people in society to learn about problems from the media, and to mobilize responses to the problems, will decrease.

The result, according to this view, is that the specialization emphasized by the new technologies will push people into their own little worlds, where they will have little appreciation for the interests and concerns of others. Consequently, Stephen Ephros, a former attorney for the Federal Communications Commission, predicts: "If my personal computer focuses on one area, and your personal computer focuses on something else, we will see what we want to see. We will not know about anything else."[7]

Another View

At first glance, it may seem difficult to know whom to believe when it comes to forecasting how new media will develop and how they will influence society. You might even be tempted to pick one view or the other depending on whether you think you are an optimist or a pessimist. But there is a third, better way: not to choose either version of the future.

This way is better because, like the futurists decades ago, neither camp takes into account the two principles set forth earlier. While they may revel in the interconnection of media technologies, they do not consider seriously the interrelationship of media *industries*. As a result, they ignore forces within the industries and the society at large that control the development of these media technologies and the materials they create—the actual movies on the laser discs, the actual data bases available through the computer, and so on. The resulting impression is that media technologies virtually spring up out of thin air and create materials in a vacuum. Not considered are the organizational, legal, and political forces that help define the actual role those media play in society from their point of conception onward.

Consider just a few of the forces buffeting the new technologies mentioned earlier:

- There exist fierce international arguments about the standards for high-definition television. These debates, coupled with the high cost of the system, may greatly delay the introduction of HDTV technology into the U.S. and world TV markets. In addition, some scientists believe that other technologies will soon surpass HDTV and that the United States should not devote substantial resources to it.
- The future of some of the most advanced methods for recording and playing music is guided more by the politics and economics of the marketplace than by quality of sound. Consider digital audio tape (DAT), mini discs, and the digital compact cassette (DCC). The first brings noise-free sound to home tape machines, though in a format not compatible with standard analog cassettes. The second, also not compatible with existing products, allows consumers to record as well as to play 74 minutes of audio on 2½ inch discs. The third, DCC, allows sound reproduction of a quality that lies between that of analog and DAT. DCC has an important advantage over DAT, though: its machine can also accommodate the existing analog tapes that most consumers own.

Each technology represents an advance in consumer electronics. That does not mean all will succeed in a consumer marketplace where analog tapes and standard compact discs (CDs) have been the favorites for several years. Recording executives fear that consumers may not want to spend the hundreds of dollars required to buy into the new formats. The recording companies themselves may well balk at having to spend the extra money required to release albums in five, rather than two or three, formats. Similarly, retailers may object to stocking the same recordings in a wide variety of formats; it takes up a lot of store space and costs a lot of money. Finally, competition between rivals over patents—Sony's mini disc versus Philip's DCC, for example—may lead firms choosing alliances to favor one format over another. All these considerations will determine the shape of home player-recorder gear more than will sheer technological possibilities.[8]

- The future of narrowcasting has to be evaluated in terms of the expense of providing media materials to very small audiences. When it comes to "network quality" movies or other entertainment materials, the cost of creating programs (over a million dollars an hour) might make narrowcasting prohibitive for very small audiences. On the other hand, producers of news, entertainment, and information (such as talk shows and travelogues) have found several ways to recoup their costs and spread their risks; these methods will be described in the course of this book. The answers that producers are formulating, depending on the materials they are creating, will guide the future of narrowcasting as much as the availability of multiple channels will.

Do not interpret the foregoing comments to mean that futuristic media will make no imprint. The new technologies may well cast large-scale impressions on society, even along lines that futurists have mentioned. Whether signs point to that happening, however, and what the social consequences might be if it does happen, are matters for intense examination and discussion. What is important to stress is that we should jump to neither optimistic nor pessimistic conclusions about the new media's implications based on a view that the social "impact" of a mass medium is built into the technology. If we want a evenhanded picture of the role that mass media technology will play in society, we should learn to look systematically at the forces shaping the development of technology, its use, and the content created for it.

That means asking a number of questions:

How are changes in media technology, in national and global politics, and in society at large affecting existing ways of working in mass media industries?

How will the menu of songs, stories, and reports available to different audiences change in the face of new media?

How will the nature of the materials themselves change?

Answering these and other questions about the present and future requires a language to talk systematically about mass media systems and industries. Such a language can help raise questions about how mass media industries operate today, how they relate to one another, and how they relate to society at large. We start our journey into the world of media organizations, strategies, and power at the very beginning: with an examination of the basic words we use, the basic process we study, and the way they link up to crucial processes in the society at large.

DEFINING MASS MEDIA AND MASS COMMUNICATION

The reason for using a term like *mass media* instead of simply naming specific items such as magazines or books is that it indicates similarities between the items. In our minds, they are grouped together, and we have chosen to call that group mass media. One advantage of having such an umbrella word, or **concept**, has to do with confronting the future. Once we understand what characteristics in these items lead us to group them together, we will have a way of deciding whether newly invented items should also be called by that word and analyzed according to similar patterns.[9]

Definitions help to make that decision. They are aids to exploring the world. As concepts, they have ideas on how to see things built into them. Those ideas, or points of view, guide us to look at certain parts of the world and not others. Definitions lead us to include particular things in our thinking, and they lead us to exclude other things. Thoughtful inclusion and exclusion often lead to innovative questions that can help us make sense of the changes that are going on around us.

Definitional issues arise all the time. In 1950, people thinking about mass media never heard of a video cassette recorder. Twenty-five years later, when VCRs were making their way into homes, writers began to casually tag them as mass media along with the more traditional forms. Were the writers correct? Are VCRs *always* mass media? If VCRs are excluded or included as mass media, what are some of the implications for an understanding of the strategies of mass media industries?

Answering these questions requires a definition of mass media. The one to be proposed here is fairly straightforward: **Mass media are the technological vehicles through which mass communication takes place**.

This definition may seem like it merely passes the buck to another term, *mass communication*. In an important sense it does. Already, though, we have begun to offer an answer to the questions about VCRs. Video cassette recorders are certainly examples of technology, and from that standpoint they fit the definition. But the definition allows that VCRs are mass media only when they are vehicles for mass communication. The key issue now is to decide what that means.

Mass communication is a concept that lies at the heart of this book. There are many definitions of mass communication. All see it as a process that involves the creation of **messages**, which are arrays of symbols that appear to be purposefully organized. In addition, conceptions of mass communication emphasize the use of technologies in the process as well as the involvement of large numbers of people.

The definition to be presented here does not necessarily cancel out or contradict other approaches. It has two purposes. One is to focus on those aspects of the process that we believe make mass communication *different* from other activities. The other is to highlight aspects of the process that we believe are the most relevant for learning about the **creation of messages**, the **use of technologies**, the **involvement of large numbers of people, and the implications** of it all.

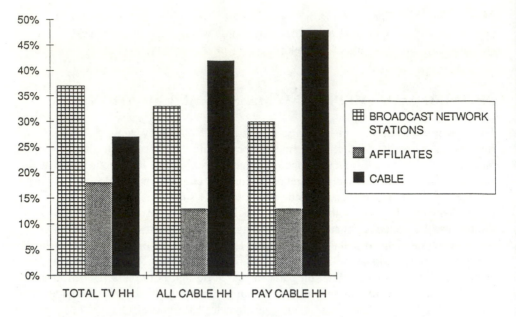

CHART 1.3 The TV Networks Lose Audiences in Households with Cable

These charts, adapted from charts created by the Cabletelevision Advertising Bureau, show in dramatic fashion how cable TV's many channels have been cutting into broadcast network TV audiences and the audiences of their affiliates.

The bars reflect the distribution of all TV viewing, throughout the week, 24 hours a day. The percentages refer to the proportion of households (HH) in which a television set is tuned to a cable station or network-affiliated broadcast station. The network bar indicates the proportion of households in which someone watched programs on ABC, CBS, or NBC during the time this study was conducted. The affiliate bar indicates the proportion of households in which viewing was taking place when the affiliates were airing nonnetwork programming. Pay cable households are those that pay for special movie or sports channels in addition to basic cable stations.

The charts indicate that when households have cable TV, and particularly when they have pay cable, the percentage with sets tuned to the networks and their affiliates declines. Such findings have been causing major dislocations among network executives, local broadcast executives in the advertising industry, and throughout the media system. One aim of this book is to lay out a framework for understanding the impact of these changes on the mass media system as well as on the rest of society.

SOURCE: *Advertising Age*, February 11, 1991, p. Cable 25.

The definition is as follows: **Mass communication is the industrialized production, reproduction, and multiple distribution of messages through technological devices.**

It should already be clear that the definition is in sync with this book's focus on media industries. This is no coincidence. What we are arguing through the definition is that mass communication's industrial nature is its most important feature.

An Industry Focus

It will be useful to clarify what we mean by industry. An **industry** is a conglomeration of organizations that work together in a regularized fashion to create and distribute products or services. So, there is the newspaper industry, the magazine industry, the billboard industry, the book industry. The industries are comprised of organizations that are involved in different phases of producing and distributing multiple copies of the messages.

In the case of newspapers, the same firms may control both the production and distribution of papers. Still, many other organizations are also strongly involved in the newspaper industry. Among them are firms that sell newsprint, wire services that sell copy, advertisers that purchase space, newsstand companies that sell the papers to the public, and truck dealers who rent or sell distribution vehicles.

Each production and distribution phase in a media industry is carried out with the use of technological devices. Radio broadcasters use audiotape recorders, compact discs, and transmitters, among other equipment; newspaper companies count word processors and delivery trucks as essential technology; and cable networks look to television cameras, videotape, and satellites for help in producing and distributing their product.

At this point, the question of whether video cassette recorders are mass media can be answered straightforwardly. Our definition emphasizes that production and distribution must be carried out by an industry in order for an apparatus to be called a mass medium. Therefore, a VCR that plays a movie created and distributed by a major film studio is certainly a vehicle of mass communication. On the other hand, a VCR that plays a program created by an individual or small group for distribution by hand to neighborhood friends and co-workers would not be considered a mass medium. Similarly, a TV set used for closed-circuit television presentations created by a company for its employees would not be considered a mass medium. In the last two cases, the VCR and TV are involved in an activity that uses technology for group communication or organizational communication, not mass communication.

Some people might find reason to argue with this distinction; controversies are almost inevitable with every definition of mass communication. At the same time, the definition expands the scope of our inquiry by directing us to consider as mass media a wide range of products that have not been tagged this way. Greeting cards, toys— even computer word processors—can under certain conditions of production and distribution be considered mass media. To say that is not to deny that these products can be grouped under other concepts. Toys might also be termed part of the recreation industry, for example. What we are doing here is applying a **mass communication perspective** to these activities. It highlights the aspects of the phenomena that are involved in the industrialized production, reproduction, and distribution of messages through technological devices.

A Mass Communication Perspective

The mass communication perspective can help us see the world around us in a new light and ask new questions. Consider, for example, the point we stressed earlier about mass media industries being increasingly interrelated. Looking at various phenomena from this point of view leads us to pay attention to the variety of industries that messages might cross, not all of them typically thought of as mass media. A character created for a cartoon—say, Donald Duck—might also find distribution in a TV program, on a video cassette, as a toy, in a magazine, and on an ice cream bar.

Notice the emphasis on production and distribution in the previous paragraphs. Unfortunately, people who discuss mass communication often ignore distribution. To neglect distribution, however, is to pass over a critically important aspect of the mass communication process. Often, in fact, it is expertise in the industrialized distribution of messages through technological devices that determines the power of various players in a mass media industry.

To illustrate, consider what would happen if you tried to be a publisher of a trade book—a work aimed at general readers that is typically sold in bookstores. If you have a laser printer and a computer with a "desktop publishing" program, it will not be difficult to make the pages look like a typical trade book. All you have to do is take the handsome camera-ready manuscript (or just the computer disk) to a photocopy shop. The photocopy shop can use fine paper and will probably be able to bind the copied pages in a respectable manner. A bindery, though more expensive, can give you a product that is almost indistinguishable from a volume you might find in a store. If you are willing to spend more money, you might have an artist design a jacket which the bindery will attach to each copy.

Realize, then, that the major difference between your publishing activity and that of major publishers such as Random House and Simon & Schuster does not lie in production. One person with the cash to pay a photocopy store and perhaps a bindery can create a product that can compete favorably in looks, and possibly in content, with something that professional publishers might turn out. Rather, it is in distribution that the fundamental distinction between a sophisticated publishing organization and a first-time operation shows itself.

As a distributor, you might want to plant your home-grown books in the B. Dalton national bookstore chain. Chances are, however, that B. Dalton's buying agents will have nothing to do with you; neither will most bookstores around the United States. Shelf space is too valuable for them to take a chance on an unknown writer from an unknown publisher. You could try to sell your book by hawking it on street corners, and perhaps you would sell a few copies. On the other hand, Random House would likely have a much easier time placing your book. The reason is that Random House has a reputation with bookstore firms of choosing books that will sell. Bookstores also assume that Random House will promote its books to help them move off the shelves.

Distribution clout within the media system is often an important by-product of distribution clout within a mass media industry. As a first-time publisher, you would have the slimmest chance of getting your work adopted by a book club or, better still, by a movie company and a TV production firm. Random House, by contrast, has a strong reputation as a releaser of books suitable for book clubs, movies, and TV. Excerpts in magazines and newspapers are also standard fare for such a large publisher.

CONNECTING MASS COMMUNICATION TO SOCIETY

The example just presented illustrates a crucial point about the mass communication process: It has the potential to distribute the same message to millions, even billions, of people. Note the word *potential*. A media industry may produce and distribute materials that may reach relatively few individuals. That may be purposeful, as when a newspaper is directed to only a couple of thousand people. It may be unplanned, as when a trade book that a publisher had high hopes for fails to move off the shelves. It is important to stress, though, that while mass media may not always reach the largest possible audiences, reaching huge populations within a relatively short period is impossible without the coordination of technologies by a variety of specialized organizations. Pursuing this point a bit deeper will lead us to yet another set of important questions to explore, this time about the connection of mass media to the larger society.

Live Aid

It might be useful to start with an example. A striking case where specialized technologies and large organizations were used to reach large populations is the Live Aid concert that was mounted in 1985 to benefit victims of an African famine. The concert was the idea of one person, British rock musician Bob Geldof. His goal was as intimidating as the need was grave: to mobilize tens of millions of people around the world to contribute money for relief efforts.

Geldof enlisted the talents of music impresario Bill Graham and producer Michael Mitchell. They realized quickly that they needed a lot of help to realize Geldof's goal. First, they had to create an organization that could command the support of other organizations from media industries around the world. Locations for the benefit had to be scouted and arranged; talent agencies had to be approached to coordinate the appearance of their clients; broadcasting firms throughout the world had to be contacted in the hope they would carry the concert live; satellite facilities and other telecommunications equipment had to be rented or borrowed; facilities and logistics for collecting and utilizing donations had to be planned—all this and more had to take place before, during, and after the concert of stellar performers was beamed live from Wembley Stadium, London, and JFK Stadium, Philadelphia.

It was, it turned out, a monumental technological and organizational achievement. Donations of time, facilities, and energy came from corporations, celebrities, even sailors of the Philadelphia Navy Yard. They helped Geldof and friends pull off what proved to be the most complicated live broadcast ever mounted. Fourteen satellites were used to link JFK with Wembley and the world. When it was all over (with remarkably few glitches), journalists reported that Live Aid stood to make as much as $50 million dollars and that, more astonishingly, an estimated 1.5 billion people were able to watch the show.[10]

While the sheer size of the potential viewing audience was mind-boggling, its diversity was at least as amazing. People from 150 countries as far-flung as Iceland and Ghana tuned into world-class rock groups. They also listened to internationally known political figures—from Bishop Desmond Tutu of South Africa to Indian Prime Minister Rajiv Gandhi—deliver prerecorded messages on world hunger. "We're using television to catalyze the world," said Mitchell before the concert. That was certainly an exaggeration. Still, Live Aid was the closest that one broadcast had ever come to trying to do just that.[11]

The Sharing of Messages

Ten years before Live Aid, technological drawbacks would have made such instantaneous international sharing of messages unthinkable. Even today, this kind of event is rare, for monetary and political reasons that we will explore in Chapter 9. Within technologically developed countries such as the United States, however, linking large numbers of people to share the same materials virtually instantaneously has become routine for the broadcast television, radio, and cable TV industries. Just as significant is the sharing that takes place relatively more slowly when newspapers, magazines, books, movies, billboards, and other mass media diffuse their messages across society.

Because of mass communication, millions of people within the United States who are anonymous to and separated physically from one another have the possibility of receiving the same messages within a fairly short period of time. This everyday situation holds profound implications for the way we think about the world around us. For one thing, it means that huge, geographically dispersed populations can focus on the same issues at around the same time. So, for example, people around the country can watch and read the same news reports about a presidential campaign while the campaign is taking place.

This sharing of messages does not mean that people share the same understanding of the messages; nor does it mean they agree with the messages. It hardly needs stressing that notions of preferred ways to behave come from many areas of society, including the family, the church, and the school. What is shared, then, are depictions of the world, and these depictions are presented more broadly and more quickly through mass media than through any other vehicles of communication.

A major upshot of this sharing is that mass media create the subjects that are grist for our everyday conversation mill. Because of mass communication, individuals have a common opportunity to develop opinions about the same messages. The ideas that people come into contact with in print, on the radio, on records, and on TV become a springboard for discussions, and arguments, with others. The talk may be ignited by anything—news, other types of nonfiction, advertising, and fictional materials such as movies and TV sitcoms. We should not assume, in fact, that news is necessarily the most common media-generated conversation piece. We can all think of how soap operas and prime time TV shows have often ignited everyday talk with friends, relatives, and work colleagues.

Some topics are covered so intensely by so many media that they take on a special importance as conversation pieces, if only to enable people to argue about whether so much attention ought to be devoted to the subjects. Mass media researchers call this process **agenda setting**. Fictional materials sometimes are raised to such significance. Special TV presentations, such as the *Roots* and *Holocaust* miniseries,

are just two examples. On a daily basis, though, nonfiction is most obviously involved in agenda setting.

Igniting Anger and Action

Agenda setting happens, for example, when all three national network news broadcasts and the front pages of major newspapers deal over several weeks with drug
addiction, Middle East wars, South African riots, American struggles over abortion,
and the baseball World Series. Viewers and readers might talk with others, even act
toward others, as if these were to be considered the most nationally and internationally critical of subjects.

**A corrollary to the importance of mass media in setting discussion agendas
is that they sometimes ignite people to anger and action.** When individuals use the
mass media, they are often aware that many others are confronting the same material.
Moreover, many people believe, correctly or incorrectly, that the mass media materials
they dislike have the ability to affect readers or viewers in harmful ways. People have
accused those who create news and nonnews materials of encouraging or reinforcing a
multitude of social ills—violence, rape, illiteracy, rampant consumerism, insulting and
depersonalizing advertising, political noninvolvement, cultural imperialism, and more.
The claims have led to vigorous social debates, many of which have themselves been
aired through one or another mass medium. Imagine a conservative religious minister
who is horrified to read in the local newspaper and see on statewide TV news
programs that a gubernatorial candidate's unwavering "pro-choice" position on abortion is increasing contributions to the candidate's primary campaign substantially. The
minister is additionally angered by what he feels is the press's characterization of
"pro-lifers" as fanatics. At the same time, the director of Planned Parenthood in the
same town might be elated with the widespread news that the liberal candidate's
popularity in the state has been helped by her stance on abortion. Both the minister
and the Planned Parenthood director may feel that the appearance of the story on the
newspaper's front page signals an important development in the primary, since it
focuses the attention of many people on the issue. That evaluation may cause them to
try to gain media attention for their own particular points of view. It may also lead
them to try to raise funds for their causes during this period when the issue has
garnered especially high visibility.

Clearly, the reactions by the minister and the Planned Parenthood director are
peculiar to their interests and their backgrounds. Notice, though, that both are responding to depictions by the newspaper of parts of the world that they cannot know
first hand. Notice, too, that they are drawing conclusions about the social action they
should take as a result of a news report about large numbers of people whom they do
not know, do not necessarily agree with, but with whom they feel linked politically
and economically.

Shaping Notions of Society

We typically use the word **society** to refer to large numbers of individuals, groups,
and organizations that see themselves linked politically and economically. One larger

point of the minister and Planned Parenthood tale, then, is that **mass media continually help shape people's understanding of the elements that make up their society**. Mass media do that by suggesting what individuals, groups, and organizations should care about politically and economically, and why. Mass media also tell people what others think of them, and they tell individuals what people "like themselves" think of others. Finally, mass media shape people's conceptions of their society by directing their attention toward certain concerns and away from others, leading people to consider what, if anything, they ought to do about the concerns.

Doing all that, mass media systems take on the powerful role of an **institution** in society. Other institutions include the military, education, medicine, and law. As these examples suggest, an institution is a loose-knit set of organizations that exercise authority over key aspects of life. Whereas medicine covers health care concerns and the law sees the formal rules in society as its domain, the mass media institution has as its territory the depiction of these and all other institutions. The mass media, in short, portray the life of society *to* society.

Many people accept the media presentations as "common sense," or "the way it is," for others, if not for them. But for some the media images underscore what is at stake in the battle over society's self-definition. The media images lead them to want to place their version of society alongside the others in the media, to call attention to themselves, and to gain legitimacy for their cause.

Far from being transmitters of passively accepted images, then, mass media are platforms for arguments about the patterns of beliefs and activities in society, what can be called its **culture.** A key reason for studying mass media systems, then, is to understand this process of **cultural argumentation** and its relationship to conflicts over beliefs and activities elsewhere in the society.

A galaxy of fascinating and important questions flow out of this realization, several of which are mentioned here:

What considerations shape the materials that different mass media create?

What factors cause certain parts of the media system to link up with one another more than with others?

How do other institutions in American society relate to different mass media? For example, do physicians concerned about their public image encourage major organizations within the medical institution to influence medicine's images via various mass media? If so, how is this attempt at influence carried out, and to what extent is it successful?

How, in general, do mass media relate to centers of power in society?

How might we understand the influence of the many "pressure groups" outside the media on media personnel?

What is the role of the audience in all this, and what part does it play in encouraging change or continuity in various forms of mass media materials? How, too, do the interests of international audiences and governments affect the creation and distribution of material?

TABLE 1.1. Channel Capacity of Existing Cable Systems As of April 1, 1990

Channel Capacity	Subscribers	% of Total
54 and over	11,677,066	24.02
30–53	31,765,994	65.34
20–29	3,540,389	7.29
13–19	180,199	0.37
6–12	638,207	1.313
5 only	5,901	0.013
under 5	1,333	0.003
Not available	804,350	1.66
Total	**48,613,439**	**100%**

By 1990, nearly 90% of all cable subscribers received 30 or more channels. Because of new technologies, observers predict that in the 1990s the number of channels people get in their homes will multiply several fold. What will be the consequences of this increase for the way society talks to itself and looks at itself?

SOURCE: *Television & Cable Factbook, 1990 Edition* (Washington, D.C.: Warren Publishing, 1990), p. C-332.

THE PLAN OF THIS BOOK

The following pages are designed to help you explore answers to these and many other questions about mass media systems in society. Later chapters will explore the systems' processes as they relate to key activities that occur within and across media boundaries. Finance and support; the distribution and exhibition of media materials; government regulation; public advocacy groups; the nature of the audience and its importance; the day-to-day work of writers, directors, actors, book editors, journalists, and other production personnel; their various subcultures and hiring patterns; the risks media executives find in encouraging both continuity and change—these and other topics will be discussed and interconnected through a great number of examples from around the media world.

The emphasis will be on American mass media, but the framework developed here is applicable to all sorts of media systems. If your goals are to be a media manager, you will find challenging perspectives for understanding how media operate and interrelate, perspectives that will help you address even mass media that do not exist yet. If your interests lie primarily in becoming a more aware consumer of media materials, the approach here is aimed at leading you to see your environment of symbols in fresh ways. The subject is important and exciting. Read on.

NOTES

1. *Social Indicators, 1976.* (Washington D.C.: U.S. Government Printing Office, 1977) p. 492.
2. Gardner Spring, quoted in James Carey and James Quirk, "The History of the Future." In G. Gerbner, L. Gross, and W. Melody (eds.), *Communications Technology and Social Policy* (New York: Wiley, 1973), p. 488.
3. Carey and Quirk, p. 492.
4. Carey and Quirk, p. 489.
5. Teresita Hermano, quoted in Michael Traber (ed.), *The Myth of the Information Revolution* (London: Sage Publications, 1986), p. 1.
6. Daniel Pope, *The Making of Modern Advertising* (New York: Basic Books, 1983), pp. 295–296.
7. Stephen Ephros, quoted in Martin Koughan, "The State of the Revolution, 1982," *Channels* 1 (December 1981–January 1982), p. 70.
8. See Jeff Clark-Meads and Susan Nunziata, "Philips Reveals Details of DCC Launch," *Billboard*, February 16, 1991, p.1; and Susan Nunziata, "Sony Launching New Disc Format," *Billboard*, May 25, 1991, p. 1.
9. For more on this subject, see Joseph Turow, "A Mass Communication Perspective on Entertainment Industries," in J. Curran and M. Gurevitch (eds.), *Culture, Society, and the Media*, 2nd ed. (London: Methuen, 1992); Joseph Turow, "Media Industries, Media Consequences: Rethinking Mass Communication," in J. Anderson, ed., *Communication Yearbook* (Newberry Park, CA: Sage Publications, 1990); Joseph Turow, "The Critical Importance of Mass Communication as a Concept," in B. Ruben and L. Lievrow (eds.), *Information and Behavior* (New Brunswick, NJ: Transaction Books, 1990), pp. 9–20; Joseph Turow, "The Challenge of Inference in Interinstitutional Research on Mass Communication," *Communication Research*, 18:2 (April 1991) 222–239; and Joseph Turow, "Cultural Argumentation and the Mass Media: A Perspective for Research," *Communication*, 8:2 (Autumn 1985) 139–164.
10. "Rock Around the World: Live Aid Was the Biggest Charity Extravaganza Ever," *Newsweek* July 22, 1985, pp. 56–58.
11. "Banding Together for Africa," *Newsweek* July 15, 1985, p. 52.

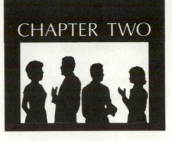

CHAPTER TWO

Power Roles:
A Framework for Strategic Thinking

Mass communication is, above all else, a process that involves organizations and industries. Thinking strategically about the present and future of mass communication therefore requires an understanding of what organizations and industries are, how they operate, and how they relate to society at large. This chapter introduces the concepts required to gain such understanding. Building on these concepts, it presents a "power role framework" as a way to explore considerations that shape the creation and distribution of mass media materials.

A CRUCIAL IDEA

A crucial idea lies at the core of the framework: **The creation, distribution, and exhibition of mass media materials is essentially a struggle by organizations over a broad range of society's resources**.

To grasp what is meant by this struggle, it is useful to think a bit about what an **organization** is and what it needs. An organization may be described as **an activity system that is goal-directed and boundary-maintaining**.[1]

The term *activity system* means that as members of an organization individuals carry out certain patterns of behaviors in relation to one another. All the work that goes on within The Chicago Tribune Company to create, distribute, or plan its broad array of media operations (from a daily Chicago newspaper to national TV syndication) comprises the activity system of that organization.

Goal-directed refers to the idea that the members of the organization typically act as if it has one or more goals. People who work for a newspaper company, for example, direct their work toward the creation of one or more daily newspapers. An observer would probably have no trouble figuring out that getting the paper out on time is an important goal.

There may well be other goals, and they may conflict with one another. Generating an unimpeachably accurate product may conflict with the paper's timely appearance, for example. Even with these conflicts, the outside observer should be able to infer that the members of the organization are not merely aimless.

Use of the word *members* raises another defining feature of organizations, the idea that they are *boundary-maintaining*. This phrase indicates that some people are allowed to participate in the organization whereas others are excluded. Chicagoans cannot walk off the street to work on the next day's *Chicago Tribune*. Guards in the Tribune building would likely prevent people without permission from gaining access to the editorial floors. Anyone who insisted on entering might get arrested.

At base, then, an organization needs the wherewithal to keep itself intact and carry out the activity system that helps it accomplish certain goals. That is where **resources** come in. Resources are the people, supplies, information, services, and money that an organization must use to carry out its tasks. No mass media organization can possibly create all the resources it needs from scratch. Instead, the organization must try to get those resources from outside its boundaries, that is, from its **environment**.[2]

It is the environment that provides people for recruitment into the organization; supplies used in the performance of organizational activities; required information, permission, and services to help gain the acceptability, or permissibility, of its activities in that environment; and money to pay for it all. At the same time, it is to the environment that the organization directs products of its activity system, often to exchange those products for resources, or to gain money to purchase other resources elsewhere.

It should be clear that resources are not randomly distributed throughout the environment. Rather, they are concentrated in various areas of the environment and often under the control of other organizations. Consider, as an example, just a few of the resources The Chicago Tribune Company must acquire to operate only its newspaper business. Clearly, money must be found. Reporters, editors, business managers, delivery drivers, press workers, receptionists, and other personnel must be hired. Paper, photographic film, ink, and other exhaustible materials must be bought. Delivery trucks have to be maintained and fueled. Telephone and newswire services must be purchased.

Other requirements may not be as transparent, but they are necessary to the survival and growth of the Tribune Company. For example, the newspaper organization needs law firms to protect and defend its ongoing activities. It needs lobbyists to protect its interests in government circles. It needs advertising and public relations companies to encourage target audiences to buy its product and enhance its reputation. It needs consulting firms to help its executives make decisions about the direction of the company—whether to buy other newspapers, whether to continue branching out into nonnews operations, what to do with other media properties, and how to arrange those deals.

In other words, the Tribune organization must rely on entities in its environment for resources. Moreover, those entities might demand substantial recompense for their help. This will be especially true if other organizations are trying to compete for the same resources, or even if they are simply trying to block that firm from obtaining resources. The Tribune Company must consequently cope with such demands by exchanging its own resources or dealing with its needs in other ways, such as reducing them.

UNDERSTANDING POWER

Here we arrive at the concept of **power** in interorganizational relations. Power involves the use of resources by one organization in order to gain compliance by another organization. An example of the exercise of power is a truckers' union that refuses to allow its members to deliver a news company's daily papers unless the firm agrees to pay them a higher salary. The union in this case is relying on the importance of a resource it controls—distribution personnel—to gain the firm's compliance.

Not all exercises of power are so obvious. In many situations, the most effective influence is the kind where the people being influenced do not even realize it. That happens when personnel in the more powerful organization or group of organizations are able to shape the structure of relationships so that the affected parties see the situation as "common sense" or simply "the way things are." A typical way for a company to exercise such **structural power** is for its personnel to ensure that laws governing their industry benefit their firm. The rules of day-to-day industry interactions would therefore carry the imprint of that firm's power, though many who deal with the company would not remember that.

This example along with the one about the union can give but a hint of the broad-ranging interorganizational struggle over resources that guides the production and distribution of mass media material. In developing a way to examine this struggle in more detail, we can locate the exercise of power in resource-controlling relationships that certain organizations hold vis à vis other organizations. So, for example, certain firms in the record industry have developed power over the creation of product, while others hold resources that allow them to excel at distribution. Still other companies may be involved in both the production and distribution processes.

Such resource-controlling relationships can be termed **power roles.** A first step understanding a media industry, then, is to generate a vocabulary that allows for systematic discussion about a wide range of power roles in media industries. That done, it should be possible to identify actual organizations in those roles that are struggling over resources with organizations that have taken on the same or different power roles. Then questions can be asked about the way those interorganizational activities affect the messages that are created and distributed to target audiences.

A POWER ROLE FRAMEWORK

A framework for accomplishing the first step is presented in Table 2.1. It is based on a scheme developed by communication researcher George Gerbner.[3] Note that each power role an organization might take on is characterized by a label for the role and

TABLE 2.1. The Power Roles of a Mass Media Industry

Power Role*	Typical Activities	Leverage
1. Producer	Create material for release to the public via mass media. Set and supervise content and selection guidelines.	Control over people and ideas that might get exposure to the public via mass media.
2. Authority	Provide government (or governmentally sanctioned) regulation and arbitration among other power roles.	Political and military power.
3. Investor	Contribute money in anticipation of production and purchase of material by clients. Set general conditions for the supply of capital and operating funds.	Control over monetary resources.
4. Client	Make organizational purchases in support of specific products. Contribute to producers' most direct cash flow in exchange for media material created.	Control over monetary resources.
5. Auxiliary	Provide material supplies to producers.	Control over access to supplies.
6. Creator	Provide producer with talent to conceive and arrange mass media material.	An individual creator's decision to join a production organization.
7. Union	Regulate the provision of personnel to producers. Set work standards; provide worker protection.	Solidarity and threats of work stoppage.
8. Distributor	Select and coordinate dispersal of material to the point of exhibition.	Control over channels by which material can reach exhibition.
9. Exhibitor	Offer material for public viewing or purchase.	Control over outlets through which the public chooses materials.
10. Linking pin	Move completed mass media material or people representing that material from production firms in one industry to production firms in another industry.	Control over access to new markets, new possibilities.
11. Facilitator	Help production firms carry out or evaluate mass media material.	Control over intermediary services.
12. Public advocacy	Demand favorable attention, portrayal, policy support.	Pressure through boycott, appeal to authorities.
13. Public	Purchase and/or attend to distributed messages in an unorganized fashion.	An individual decision to choose or not choose particular content. An individual decision to complain through legal or other channels.

*All but the *creator* and *public* power roles are typically carried out by organizations. See text for further details.

the typical activities that describe it. Also listed in the table is each power role's leverage in the industry. An organization's leverage is the resources it can use to gain compliance from other organizations. An organization taking on the authority power role, for example, may be able to marshall resources of the legislative system and the police to enforce its will on producers.

The descriptions in Table 2.1 make it clear that the framework revolves around the **producer** power role. Of chief concern is the way organizations taking on different roles within a media industry influence the amount or nature of mass media materials created for release to the public. Organizations acting as **distributors, exhibitors, clients, unions**, and the rest sometimes involve themselves in actions that have no impact on mass media producers. They all pay bills to the electric company, for example. Here, however, the concern is only with activities by them that may affect the output of an organization taking on the producer power role.

The power role framework charts activities and lines of leverage between organizations. That is, it is essentially an **interorganizational** scheme. Nevertheless, two power roles in Table 2.1—**creators** and **publics**—are included because of their importance even though they cannot by their very concepts be filled by any organizations. As the descriptions in the table indicate, creators and publics are by definition unorganized. Creators are people who make individual decisions about lending their talents to production firms. Publics do not even join organizations. They are consumers who, individually or (at most) in scattered small groups, make decisions about whether to buy a book, subscribe to a magazine, or watch a particular TV program.

Clearly, decisions by individual consumers have important implications for a producer's ability to survive. Directly or indirectly, publics provide a crucial resource, money. Still, it is worth stressing that when individuals go beyond making these kinds of yes/no decisions or registering individual complaints, they are not acting as publics any more, according to this scheme. Rather, when consumers band together to affect production, distribution, or exhibition choices, they are acting as organizations that hold the public advocacy power role. Similarly, creators who band together take on the union power role.

Taking On Power Roles

The language about organizations *taking on* power roles is purposeful. It is important to stress that organizations are not in themselves power roles. Rather, they carry out role-related activities. This means that organizations can take on more than one role within a mass media industry. Firms acting as producers, for example, can also be distributors and exhibitors. The ability to do that can increase an organization's power within a mass media industry, as will soon become apparent.

The power role scheme sees mass media industries as systems—that is, as organizational forces that interact continually to accumulate and exert influence over production. Exploring the elements of the industry systems in greater detail will reveal how the industries relate to one another to create the larger mass media system in society. The following sections of this chapter begin this exploration. The focus is on specific influences that organizations in various power roles exert over mass media content.

To keep the scope manageable, the sections will draw examples from mass media industries in the United States alone. The aim is not to present exhaustive descriptions of activities and leverages associated with these roles. In fact, several especially powerful roles will be introduced rather briefly, since later chapters will treat them at length. Roles that take up less attention later in the book, or roles that must be described in some detail now in order to develop key points later, will receive somewhat disproportionate attention in this chapter. The tack, then, is to set up avenues for further analysis and generalization.

THE PRODUCER ROLE

The producer is the central power role in this interorganizational scheme. Producers in a mass media industry must compete with one another for resources. How fierce the competition is between particular production firms depends to a large extent on the similarity of their goals and activities. The more alike two companies are in what they make and how they make it, the more fierce their competition is likely to be. The reason is that the producers would be competing for very similar, and by nature scarce, resources. The more difficult (or "expensive") it is to procure resources, the greater the likely competition.

An Example from Book Publishing

Take two publishing firms. Executives of both decide to produce an expensive title—a large "coffee table" book on candle making. Moreover, executives of both firms decide that the best way to market the title is through bookstores. Here are grounds for competition. Grounds for even fiercer competition might be imagined.

Suppose that to make a good profit the firms must convince the top five national book outlets to carry their products. Suppose, further, that each chain will carry only one such candle-making title. In other words, a key resource—exhibition service— would be highly concentrated. Or suppose that the number of people interested in buying expensive books on candle making in bookstores is smaller than the number of books the two publishers must sell to make a profit. That is, the **environmental capacity** is lean from the standpoint of another key resource—the public's money. Both of these situations would increase competition between the two publishing firms.

Competition would be *reduced* if the companies did not have similar goals and activities—for example, if they chose different kinds of books to create and sell. Similarly, competition would lessen if the environment's distribution resources were less concentrated and if a larger public willing to buy the book could be found. One way this might happen is if one of the publishers decided to use book club rather than bookstore channels to reach potential customers. The book club strategy would allow the firm to use different outlets from its competition. That would provide a group of potential customers who might be quite different from bookstore browsers.

Let us assume that both publishers decide to produce only coffee table hobby books on candle making, car repair, and flower arranging. One publisher aims at the bookstore market while the other aims at the book club arena. Under such circumstances, one can say that each publisher had its own rather specialized **niche** within the book industry. The concept of niche refers to a distinct combination of resources that can support organizations with similar goals, boundaries, and activities.[4] Generally, when one production firm perceives a niche, attempts to exploit it, and thrives, other firms enter to compete in the niche.

Competition over Niches

In the newspaper business, an example of a much-contested niche is the suburban audience. In many areas of the United States, the growth of upper-middle-class suburbs during the 1950s and 1960s provided fertile ground for small daily and weekly papers to grow and prosper. The growth of that niche often meant the loss of resources for urban papers, as advertisers pursued their prime audiences into the suburbs. When the big city papers counterattacked, it was by expanding into the suburban niches themselves. Sometimes they did it by increasing coverage of the suburbs in the main paper, sometimes by creating special zoned editions. In some regions the strategy worked better than in others. Sometimes it backfired. One suburban paper, Long Island's *Newsday*, became so powerful that in the late 1980s it began to challenge New York City papers for the resources of their own niche.

The growth of the suburbs is a case where the resources of a niche were created through geographic movement. A case where resources were created through the changing nature of people in the population can be seen in the development of periodicals for Americans 55 years and older. This group was a growing, increasingly affluent segment of the U.S. population during the 1980s. A magazine market that offered *Modern Maturity* to them early in the decade included by the late 1980s *Modern Maturity, Longevity, Second Wind, Renaissance, Lifewise, Memories, McCall's Silver Edition, 50+, Mature Outlook*, and *Grandparents*, among others.

Executives in magazine publishing firms perceived that with increased longevity and burgeoning pension funds, a new resource became available to them—upscale people over 55 who were attractive to magazine advertisers and who might subscribe to magazines that discussed their interests and problems. As a result, the several magazines mentioned came into being.

Organizations stop competing in a niche (or go broke) when they no longer find it profitable. To survive in a crowded environment, producers might try to broaden or narrow the conceptions of their niche to take advantage of resources others are not pursuing. Titles such as *Grandparents, Memories*, and *Longevity* show that their publishers were trying to carve out special niches within the broad arena that advertisers call the "mature market." The positioning was designed to attract mature readers with specific interests as well as advertisers interested in paying to reach them.

As this example indicates, niche is a slippery concept. It is not at all obvious where one niche ends and another begins. For example, did *Longevity* and *Lifewise* really share the same niche with *Modern Maturity*? Or did they more properly seek the same resources as magazines such as *American Health* and cable channels such as Lifetime?

The answer is that the description of a niche is negotiated territory. How a magazine company sets itself off from competition, argues the value of its existence, and seeks the resources it needs depends to a large extent on how organizations and publics that provide it with resources are willing to see it. This point directs our attention to organizations and groups that hold other power roles by virtue of their ability to supply resources to, and withold resources from, the producers.

THE AUTHORITY ROLE

One of those power roles is that of authority. It involves regulating the other roles within a mass media industry. Simply put, authorities are governments. The most important resource they provide is permission—permission to publish, permission to broadcast, permission to film and record. Authorities can provide other resources as well:

> **Information** on the society or the world that production firms might find impossible or too expensive to bring together by themselves
>
> **Tax benefits** that might improve the cash flows of production firms
>
> **Training programs** to supply personnel

Of course, authorities can also withold these resources. Such broad abilities, plus the political and military leverage to enforce decisions, make organizations taking on the authority role important for mass media organizations to have on their side. Authorities set the ground rules for the activities that go on in mass media industries.

The term *authority* covers a wide and complicated territory. It refers to various levels of government—federal, state, county, city. It also refers to several types of organizations—courts, legislatures, executive agencies, police. The different types of government arms are involved in setting policies, drawing up regulations, interpreting them, and enforcing them. These arms are found at all levels of government, and the different levels might have different jurisdictions over mass media industries. So, for example, licenses to broadcast commercial television signals in all communities across the nation are issued and regulated at the federal level by the Federal Communications Commission (FCC). By contrast, franchises for cable systems are granted at the state and/or local (city-county) level, with the understanding that those authorities adhere to minimum FCC guidelines. Similarly, expectations about the kind of material that can

---

Talking Point 2.1   A Newspaper Tries a New Niche

Mass media production firms are continually searching for ways to increase their revenues, and that sometimes means trying to identify and exploit new niches. An example
is The New York Times Company, which tried to expand the market for its news in a
novel way. Executives of the firm were aware that their use of satellites to print editions
of *The New York Times* around the United States on the same day was making their
product increasingly a truly national newspaper of record. That kind of timeliness was
not available in other countries, especially in the Far East, where even with shipment by
air the *Times* was arriving long after its release in the United States.

   Times executives reasoned that they had a new niche, that influential executives and
politicians in the Far East would pay to receive the paper when their counterparts in New
York, Chicago, and Los Angeles did. The most cost-efficient way to begin, they concluded, was through a facsimile service—sending synopses of the *Times* by phone lines
to fax machines in the Far East. The service, begun in 1990, was called *TimesFax* and
consisted of six to eight letter-sized pages of material gleaned nightly from the next
morning's issue of the *Times* and transmitted from New York about 10:00 P.M. That
schedule would make it available in midmorning to Tokyo subscribers.

   When the new service was announced, executives said the publication would include
a summary of articles that appear on the front page of the *Times* and articles on
international news, U.S. news, and business news. It was also to include some editorial
commentaries and columns by business writers. It is possible that *TimesFax* represented a
relatively low-cost attempt to test the Far East waters. Perhaps *Times* executives wanted
to determine if the new niche justified building a printing plant in the region that, with
the aid of a satellite, could reproduce the entire paper instantly from New York.

SOURCE: *The New York Times*, November 11, 1989.

---

be carried on a local television station are found broadly in FCC documents; local
complaints about programming are evaluated on a case-by-case basis at the federal
level. On the other hand, expectations about the kind of material that can or should be
carried on a channel originating from a cable system are generally a nonfederal affair,
though federal laws might prevent state or local authorities from prohibiting certain
programming.

Three Levels of Regulation

Authorities may be said to regulate mass media industries on three levels: structural,
technical, and content. The **structural** level involves rulings that dictate actual organizational processes and relationships in a mass media industry. One example is the
decision by Congress in 1919 that broadcasting should be a commercial enterprise
rather than a government monopoly.[5] An example narrower in scope was a 1945
decision by the United States Supreme Court that encouraged competition between
newspapers. The decision struck down an Associated Press bylaw that permitted the
wire service to grant exclusive service to a particular newspaper for a particular area.[6]

   At the **technical** level, rulings relate to standards of a mechanical, electronic, or otherwise scientific nature that organizations of a mass media industry must uphold. A relevant case is the decision by Congress in the early 1960s to require that all television set manufacturers involved in interstate commerce equip the sets with receivers capable of receiving both UHF (Ultra High Frequency—Channels 14-83) and the more popular VHF (Very High Frequency—Channels 2-13).[7] More generally, postal edicts relating to weight, size, and construction represent technical regulations that affect the operations of book, newspaper, and magazine publishers, as well as direct marketers.[8]

The third level of regulation, the **content** level, involves specific messages and message policies. An example from broadcasting is the Federal Communication Act's requirement that broadcast licensees program "in the public interest, convenience, and necessity." More specific is the Communication Act's demand that stations that provide time to one candidate during an election allow opponents the same amount of time.[9] Relevant to all mass media are content rulings concerning free speech and its limitations on subjects such as libel, copyright, obscenity, pornography, and deceptive advertising.[10]

Content regulations obviously affect the kinds of materials mass media production organizations create. Less obvious, but equally important, is the impact that structural and technical regulations can have on content. For example, the 1919 decision by Congress to allow a commercial structure in broadcasting had profound long-term consequences for the materials sent over the air. It ignited a long and complicated series of events through a number of decades. They led to the radio and TV networks, to the advertiser-supported system, and to the commercial approach to programming that guided the broadcast media through the 1980s. Exactly how that happened will be explored in more detail as you move through this book.

Postal rules illustrate how technical regulation can shape mass media material. Relatively lower postal rates for books, magazines, and newspapers compared with other commercial matter have historically helped encourage the growth of those media. For example, postal laws have traditionally held that magazines sent to paying subscribers ("paid-circulation magazines") may pay lower rates than magazines circulated free to a designated group of people ("controlled-circulation magazines"). That is one reason many magazines prefer paid to controlled circulation. At the same time, magazine publishers wishing to be eligible for the lower (second-class) rate must make sure that the shape and orientation of their products conform to the technical standards the post office uses to define a paid-circulation magazine:

1. It must be regularly issued at stated intervals, as frequently as four times a year. It must bear a date of issue and be numbered consecutively
2. It must be formed of printed paper sheets, without board, cloth, leather, or other substantial bindings. Moreover, it may not be produced through the stencil, mimeograph, or hectograph process or in imitation of typewriting.
3. It must be originated and published for public dissemination, or devoted to literature, the sciences, or some special industry. It must have a legitimate list of subscribers. Also, it should not be designed primarily for advertising purposes, or for free circulation or for circulation at nominal rates.[11]

Clearly, these technical standards were created with a viewpoint about what proper magazines should look like and what they should contain. How regulatory approaches develop and how they differ among media industries are topics that will be addressed in Chapter 3.

THE INVESTOR AND CLIENT ROLES

The leverage investors and clients hold is quite straightforward: They control the money producers need to make material for release to the public.

Investment organizations include banks, stock brokerage firms, insurance companies, government and private foundations, and investment syndicates. Generally, they provide money only when the expectation is that the production firm's overall activities will yield an attractive return on their initial outlays. As a result, their power to veto or approve of a production company's long-range plans is enormous. The importance of the investment community is so critical, in fact, that top executives of media firms of all sizes make a point to brief their major investment communities regularly on their firms' progress and plans. It is not unusual to see the presidents of CBS and Paramount Communications giving talks to top Wall Street brokers and bankers on their firms' future. Nor is it unusual to see the heads of smaller companies trying to catch the interest of international lenders at one of the many movie and television conventions in Europe and the United States that take place throughout the year.

Sometimes, even one investment organization's loss of confidence in a company can spell disaster for that firm. That happened in 1989 to Vestron, Inc., a medium-size film producer and video distributor. During the summer of that year, Los Angeles-based Security Pacific National Bank promised the firm a six-year, $100 million line of credit. A few months later, Security Pacific withdrew its offer, arguing that Vestron's financial situation had worsened to such an extent that the bank had grounds to abort the agreement out of fear it would not be repaid. Vestron executives were stunned. Not only did they lose the promised loan, but Security Pacific's action made all other investors wary of offering Vestron long-term financing. With survival at stake, Vestron decided to sue the bank for breach of contract and fraud.

"We relied on [Security Pacific's] contractual commitment," said Vestron's chief executive officer in a statement issued by the firm. "It was central to the company's business plan, and when the bank reneged, Vestron's long-term financing collapsed. This has forced us to abandon significant elements of our business plan and has triggered massive financial losses."[12]

The power of organizations taking on the **client** role is different from that of organizations acting as investors. Whereas investors lend cash in support of general long-term growth, clients provide money in support of *particular* products before the producer releases them for public consumption. By far the dominant client group in American mass media is the advertising industry. In many sectors of the newspaper, magazine, and broadcast television industries, banks and insurance companies invest in particular production firms on the conviction that enough advertisers will pay to be identified with the mass media material to make the investment profitable. But advertisers are not the only media clients. The "trade" sector of book publishing is a case in point. Investors provide capital to publishers with the expectation that a profitable number of stores will purchase the books and place them on sale to the public. For these publishers, their exhibition outlets (the stores) are also their clients.

In essence, then, clients are customers of producers. Dominant media clients decide by their purchases whether particular mass media materials will be released to the public. It follows that the clients' importance relates to their being most directly responsible for the production organizations' solvency. This pivotal position holds profound implications for both the process and product of mass media producers. Chapter 4 examines those implications in detail.

THE AUXILIARY ROLE

At this point, attention shifts from power roles that regulate or sponsor mass media production to roles that contribute to a production firm's technical ability to do its job—auxiliaries, creators, and unions. As in earlier sections, our interest is in the way these relationships may affect the amount and nature of mass media material released to the public.

There is much to consider about the ability of auxiliaries to influence mass media content. Simply, mass media material could not be created if auxiliaries did not provide producers with supplies. Take, for example, the many supplies required to put together a movie. Of course, plumbing, air conditioning, telephones, and office equipment are needed to run the facilities from which the movie is coordinated. Typical preproduction as well as in-production demands include camera, sound, lighting, setting, wardrobe, makeup, hairdressing, and transportation equipment. Other production operations require equipment for editing, special sound and visual effects, and dubbing.

Moreover, if the film is shot on location, many **ancillary services** will be needed—services that support, but do not contribute directly to, actual production procedures. Transportation must be provided for cast and crew; hotel and meal accommodations must be established; preparations must be made to use the location setting; and facilities for screening daily "rushes" by the producer and director have to be set up. Even if the entire movie is made in a studio, ancillary services as diverse as security, accounting, maintenance, and film developing will be required.

The ability of a production organization to afford auxiliaries' resources typically determines whether it will get them. That, in turn, may determine whether the film is produced in the manner originally conceived. During the mid-1970s, for example, sharply rising costs of silver forced auxiliaries to charge more for photographic film. That led to the cancellation of a number of tightly budgeted movie projects. Of course, the chance also exists that auxiliaries will develop new supplies or services that will revolutionize the way mass media material is produced.[13]

The Case of Printing

Another illustration can be taken from the newspaper and magazine industries. The ability of auxiliaries such as IBM, Merganthaler, Compugraphic, and Atex to wed data gathering, storing, retrieving, and printing capabilities of computers to newspaper and magazine situations has helped create significant changes in the content produced.[14] A computer-run system has encouraged editors to experiment with changes in the graphic design of periodicals much more than before. Computer facilities allow them to translate new ideas into print without going through previously required time-consuming steps involving composition and press workers.

Computers are also beginning to give magazine publishers the ability to offer "selective binding" services to their advertising clients. Ads personalized with names of subscribers and phrases of special interest to them can be inserted automatically into a periodical. As this technology develops, it is possible to imagine that issues of major magazines will be customized as a matter of course. Computers will adjust the ads of marketers trying to reach specific types of individuals, or specific individuals. Even changes in the articles will be made by the computer to conform to the publisher's or the advertiser's knowledge of particular readers' interests.

During the past two decades, computer-run production systems were oriented toward a different goal: allowing editors and writers in large firms to work closer to printing and distribution deadlines than ever before.

Take the case of *U.S. News & World Report*. Before the introduction of computer production into the weekly magazine's operation, the editorial deadline (the "closing") began at noon on Thursday and ended at 9:00 P.M. that day. Printing took place over the weekend. When new equipment came in in the mid-1970s, final page composition and printing took much less time. As a consequence, editors and writers did not need to *begin* closing until late Friday.

This gain of more than a day was quite substantial for a weekly newsmagazine. It allowed editors much greater leeway to update changing circumstances and integrate "late breaking" stories into the body of the periodical. Such flexibility is increasingly important as other forms of advanced technologies—laptop computers, satellite communications, mobile phones, fax machines—allow reporters to transmit stories to their news organizations from around the world at the speed of light.[15]

THE CREATOR AND UNION ROLES

The key consideration that has moved newspapers and magazines toward computers in composing and printing has been their ability to lower labor costs substantially. Of course, there still remain areas of content selection and production where the substitution of machines for people is prohibitively expensive, if not downright impossible. At the very least, people must participate in coming up with the ideas and deciding how they should look in the final products. Such individuals hold the creator power role. Examples are magazine writers, TV actors, news reporters, set designers, television producers, movie directors, movie stuntpeople, news photographers, book editors, and record producers.

Some mass media creators become more highly recognized than others for their individual achievements. As a result, they take on power that makes them independent forces within their industries in the creation of mass media material. Actors such as Gene Hackman, movie producers such as Steven Spielberg, movie directors such as

Spike Lee, and broadcast journalists such as Dan Rather and Diane Sawyer have "clout" to personally initiate, shape, and finalize mass media works. Their clout often exceeds the leverage carried by entire organizations that deal with production firms. That is the reason for including the creator power role in this essentially interorganizational scheme.

It is important to stress that the kind of leverage that Hackman, Spielberg, Lee, Rather, and Sawyer hold is possessed by a very small percentage of personnel in any media industry. Most creators must work within the confines of rules they find within the organizations that hire them. In fact, the relative lack of leverage that most creators find in their jobs has led them to form unions or guilds in attempts to wield collective power with respect to production firms.[16]

Union Clout

Whether they represent creators or other personnel, organizations taking on the union power role can have substantial leverage. In 1989, an article in *The New York Times* about union problems at *The Daily News* commented that "it has been conventional wisdom in New York that no newspaper can publish without the truck drivers, a particularly tough union." Fear by *Daily News* executives that they would not be able to reach an easy agreement with their ten labor unions resulted in a campaign of "tough talk and sophisticated public relations" more than two months before the strike. The aim was to intimidate union leaders toward concessions.[17]

The ability of mass media production organizations to make use of an auxiliary organization's resources will sometimes depend on the terms that organizations holding union roles negotiate with producers about the use of those resources. This point was demonstrated dramatically in the newspaper industry. Craft union anger over executives' desire to replace Linotype machine operators with computers led to bitter disputes. In a flurry of incidents during the late 1960s and 1970s, the International Typographical Union and the National Newspaper Guild tried to use the leverage of solidarity they had with union workers throughout their firms to set standards for retaining printers in the face of the new technologies.

Arguments with management over the proper introduction of automation generally led to compromises acceptable to both sides. In a minority of cases, however, the disagreements ignited in bitter strikes. For a combination of reasons, the strikes resulted in the suspension or merger of newspapers, particularly in large metropolitan areas. By the 1980s, it had become clear to all involved that traditional newspaper craft unions had been forced to give way to automation. Some writers suggested that the best way for the weakened unions to retain significant leverage in the current technological era was for them to merge.[18]

Most union demands revolve around defining and ensuring satisfactory wages for their members under nonexploitive working conditions. One way to do this is to develop industry standards for creative or technical quality that a small percentage of the potential worker population can meet. Sometimes, union admission requirements and apprenticeship tracks protect these standards and regulate worker entry. The activities make the needed resources (employable workers) scarce, and drive up their minimum price. In turn, the finished product reflects a "professional" approach.

TABLE 2.2. Network TV's Major Unions

ABC, CBS, and NBC negotiate labor agreements with locals of more than a dozen unions. Below is a list of the nine largest national unions they face at bargaining tables.

- National Association of Broadcast Employees and Technicians (NABET): technicians and clerical workers at NBC and ABC.
- International Alliance of Theatrical Stage Employees and Moving Picture Machine Operators (IATSE): camera, sound, and lighting techicians and stagehands at the networks, their affiliates, and the production firms.
- International Brotherhood of Electrical Workers (IBEW): technicians at CBS.
- American Federation of Television and Radio Artists (AFTRA): actors in soap operas, game shows, and programs shot in video as well as network and affiliate news correspondents.
- Screen Actors Guild (SAG): actors in movies, commercials, and TV shows shot in film.
- Directors Guild of America (DGA): directors, stage managers, and production assistants.
- Writers Guild of America (WGA): script, promotional, and news writers, and graphic artists, with separate divisions on the East and West coasts.
- American Federation of Musicians (AFM): network studio musicians.
- United Scenic Artists (USA): art and scenic directors and costume designers.

SOURCE: *Channels Magazine*, November 1986, p. 44.

The ability of unions to fix specific minimum wages and other terms for their members varies within and across media industries. In book publishing, for example, the Authors League has created a "model contract" for royalty terms and other aspects of writer–publisher agreements. However, the contract has no binding value, and many publishers successfully negotiate terms less generous to authors.[19] By contrast, the Writers Guild, which operates in the movie and television industries, has successfully established minimum rates that producers must pay for a "treatment" (a brief description of a proposed screenplay), for an actual screenplay, and for revisions. In addition, the guild has helped create rules about the on-screen credit that writers will be given and about the kinds of rights over an original screenplay that a writer may retain when a producer buys that writer's material for a movie.[20]

At the same time, the Writers Guild has tried and failed to get production firms to agree that the writer of a movie screenplay retains creative control over that screenplay even after the material is delivered to the production firm. Production firm executives have insisted that the writer is simply an employee, not an executive. They have maintained the right to alter a screenplay any way they wish once they have paid for it.[21]

In the nature of things, compromises must be made. A union's bargaining position toward a compromise is only as strong as the collective importance, and solidarity, of its members as production resources. Many times, the way the arguments are resolved influences the content that is created. The most drastic consequence of negotiations or work stoppages over wages might be producers' decisions not to work on certain products at all because of high labor costs. The producers might, however, respond to higher costs in one or more of the following ways: They might scale down the material to versions more in line with current prices. They might keep the material unchanged but raise its price to the public to meet extra costs. They might keep the material unchanged but raise the price of advertising inserts to help defray expenses.

Or they might keep the material unchanged but create it in ways that reduce reliance on the unions.

Getting Around the Unions

One way to get around the union involves turning to auxiliaries for substitutible automated resources. Another way is to create the material in places where union regulations are absent or not as stringent. We have already seen that the use of new technologies can themselves lead to important changes in mass media material. Choosing a production location because of a favorable union environment also may affect what the public sees, hears, or reads.

The shifting of television series programming between Los Angeles and New York during the past three decades is to a significant extent a tale of shifting union costs. Between the late 1950s and late 1970s, producers generally considered the major New York union, the International Alliance of Theatrical Stage Employees (IATSE), to be more troublesome and a lot more expensive than its counterparts on the West Coast. That, plus a parallel decline in available studio facilities, encouraged producers to forsake the "Big Apple," birthplace of TV production, for Hollywood.

In the early 1980s, however, as part of a bid by the mayor's office to attract motion picture and television work to the city, the management of the IATSE became more flexible in meeting filmers' demands. Moreover, a second union became more prominent, and competition between the two created an even more flexible attitude toward production. An umbrella organization, the Conference of Motion Picture and Television Unions, was formed to provide a forum for production executives and members from both unions to discuss problems of mutual concern. These activities, along with an increase in studio space, helped establish near parity in production costs between New York and Los Angeles. As a result, the number of series, specials, and movies with a New York City backdrop increased.[22]

The increase may not have been permanent, though: A strike by technicians in 1991 brought moviemaking in New York to a standstill for many months. It threatened to jeopardize previous gains, as producers learned to use less expensive alternatives to Hollywood and the Big Apple.[23]

The lure of relatively low labor costs has made Toronto, Canada, and the state of Florida major motion picture and TV production sites. Toronto won popularity during the 1980s because of favorable U.S.-Canadian money exchange rates, Florida because of laws allowing nonunion workers. Most stories that were shot in these areas were represented as taking place elsewhere. In the case of Toronto, some people in the movie business snickered privately that Toronto was too clean a city to stand in for a U.S. counterpart, which was often New York.

THE DISTRIBUTOR AND EXHIBITOR ROLES

Along with concern by producers of mass media material about the costs of auxiliary and union resources must come an awareness of the critical importance of distribution and exhibition. If garnering specific resources to create a product is a necessary early step toward achieving influence and making a profit, placing that product in front of the people who will potentially choose it is the equally necessary later step. Consequently, to remain viable, production firms in every industry must exert influence over the distributor and exhibitor power roles. Here we are concerned with the way such controls, combined with leverage on *producers* by distributors and exhibitors, can influence the amount and kind of mass media materials producers make.

The subject, put concisely, is spectrum of choice. For executives in a production firm, the question is this: How can we ensure that the spectrum of materials which the public gets to choose from will include our company's products? One answer is for them to oversee an entire chain of activities leading to the marketplace, from production to distribution to exhibition. This approach, called **vertical integration**, is common in many industries. A logical next step for a vertically integrated production firm is to inhibit other firms from competing with it at the production, distribution, or exhibition levels. When only one company remains, it is called a vertically integrated **monopoly**. When a few firms compete and keep others out, they are vertically integrated **oligopolies**. To greater or lesser degrees, both scenarios maximize the chances that the public will choose the production firm's products.

The Movie Majors

The Los Angeles-based (Hollywood) movie industry is an area where vertically integrated oligopolies reigned supreme for decades. Beginning in the early 1920s, a small number of production companies (Paramount, Warner, 20th Century Fox, RKO, and MGM) managed to reduce their risks greatly by owning (or being owned by) both dominant distribution firms and major nationwide theater chains (exhibition outlets). Critics of their approach claimed that they were restraining trade since their lock on the marketplace was not allowing other production firms a realistic route to screens across the country. In 1948, the U.S. government, agreeing with these claims of anticompetitive behavior, forced the film industry "majors" to divest themselves of their exhibition interests.[24]

Since then, many changes in the structure and activities of the movie industry

TABLE 2.3. Top Six Production States

California gets more than twice the money from film and television production as New York State. The other four states are also-rans, relatively speaking. Still, state governments throughout the United States crave audiovisual production money.

Except where noted, the figures include direct spending for national films, TV shows, and commercials in 1989. All numbers are in millions.

1. California $4,700
2. New York $2,100
3. Florida $220
4. Georgia $141
5. Texas $116   (feature production only)
6. North Carolina $115   (includes intrastate production of commercials)

SOURCE: *Variety*, August 22, 1990, p. 69.

have taken place. RKO has dropped out of the "major" studio category; Disney, Columbia, TriStar, and Orion have entered. These majors have tried to maintain dominance as theatrical film producers by controlling a substantial, sometimes oligo-polistic, share of the distribution business. Movies financed and distributed outside this powerful circle *can* be found in theaters. In general, however, independent film-makers with ambitions to reach huge audiences try to attach themselves to a powerful distribution arm. They agree to give the major a substantial share of the profits in return for circulating the picture. Independent filmmakers who cannot or do not want to interest the majors must often content themselves with limited distribution, usually through small theaters in only the largest cities or (for "art" and foreign films) in university towns.

Three major barriers to entry protect the majors' theatrical turf. One is the huge yearly expenditure (tens of millions of dollars) each company spends to maintain a distribution and sales force world wide. Possible competitors would find duplicating such a setup on a comparably large scale extremely difficult. A second barrier, also related to cost, is the large amounts of cash studios can get (from their distribution pipelines and revolving bank loans) to support the kind of movie slate necessary to a large distribution operation. A third barrier is the strong links that the majors devel-oped with the huge exhibition chains after 1948. Although the relationships between the two parties have sometimes been stormy, the theater owners have come to rely on the studios for providing a predictable stream of movies that bring in the high numbers needed to keep the seats filled. They are wary of dealing regularly with new firms that sport no audience-luring record.

Contested Cable Terrain

Although the major movie studios have worked hard to keep control over their traditional exhibition arena, much of the terrain of battle over distribution and exhibi-tion has shifted away from the theaters. In 1948, movie theaters provided the primary audiovisual media experience of Americans. Broadcast television and cable TV hardly existed; the invention of video cassette recorders was years away. Today, these media are major entertainment vehicles for people in the United States and abroad. As such, they have become key exhibition outlets for movies.

Yet the Hollywood majors were late in understanding the power of TV and cable to threaten their positions as the dominant moviemakers. The key distribution power in television belongs to the three major networks—ABC, CBS, and NBC. While they often purchase movies and series from the major studios, they do not hesitate to purchase programs from other companies. The majors were also late in recognizing the importance of controlling the distribution of their movies to cable TV systems.

During the 1970s and 1980s, primary distribution of recent films in that industry belonged to Home Box Office (HBO), a division of Time, Inc. Time, a magazine-publishing giant, also owned American Television and Communications (ATC), one of the largest operators of cable systems in the United States. Time executives clearly realized the usefulness of the link between its HBO channel and cable exhibitors. Since subscribers were asked to pay extra for HBO, the channel increased the profits of ATC and other cable systems nationwide. From Hollywood's standpoint, however,

HBO's grip over pay cable meant that film producers were often at Time, Inc.'s mercy when it came to the selection and pricing of their pictures for cable.

By the early 1980s, strategists for the Hollywood majors were aware that it was in their firms' interests to control the movement of their product into the markets created by increasingly popular technologies, such as cable TV and home video. As a result, all the majors, individually or with other firms, created home video divisions that developed clout that mirrored their power in the theatrical marketplace. This kind of opportunity was not as easily duplicated in the cable business, which had already developed its own distribution and exhibition structure. However, a number of majors tried to make distribution inroads. Disney's creation of The Disney Channel, a pay cable distribution channel, was a notable example. An even more important development was the transaction that brought Home Box Office, the major pay movie channel, under the control of a major movie distributor.

It happened in 1989, when Time merged with Warner Communications. Through its ownership of Warner Brothers, HBO, and ATC, the new firm instantly became a vertically integrated power in the cable industry. The implications of Time Warner's status frightened a number of cable system owners. Those exhibitors worried that HBO would use its Hollywood production link to force cable systems not owned by Time Warner to pay higher rates for HBO. That would diminish cable systems'

TABLE 2.4. Top Ten Cable Television Multiple System Operators

Rank Multiple System Operator	Number of Subscribers	
1. Tele-Communications Inc.	7,014,350	(6/90)
2. American Television & Communications Corp.	4,400,000	(6/90)
3. UA Entertainment	2,688,793	(8/90)
4. Continental Cablevision	2,595,000	(5/90)
5. Warner Cable Communications	1,810,000	(7/90)
6. Comcast	1,629,600	(5/90)
7. Cox Cable Communications	1,598,417	(9/90)
8. Storer Cable Communications	1,550,000	(5/90)
9. Cablevision System	1,530,432	(9/90)
10. Jones Intercable/Spacelink	1,516,183	(9/90)

Multiple system operators (MSOs) are firms that own more than one cable television system. The very biggest MSOs are especially powerful cable exhibitors, since their agreement to carry channels can sometimes make the difference between success or failure for distributors of programming. Taking advantage of its power, TCI, the top MSO, often demands a part of the profits as payment for carrying a new channel. The ownership of number-two ATC by Time Warner means that new cable programming ideas by HBO or other Time Warner units might have an easier chance to get tryouts than might otherwise be the case.

Table 2.4 lists the largest ten MSOs according to the number of subscribers to their basic service during certain months in 1990. A basic service is the set of channels that consumers receive when they pay a cable company the lowest monthly subscription fee. Higher fees are charged for nonbasic services, such as pay-TV channels (HBO, Showtime) and pay-per-view activities.

SOURCE: *Advertising Age*, February 11, 1991, p. Cable-25.

profits. In fact, the possibility frightened the nation's largest cable television operator, Tele-Communications, Inc. (TCI), so much that it moved to purchase half of Showtime/The Movie Channel, HBO's only serious competitor. By infusing the ailing Showtime with cash to buy films from Hollywood majors, TCI hoped to make it a viable alternative to HBO and keep the latter from raising its rates.

"The Time Warner merger has shaken up the cable world," TCI's chief executive said. "Time controls about 25% of all broadcast programming, between [subsidiaries] Lorimar, Warner, and Telepictures. . . . You tend to look for counterbalances. You are seeing new alignments take place. We need some parallel relationships."[25]

The Battle over TV Distribution

The power of HBO in Hollywood and TCI's move to shore up Showtime/The Movie Channel underscore the importance of controlling distribution in a mass media industry. By extension, the Time Warner merger illustrates the desire by companies to control production and exhibition as well as distribution in cable and in the theatrical business. A similar desire has brought increasing frustration on the part of the three major distribution powers in the television industry: ABC, CBS, and NBC.

For over thirty years, from 1948 through the early 1980s, these commercial TV networks dominated the channels that connected the great majority of TV exhibition outlets in the United States (the broadcasting stations) with TV producers. The public television network (PBS) was not a strong competitor for audiences. Moreover, there were relatively few other broadcast channels to draw viewers away from those affiliated with one of the networks. Of 988 television stations broadcasting in 1979, only about 100 were independent of the networks.[26]

One upshot of this situation was that on a typical evening in the mid-1970s, 90% or more of people watching television in the United States could be found viewing ABC, CBS, or NBC. Another result was that the networks were the major game in the industry as far as big-money production was concerned. The power of the networks over TV distribution was so strong, in fact, that in the late 1960s the Federal Communications Commission set forth rules to limit their dominance over the availability and distribution of TV programming.

The rules stipulated that a network could not syndicate or have a financial interest in programs that it had not solely produced, and could syndicate only in foreign countries any programs that it had solely produced. The Justice Department, however, was not satisfied that even these "fin/syn" rules would dampen network dominance. Concerned that the ABC, CBS, and NBC were using their right to produce programs themselves to inhibit competition in Hollywood, the Justice Department instituted antitrust proceedings against them. In 1978, the suit was dropped when the networks agreed to refrain until late 1990 from owning most of the entertainment programming they aired.[27]

Their control over production was, nevertheless, great. Production companies that wanted to create for commercial television—companies that included the major film studios—were at the mercy of the networks for decisions about the number and kinds of shows that would be acceptable, and the price that would be paid for them. Producers choosing to sell programs elsewhere in commercial TV had to go the

syndication route exclusively. That is, they had to distribute their programs to individual stations or station groups market by market with the hope of obtaining enough reach and advertiser support to make the project viable.

The problem for producers through the early 1980s was that the number of independent stations along with the percentage of national population they reached was not enough to support syndication of expensive programs that might compete with network fare. Success in this regard would be possible only if some network affiliates preempted network programs. Affiliates did have an incentive to do that occasionally, because syndicated pickups do not require the station to share advertising time and revenues with the network. For the same reason, however, the networks discouraged replacement of their shows with syndicated material. Their powerful leverage lay in an ability not to renew the station's affiliation contract. Loss of affiliation would stop the station's continuous supply of expensively mounted programs that reached large audiences and attracted local as well as national advertisers. An added element of network power was that affiliates in the very largest markets were owned by the networks themselves. The upshot of this distribution clout was that all affiliates generally "cleared" every network prime time program, and syndicating a prime time show was very difficult.

The possibilities of prime time syndication are still quite limited, for many of the reasons mentioned. However, the broadcast TV environment has changed drastically since the early 1980s, and the networks are finding their supremacy seriously challenged. We have already noted some of the challenges to network TV's audience-grabbing power: the spread of both cable television and video cassette recorders to over 50% of American homes by the 1980s. An added challenge was the proliferation of independent television stations, usually on the UHF band. From only about 100 in 1979, the numbers soared to 904 just six years later.[28] The increased number allowed a major Hollywood studio, 20th Century Fox, to buy a number of UHF broadcast outlets in major cities and launch a new commercial TV network. Scheduled initially for prime time on only Saturday and Sunday, the Fox network successfully challenged its full-scale counterparts for audiences and advertisers. It marked yet another attempt by a Hollywood TV studio to try vertical integration outside the theatrical film business.

Fox's activities were yet another force—along with cable, video, and independent TV stations generally—that steadily diminished the percentage of Americans who watched network television even in prime time. By the late 1980s, the three major networks together reached between 65% and 70% of TV viewers during a typical evening. The numbers represented a drop of over twenty points in viewing audience share from a decade earlier.

From the standpoint of ABC, CBS, and NBC executives, the erosion of their audience share meant, bluntly, that their power over television distribution and exhibition was dropping. Unlike the Hollywood majors, however, the three networks were prevented by government rulings from creating or owning most of the materials they distributed. They realized that power over distribution in the evolving media system is increasingly tied to a company's ability to link it to production clout—that is, to generate and control the creative product it distributes. Network executives therefore saw themselves hampered from competing with other large media organizations (such as Fox and Time Warner) for part of the changing media pie. As a result, they urged the FCC not to renew the regulations prohibiting them from owning a financial interest in, or syndication rights to, TV materials which they air.

For their part, the network's Hollywood suppliers lobbied the FCC not to change things. They argued that giving the networks the right to own and syndicate all their programming would lead them to insist on financial equity in everything they put on the air. This would lead, in turn, to the disappearance of independent production firms, they said, as well as to the needless growth in the already substantial power that ABC, CBS, and NBC have over American culture.

In the face of the lobbying by powerful constituencies on both sides, the FCC came up with a compromise in 1991 that pleased none of them. It allowed the Big Three the right to negotiate ownership and syndication rights with production firms that bring shows to them. It also allowed the networks to negotiate with producers for 100% of the profits from foreign syndication.

However, the FCC placed restrictions on the number of prime time shows ABC, CBS, and NBC could own and syndicate domestically. For example, the networks could not themselves create more than 40% of their prime time lineup. Nor could they syndicate more than 40% of their prime time shows to the U.S. market. In addition, to protect independent production firms from being forced to surrender equity in their projects, the FCC required that network executives not be allowed to negotiate for part ownership of a program until thirty days after making a deal to place the program on their schedule. Finally, to protect the Fox network, the FCC ruled that Fox would not be bound by any of those limitations because it did not produce more than fourteen hours of prime time entertainment programming.

Hollywood production firms as well as the Big Three networks decried the FCC ruling and promised to fight it, in court and in Congress.[29] At the same time, rumors flew that one of the Big Three networks would reduce its prime time programming to fourteen hours in order to be able to enter into the domestic syndication business—or to merge with a huge Hollywood studio that syndicates TV programming.[30] At this writing, the battle over the future of the networks in program ownership and distribution was still raging.

Distribution in Print and Radio

The broadcast television, cable television, and theatrical movie industries reveal intensely public bids for control over distribution. Control over distribution with the aim of maintaining a producer's access to distribution outlets is not as dramatically evident in the print media. This does not mean that control over the distribution process is not important. It does mean that many more producers have an opportunity to exert control. Four differences between print media industries, on the one hand, and the cable, broadcast, and theatrical film industries, on the other, seem to explain the difference in access to distribution:

The relatively low cost of production and promotion that is possible in print

The relatively greater number of units of material that print outlets will accept

The relatively larger number of outlets that exist to exhibit print materials

The relatively larger *variety* of outlets that exist to exhibit print materials

Comparing the theatrical movie industry with book publishing will illustrate these points. Books are substantially less expensive to create than movies; bookstores, libraries, and schools will carry more new titles a year than will movie exhibitors; there are more outlets for new books in the United States than there are theatrical movie outlets; and the variety of book outlets (bookstores, libraries, schools, a wide spectrum of commercial locations, book clubs, and direct-to-home sales) is much greater than the variety of first-run theatrical film outlets (essentially "hard top" movie houses and drive-ins).

In magazine publishing, the ability to distribute material to consumers directly through the mail, as well as through racks in stores, also makes it more difficult for a small number of companies to own all distribution routes. Similarly, the situation in radio, though once comparable to the contemporary TV and movie industries, is closer today to book publishing in its range of outlet diversity and production costs. The change came about as a result of two parallel developments that began in the mid-1950s. One was the new advertising role for radio that emerged during the rise of television—reaching narrower publics than TV for short periods of time. The other was the increased government allocation of AM and (particularly) FM licenses. By 1989, over 10,500 radio stations existed in the United States.[31] While traditional radio networks (ABC, Westwood One, CBS) certainly exist, a tremendous number of other production and distribution services with a wide variety of long and short programming forms also compete for stations' interests.

Note, however, that a general atmosphere of easy entry for producers at both the distribution and exhibition levels of a mass media industry does not mean that all segments of the industry are so competitive. To the contrary, it is quite likely that even in these industries distribution channels to certain types of outlets are controlled by a small number of production firms. Mass market paperback publishing—a sector of book publishing in which different types of retail stores are the major outlets—serves as a good example. In 1990, eight paperback publishers accounted for 75% of all best-selling mass market paperbacks in the United States. Of those, six publishers—Pocket Books, Bantam, Berkeley, Fawcett/Ivy, Penguin, and Avon/Ballantine/Del Rey—accounted for 66% of the best-sellers. Pocket Books itself managed to rack up almost one out of five of the hits.[32] Parallel examples of such power by producer-distributors over their markets could be brought from the general bookstore ("trade") outlet sector of book publishing and the record store area of the record industry.

When distribution channels are not controlled nationally by a small number of firms, a wide range of producers can be encouraged to try to reach the public. So, for example, a small firm wanting to market a magazine for first and second graders might be able to convince distributors in different cities to carry the magazine. Some might carry it, some might not. Failing that, the firm might be able to succeed by advertising and selling the magazine through the mail. Or, perhaps, the firm might decide that the best approach is through toy stores, where another kind of distributor will carry the material.

TABLE 2.5. Best-selling Paperback Publishers, 1990

Publisher	No. of Books	Publisher	No. of Books
Andrews and McMeel	7	Lasser Institute	1
Anchor	1	Little, Brown	3
Avon Books	15	Modern Publishing	1
Ballantine/Del Rey/Fawcett/Ivy	26	W. W. Norton	1
Bantam Books	29	Penguin USA[2]	18
Berkley[1]	27	Pocket Books	39
Bridge Publications	1	Rand McNally	1
Dell Publishing	13	Rizzoli/Kodak	1
Doubleday Publishing	2	St. Martin's Press	7
Earthworks Press	1	TSR	1
Fireside	2	Tor	1
Harcourt Brace Jovanovich	1	Touchstone	1
Harlequin	1	Vintage	1
HarperCollins Paperbacks	7	Warner Books	8
Harper/Hazelden	1	Workman	3
Harper/Perennial	3	World Almanac/Pharos	2
Health Communications	1	Worldview/Perigee	1
Houghton Mifflin	1	Yankee	1
		Zebra Books	2

[1] Includes Ace, Charter, Jove.
[2] Includes NAL, Signet, Onyx, Penguin.
SOURCE: *BP Report*, January 14, 1991, p. 4. Reproduced with permission from SI Inc., Wilton, Connecticut

There are, in fact, a number of child-oriented periodicals that are sold more in toy stores and through the mail rather than on newsstands. *Sesame Street Magazine*, *Barbie Magazine*, and *Toys R Us Magazine* are the ones found in the Toys R Us toy chain, for obvious reasons. Another, more unusual, example of a periodical sold through nontraditional retail outlets was *It's Me!*, a bimonthly aimed at large women. While it was marketed in 1981 on a test basis through magazine stands in Chicago, *It's Me!* was released in Los Angeles, New York, and Chicago through stores of its charter advertiser, the Lane Bryant clothing chain for larger women.[33] Neither the in-store nor the newsstand tests were considered successful, though, and the magazine disappeared after its first year.

Producers' Power over Exhibition

The control production firms exercise over exhibitors varies. Producers have much power over exhibitors in areas of media industries where they face little competition in the production and distribution of their products. The distribution of films provides an example. The major movie companies have managed to exert quite a lot of influence over the policies of theater chains, from the amounts they charge for tickets to their right to show commercials in the theaters. The reason is that the theater chains, as large as they are, are dependent on a handful of firms for the bulk of their money-making product and do not want to alienate them.

The broadcast television networks, as producers and distributors of a flow of programming, also exercise a good deal of influence over their affiliate stations.

Those exhibitors rely on network fare for the bulk of their programming and a large percentage of their revenues. While the money-making capabilities of a TV network are not what they used to be, losing a link to a network could represent a major monetary blow in many markets.

Still, such power does not mean that the broadcast networks or major movie companies totally ignore the outlets that carry their programming. Sometimes the exhibitor/distributor relationship can strongly influence the material released to the public. For example, for years the objection by affiliates that an hour-long newscast would not enhance their profits has stopped ABC, CBS, and NBC from implementing what their news divisions have sorely wanted.

Coping Strategies

Generally, though, exhibitors have more influence over what they carry (and, thus, more leverage with producers) in industries where production and distribution is not dominated by a few companies. In situations where exhibitors have such power, producers must develop ways to reduce the uncertainty over whether outlets will carry their products.

Following sociologist Paul Hirsch, we can suggest four **coping strategies** that production firms employ to deal with this kind of uncertainty:

Deploying contact personnel to organizational boundaries

Overproducing and differentially promoting new items

Co-opting mass media gatekeepers

Bypassing outlets altogether through direct marketing[34]

It might be useful to start with the last, since it ignores distributors and exhibitors totally. **Bypassing outlets through direct marketing** means using the mail or other advertising vehicles (including mass media) to inform members of the public that the item can be purchased directly from the producer.

This can be a useful strategy for media production firms with products or audiences that need special handling. It may be that a firm's product is aimed at publics that do not frequent predictable outlets in numbers high enough to make the material profitable. (Example: albums of big band music aimed at retirees who do not visit record stores.) It may be that the target audience is well known to, and easily reached by, the producer. (Example: an audience of mass communication professors whose addresses are made available to a publisher of a scholarly book relevant to them.) Or it may be that the product typically requires more explanation than can be obtained by looking at it in an outlet. (Example: an encyclopedia.) In any of these cases, a direct-marketing approach will be the strategy of choice for the producer.

If, however, getting the product to the public via distributors and exhibitors is the goal, the other coping strategies may well come into play. The first strategy, **deploying contact personnel to organizational boundaries**, involves the production firm's sales representatives.

Part of a sales representative's role might be to build trust with buyers in distribution and exhibition organizations so that the buyers will want the producer's products. Doing that might mean circulating information that tries to justify high optimism for the products' sales. The sales representative might give assurances that impressive advertising campaigns will bring the public to exhibitors in search of the product. The rep might offer outlets or distributors special discounts for carrying the product. More darkly, gaining favor might involve bribing people with money or drugs.

The second coping strategy, **overproduction and differential promotion of new items**, means producing a large number of items (many book titles, many record album titles) and promoting only the ones that seem to be catching on. The hope is that at least some of the products will be accepted by distributors, outlets, and, ultimately, members of the public. Sociologist Serge Denisoff has offered a good illustration of how this approach has worked in the recording industry; his example applies to many areas of book publishing as well.

He pointed out in the mid-1970s that despite control by five record conglomerates of over 50% of the business, those firms found it imperative to follow what Denisoff called "the buckshot theory of record releasing."

> CBS Records, with its plant and catalog, must produce an enormous amount of product to keep its various bureaus, agencies, and departments busy. Of every 10 records released, only 2 or 3 will sell. Consequently, large companies must produce massive amounts of product to sustain their large corporate bodies. Huge investments are made and must be maintained. A concentration upon proven talent, coupled with the 7 to 3 ratio, motivates the larger companies to treat newcomers indiscriminately, at the same time competing with each other for surefire sellers. . . . Capitol [Records] operates on what [an executive] calls Formula 10, which is nearly identical to Columbia's 7 to 3 ratio. Capitol's advertising department head believes that in 10 releases at least one should be gold with several others bringing in a sizable return.[35]

As Denisoff's description suggests, use of the overproduction strategy can have both positive and negative implications for new artists breaking into the media business. The need for a large slate of releases may encourage firms to look for new faces. On the other hand, the firms' tendency to let certain releases sink or swim in the marketplace may mean that that the artists do not get the kind of publicity and marketing support they need to gain the notice of distributors, exhibitors, and segments of the public.

The third strategy Hirsch mentions, **co-opting mass media gatekeepers**, is likely to be employed in combination with other strategies. **Gatekeepers** are people who make decisions about whether or not to select certain materials for production. Co-opting mass media gatekeepers involves convincing them to promote mass media items that are available for sale, rent, or viewing elsewhere.

Examples are easily found: a record album promoter who persuades a radio station program director to play a particular record; a public relations agent who convinces a talk show coordinator to schedule the author of a new book on the show; and a movie studio publicist who convinces television network programmers to produce a special about how a new movie was made.

THE LINKING PIN ROLE

The previous examples of co-opting mass media gatekeepers point to factors that are often underestimated when people consider influences on mass media production organizations. The term that will be used here to describe these factors is **linking pin activities**. They involve the movement of completed material, or people representing that material, from production firms in one industry to production firms in another industry.

Linking pin activities are key aspects of a mass media cross-fertilization process that serves to tie together publics that might have little in common. Consider how often you have seen people or subjects appear on television, in magazines, on book covers, and in the movies during a particular period. This phenomenon exists regarding what journalists call "hard news" (the government, economic, and crime reports of the day), "soft news" (tales of ordinary people and discussions of the arts), and even fiction. For example, Jane Fonda might appear in a new movie, on a magazine cover, and on a TV talk show in the course of the same week. Similarly, Tom Wolfe might discuss his new book on TV's *Good Morning America*, on Mutual radio's *Larry King Show*, and with *Time* magazine all on the same day.

As these examples suggest, much linking pin activity is promotional from the standpoint of the organization that initiates the interconnections. Production firms that want to ensure large audiences for their creations often turn to other mass media to spread the word. Typically they will devolve this linking pin power role upon public relations companies or promotional agencies specialized in this task. At other times, the production organizatons act as linking pins. Special units of the organizations arrange to tout the firms' creations in other media. In the case of the largest media conglomerates, transactions might even take place among various arms of the company. An example is when Home Box Office, a cable TV subsidiary of Time Warner, carries a program about the history of *Life*, one of Time Warner's magazines.

A major impetus for linking pin activity is the mass media's need for information. Production organizations often pursue the output of other media. They might do so because they want assuredly popular materials. Too, they might find that borrowing from other media is the easiest way to fill time or space in their own medium. Producers of TV's *Phil Donohue Show,* for example, who need to come up with controversial guests for five hour-long programs each week, might rely on a variety of magazines and books as sources for suggestions. And a company might buy the rights to make a film based on a popular new novel in the hope that its popularity will carry over to the movie.

Firms that are the objects of such linking pin pursuits do not discourage the situation; it means free publicity and sometimes lots of money for them. Richard Snyder, president of the Simon & Schuster book publishing concern, recognized the importance of interindustry connections when he said, "In a certain sense, we are the software of the television and movie media."[36]

Probably the most important linking pin organizations in the world are the major international news wire services: the Associated Press, Reuters, United Press International, Agence France Presse, and TASS. These firms are producers in what might be

---

Talking Point 2.2   Simon & Schuster's Linking Pin Role

Simon & Schuster is a book publishing division of Paramount Communications. When it released Kitty Kelly's explosive biography of Nancy Reagan in 1991, the intensive coverage was marked by an unusual contract to control how reporters got advance copies of the book.

The document said that in order for them to get an advance copy of the book, reporters could not talk or write about it until April 8, when the book was to be released. As the Associated Press commented a number of days later, the contract represented the latest example of covenants aimed at controlling news coverage.

To limit access and leaks of the book's contents, Simon & Schuster imposed stringent security on the editing and printing process. Only five manuscripts were prepared. They were numbered and a log was kept of each copy's whereabouts.

To ensure that stories about the book would appear in unison, the publisher asked the Associated Press, *The Washington Post, USA Today, The Los Angeles Times, The New York Times, The New York Daily News, Newsweek Magazine, Women's Wear Daily,* and *Entertainment Tonight* to sign the agreement. All agreed except the two New York dailies. They published stories about the book on April 7th.

Nevertheless, Simon & Schuster had orchestrated a publicity coup.

SOURCE: *Editor and Publisher*, April 27, 1991, p. 11.

---

called the **raw materials news industry**. That industry generates thousands of nonfiction stories that are sold across mass media boundaries as building blocks for newspapers, magazines, even books.

Examples of a few other linking pins in the raw materials news industry are:

The **investigative journalism collectives** (the Community Information Project, the Center for Investigative Reporting, and the Better Government Association), which sell their reports to newspapers, magazines, and television networks

The **major international picture agencies** (Sygma, Magnum, Gamma-Liaison, Sipa, Black Star, and Contact), which, for a fee, will help photographers sell their work to newspapers, magazines, and book publishers throughout the world

Picture libraries, such as the Bettmann Archive, which rent historical pictures on a variety of subjects to production firms in various mass media industries

THE FACILITATOR ROLE

The role of linking pin organizations is to move mass media material, or people representing that material, from one mass media industry to another. By contrast, organizations that take on facilitator roles work *within* mass media industries. They help initiate, carry out, or evaluate mass media material in the first place—sometimes even before it is produced or distributed. Organizations taking on a facilitator role include:

Talent agencies that suggest artists to production firms and negotiate their contracts

Law firms that help production firms deal with investors, authorities, and distributors

Consulting firms that help producers create mass media material

Market research firms that survey the environment for mass media material, evaluate how previous material has fared, project how current material might do, and suggest why

The consequences of these facilitation activities for mass media material can sometimes be profound. Consider the position of a large talent agency (say, William Morris or Creative Artists) in the process. On a basic level, a talent agency's purpose is to serve as a negotiating intermediary between a particular creator—for example, an actor, director, composer, or writer—and the production organization. The agency's mandate is to get the client work and then extract the best deal possible from the firm that wants the client's services. Over the years, though, large talent agencies have developed the ability to go beyond suggesting and negotiating for individual clients. Now they often parlay their influential client lists into **packages of talent** that they market to production firms.

A **package** is a combination of two or more creators who come together to work on a mass media project. Through clients who are writers, a talent agent knows what manuscripts are available. At the same time, through clients who are producers, directors, and actors, the agents can keep close tabs on developments in their creative communities. By putting these people together, the agent might yield a plan for a movie or TV series that a production firm will find attractive. The production firm, for its part, might appreciate the agency's packaging activities, since it saves producers time, effort, and money involved in trying to do the same thing.

Talent firms often act as linking pins as well as facilitators, since they frequently parlay particular groups of talent into packages that cross media boundaries. Thomas Whiteside has described that activity well:

A script is an "element," so is a writer, so are a book, a producer, an actor or group of actors, a director. In contrast to simpler times, in which it was taken for granted that a published book originated with the author . . . [the package] does not have to take place in the mind of a writer; it can occur around a conference table in the office of a producer or an agent, who may then add to it "elements" including the writer, who is "acquired" sooner or later in the packaging process.[37]

Not all packaging deals are completed, of course. Such negotiations are very delicate for the agents involved, since they involve placing value on every person in the package in relation to the others in the package. In addition, production firm executives might not want certain individuals in the package, preferring to substitute their own choices in those creative slots. Nevertheless, use of talent agencies to facilitate the production of material has become a pervasive fact of life in mass media industries.

THE PUBLIC ADVOCACY AND PUBLIC POWER ROLES

The last two power roles in Table 2.1—public advocacy and public—have already been introduced in this chapter. Little more will be said about them here. This is because the task of drawing out their actual implications for mass media material is so great that it demands a separate discussion (see Chapters 5 and 6). At this point, it is useful to note only that **publics** come into existence when scattered groups or individuals share certain mass media materials. By contrast, **public advocacy organizations** are created when those individuals or groups band together systematically. Typically, their aim is to demand that producer, distributor, or exhibitor organizations change certain approaches to mass media content.

As a member of a public, a person's leverage regarding the media will be expressed in individual ways. If you like a TV show, you may view it; if you don't, you may not. If something about a program makes you especially angry, you might write a letter to the people in charge. Public advocacy organizations might have the same aims with respect to the TV show, and they might utilize the same tactics. In addition, they might try to force change through boycotts of the firm that creates the program, the network that distributes it, the stations that air it, and even the advertisers that support it.

It should be noted that the word *audience* is not the same as *public* as it is used in the power role framework. The term *public* refers to the individual viewers, readers, and listeners to the mass media material, *as they see themselves*. By contrast, the word *audience* refers to the viewers, readers, and listeners *as they are understood and targeted by media executives*. Chapter 5 will take up the meaning of audience in much more detail, explain how it differs from public, and show the surprising importance it has for helping us make sense of mass media activities.

SOME IMPLICATIONS OF THE FRAMEWORK

I hope that this chapter has shown the usefulness of the power role approach for examining how interorganizational activities within and across mass media industries influence the creation of media materials. The power role framework developed here will serve as a constant backdrop to the journey through media systems in the chapters that follow. Before ending Chapter 2, it will be helpful to step back and examine the power role framework as a whole after becoming familiar with its parts. Doing that will allow us to see issues regarding the media and the larger society that might have been missed when analyzing particular power roles.

A point made earlier bears repeating: Power roles represent interdependent *activities* of organizations. They are not in themselves organizations or groups. A corollary of this point is that organizations may take on more than one role within a mass media industry. Illustrations throughout this chapter have shown that producers are sometimes also distributors, exhibitors, and linking pins; that linking pins are sometimes also facilitators; that exhibitors are sometimes also patrons. The overlapping of other roles might be harder to imagine. For example, it is rather unusual to to find a case in the United States where a producer also acts as a client and auxiliary.

However, in today's world of many-leveled, vertically integrated conglomerates such combinations are not at all out of the question. In countries outside the United States, organizations take on the authority, producer, client, and auxiliary power roles across a variety of media industries. Only the public, public advocacy, and creator roles are, by the very nature of their definitions, not able to be carried out by organizations that also act as producers.

Coalitions and Power Centers

The accumulation of roles by an organization means an accumulation of the organization's ability to obtain resources. That, in turn, means an accumulation of the organization's ability to exert leverage within (and possibly across) mass media industries. Organizations can also increase their influence by forming coalitions with other organizations holding the same or different roles. For example, a union might increase its leverage with a production firm by marshaling the support of another union. The other union might agree to help out of genuine concern for the cause, or out of an assurance that the help will be repaid.

This view of mass communication as an interorganizational struggle over resources leads us to look for power centers and alliances. Awareness of this ever-moving and often shifting struggle should put to rest any notions that mass media material results from the process of "giving the public what it wants," as some media firms would have us believe. As the power role framework shows, the public is certainly a factor in an industry's scheme of things. It is, however, only one factor. Other power roles may at time be more evident, and carry more leverage, than do scattered, individual consumers.

In every established mass media industry there is a pattern of roles that the organizations maintain with one another. That role pattern is what we mean when we refer to an industry's **structure**. The broadcast television's structure, for example, is found in the rather predictable relationships that networks, Hollywood production firms, communication law firms, market research firms, pressure groups, and other entities have with one another. An important step toward understanding the structure of an industry and its function in society lies in assessing the events that have caused various relationships to evolve. Relationships not developed, leverage possibilities not pursued, resources not exploited—these and other omissions may have their roots in incidents, power struggles, and national philosophies that shaped an industry at its birth or at later critical points. Insight into the historical processes shaping mass communication is therefore necessary if you want to develop a firm understanding of the processes and strategies of media systems. To learn more about this subject, turn to Chapter 3.

NOTES

1. Howard Aldrich, *Organizations and Environments* (Englewood Cliffs, NJ: Prentice Hall, 1979), p. 4.
2. See Ephraim Yuctman and Stanley Seashore, "A System Resource Approach to Organizational Effectiveness," *American Sociological Review*: 32 (December 1967), p. 900.

3. George Gerbner, "Institutional Pressures upon Mass Communicators," *The Sociological Review Monograph* 13 (1969), pp. 205–248.

4. Michael Hannan and John Freeman, "The Population Ecology of Organizations," *American Journal of Sociology* 82 (March 1988), pp. 929–962; and Aldrich, *passim*.

5. Erik Barnouw, *A Tower in Babel* (New York: Oxford University Press, 1968).

6. Richard Allen Schwartzlose, *The American Wire Services* (New York: Arno Press, 1979), p. 239.

7. Kenneth Cox, "The Federal Communications Commission," *Boston College Industrial and Commercial Law Review* 11 (May 1970), pp. 605–666.

8. Ernest C. Hynds, *American Newspapers in the '80s* (New York: Hastings House, 1975), p. 157.

9. Cox, p. 631. See also Erik Barnouw, *The Golden Web* (New York: Oxford University Press, 1970), pp. 311–347.

10. Don R. Pember, *Mass Media Law* (Dubuque, IA: William C. Brown, 1977).

11. J. W. Click and Russel N. Baird, *Magazine Editing and Production*, 2nd ed. (Dubuque, IA: William C. Brown, 1979), p. 281.

12. "Vestron, Saying Nixed Loan Triggered Woes, Sues Bank," *Variety*, June 17 1989, p. 66.

13. Lewis Jacobs, *The Rise of the American Film* (New York: Teacher's College Press edition, 1968), pp. 302–305; and Arthur Knight, *The Liveliest Art* (New York: Signet edition, 1957), pp. 142–187 and 274–312.

14. Hynds, p. 273.

15. On *U.S. News*, see Click and Baird, p. 215. Also see Jim Rosenberg, "System Changeover Under Way At AP," *Editor and Publisher*, July 8, 1989, p. 20.

16. See Charlton Heston, "Actors as Union Men," in A. William Bleum and Jason Squires (eds.), *The Movie Business* (New York: Hastings House, 1972), pp. 85–91.

17. Alex S. Jones, "New York's *Daily News* Prepares for a War with Its Unions," *The New York Times*, September 25, 1989 p. D-9.

18. Hynds, p. 164.

19. John Dessauer, *Book Publishing* (New York: Bowker, 1974), p. 345.

20. M. William Krasilovsky, "Motivation and Control in Creative Writing," in Bleum and Squire, eds., p. 33.

21. J. Kenneth Rotcap, "The Story Editor," in Bleum and Squire, eds., p. 22.

22. Amy Kaufman, "It's Easier Now Than It Used to Be," *Emmy Magazine* 3 (Fall 1981), pp. 38–41.

23. Michael Fleming, "Pact Prods Pix Back to Gotham," *Variety*, May 20, 1991, p. 1.

24. Thomas Guback, "Theatrical Film," in Benjamin Compaine, ed., *Who Owns the Media?* (White Plains, NY: Knowledge Industry Publications, 1979), p. 183.

25. Geraldine Fabrikant, "Cable Hungry for Programs," *The New York Times*, November 16, 1989, p. D-1.

26. *Broadcasting Yearbook*, 1979, pp. A-1 and D-49.

27. Christopher H. Sterling, "Television and Radio Broadcasting," in Compaine, ed., p. 201.

28. Christoper H. Sterling and John M. Kittross, *Stay Tuned: A Concise History of Broadcasting* (Belmont, CA: Wadsworth, 1990), p. 637.

29. Michael Fleming, "Finsyn Peace Treaty Kinder to the Networks," *Variety*, April 8, 1991, p. 1.

30. J. Max Robins, "Would NBC Pare to Pact with Par?" *Variety*, April 29, 1991, p. 1.

31. Sterling and Kittross, *Stay Tuned*, p. 633.

32. *BP Report*, January 14, 1991, p. 4.

33. "New Women's Magazine Aiming Big," *Advertising Age*, March 2, 1981, p. 40.

34. Paul Hirsch, "Processing Fads and Fashions, *American Journal of Sociology* 77 (January 1972), pp. 639–659.

35. R. Serge Denisoff, *Solid Gold: The Popular Record Industry* (New Brunswick, NJ: Transaction Books, 1972), pp. 97–98.
36. Thomas Whiteside, *The Blockbuster Complex* (Middletown, CT: Wesleyan University Press, 1981), p. 70.
37. Whiteside, p. 70.

CHAPTER THREE

A Bit of History:
Government, Business, and Mass Media

Some people think of history as a collection of disconnected facts about eras that no longer exist. They are wrong. History is the study of the past, but seen through the eyes of the present. Good historians see that study not merely as a sequence of facts, but as a tapestry of stories built on those facts. The stories illuminate the way people used to think and live. But they do more. They serve as tools for trying to make sense of how and why we think and live today.

When it comes to mass media, a study of the past can help us understand how media industries developed the structures that currently guide them. Recall from Chapter 2 that when we talk of the structure of a media industry we mean the roles that organizations take with one another in the course of producing, distributing, and exhibiting mass media materials. In every society, these roles have a history behind them. They develop over time in response to political and economic conditions.

In the United States, present-day power role relationships did not begin with the organizations that currently exist within mass media industries. Rather, the bases of those relationships were set decades, even centuries, ago. The approaches that were instituted back then contained possibilities for activities by media industries that are only now beginning to emerge. In fact, some implications of the media structure have yet to be revealed. If the aim in this book is to understand present and future trends in mass media industries, part of our exploration must involve examining the ground upon which the contemporary media system was built.

Deciding where to begin is difficult. Strictly speaking, the industrial activity called mass communication began in the nineteenth century, as will be seen. Yet to understand mass communication it often helps to look further into the past. One can trace influences on American mass media all the way back to the invention of writing about 6,000 years ago. Another starting point might be the invention of the printing press by Johannes Gutenberg in the mid-fifteenth century region of Europe that is now Germany.

Here the scope must be more modest. The purpose will be to sketch how the fundamental power role relationships of American media industries—those that relate to authorities and clients—came to be. Accordingly, this chapter will trace the beginnings of government-media relations and media-business relations in the United States. In many ways, it is impossible to understand the government's role without understanding the role of business in the activities of U.S. mass media. That is because the business of media is sanctioned and regulated in a variety of ways by the authorities. Knowing why that is and how it came to be is crucial for being able to think creatively about contemporary relationships among government, business, and media.[1]

AN ADVERSARIAL RELATIONSHIP

In considering the development of government-media relations in the United States, it is instructive to think back to the American colonies of the eighteenth century and their most influential ruler, England. This was a period when crucial ground rules were set about the relationship between the government and newspaper printers. The newspaper was a relatively recent phenomenon in England at the time.

News historians agree that a newspaper can be defined as a printed product created on a regular (weekly or daily) basis and distributed to large numbers of people. By these criteria, the newspaper is almost by definition the most novel product of the printing press. Books, handwritten for a select few, had existed long before the 1400s; so had circulars, posters, and broadsides. The newspaper, on the other hand, could not exist before Gutenberg adapted the wine press to the idea of movable type, because regularized creation of large numbers of copies requires the use of machines. Gutenberg lavished attention on printing a revered book, the Bible. Others, though, used the press for relating contemporary events and ideas to the growing (but still very small) number of people who could read.

Newspapers of those days were little like the ones we see today. Illustrations (from block carvings) were few; the print was small and dense. Often, articles were simply reprints or translations of pieces in other newspapers, and they were not in the style we associate with contemporary reportage. Merchants were a primary audience, since the papers informed them about events in other countries that could influence their ability to travel and sell goods.

Political dissenters were also drawn to newspapers. One reason was that papers could bring information about the activities of enemies and allies, within or outside their territory. Another was that through newspapers they could circulate expressions of dissent among supporters and would-be supporters.

Commerce and Dissent

This dual function of newspapers—information provider for merchants and rallying point for political dissenters—helps explain the slow development of the medium in England and British colonial America. Although William Caxton set up the first press in England in 1476, nearly two centuries elapsed before the country had a newspaper printed regularly within its borders. One reason was that England was still not a mercantile power. What interest there was among the British in merchant news was supplied from abroad in English by the enterprising Dutch.

Another, more important, reason for Britain's failure to develop newspapers for any length of time during the sixteenth and seventeenth centuries had to do with the British Crown's fear of dissent and desire to fully control all printing. In 1509, for example, King Henry VIII put out a list of prohibited books and established a **licensing** system. Licensing meant that only people with written authority of the Crown could use a printing press. Queen Mary Tudor, who came after him, established the Stationers Company, whose members were the elite of printers. They were chosen for their loyalty to the monarchy and acted as police in the Crown's benefit. In the late 1500s, the Stationers adopted an order for a weekly search of London printing houses to report on work in progress, the number of orders on hand, the number of employees and their wages—even the identity of customers. Through the early 1600s, the crown passed from the Protestant Tudors to the Stuarts, who were Catholic. Political and religious disputes ensued and the power of the monarchy bined with a merchant class that was still not yet preoccupied with affairs on the European continent inhibited the creation of long-lasting, openly available newspapers.

By the 1600s, though, England was beginning its ascent to greatness as a trading nation. The atmosphere was ripe for more channels of communication that would inform the growing merchant class about conditions affecting their work outside England. Also on the rise were public arguments in print by various factions of British society. That was because the climate of governance was changing. In the early 1600s, the crown passed from the Protestant Tudors to the Stuarts, who were Catholic. Political and religious disputes ensued and the power of the monarchy deteriorated. Paralleling the Crown's decline, the power of other elites rose as Parliament gained a voice in British society that was more substantial than in the past.

Truth in the Field

Throughout this tumultuous century, British elites argued bitterly about the extent to which the press should be allowed to publicly reflect disputes. Embattled groups that supported the right of their side to be heard developed the argument that the free expression of ideas would necessarily help leaders of society and the people to see which side contained the truth. This was the theme of John Milton in the following passage of his famous 1644 pamphlet, *Areopagitica*:

> And though the winds of doctrine were let loose to play upon the earth, so truth be
> in the field, we do injuriously by licensing and prohibiting to misdoubt her strength.
> Let her and falsehood grapple: who ever knew truth put to the worse in a free and
> open encounter. . . .[2]

The idea that truth would always win out in a printed debate became the rallying cry behind those in England and America who wanted press freedoms. Among the British, it contributed directly to the establishment of the first English Bill of Rights in the 1680s, which endorsed free expression for members of Parliament. In the American colonies, it lay behind the glorification of a press system that was not only free from government control but was also free to attack the government.

This ideal was established slowly in the colonies during the eighteenth century. At the century's start, newspapers such as the *Boston Newsletter* carried the phrase "by authority of the Crown" even after such announcement of fealty was not required in England. Good will toward the political establishment was further assured by the fact that the publishers of many colonial papers were either postmasters appointed by the royal governor or printers who had succeeded in winning government printing contracts. In neither case was the person likely to circulate ideas that were politically suspect.

Nevertheless, there did appear printers who dared to challenge the authorities, and they set important examples. One was James Franklin, printer/publisher of the *New England Courant* in the 1720s. Franklin, brother of the more famous Ben, released articles that criticized Cotton and Increase Mather's leadership in Boston during a smallpox epidemic. Franklin was imprisoned, then exiled from the city, but not before he printed a ringing defense of his actions that echoed Milton.

> Even errors made publick, and afterwards publickly expos'd, less endanger the constitution of church or state, than they are (without opposition) industriously propagated in private conversation. Hence, to anathemize a printer for publishing the different opinions of men, is as injudicious as it is wicked.[3]

Public support for this position seems to have accelerated as a result of the trial of New York printer John Peter Zenger in 1735. He was charged with seditious libel for presenting information in his newspaper that criticized the generally disliked royal governor. The jury should have deemed Zenger guilty, since by British Common Law the truth of a published remark was not a relevant defense. Yet Zenger's renowned Philadelphia lawyer, Andrew Hamilton, persuaded the jury that his client was not guilty by reason of the value of exposing truth. Hamilton argued that Zenger should be set free because "Nature and Laws of our Country have given us a Right—the Liberty—both of exposing and opposing arbitrary Power (in these Parts of the World, at least) by speaking and writing Truth."[4]

Hamilton's comments and the jury's verdict point to an idea that was gaining strength through the 1700s in the American colonies: that the newspaper could and should be used as a weapon of truth against unfair aspects of British colonial rule. Many American intellectuals were influenced by European "Enlightenment" philosophers of the day. They agreed with the endorsement by Bacon, Descartes, and others of the empirical methods of scientific, rational inquiry. They agreed, too, with the affirmation by Locke, Montesquieu, and other thinkers that truth, as shown by reason, would inevitably triumph when challenged by error—and that it would be recognized by the majority. As they saw it, reason would triumph in human affairs through the action of the majority in political decisions. This was, in fact, the extension of Milton's *Areopagitica* argument, and the British parliamentary Bill of Rights, to the people at large in relation to the government.

Toward the First Amendment

The contention that the press could and should play an adversarial role toward the government became particularly strong in the wake of British attempts to impose taxes on paper to pay for its expensive war with France during the 1760s and 1770s. Lawyers and printers (who were most hurt by these rules) banded together to publish strong condemnations of the British colonial policy of taxation without representation.

Their concern with the right to move their arguments into the public arena carried over to the postrevolutionary era. Each of the various ideological factions and state governments that vied for primacy in the new union that was being established were concerned that it not be prevented by more powerful parties from using the press and orator's box. American newspapers of the late eighteenth century tended to voice the opinions of particular political parties, with no pretense of impartiality. Their owners, and the parties they stood for, wanted to keep doing that.

As a result, the framers of the United States Constitution of 1787 found it necessary to agree to a Bill of Rights that would include the following words: "Congress shall make no law . . . abridging the freedom of speech, or of the press." This First Amendment to the Constitution, largely the work of James Madison, points very clearly to concern by the Founding Fathers over government manipulation of the press. The amendment does not insist that speech and the press ought to be free in some broad, abstract sense. Rather, it specifically refers to freedom from congressional control, just as many of the state constitutions specify freedoms of speech and of the press from government control within their borders. The issue of private control over the avenues of knowledge—by advertisers, media conglomerates, or other means—is not a concern of the First Amendment.

The point of the First Amendment, in other words, was to ensure that the adversary relationship between the press and the authorities which had evolved during colonial times and continued into the early days of the republic would continue. Congressional prohibitions that restrained the press but did not impede this adversary relationship were allowed. Laws regulating slander, libel, and indecent language were elaborated and interpreted through the nineteenth and twentieth centuries. **Plagiarism**—copying someone's work without permission—likewise was disallowed, as it had been under English common law. By extension, the idea that Congress could set forth the terms whereby a person could control a work—a notion called **copyright**—was not felt to be an abridgment of press freedoms.

Even when it came to the cherished adversary relationship, government actions were not always in harmony with the celebrated ideal. For one thing, when the Constitution was written, it seems clear that the framers saw the Bill of Rights as reserved for cultured, literate white males only. They believed that such people were the only ones who ought to have access to a press. Moreover, within seven years of the adoption of the First Amendment, the threat of war with France led President John Adams to secure congressional approval of the **Sedition Act**. It threatened journalists with prison for writing material that cast aspersions on the political leadership of the United States.

Consider, too, that even national leaders who stressed the importance of press freedoms could sometimes voice exasperation and impatience with the potpourri of scurrilous accusations that the nation's highly politicized newspapers were serving up.

President Thomas Jefferson, for example, was distressed in 1803 by the vitriol of the Federalist press. He toyed with the thought that "a few prosecutions of the most prominent offenders" would bring the rest of the newspaper community into line. That he, and George Washington before him, did not follow this tack is testimonial to his deep belief that contending political viewpoints would help the nation arrive at truth. But the tension that Washington, Jefferson, and many government leaders after them felt over this adversarial relationship with the press has continued through today.

TOWARD A NEW SUPPORT SYSTEM

One reason the press's adversarial relationship with the government could continue was that newspapers and other public media developed forms of monetary support that were not connected directly to the government. The First Amendment ensures only that the government will not enact laws directly controlling the content of the press. The amendment does not say anything about other methods politicians can use to control what is printed. A key avenue of such control is cash. If the major leaders of the government are the only ones who can support newspapers (or magazines or TV stations), the views expressed through those communication channels will effectively be controlled by those leaders.

From the start of the republic, however, it was clear that newspapers could find funds from a variety of sources to keep the adversarial relationship going. Newspapers of the early United States reveled in the kinds of political attacks that today we associate with entertainment/gossip tabloids such as *The National Enquirer*. For example, a *New York Evening Post* article reported that President Thomas Jefferson, a Republican, had paid a Richmond, Virginia, newspaper editor to spread the word that George Washington, a Federalist, had been a robber, traitor, and perjurer.[5] The combativeness within the highly politicized American press could have implications for physical harm. When Benjamin Franklin Bache wrote in the *Philadelphia General Advertiser* of 1796 that "the American nation has been debauched by Washington," Federalists wrecked his office and beat him in retaliation.[6] Similarly, when Vice President Aaron Burr challenged Treasury Secretary Alexander Hamilton to the duel that took the latter's life, it occurred after an Albany newspaper published an alleged remark by Hamilton that Burr found personally insulting.[7]

Early American newspapers were typically small operations run by publishers who were also printers and editors. They drew their support primarily from the upper-class aristocracy or the upper-middle-class merchants. Many of the papers were allied with political parties. That explains why, apart from commercial notices, much of the "news" that appeared was phrased in the form of fierce political arguments against the opposition.

Some newspapers were even supported by party officials, who helped arrange lucrative government printing contracts for the editors. Readers who picked up the *Gazette of The United States* during the 1790s knew they were reading the organ of the Federalist party sponsored by Alexander Hamilton. Similarly, readers knew that *The National Gazette* was a Jeffersonian Republican mouthpiece.

The great majority of Americans did not read any of the newspapers that were printed during the closing years of the eighteenth century and the first few decades of the nineteenth. Much of the reason was illiteracy, though the number of working-class citizens learning to read was growing rather quickly. Even among those who could read, however, the cost of getting a newspaper was out of reach. The reason was that newspapers were still created in an expensive, labor-intensive manner—by hand-driven presses that as late as the 1790s were still not that much different from Gutenberg's.

Publishers charged from $6 to $10 a year *in advance* for a newspaper subscription. That was more than most skilled workmen earned in a week and, in any case, a person of limited means could not pay all of that up front. One result was that circulations were not impressive by current standards. A circulation of 1,500 was considered adequate in all but the biggest commercial centers. Another consequence was that most of the papers tended to reflect the editorial slant of the conservative political party (the Federalist party), since the prosperous class seemed to gravitate toward that viewpoint.[8]

A Sea Change

By the 1830s, however, a number of factors were converging to encourage a sea change in American journalism. The 1820s and 1830s marked the rise of an emphasis on the power of the "common man." Andrew Jackson's presidential victory in 1829 signaled the utility of appealing to more than just the wealthy in a nation where white male suffrage was the rule. Literacy among the working class continued to climb. In fact, the interest of workers in newspapers was evident in a number of early union-supported newspapers that had appeared briefly during the previous decade.

Adding to this fascinating soup of change was the steam-powered press. Invented in Saxony (today a part of Germany), improved in England and the United States, a steam-powered press in 1830 was able to produce 4,000 double impressions an hour. The labor-saving speed of the technology lowered the per-page cost of printing drastically, making a newspaper that huge numbers of people could afford possible. During the late 1820s and early 1830s, in fact, a number of entrepreneurs tried to create a paper that sold for a penny, but with little success.

Then, in 1833 Benjamin Day, a struggling printer, founded the *New York Sun*. Hugely successful (within six months its circulation reached 8,000) and quickly imitated, it pointed the way toward drastic changes in the look and content of the American newspaper. Doing that, however, it did more: It led to a revolution in the way many mass media in the United States were financed.

The slogan on the *Sun*'s masthead was "It Shines for All." It reflected the newspaper's desire to entice great numbers of people, rather than only the merchant class, to its material. To the typical newspaper of the early nineteenth century, the *Sun* was shockingly different. Following the example of an emerging British popular press, Day's product and its imitators emphasized not partisan politics but sensationalism, human interest, and humor. In the earliest years, hoaxes and exaggerated stories were fairly common. Over the next few decades, however, the *Sun* and other papers in this new generation (such as the *New York Herald* and *New York Tribune*) developed a basic approach to the organization of American journalism and the presentation of news that still obtains today.

A consensus emerged about the importance of such characteristics as speed in identifying and processing news; the proper use of headlines, datelines, and bylines; distinctions between "hard news" and "features"; the optimal adversarial stance between government and journalist in a nonpartisan press; and the procedure for writing an "objective" story. These approaches became the backbone of a prosperous new newspaper industry. By the end of the century, the values and writing standards of American journalism were shared so widely that they were used to justify the professionalization of newswork as taught in special journalism schools.

The nature and implications of these values and standards will be discussed in Chapter 7. Here it is important to point out that **the new nonpartisan approach to journalism encouraged a new, industrialized, way of organizing and supporting production, one that could truly be called mass communication**.

From the start, Benjamin Day's slogan "It Shines for All" reflected his philosophy for financing the paper as well as creating its content. He and his partners believed that a penny publication would thrive by making its money back one issue at a time. The paper was sold on the streets for a penny by ambitious hawkers who made about 37 cents for every hundred copies they sold. As new presses offered faster, larger, and cheaper print runs, increased circulation meant increased profits for the publisher. Day and his competitors tried to entice more and more readers to their product by adding new sections to match a variety of possible interests, including those of the wealthier classes. The *New York Herald* was particularly innovative in appealing to different segments of the population in different portions of the same issue. By the late 1840s, it had a sports section, a critical review column, society news, and a strong financial section, among others.

One consequence of such developments was that newspapers became complex organizations. The single printer-publisher-editor-reporter of the early 1800s gave way to a hierarchy of specialized positions needed to create, print, and market the newspaper. A related change was that through the middle and late nineteenth century and the early twentieth century the newspaper world became industrialized. Newspaper organizations entered into regularized interactions with a variety of organizations and industries that provided the symbolic and material supplies necessary to do their work. From the standpoint of actual editorial product, the chief new organizational contributors were the telegraph company (Western Union), the newswire services (such as Reuters and the Associated Press), and syndication firms (such as King Features). Just as significant, the money to pay for these services came increasingly not from readers but from a new set of organizations that wanted to reach them: the advertising industry.

The Rise of Advertising

Advertising had actually begun well before the nineteenth century. Merchants had advertised in newspapers from their inception, and by the time Benjamin Day arrived on the scene ads were taken for granted as a fact of journalistic life. In those days, advertising was a source of extra money for a newspaper firm; the real source for financing the operation was from the readership. In the decades after the rise of the penny press, however, the emphasis of financial support shifted, and advertising became the monetary lifeblood of the journalistic enterprise.

Talking Point 3.1   A Whistler

The penny papers were as different from today's major dailies as from the traditional political-commercial papers of their day. Editors had no qualms about running unattributed stories about unnamed people doing things at unnamed times who seemed to be news simply because they were interesting. The following story ran on the front page of the *New York Sun*'s first issue, September 3, 1833:

> A Whistler—A boy in Vermont, accustomed to working alone, was so prone to whistling, that as soon as he was by himself, he unconsciously commenced. When asleep, the muscles of his mouth, chest, and lungs were so completely concatenated in the association, he whistled with astonishing shrillness. A pale countenance, loss of appetite, and almost total prostration of strength, convinced his mother it would end in death if not speedily overcome, which was accomplished by placing him in the society of another boy, who had orders to give him a blow as soon as he began to whistle.

Many considerations led to the changed relationship between advertisers and newspaper organizations. One was simply that advertisers were impressed by the large circulations of the new penny press and its descendents. It allowed them to reach more people through one vehicle than was previously possible. The news merchants, for their part, saw advertising revenue as a the way to get the large amounts of cash required to purchase the faster printing presses and other technologies necessary to stay ahead in what had become a highly competitive business.

The competition typically revolved around speed. Publishers, editors, and reporters increasingly saw news in terms of getting stories to the public faster than their counterparts in other papers did. Boasting about having "the latest" news seemed to increase circulation. So did emphasizing that coverage was "objective," even when pursuing an adversarial relationship with government, so that people of all political persuasions could read the same paper for "the facts."

Increasing circulation was the way to increase advertising revenues. Increased ad revenues, in turn, allowed for more speed-oriented technologies that could bring the latest news along with a kaleidoscope of cartoons, human interest columns, and pictures. That, publishers felt, would lift circulation to still greater heights. It was a continuing cycle.

Advertising as an industry evolved hand in hand with the new U.S. world of journalism. Central to that industry was the advertising agency. The first one was conceived in 1849 as a middleman between papers and businesses looking to purchase space for ads. In the decades that followed the American Civil War ad agencies developed into marketing arms for companies trying to sell goods.

Innovative persuasive strategies for newspaper ads were most often used to hawk patent medicine products—drinks and other commodities that were supposed to cure bodily ailments but most often could cause them if they did anything at all. Ineffective and illegal patent medicines were outlawed in 1905 by the nation's first Pure Food and Drug Act. However, the legacy of patent medicine advertising remained—in advertisers' strong financial influence over the newspaper business, in the persuasive

---

Talking Point 3.2   *The Ladies' Morning Star*

The phenomenal success of the first penny papers in New York City—the *Sun*, the *Transcript*, and the *Herald*—soon resulted in a number of others in New York, all of which were short-lived. The most novel of those failed undertakings was a penny paper for women, *The Ladies' Morning Star*, established by William Newell in April 1836. Two years earlier, a similar attempt, edited by an "Ann Oddbody," had failed. Newell was trying again.

Newell's idea was that the general penny press did not address what he (and others of the day) saw as the more refined sensibilities that women had over men. The police reports of the typical penny papers were, he stated in an editorial, written in a way that degraded those sensibilities. Echoing Benjamin Day's motto "It Shines for All," Newell wrote that his paper was aimed at all types of women, those married as well as "that class of young women who live by their daily labor."

The paper was praised at the time by the editor of the Philadelphia *Public Ledger*. Unfortunately for Newell, he could attract neither advertisers nor readers. Merchants apparently objected to advertising in a paper intended exclusively for women. Newell, after six months, changed the name to *The Morning Star*. That still did not help pay the bills, though, and the paper died by the end of the year.

SOURCE: William Grosvenor Bleyer, *Main Currents in the History of American Journalism* (Boston: Houghton Mifflin Company, 1927), pp. 168–171.

---

strategies that showed up in ads for a variety of products, and, not least, in the taint of unscrupulousness it lent to the advertising business within society at large.

By the time of patent medicine advertising's demise, many other goods had come on the advertising scene. The late nineteenth century was a period of rapid expansion of the U.S. economy. The Industrial Revolution was moving at full speed, and a flood of new consumer products was being released to the marketplace that needed to get public awareness to succeed. Advertising agencies became vehicles to try to create that awareness. The space that ad agencies bought encouraged huge circulation growth and rapid competition among big city newspapers of the late nineteenth century. Advertisers also sponsored weekly and monthly magazines (*The Saturday Evening Post*, *Collier's*, *The Ladies' Home Journal*) that reached millions of people. Keeping this boom going were a rapidly growing population of readers, favorable postal rates, further developments in high-speed printing, and the ability to reproduce photographs on high-speed presses.

The result was that newspapers and magazines entered the twentieth century with the largest audiences in history to that point. What is more, the audience was paying a minor portion of the actual costs of producing what it was reading. Advertisers, searching for huge numbers of likely consumers, were footing most of the bill. In about a century American mass media had developed a support system that separated media control from political parties. A new source of financial control—advertisers and the advertising industry—had risen to take its place. One broad consequence was obvious. Rather than politics guiding the creation and content of newspapers, now commerce set the ground rules. Newspapers and magazines had become vehicles in a people-catching activity.

BUSINESS, GOVERNMENT, AND NEW MASS MEDIA

Not all U.S. mass media used advertising as their primary support at the turn of the twentieth century. The book industry mostly continued its centuries-old tradition of printing only announcements of related titles by the same publisher. Similarly, the new music recording industry carried no ads on its discs, although the records' paper jackets often advertised the companies' other offerings. One reason for the absence of ads on the recordings themselves might simply have been the initial shortness of a disc's playing time. Early records had only one side, and a song plus a commercial would not fit on the same side.

That kind of constraint did not apply in the film industry. In fact, film entrepreneurs did experiment with using moving images to sell consumer products as early as the 1890s.[9] Still, even though the advertisement of "coming attractions" became standard in U.S. theaters, the practice of presenting commercials for nonfilm products did not catch on in U.S. theaters until the 1980s. One can speculate about the reasons, but no one seems to have investigated them systematically.

Government, Business, and Radio

In not encouraging advertising, the recording and movie industries stand out as unusual when compared with almost all other mass media that developed in the twentieth century. Radio, which emerged in the 1920s as a major mass medium, was the new technology that set the pattern in favor of ad industry sponsorship. Today, Americans may think of commercials as a natural part of radio and its offshoot, television. Advertising was never a necessary part of that invention, however. In England, radio was operated through a government-run organization (the British Broadcasting Corporation), supported by a tax on receivers. It did not evolve a commercial side until the 1950s.

In the United States, neither private ownership nor commercial sponsorship was taken for granted, either. The U.S. Navy, which had been authorized control of radio broadcasting for reasons of national security during World War I, lobbied Congress vigorously to retain that monopoly after the war. When Congress denied the Navy's request and decided that broadcasting to the public ought to be developed privately, many observers within the radio business and outside it stated their hope that radio waves would never be used to sell products. They felt that radio stations could be financed by stores and equipment manufacturers that needed to give consumers something to listen to after they purchased sets.

Looking back on the congressional debate about the future of radio in 1919, one can see quite clearly how a view of the past combined with concerns of the present shaped the nation's approach to a new mass medium. The United States at the time was an increasingly wealthy, business-oriented society. Radio was undeveloped, with unwieldy technology, listeners who saw it as a curiosity, and no regularly scheduled programs. It was clear, though, that the medium was on the threshold of great changes.

Leaders of commerce and government believed that the best way to develop radio's great potential was to move it from the public to the private sector. In addition, members of Congress were acutely aware of the American tradition that kept mass media away from direct government control. A broadcast station could spread words further than any individual newspaper or magazine could. Moreover, it could reach the illiterate as well as the literate. Allowing the Navy to dictate decisions about use of the airwaves would mean getting a government agency into the potentially controversial area of controlling ideas to large segments of the population.

As the result of this debate, Congress decreed in 1919 that broadcasting was to be a privately sponsored enterprise, available to any citizen who paid for a license. Radio's split from government was not straightforward, however. Leaders at the U.S. Navy feared that opening broadcasting to all comers might mean that power over this potentially important medium could fall to parties with ill will toward the nation. To ensure that dominant control of radio would remain in friendly hands, the Navy encouraged a number of American firms that owned the major broadcast patents (notably, American Telephone and Telegraph, General Electric, and the Westinghouse Company) to form a patent **trust**—that is, a company that would rule U.S. radio through patents.

They called the trust the Radio Corporation of America (RCA). The idea was to force anyone interested in setting up a broadcasting operation to pay RCA for the infringement on RCA's radio patents. RCA, in turn, would impose certain agreed-upon conditions on the use of the airwaves. In addition, RCA would be the most powerful force developing the airwaves, thereby ensuring that an entity close to the Navy would remain in the driver's seat.

The use of a patent trust to control a media industry was not new. Thomas Edison, for one, had tried it in both the record and movie industries. Moreover, like the movie and record trusts before it, the radio monopoly was broken up by the courts within a decade of its inception. The creation of RCA was different from the building of the other trusts because it was orchestrated by an arm of the federal government. Still, both the construction and destruction of these early media monopolies were indicative of a new federal approach to media in the late nineteenth century. It involved attempts by one or another branch of the government to sidestep the prohibitions of the First Amendment through **structural regulation**—that is, through laws or rulings that would guide the creative output of the industry *indirectly* by dictating the industry's structure.

TENSIONS OVER CONTROL

The trend toward structural regulation reflected a complex social tension that developed around new media during the early 1900s. The tension was rooted in the same uneasiness about alleged political excesses of the press that had agitated American leaders in the early years of the republic. Added to it, however, were new concerns that moved government officials and others to search for ways to influence the mass media beyond copyright, libel, and obscenity statutes.

Talking Point 3.3   Defending Patent Medicine Advertising

Like many newspapers of the nineteenth century, *The Boston Daily Times* printed much advertising from patent medicine firms. Also like many of the papers, the *Times* received angry letters for doing that. In an 1837 editorial, it defended its practice in this way:

> Some of our readers complain of the great number of patent medicines advertised in this paper. To this complaint we can only reply that it is for our interest to insert such advertise-ments as are not indecent or improper in their language, without any inquiry whether the articles advertised are what they purport to be. That is an inquiry for the reader who feels interested in the matter, and not for us, to make. It is sufficient for our purpose that the advertisements are paid for, and that, while we reserve the right of excluding such as are improper to be read, to the advertising public we are impartial, and show no respect to persons or to the various kinds of business that fill up this little world of ours. One man has as good a right as another to have his wares, his goods, his panaceas, his profession, published to the world in a newspaper, provided he pays for it.

SOURCE: William Grosvenor Bleyer, *Main Currents in the History of American Journalism* (Boston: Houghton Mifflin Company, 1927), pp. 174–175.

One difficulty critics voiced was that the popular new media, especially motion pictures and radio, did not use the printed word. Consequently, the argument went, they could reach huge numbers of children and illiterate adults with dangerous ideas that they would not be able handle intelligently. Another part of the problem was that increasingly large companies were dominating the news and entertainment businesses. Critics from several quarters worried about the implications of having powerful pri-vate corporations in charge of wide-reaching communication technologies, especially if their goal was to reach the intellectually vulnerable of the society.

Activists of many political stripes called for structural regulation and direct content regulation to protect the nation from problems they alleged the new technolo-gies were bringing. Conservatives saw both approaches as ways to ensure government control over potentially disruptive media. Liberals tended to prefer structural regula-tion when it was used to break up monopolistic activities. They argued that federal trust-busting encouraged freedom of the press, even though it meant getting the government involved in setting a media industry's rules. By fostering competition, they reasoned, the government would encourage diversity in the production, distribu-tion, and exhibition of cultural materials. Despite their insistence on First Amendment rights, however, some liberals also believed that structural edicts might not be enough to erase problems such as racism and violence in movies or on the radio. They insisted that certain abuses demanded direct regulation of content by government.

Inviting Government Interference in Radio

These types of arguments and concerns had much to do with shaping the structure and content of the American movie and radio industries during the 1920s. In the case of radio, private interests actually invited government interference. As the medium moved into the private realm, the Department of Commerce, which administered radio, felt it had no right to turn anyone down for a license. That led to an oversupply of parties willing to pay for a broadcast license and air programming. The result in many localities was that radio stations were broadcasting on top of one another.

The interference caused cacophony over the airwaves. This, in turn, hindered the development of stations and networks whose owners were trying to make radio broadcasting into a stable business supported by advertisers interested in reaching large numbers of people. The situation was so annoying to those powerful stations that they pressured Congress to pass a law that would allow the federal government to allocate radio frequencies selectively with the aim of bringing order to the airwaves.

By the middle 1920s it had become clear that RCA would not be the government's answer to influence and order over radio. Wanting to aid the evolving radio industry while not losing power over it, congressional leaders adopted the argument that federal jurisdiction over the medium's structure and content was justified by the nature of the technology. Radio waves, they argued, make up a scarce public resource and, as such, should have their use guided by the government.

The ensuing deliberations led to the Federal Radio Act of 1927. It established a Federal Radio Commission as the presidentially appointed, congressionally confirmed body that would decide who should get frequencies and who should not. It was clear that Congress intended most licenses to be in private hands. Relatively few spots on the dial went to universities and nonprofit foundations.

At the same time, lawmakers composed the act to allow continuing government influence on the materials those businesses were sending out. One specific paragraph required that broadcasters give "equal time" to political candidates. The other rulings relating to content were more general. A radio license was given to the broadcaster for five-year terms. It could be revoked, the act warned, if the licensee did not broadcast "in the public interest, convenience, and necessity."

Exactly what that phrase meant was not made clear; its meaning has never been spelled out. Yet the ambiguous language was carried over into a revised Federal Communications Act of 1936, when the name of the regulatory body was changed to the Federal Communications Commission. It seems clear that the ambiguity was retained because it served as an important safety valve in relation to the tension between government and private control over the mass media content.

The phrase allowed the executive branch and Congress to have it both ways. That is, they could express concern and power over broadcast materials while they technically retained the "hands off" stance that had existed historically between government and press in the United States. The hope was that government influence over content would be exerted through **raised eyebrow** or **jawbone** methods. Companies afraid of losing the right to broadcast would adjust their programming in response to implied (raised eyebrow) or directly expressed (jawbone) complaints by regulators.

The Movies and Government Control

An obvious question confronting broadcasters was how to avoid more direct government controls in the future. The same sort of question had been faced by the movie industry a few years earlier. At the turn of the 1920s, the Hollywood movie studios

---

Talking Point 3.4   Sex and the Motion Picture Code

The Production Code of the Motion Picture Producers and Directors of America went through several revisions. In each, the depiction of "sex" (as the code called it) received substantial attention. They helped shape the way romance, love, marriage, sexual violence, and sexually transmittable diseases were depicted. Below are the rules laid out by the code that was in effect between 1930 and 1934. Note that Spike Lee's 1991 movie *Jungle Fever*, about a white-black romance, would have been impossible under the code.

> The sanctity of the institution of marriage and the home shall be upheld. Pictures shall not infer that low forms of sex relationship are the accepted or common thing.
>
> 1. Adultery and illicit sex, sometimes necessary plot material, must not be explicitly treated or justified, or presented attractively.
> 2. Scenes of passion
>   a) These should not be introduced except where they are definitely essential to the plot.
>   b) Excessive and lustful kissing, lustful embraces, suggestive postures and gestures are not to be shown.
>   c) In general, passion should be treated in such manner as not to stimulate the lower and baser emotions.
> 3. Seduction or rape
>   a) These should never be more than suggested, and then only when essential for the plot. They must never be shown by explicit method.
>   b) They are never the proper subject for comedy.
> 4. Sex perversion or any inference to it is forbidden.
> 5. White slavery shall not be treated.
> 6. Miscegenation (sex relationship between the white and black races) is forbidden.
> 7. Sex hygiene and venereal diseases are not proper subjects for theatrical motion pictures.
> 8. Scenes of actual childbirth, in fact or in silhouette, are never to be presented.
> 9. Children's sex organs are never to be exposed.

SOURCE: Garth Jowett, *Film: The Democratic Art* (New York: Little Brown, 1976), p. 469.

---

had been besieged by angry groups throughout the nation. They were upset about what they considered the unwarranted violence and sexual displays in motion pictures of the day. Murder and sex scandals among a few popular actors further encouraged demands by those advocacy groups that the studios be restrained by city, state, or federal government agencies from distributing what the critics insisted were films injurious to the nation's health. Between 1909 and 1922 eight states passed some form of film censorship legislation.[10]

Legal justification for this sort of content regulation was necessarily different from the one used regarding broadcasting. Movies did not involve scarce radio waves. They did mostly involve "entertainment," though, and in 1915 the U.S. Supreme Court ruled that motion picture fiction was "a spectacle, a show," not part of the "press," and therefore not protected by the First Amendment. As a result, the Court continued, films might legally be censored and regulated by authorities at the federal, state, or local levels.

Fearing that a patchwork of state rules would make the separate editing of films for release to different regions of the country unmanageably expensive, the heads of the major Hollywood film studios turned for protection to self-regulation. Their vehicle, created in 1922, was the Motion Picture Producers and Distributors of America (MPPDA). To underscore the MPPDA's allegiance to government authority, they followed (probably unconsciously) a course similar to the one that British colonial governors had used in the early eighteenth century: they chose a postmaster with other strong ties to the establishment. Will Hays, the former U.S. postmaster general, Republican party chairman, and Presbyterian Church elder, became so identified with the MPPDA that it was called the Hays Office during his twenty years there.

Hays set forth elaborate criteria that the major motion picture studios agreed to accept as indicating the boundaries of good taste in their films. A member studio could be fined for releasing a film that had not passed MPPDA inspection. The Hays Office criteria were formalized into a code in 1930. Although the code and the MPPDA's other activities did not eliminate public anger and calls for censorship over movies that groups felt were harmful, the Hays Office nevertheless was successful in staving off direct government control over the content of films. It is not surprising, then, that radio broadcasters followed the film industry's precedence of **self-regulation**. In fact, the National Association of Broadcasters announced a "code of ethics and standards of commercial practice" a year before the Hays Office released the public version of its code. Through these actions, the rhetoric of self-regulation became an integral part of the complex tug-of-war over government and private influence on the mass media.

REGULATORY SHIFTS

In 1952, the government's ability to influence films was reduced substantially when the Supreme Court ruled that a New York law outlawing "sacrilegious" movies was too vague and that it unconstitutionally abridged freedom of speech and press. The High Court did not say that all censorship by government agencies was unconstitutional. However, the ruling and others that flowed from it effectively ended government authority to interfere directly with nonbroadcast media content, except in cases relating to copyright, slander, obscenity, and certain types of commercial speech. Structural regulation was still a viable option, though; the setting of postal rates, the questioning of firms' tax status, and the implementation of antitrust suits have been among a spectrum of approaches that government agencies have used to encourage certain types of media activities while discouraging others. The threat of such tactics, and the desire for the general public's good will, has kept "self-regulation" alive among moviemakers, pop recording companies, and other media firms.

Broadcast Regulation

As noted, broadcasting has continued to be the exception where direct government rulings on content are allowed even though they breach the First Amendment rights of the firms' owners and managers. The Federal Communications Act requires that broadcasters give "equal time" to political candidates; newspapers have no such obligation. In addition, debate at the federal level has periodically centered on whether certain types of programming—notably certain kinds of children's shows—

ought to be required. Federal actions to require programming would clearly be illegal in nonbroadcast media.

When television technology was being developed in the 1920s and 1930s, government officials and industry leaders considered it an extension of radio and so agreed that the regulatory apparatus should be the same. After the Supreme Court's landmark 1952 decision applying free speech criteria to motion pictures, regulators have realized that their legal ability to make broad rulings about new media hinges on showing those media are more like broadcasting than theatrical film. That means developing a justification similar to the "natural scarcity" reasoning used for broadcasting.

Home Video and Cable

Home video and cable television are two technologies that provide interesting contrasts regarding government application of this rationale. Home video, which emerged as a popular medium in the mid-1970s, has managed to position itself as a counterpart to movies, magazines, and sound recordings. Inasmuch as the print model of "freedom of the press" applies to those media, legislators and the courts have accepted that it applies to video cassettes.

The situation with cable television is quite different. Cable was introduced during the late 1940s as a way to use a special wire (a coaxial cable) to bring over-the-air TV signals to populations too far from TV transmitters to receive them normally. Reflecting its role as a retransmission service, the technology was called **community antenna television** (CATV). Since then, much jockeying has gone on between government and private interests to decide how cable ought to be treated and who (if anyone) at the government level should have jurisdiction over its programming.

Until the late 1950s, the Federal Communications Commission refused to address regulatory issues regarding cable. Then, prodded by broadcasters who saw the medium as a potential competitor, the FCC announced the following logic: Since CATV was basically delivering broadcast signals to people, it was a service *ancillary* (or related to) broadcasting and therefore could be regulated like broadcasting.

In the 1960s and 1970s, many cable operators began moving out of the business of simply retransmitting broadcast signals from the nearest large cities. They enticed viewers in major metropolitan areas to their service by offering stations from around the country and by adding channels (the weather, the Cable News Network) that were unique to cable. Nevertheless, the FCC continued to regulate the cable industry under the "ancillary" justification. Many cable TV executives saw the regulatory link to broadcasting as a hindrance. Gaining lobbying strength as it gained economic power, the cable industry began to fight this comparison with broadcasters and the restrictions that came with it. Cable executives felt the restrictions were aimed at slowing their industry's growth to protect over-the-air broadcasters.

The lobbying effort was helped by the deregulatory climate of the 1980s. One important result was the Cable Communications Policy Act of 1984. The act clearly divided the regulatory authority for cable. It gave the FCC overall jurisdiction but allowed state and local governments to control **franchising**, the process of drawing up contracts. Contrary to what many local regulators had wanted, the act allowed cable operators to set their own rates. The act did say that franchising authorities could require systems to provide channels for public, educational, and government use, but this provision was later challenged in court.

The deregulatory trend continued in 1985 when a federal appeals court struck down the FCC's "must-carry rules." Based on the idea that cable was ancillary, the rules required that cable systems carry all local stations and any others significantly viewed in the community. A revised set of must-carry rules drafted by the FCC in 1987 was also declared unconstitutional. The courts did not accept the commission's argument that cable's ancillary status to broadcasting justified the forcing of systems to carry particular channels.

Still, neither the act nor the court decisions refuted the idea that the cable business is an ancillary service to broadcasting. Many in the industry, however, have argued that the ancillary tag is outmoded. Some have gone so far as to say that the government should view them as similar to newspaper companies, with all the First Amendment rights that apply to the print media. More commonly, cable industry leaders have felt a need to keep some form of direct regulation, since they want to be able to sign near-exclusive franchises with the communities they serve. They have therefore argued that cable television should be regulated, but only with the minimum safeguards necessary to ensure that a cable operator adheres to its franchise. That would make cable firms far less regulated than broadcasters, but more controlled than newspapers.

Other parties have taken yet a third position. They suggest that the contemporary cable TV situation is most similar to the "natural monopoly" position of a telephone company, since cable firms typically operate with no cable competition in the areas they serve. Those who take this position contend that cable TV firms should act as **common carriers**—that is, as message conduits, like telephone companies, rather than as program creators.

Cable firms are wary of this notion even though it frees them of most content regulation. One reason they reject it is that it implies they should have little control over the materials they send over the wires. Another reason they reject this conception of cable TV is that it virtually invites the powerful regional phone companies to get into the business of delivering TV signals to the home. While this activity is quite possible from a technical standpoint, it has been prohibited by the 1984 ruling that broke up the American Telephone and Telegraph Company and created the "Baby Bells"—Bell Atlantic, Nynex, Bell South, Ameritech, US West, Southwestern Bell, and Pacific Telesis.

The U.S. district judge who oversaw the breakup, Harold Green, imposed the ban out of a concern that these wealthy "telcos" would use their technological and monetary might to drive cable companies out of business. In mid-1991, however, Green decided that an appeals court decision of the previous year along with changing competitive circumstances—including the increased wealth of cable firms—now justified allowing the regional telephone companies to offer information services such as cable programming and news by phone. Recognizing the turmoil his ruling would cause, Green ordered it not to go into effect until parties unhappy with the decision could appeal it. Many cable firms and newspapers were wary that the phone companies would infringe on their turf. They immediately announced their intention to fight the change in Congress, at the FCC, and in state public utility commissions, as well as in the courts.[11]

GOVERNMENT AND THE BUSINESS OF MEDIA

Such a struggle over the regulatory approach to a medium recalls the critical debates Congress held about the structure of radio in 1919 and 1927. There is a substantial difference, though. In the 1920s, radio was a medium in relative infancy, while in the 1990s cable television has been on the American scene for more than forty years. What has happened with cable is that the medium has been regulated differently during different decades, as various business constituencies have risen to support of one or another regulatory approach that would fit their interests. With so many powerful interests exerting leverage on lawmakers regarding the future of cable TV, it is not clear that the medium's regulatory roller coaster ride will end soon.

Two points are useful to emphasize about this situation. One is that the various regulatory alternatives for cable television in America—the ancillary-to-broadcasting model, the common carrier model, the newspaper model—are very much solidly anchored in the history of government-media relations; to understand them, one must understand the history of the government and media in America. The second point is that the regulatory uncertainty facing cable is highly unusual for an American mass medium.

As this chapter has shown, the structural, technical, and content regulations that authorities enforce in a mass media industry are generally the result of struggles by various groups within the industry to achieve conditions favorable to them within the broad context of mass media law and tradition. In societies torn by political turmoil—in Africa and Eastern Europe, for example—the regulations may vary from month to month as the shifting fortunes of those in power are reflected in the shifting fortunes of people in the media who support them. Relatively stable societies tend to have more predictable media rules.

Forces Promoting Regulatory Stability

In the United States, two forces operate to ensure that the regulations and the organizations in power are not likely to change dramatically. One force is the **self-perpetuating activities of the groups that benefit most from the regulations**. Successful media organizations typically channel some of their profits into trying to make sure the rules that have allowed them to become successful continue to guide the industry. When this activity involves channeling resources into achieving good will with government circles or among the population at large, it is called **public relations**. When the work involves attempts to persuade government officials on specific issues, it is called **lobbying**.

Public relations is often itself carried out through mass communication. An example is the large-scale persuasive effort that commercial television broadcasters carried out in the 1950s to stop competition for their audiences from over-the-air and cable services that charged for access to additional programming. "Save Free TV"

BOX 3.5   Movies, the Government, and World War II

Direct government control over entertainment has been rare in the United States. During World War II, however, the U.S. government, through its Office of War Information (OWI), exercised immense control over the images Americans received at their local theaters.

Technically, the OWI's Bureau of Motion Pictures was just a liaison office with the Hollywood studios. In practice, though, Hollywood's producers paid strict attention to the guidelines, since they supported using celluloid to help win the war at home and abroad. They found their instructions in a thick manual distributed in August 1942. Called *The Government Information Manual for the Motion Picture*, it advocated the casual insertion of a constructive "war message" in a picture whenever possible. For example:

> At every opportunity, naturally and inconspicuously, show people making small sacrifices for victory—making them voluntarily, cheerfully and because of the people's own sense of responsibility, not because of any laws. For example, show people bringing their own sugar when invited out to dinner, carrying their own parcels when shopping, traveling on planes or trains with light luggage, uncomplainingly giving up seats for servicemen or others traveling on war priorities; show persons accepting dimout restrictions, tire and gas rationing cheerfully, show well-dressed persons, obviously car owners, riding in crowded buses and streetcars.
>
> In crowds unostentatiously show a few wounded men. Prepare people but do not alarm them against the casualties to come. . . . Show colored soldiers in crowd scenes; occasionally colored officers. Stress our national unity by using names of foreign extraction, showing foreign types in the services.

The OWI suggested that each filmmaker ask himself seven questions before undertaking a movie, especially, "Will this picture help win the war?" Thinking of the office and its guidelines makes viewing all sorts of movies made from late 1942 through 1945 especially interesting.

SOURCE: Richard R. Lingeman, *Don't You Know There's a War Going On?* (New York: G.P. Putnam; 1970), pp. 221–222.

---

was the nationwide rallying cry that could be read and heard across several media. The hope was that rank-and-file Americans would pressure their elected representatives to quash any regulations that would encourage alternatives to broadcast television.[12]

Lobbying is a narrower and more direct activity. Just about every U.S. media industry maintains a lobbying effort. Most of it takes place at the federal level, in Washington, D.C. Sometimes, state and local lobbying is also necessary.

An example is the attempt by the Direct Marketing Association to keep out-of-state catalog goods from being taxed. Previous to the 1980s, taxes had not been levied. However, with the boom of the catalog business during the decade, local merchants, who must charge state tax because they are located in the state, began to lose business to catalog firms. When local merchants tried to change the law, direct marketers and their allies worked to persuade legislators in several states not to impose taxes on goods bought by citizens of those states from mail-order firms outside their boundaries. As of the late 1980s, they had remained successful in holding back taxation that would harm most of their business.

The second force operating to ensure the stability of fundamental operating principles for U.S. media is the logic of the American judicial system. It places high value on rules of the past, or **precedents**, established by English common law, the United States Constitution, and previous decisions in U.S. courts. Expressing this approach is a Latin phrase well-known in legal circles: *stare decises et nonquieta movere*. It means "to stand by past decisions and not disturb things at rest." The idea is that a judge should resolve current problems in the same manner, or along similar lines, as other problems were resolved in the past.[13] This approach, like lobbying and public relations, guides authorities toward behavior that is conservative, predictable, and imbued with support for the business of media that has woven through American history.

Such predictability means authorities typically set conditions for the operation of mass media industries that producers can work into their approaches to content. Authorities can therefore become minor considerations in producers' day-to-day profit-and-loss decisions. Of course, discontented groups might launch challenges to the regulatory status quo. Those benefiting from it will then have to use public relations, lobbying, or the courts—or all three—to defend their traditional claims on the authorities' resources.

Lobbying, public relations, and legal efforts for a production firm are usually carried out by personnel or organizations that specialize in dealings with authorities. Their contentions with regulators and others who want to change things might stretch over a period of several months, or even years. These defensive approaches hold a number of advantages for production firms with regulatory challenges before them.

First, the approaches provide production firms with maximum opportunity to redirect rulemaking in their favor. Second, during that time, people involved in the actual creation of mass media material by and large continue along traditional paths, though sometimes a few authority-pleasing modifications are engineered by the firms' most important policymakers. Third, if the rules go against the production firm, the approaches provide the time that the firms' policymakers need to plot long-term changes to fit the rules and integrate them into the organization's creative activities with as few disruptions as possible.

The ability of mass media production firms to integrate authorities' expectations into the very fabric of decision making about content is, then, generally a stable element in the production process. Less predictable, and therefore more crucial, subjects in daily production decisions are the expectations and activities of organizations that can withhold or provide critical resources to support individual products on a daily basis. It is to the influence of these organizations, the ones who take on the client power role, that we turn in Chapter 4.

NOTES

1. Among the sources for the facts presented in this chapter are J. Herbert Altschull, *Agents of Power: The Role of the News Media in Human Affairs* (New York: Longman, 1983); Edwin Emery and Michael Emery, *The Press and America* (Englewood Cliffs, NJ: 1978); Daniel

Pope, *The Making of Modern Advertising* (New York: Basic Books, 1983); Erik Barnouw, *The Sponsor* (New York: Oxford University Press, 1978); Erik Barnouw, *A Tower in Babel* (New York: Oxford University Press, 1968); Garth Jowett, *Film: The Democratic Art* (Boston: Little Brown, 1976); Christopher H. Sterling, *Stay Tuned: A Concise History of Broadcasting* (Belmont, CA: 1990); and Joseph Dominick, Barry Sherman, and Gary Copeland, *Broadcasting/Cable and Beyond* (New York: McGraw-Hill, 1990).

2. Quoted in Altschull, p. 11.
3. Quoted in Altschull, p. 24.
4. Quoted in Altschull, p. 23.
5. Quoted in Emery and Emery, p. 97.
6. Quoted in Emery and Emery, p. 95.
7. Quoted in Emery and Emery, p. 96.
8. Quoted in Emery and Emery, p. 97.
9. See Albert E. Smith in collaboration with Phil A. Koary, *Two Reels and a Crank* (Garden City, NY: Doubleday, 1952).
10. Jowett, p. 119.
11. Christy Fisher, "Bell Ruling Rings Alarm," *Advertising Age*, July 29, 1991, p. 1.
12. Erik Barnouw, *The Image Empire* (New York: Oxford University Press, 1970), p. 246–247.
13. Don R. Pember, *Mass Media Law* (Dubuque, IA: William C. Brown, 1977, pp. 3–4.

CHAPTER FOUR

Media Support:
Paying the Piper, Calling the Tune

"**M**oney talks." Maybe that well-worn phrase is the best way to explain this chapter's title. The idea is that the relationship mass media production organizations (film studios, book companies, newspaper firms) have with their client organizations is typically the most important relationship they maintain with their environment. Of course, *all* the power roles discussed in Chapter 2 influence the output of producers. Authorities are unquestionably crucial, since, as we saw in the previous chapter, they set the basic terms under which all mass media in the society operate. Once the most basic of the authorities' conditions are set, however, the interactions between clients and producers take over as the most pivotal interorganizational forces shaping mass media materials.

The reason for this contention lies in what client organizations do. Recall that clients make purchases in support of existing products before these products reach the public. Clients help producers accomplish certain activities. For example, advertisers purchase space in newspapers and magazines in the hope that readers will buy their products. Bookstores purchase books from publishers with the aim of retailing them profitably. Record stores buy discs and tapes to sell profitably to the public.

In acting as clients, these organizations provide production firms with the cash flow that is most directly responsible for their survival. Examination of the producer-client relationship will show that while the phrase "money talks" might be a rough indicator of clients' importance to producers, a better way to describe it is to say money starts an key interorganizational conversation. That is, influence in the producer-client relationship runs both ways—from producers to clients as well as from clients to producers. Too, the influence runs deep, even to the decision-making structures of production organizations and to the images producer and client executives hold of their audiences.

THE VARIETY OF PRODUCER-CLIENT RELATIONSHIPS

The examples of clients in the newspaper, magazine, book publishing, and record industries show that there is no uniformity to the kinds of organizations that take on the client role. In fact, even within an industry one sector may have different kinds of patrons from another sector. Take the book industry as an example. While bookstores as a broad class are important to the solvency of many publishers, there are also many publishers that rarely turn to bookstores as key monetary supporters of their products' public release. For example, libraries are crucial to publishers of certain technical monographs, digests, encyclopedias, and other volumes. By contrast, school boards and schools are crucial in the elementary and high school ("el-hi") market.

The complexity does not stop here. Even within a sector of an industry, different kinds of clients may exist, and they may hold different levels of importance. Trade book publishers that have bookstores as their major clients may also sell a fair amount to public libraries. Similarly, children's book publishers that aim mostly at the library market may, at times, find that stores are also profitable clients for some titles.

It is useful, then, to speak of *primary* and *secondary* producer-client relationships. One type of client is primary in a producer's scheme of things if it contributes more than any other type of client to the solvency of the production firm. So, for example, if libraries contribute more than bookstores to the profits of a particular publisher, libraries are the primary and bookstores are the secondary client organizations for that publisher.

As the preceding illustrations suggest, clients become supporters of mass media producers with the aim of using them to carry out other activities. In the United States, these activities relate most often to one of three forms: exhibition, distribution, or advertising. The general trade sector of book publishing is a case where the primary clients are exhibitors (stores). The mainstream U.S. movie industry is different. There a group of major distributors rather than the exhibitors (the theaters) take on the primary client role.

Clients in the Movie Industry

The "majors" are nine powerful distribution firms—Columbia, TriStar, Paramount, 20th Century Fox, MGM-UA, Universal, Orion, Warner Brothers, and Buena Vista (Disney)—that are owned by movie production firms. The majors direct about 90% of Hollywood's product to the overwhelming number of American movie theaters.[1] Drawing on money made on previous films and on long-term bank finance arrangements, the major distributors provide cash for making films to their own production firms. Other revenues used by those production firms to make movies come from two other types of distribution subsidiaries: those that direct product to theaters in foreign countries and those that direct films to the homevideo market.

The high cost of distributing movies to the mainstream market means that independent production companies (those that do not own distribution firms) must try to convince one of the majors to carry their output if they are aiming at huge audiences. Such arrangements can benefit both parties. A major might be interested in taking on an independently produced movie because it adds to the inventory that the distributor will have for theaters while it frees the major's parent from the high cost of making a greater number of its own films in one year. Moreover, the cut of the box office gross that the distributor gets for the film is substantial; it typically falls around 47%.[2]

For their part, independent producers forego that whopping royalty for the privilege of plugging into the most powerful and efficient method of theatrical distribution available. In addition, the distributor will often finance a portion of the film (for a higher cut of the profits). Frequently, the distributor's power as a client comes indirectly as well. When a bank finds out that a major has agreed to carry a film by an independent producer, the film's success becomes more plausible, and the bank is more willing to extend credit for making the film.

Advertisers as Clients

The third form of media clients—advertising—is without question the most pervasive form in the United States. Advertising involves payment for calling attention to a product, service, or need. Whether the subject is Coca-Cola, a cleaning store, or the United Way, the goal of advertising is straightforward—to persuade people to purchase or otherwise support the product, service, or need.

Advertising is itself a media production activity. In fact, it is sometimes carried out by itself, separate from other kinds of mass media materials. Mass-produced billboards, handbills, catalogs, audio cassettes, records, even video cassettes, are part of a blizzard of media that carry only advertising messages. At the same time, advertisers find it useful to place their announcements alongside material that does not carry overtly persuasive intent—material such as newspaper and magazine articles, radio programs, and television shows. Their hope is that the people using those media will also attend to the commercial messages and act favorably in response to them.

Clearly, then, advertisers' client relationships with mass media production firms is a direct outgrowth of their desire to reach people who might respond favorably to their messages. In 1989, the 100 companies that led in United States advertising spent an estimated $34 billion on that activity. Most of that money was used to purchase time or space among attractive nonadvertising material on broadcast television, on radio, in magazines, or in newspapers. For example, the twenty-five top newspaper advertisers spent $1.8 billion. The twenty-five top magazine advertisers also spent $2 billion. The twenty-five top local radio advertisers spent $537 million. The twenty-five top network TV advertisers spent a bit over $4.8 billion.[3]

These numbers do not reflect the thousands of companies that spent much smaller amounts supporting media through advertising. Still, it is worth paying attention to the largest mass media customers, since the amounts they spend might be of particular significance to the survival of production firms within a media industry, or even to the health of the industry as a whole. It is hard for television executives to ignore Philip Morris, for example, which spent about $2 billion on advertising in 1989, 19% percent of it going to network TV and 8% percent going to local stations. Similarly, newspaper executives might find it difficult not to consider the May Department Stores Company, which placed about 60% of its $386 million ad budget into that medium. Even more difficult to ignore are classes of advertisers—food firms, airlines, tobacco companies, and the like—that pack a lot of financial clout in certain mass media industries. For example, only five department stores (May, RH Macy, Sears, Campeau, and Dayton Hudson) together contributed about $819 million to newspaper coffers in 1989. And only five auto companies (General Motors, Ford,

TABLE 4.1. National Advertising Spending By Major Medium, 1989

Category	Total Spending in Millions	% of That Spending Represented by Top 100 Advertisers
Magazine	$6,594.9	44
Sunday magazine	737.0	32
Newspaper	8,777.3	24
Outdoor (billboard)	705.8	39
Network TV	9,559.0	76
Spot TV	9,030.4	41
Syndicated TV	1,286.7	73
Cable TV networks	952.6	54
Network radio	696.2	62
Spot radio	1,841.2	39

The table gives a snapshot view of the comparative value that different mass media hold for advertisers trying to reach audiences across the United States. It also shows how critical the 100 leading national advertisers are to national media spending.

It pays to stress that these figures represent spending to reach nationwide audiences; they do not represent ad spending confined to local areas. **Syndicated** TV deals are advertisements placed within particular TV or radio programs that are placed individually on stations around the country, as opposed to through a single network buy. If a company creates a show, gets an advertiser to sponsor it, and then places the program on stations around the country who may show it at different times, that is a syndicated TV deal.

Spot purchases are national purchases made during network programming as a result of deals with local station representatives, not through TV or radio networks. Time for spot ads exists because networks typically allow their affiliates to sell a few minutes an hour to advertisers during network programming. Some advertisers may buy spot ads because they want to advertise in just a few localities, not on the entire network. For example, a supermarket chain might get involved in a spot deal because it wants to advertise during prime time but only in the five cities in which it has stores.

SOURCE: *Advertising Age*, September 26, 1990, p. 8.

Chrysler, Honda, and Toyota) provided about $590 million of support to magazines in the form of advertising space purchases.[4]

Less obvious, but even more concentrated in their ability to direct the flow of cash to mass media, are the leading advertising agencies that service the national advertisers. These organizations clarify, crystallize, even create, the advertising plans of their clients. They produce advertising material based on those plans, purchase media space or time for the material, and evaluate the success of the efforts with the aid of market research firms (which they sometimes own). In the process, they direct hundreds of millions of dollars toward, or away from, various mass media industries. In 1988, fourteen advertising agencies each paid over $1 billion to various American mass media firms for carrying their commercial announcements. The range of manufacturers whose cash the agencies controlled was quite broad. For example, Young and Rubicam, with $1.8 billion in ad placement billings, operated in support of firms as diverse as Bell Atlantic, Kodak, Nestlé, Ford Dealers Association, National Yellow

TABLE 4.2. Top Advertisers in Four Media, 1989

	Dollars (in Millions)
Network Television	
General Motors Corp.	506.5
Proctor and Gamble	449.1
Philip Morris Cos.	368.4
Kellogg Co.	324.8
McDonald Corporation	252.1
Newspapers	
May Department Stores Co.	230.9
RH Macy & Co.	183.6
Sears, Roebuck & Co.	153.6
Campeau Corp.	144.0
Dayton Hudson Corp.	106.5
Magazines	
Philip Morris Cos.	281.5
General Motors Corp.	213.5
Ford Motor Co.	135.2
RJR Nabisco	132.8
Chrysler Corp.	131.3
Outdoor (Billboards and Related Activities)	
Philip Morris Cos.	70.9
RJR Nabisco	49.1
Loews Corp.	34.2
B.A.T. Industries PLC	27.7
American Brands	10.7

The largest producers and sellers of consumer goods are often the largest advertisers. Marketers often use different mass media for different purposes. Note, for example, that all five of the top outdoor advertisers are firms that create and sell cigarettes.

SOURCE: *Advertising Age*, September 26, 1990, pp. 36, 24, 17, 70.

Pages, Connecticut Mutual, Health and Tennis Corporation, and Cellular One. The agency allocated 34% of its billings to network television, 23% to local ("spot") television, 5% to radio, 14% to consumer magazines, 6% to newspapers, 6% to direct response ("mail order") advertising, and 3% to cable television. The rest went to business publications, medical journals, farm periodicals, billboards, and transit advertising. Other agency leaders doled out money in rather similar proportions.[5]

The interconnection of advertisers, advertising agencies, and market research firms in supporting the production of newspapers, magazines, television programs, and other mass media material indicates that when it comes to advertising, the "client" can be seen as an industry in itself, rather than a single type of organization. While advertisers put up the money to proclaim their products or services, ad agencies often set the agenda for using the funds. Small wonder, then, that many production firm executives see the major advertising agencies collectively as the key forces to influence for support.

Don Lachowski, a vice-president of sales at Turner Broadcasting System, reflected this idea somewhat bitterly in 1980, when his company's advertising-based cable TV channel was struggling for recognition and support from Madison Avenue.

TABLE 4.3. The May Department Stores Company's Media Spending

Department stores tend to advertise locally, where their stores are, and not nationally. Therefore, they are crucial clients to local advertising media, particularly newspapers, as this table shows. The May Department Stores Company, the case in point, is based in St. Louis. It owns different chains in cities around the country, from L.S. Ayres in Indianapolis, to May D&F in Denver.

It ought to be noted that these data, adapted from *Advertising Age*, break out only certain media and not others. For example, not listed here are monies spent for direct-mail letters, catalogs, and business publications, to name a few places ad monies could go. May Department Stores spent 30% of its approximately $386 million ad budget on these "unmeasured" media. It spent the other 70% on the following media, in the following proportions. Spending amounts are in thousands.

Medium	Ad Spending	% of Total
Magazines	$3,133	1
Sunday magazines	5,009	2
Newspapers	230,874	86
Outdoor	54	—
Network TV	5,259	2
Spot TV	24,156	9
Spot radio	1,473	1
Total	**269,957**	**101***

* The number is greater than 100% due to rounding.

SOURCE: *Advertising Age*, September 26, 1990, p. 92.

Speaking to a group of advertising industry executives, Lachowski complained that major advertising agencies had been deliberately understating the movement of audiences to cable from broadcast TV because they did not want to change their media buying patterns. The frequent attitude, he said, had been that "if we ignore it [cable as well as other new technologies] and pretend it doesn't exist, maybe it will go away."[6]

THE PRODUCER-CLIENT RELATIONSHIP AND MASS MEDIA MATERIAL

Lachowski's concern about the flow of advertising dollars into the cable TV industry points to the clearest influence of the producer-client relationship on mass media content. Simply, if there is no money to create the material, it will not be created. It is worth stressing that Lachowski's comments came at a point in cable TV's history when the advertising industry was still unsure as to how broad and deep a commitment it was willing to make to the medium. Things have changed since then; in 1989, the top 500 ad agencies spent $617 million on cable TV commercials, many times the amount of a decade earlier.

Still, the general tension Lachowski was addressing is not unusual. Every year, book publishers, magazine publishers, record producers, and newspaper publishers go out of business because not enough clients exist to support them. Once in a while, entire niches within mass media industries see their client resources dry up. Overall, though, many mass media producers do thrive. It is to the influence of the producer-client relationship on mass media output that we now turn.

The Relationship as a Communication System

As a first step, it will be useful to try to understand what it really means to talk about a relationship between production and client firms within a mass media industry. Throughout this book we have described dealings of one organization with another organization as exchanges between faceless entities. Here, however, it pays to be more systematic about this point, since it bears strongly on an ability to know how producer-client links operate in the media on a daily basis.

The key to understanding the influence of the producer-client relationship lies in seeing it as a communication system involving **boundary personnel** from the client and production organizations in a mass media industry. Boundary personnel are workers who communicate with workers in companies other than their own.

To understand the function the communication system holds for each organization in the relationship, it pays to note sociologist Howard Aldrich's proposition about executives and resources. The major goals of organizational leaders, Aldrich said, "are avoiding dependence on other [organizations] and making others dependent on one's own organization."[7] For planners in both production firms and client firms, that means dispatching people to find out about other organizations in the environment so that concerns about resources can be identified and dealt with successfully.

Mass media production firm executives worry particularly about their firms' primary clients because they affect the solvency of the production firm quite directly. These clients become what sociologist William Evan has called **normative reference organizations**.[8] That is, they become entities that production executives see as generating requirements that they must contend with if they are to bring in the cash necessary for survival. What the clients need depends on the kind of client organizations involved. Sometimes (as when book or record stores are clients) their overall goal is the profitable retailing of products. Other times (as when advertisers are the clients) the goal is to reach people who will respond favorably to certain messages.

To find out about specific client aims, and to help shape them, production firms assign salespeople, marketing executives, and other employees the task of contacting people in client firms. Client firms, in turn, assign people the task of working with production firm representatives in order to clarify client needs. In view of production executives' general desire for predictable cash flow, we would expect that their boundary personnel would use talks with their counterparts in the client firms to negotiate expectations about output that would be profitable for the production firms.

At the same time, we would expect that client executives would instruct their boundary personnel to make clear that they expect certain sorts of performance from the production firm that would be profitable for the client organizations. The influence of the producer-client relationship, then, would flow from the continual interactions of the boundary people that make up the relationship. The influence would be in both directions. Each side would negotiate its expectations of the other.

A couple of important insights about the producer-client relationship flow out of the idea that the relationship is continually in the process of being created:

- One conclusion to draw is that knowing the history of a producer-client relationship is relevant to understanding its current situation.
- A second corollary is that every relationship involving one production and one client organization must necessarily be different from relationships involving any other producer-client pair. That is because the perceptions a given organization's executives hold about their environment will inevitably be at least somewhat different from the perceptions of exectives in other organizations. The differences come about simply because of the different people involved, their history together, the tradition of their organization, and the history of their organization's interactions with other organizations.

At the same time, it would be incorrect to make too much of the differences between the relationships that involve the same types of established producers and the same kinds of established clients in a particular area of an industry. Doing so would be like seeing trees but not the forest. While there are certainly differences between the producer-client relationships within an industry's niche, there are also important similarities among the various relationships. The similarities stem from needs by the same kinds of organizations to compete for the same resources. Exploring these similarities can lead to useful generalizations about the influence that the producer-client relationship has on the creation of mass media content.

SETTING LIMITS FOR THE PRODUCTION FIRM'S ACTIVITIES

One generalization that can be suggested with certainty is this: The producer-client relationship limits what a mass media production firm can do in its day-to-day activities. The limits affect the production firm in three broad areas:

The kinds of people who are the targets of the company's media output

The frequency at which the material is released to those people

The amount it costs to produce and release the material

These limits are set as a result of competition between producers over the resources (usually money) that clients can provide. The number of clients and the amount of money they want to devote to mass media are limited at any particular point in time. In exchange for spending their money, clients want the media they support to provide them with certain benefits. For instance, a bookstore chain will want to be confident that it will sell the copies of a book about antiques it ordered. Or, to give another example, an airline that purchases space in a newspaper's twice-weekly "business review" section to promote lower fares will want to feel secure that the money the ads cost will be more than regained by the number of flights booked because of the ad.

In the case of the antiques book publisher, the satisfaction of bookstore chains with the speed and number of sales will determine whether the company can continue to target antiques collectors through that type of outlet. Response from the bookstore chains will also determine how many new titles about antiques the publisher can profitably turn out each year as well as how much it should expect to be able to charge for each title.

The case of the newspaper and the airline is a bit different, since the newspaper will probably not cease publication if the airline withdraws future advertising. Nevertheless, if all airlines decide to pull their ads, and if other travel-related firms follow, the monetary shortfall might cause the paper's executives to institute strategies to target business travelers to their business section. Alternatively, they might give up on getting travel clients and look to other markets for support—to producers of copying machines and computers, for example. If they cannot convince enough advertisers that they are meeting their needs, the executives might have to cut the section's frequency to once a week or to implement other measures that would make the section profitable for the newspaper despite the decrease in advertising revenues.

The newspaper example highlights the value of a **resource-rich** environment for a production firm. A resource-rich environment is one which offers a large number or variety of interchangeable elements that can help a producer survive. When executives in a newspaper firm confront a large number or variety of potential clients interested in a broad range of publics, the executives will find it a lot easier to support their venture than when this diversity is absent. Even facing such an environment, though, production firm executives will still have to present clients with products that yield the benefits they are seeking at a price they are willing to pay.

For example, if the people that a media production firm reaches begin to be of no interest to any clients, the firm will have to fold its operation. Similarly, if the cost of reaching a target audience begins to be considered too high by relevant clients, the producers will not be able to continue their approach. Too, if the producer can interest only a few clients to sustain a frequent production of material for a target audience, the producer will have to release its material less often.

Even when the environment is relatively rich, a production firm may feel compelled to court clients. The reason is that poor relationships with clients might lead many of them to look for other options. That may encourage more competition with the production firm and lead the firm to experience a scarce resource situation. That kind of situation befell *The Philadelphia Inquirer* newspaper in the early 1990s. Advertising agencies, which had often accused the prestigious regional daily of not paying attention to their needs, began to drop their sponsorship as the economy took a downturn.

"Two years ago, the *Inquirer* had a very definite mentality of 'We're the only game in town, and if you don't like it, tough,' " according to the director of media services for a local ad agency. "They woke up because of the economic situation. They're getting hurt tremendously in retail lineage, and classified and real estate are down."[9]

"Waking up" meant trying to be more helpful and accommodating to advertising agencies. The *Inquirer* simplified its ad rate charges and assigned a sales manager as a particular contact person for each of the top twenty agencies it deals with. The firm designated someone to a new post of manager of agency relations to answer marketing and research questions for clients. Moreover, it began a hotline and a quarterly newsletter to acquaint ad people with new sections of the paper they might want to sponsor and new market research findings that might help the ad people get new business.

There are times that even the kinds of activities the *Inquirer* implemented will not hold clients. Basic client demands may actually change to the point that they can no longer support certain kinds of mass media. That loss of support, by extension, can affect the kinds of mass materials produced.

THE CASE OF MAGAZINES

The link between changing client demands and mass media output can be illustrated by looking at changes in the United States consumer magazine industry. **Consumer magazines** represent the segment of the magazine industry that is aimed at the general reading public. "They are called consumer magazines because their readers buy and consume products and services that are sold at retail and may be advertised in those magazines."[10]

Advertising represents a crucial vehicle of support in the great majority of these magazines, although an increasing amount of money is earned through reader subscriptions and, sometimes, newsstand sales. Consumer magazines generally derive about half of their revenues from advertising and half from readers. Judging by the number of consumer magazines that exist in the United States, the environment for supporting this activity is rich indeed. According to the editorial department at *Folio*, a trade magazine for magazine publishers, there were about 3,500 magazines distributed in the United States in 1991.[11] To be considered a consumer magazine by *Folio's* staff, a publication must be aimed at nonbusiness users, be released at least three times a year, have a circulation of at least 3,000, and contain at least sixteen pages of editorial (as opposed to advertising) matter.

The fields of interests of consumer magazines are diverse—from "girlie" magazines to periodicals about boxing, wrestling, and karate, to those dealing with sewing and crafts, to news magazines. Still, the environment for support by advertisers and readers is not unlimited. *Folio* reports that only 10% of the approximately 300 magazines started each year in the late 1970s survived a year.[12]

The Move to Specialization

If one trend could be said to encompass the consumer perical area in the early 1990s, it would be the increased movement to specialization in subject matter and readership. The trend is clearly associated with the movement of advertisers away from supporting large general interest magazines during the mid-1960s through the 1970s.[13]

Until then, and since the turn of the 1900s, consumer magazines with huge, heterogeneous readerships (such as *Life, Look, Coronet, The Saturday Evening Post*) had been very attractive to national advertisers. Magazine publishing firms had tried to build huge circulations by offering readers very low subscription rates. Advertisers were satisfied with this situation, since it allowed them to use just a number of magazines to reach the kinds of widespread audiences that only network radio could duplicate; and radio could not carry pictures.

To satisfy producers and clients, magazine circulation figures were systematically audited by an independent agency, the Audit Bureau of Circulation (ABC). In addition, to facilitate cost comparison of two periodicals, both parties used an efficiency measure, **cost per thousand** (CPM). CPM was (and is) simply the price an advertiser paid to reach 1,000 people through a full-page, black-and-white ad.

With the advent of television, however, the situation changed. By the late 1950s, 86% of all United States homes had at least one TV set; the number jumped to 93% in 1965.[14] Advertisers, attracted to the audiovisual capabilities of TV, realized that the new medium reached basically the same heterogeneous audience as the general consumer magazines at about the same CPM. That was the beginning of the end of those periodicals, despite their large readerships. For example, the 1963 *Coronet* ceased publication while carrying a circulation of 3.1 million.[15] *Life, Look, The Saturday Evening Post*, and others of that ilk also died a little before or during that decade.

Magazine publishing surged back beginning in the late 1960s, but it was in a new relationship with advertisers. Many advertisers saw that television filled their needs for reaching giant, diverse segments of the population quickly. Magazine executives, recognizing that the head-on battle with TV was lost, tried to persuade advertisers that certain kinds of periodicals were still worth their advertising dollars: the ones that helped them reach narrower social segments (often the wealthy segments) with specially tailored messages.

The magazine executives noted that quality-looking magazines could be produced much less expensively than could prime time television programs. CPMs could therefore be reasonable even if subscribers numbered only in the tens of thousands. This was particularly true if the magazine passed more of its costs along to readers in subscription fees. In addition, magazine executives contended that passing more costs on to readers indicated that subscribers would read the magazine (and its ads) more seriously, since they had paid significant sums to receive it.

J. W. Click and Russell Baird reflected the advertiser's point of view on this trend: "The efficiency of carrying advertising within a specialized area to persons obviously interested in that activity appeals to advertisers catering to such an area and makes these magazines ideal media for their ads at lower overall cost and with minimal waste circulation."[16]

Rethinking Audience Research

Many magazine executives, seeing the needs of advertisers in a TV age, took the initiative to establish a new relationship with their clients, based on a new perspective. As a result of this perspective, the advertising industry supported special interest consumer magazines that could prove the worth of their readership, and that area of the business grew tremendously. From *Psychology Today* to *Essence* to *National Lampoon* to *Smithsonian* to *Money* and *Omni*, the 1970s saw magazines with circulations in the hundreds of thousands (instead of the several millions) find strong support on Madison Avenue. As the key to this producer-client relationship became efficient specialization, leading magazine publishing firms, advertising agencies, and the Mag-

TABLE 4.4. Leading Magazines in Revenues, 1990

Magazine	Total	Ads	Subs
1. *TV Guide*	$913	$320	$327
2. *People*	642	346	111
3. *Time*	636	382	227
4. *Sports Illustrated*	551	336	200
5. *Reader's Digest*	436	109	306
6. *Newsweek*	403	253	125
7. *Parade*	355	355	0
8. *Business Week*	284	246	35
9. *Better Homes & Gardens*	276	144	120
10. *Good Housekeeping*	260	163	63
11. *U.S. News & World Report*	256	159	89
12. *National Geographic*	247	36	211
13. *Family Circle*	240	137	65
14. *PC Magazine*	228	190	30
15. *Ladies' Home Journal*	213	109	81

In this table, total revenues of a magazine equal money from advertisers (Ads) plus money from subscribers (Subs) plus money from newsstand sales. Dollars are in millions.

While many magazines are drawing increasing amounts of money from subscriptions and single-copy sales, a crucial part of a magazine's revenues usually still comes from advertising. Note that three of the top four periodicals (*Time*, *People*, and *Sports Illustrated*) are owned by Time Warner.

SOURCE: *Advertising Age*, October 22, 1990, p. 42.

azine Publishers Association began to devise more studies and measures that reflected the value of a magazine to a sponsor. Magazine executives wanted to present their periodicals to advertising agency people as better buys than other periodicals or other media (especially television). Agency executives, for their part, wanted to be able to justify their media-buying decisions in quantitative, "scientific" terms that would be difficult for their bosses to question.

Consequently, during the 1970s and 1980s both parties joined forces to develop various measures that go beyond circulation and CPM to chart various characteristics of the readers. Many magazine executives decided they had to tell potential advertisers such facts as how many children their readers have, how many cars they own, how often they take vacations, sometimes even what wines they buy. The emphasis on targeting specific readers that advertisers want also caused publishers to sharpen and focus their editorial product.

George Green, president of *The New Yorker*, noted the change this way: "Magazines today are often designed around the advertising, particularly with specialized magazines. [Research] studies are getting so specific that you can design magazines around readers so you can have more clearly defined target audiences for the advertisers."[17]

The Lesson Beyond Magazines

This power of clients to set the general conditions of production can be seen across media industries. Regarding network TV, for example, one can start with journalist

Les Brown's reflection that "programs come into being to deliver . . . [an audience] to advertisers."[18] Then one can show how changes in client demand over the years has influenced:

The **number and kinds** of people that the three major commercial networks have targeted as viewers

The **amount of television time** the networks take up with their programming

The **costs** of the programs the networks show at different times of day

Similarly, in the movie industry, analysis of the relationship between the major production companies and their clients (the major distributors) can show how financial interests of the distributors have guided studies regarding the costs, audience requirements, and the number of films they should produce. Garth Jowett and James Linton conducted just this sort of survey in the 1970s. They found that distributors' requirements led the major production firms to create "a smaller number of blockbusters (with higher production costs and larger audience requirements) rather than . . . a larger number of 'lesser' movies (with lower production costs and smaller audience requirements)."[19]

The popular recording industry stands out as a fascinating exception to this pattern of client influence. As noted earlier, record producers' primary clients are record stores. As a result, one might expect the stores to collectively exert a dominant influence on the kinds of people targeted, the approach to titles released, and the cost of each recording. By all accounts, though, radio stations (and, to a lesser extent, the MTV cable music service) exert the influence we have attributed to clients, even though they provide no money to the recording firms.

The reason for their clientlike clout is not difficult to perceive. Record stores do not generally provide people with ways to hear all the albums and singles that are on their shelves. Nevertheless, they expect customers to be familiar with the popular records they carry. This expectation forces producers to try to publicize their output so that stores will want to carry it. Purchasing advertising time on television and radio to play all new songs would be prohibitively expensive. The presence of popular music formats on radio allows recording company boundary personnel to do the next best thing. They try to convince radio station programmers to play the songs. Records played often and widely have a better chance of being carried in record stores than records played not so often or widely. In a large sense, then, stores have handed over much of their client-based influence to the radio stations.

CLIENTS AND MASS MEDIA CONTENT

Setting general limits for the production of mass media material is often only the beginning of the client system's impact. In many cases, client needs affect quite specific decisions that producers make about the ideas presented in the material—the kinds of arguments made, the types of topics covered. While the potential for this kind of influence exists in all kinds of producer-client relationships, it is most common when the advertiser is the client.

Direct Interference by Advertisers

Interestingly, many American media creators have contended that interference by advertisers in their work is near-immoral. They even consider it unprofessional to create specific messages with a blatant attempt to help and attract advertisers. So, for example, the editor of *The Ladies' Home Journal* said flatly that her colleagues should not plan editorial matter (the nonadvertising matter in a magazine) to interest advertisers. She contended that neither publishers nor major advertisers expect such interference because it detracts from the editorial credibility with which advertisers want to identify.[20]

The reality of the situation, however, is that it is difficult to find a mass media product supported by advertising that does not carry an imprint of the sponsors in its content. Moreover, some portion of that influence does sometimes involve direct negotiation of editorial support for a product, service, or idea in exchange for an advertiser's commercial support.

A particularly startling example can be brought from the declining days of *The Saturday Evening Post*. In order to secure $400,000 of Ford automotive advertising for the periodical's October 5, 1968, issue, *Post* executive Martin Ackerman promised the client that Henry Ford would grace the cover of the issue.[21]

Advertising executives agree that such activities are uncommon among large advertisers and mainstream media. They argue that clients and producers understand that editorial-advertising deals would become obvious and weaken the credibility of a medium as both an advertising and editorial vehicle. Nevertheless, anecdotes continue to pop up about media production firms that ensure editorial coverage for an advertiser in exchange for ads. In the magazine industry, research indicates that direct advertiser influence on editorial matter is more common among trade magazines than among consumer magazines. Trade magazines are periodicals that target readers in particular occupations (doctors, plumbers) with information about their workplace.

In 1990, an article in *Folio*, a trade magazine for the magazine industry, stated that "advertising pressure on editors is the skeleton in the closet of the magazine publishing industry: Everyone knows it's there, but no one wants to talk about it." According to the article, several editors of trade periodicals admited in private that the pressure to give in to sponsor demands to trade advertising for editorial coverage can be intense. The message to keep advertisers happy is constant, said one source. "I simply go along with the system because it's the only way I know to hold my job."[22]

The reason would seem to be the precarious monetary situation in which many small trade journals find themselves. As two academic observers of the [trade] magazine industry have noted, "Editorial integrity is much easier to maintain if the [magazine] is in solid financial condition and does not need to desperately woo advertisers."[23]

Structural Influence by Advertisers

While less startling than direct pressure, the most common way the impact of Madison Avenue on the material takes place is **structural**. Structural influence does not involve bending to demands by individual clients. Rather, it means that creators respond to their perceptions of needs of the client structure as a whole. This typically involves trying to create media materials that will be supportive environments for the commercial messages. The activity is driven by the idea that target audiences pay most attention to the ads when they are surrounded by noncommercial matter that relates to the ads in a positive way.

Typical of this approach is the newspaper publisher that initiates weekly articles about science and computers with the aim of attracting computer advertisers. A similar tack is the use of food recipes in *The Ladies' Home Journal* to serve as the appropriate environment for salad dressing and other components of meals.

Of course, one can argue that this kind of activity benefits readers as well as advertisers and producers. The purpose here is not to dispute that conclusion. Rather, the purpose is to point out that material is often created in response to sponsors, not necessarily or even primarily in response to readers.

Inserts and sections that would not tie in with advertisers' needs would likely not be created. It is difficult to imagine, for example, that a series of articles about deceptive labeling by major food brands would show up in a homemaker-oriented women's magazine that relies on food sponsorship for support. Similarly, it would be most surprising if a newspaper routinely initiated stories exposing abuses in price and quality in area food stores.

Moreover, to ensure that advertisers feel comfortable with their commercial placements, editors will often deter writers from directly criticizing sponsors or their product policies in articles that do get printed. So, for example, one editor of a magazine for young parents admitted to modifying an article about toddler's shoes so as to not alienate key shoe advertisers. The article had originally told parents to avoid purchasing shoes with stiff soles. It was a suggestion that pediatricians often offer but that could be construed to advise against the purchase of clients' shoes. As a result, the passage was changed to say that the shoes should not be too tight, a caution that, the editor thought, would offend no one.[24]

Censorship and Advertisers

We should stress that we are not talking here about censorship. **Censorship** is the active attempt by an organization or group to suppress material that a production firm has already composed. By contrast, tailoring editorial material to create an attractive environment for ads constitutes an active, willing attempt on the part of the production firm to tilt toward the needs of clients. Production executives understand that "many agencies and corporations consider it an endorsement of an editorial product if you advertise in a magazine."[25]

How far a production firm is willing to shift its editorial environment to attract certain types of advertisers depends on

- The nature of the firm
- Its need for certain kinds of advertisers
- Its perception of demands from those advertisers

So, for example, a newspaper's editors might not initiate a critical investigation of supermarkets in the area for fear the paper will alienate a key class of revenue-providers. At the same time, editors' commitment to journalistic professionalism may lead them to print balanced stories about supermarket problems if the stories have originated outside the papers. Moreover, through interaction between marketing and salespeople of the different firms, the newspapers may even convince the stores it is acceptable to do that.

Some producers actually go out of their way to alienate certain types of advertisers in order to maintain—even show off—their editorial points of view and readership. The politically left *Mother Jones*, the scandal-mongering *National Enquirer*, and the sexually and politically provocative *Penthouse* magazine are just a few of the many magazines that will not win the support of conservative mainstream advertisers such as General Motors, General Mills, and General Electric. They survive because they have found enough clients who find their editorial environment acceptable for reaching the audiences those media vehicles claim to reach.

THE CASE OF TELEVISION

A view of the wide-ranging influence of the producer-advertiser relationship on the creation of mass media material can be obtained through a brief sketch of that relationship's effect on prime time commercial network television in the early 1990s. Prime time network TV programming involves two levels of client relations. On one level, advertisers purchase time during shows on the three major networks, ABC, CBS, and NBC. On the other level, the networks use much of the money to support production firms that create programs. Those programs become the building blocks of the networks' schedules.

The Importance of Ratings

The influence of advertisers pours across both levels. To understand how, one need only begin with that basic viewership gauge, the Nielsen ratings. Over the years, broadcasters and advertisers have encouraged the development of Nielsen measurement categories that directly reflect the specific marketing concerns of sponsors. During TV's first two decades, companies that bought time on TV were interested almost exclusively in attracting huge numbers of people to their commercials. Beginning around the 1970s, their goals in reaching TV audiences began to shift toward targeting certain large segments within the TV audience—especially women or men aged 18–49. The 1980s saw an insistence by marketers in knowing more precisely than before how and when those age and gender segments viewed. Moreover, the three networks, feeling competition from cable TV, home video, and independent stations, were increasingly eager to show advertisers that they could meet advertisers' needs for reaching huge, but well-understood, audiences.

As will be seen in Chapter 5, Nielsen and a few competitors have been working hard to create instruments that will give marketers a wide variety of information about

TV viewers. At the present stage of ratings technology, though, standard Nielsen equipment aims to record just a few basic categories—the number of viewers at any particular moment as well as their age and sex. The findings are sold to advertisers, ad agencies, and the networks. They become the basis for advertiser-network negotiations over the cost of air time. Those negotiations affect not only the profits of each network but the amount of money the networks can pay production firms for programs.

The Importance of Time Periods

Network television is often the medium of choice for advertisers trying to reach tens of millions of people at a time. As a result, the number of viewers a network reaches with its shows is extremely important to TV advertisers and the networks. Both groups have tended to make capturing extending blocks of viewers' time, rather than winning a half hour slot here and there, an important criterion for network success. Winning the year in a time block (whether it is morning, afternoon, evening, or late night) means being able to charge substantially more for commercials in that block at the start of the next year.

For many national advertisers, however, the age and sex of viewers during those time blocks are also very important. The most attractive target has been 18- to 49-year-olds, since they have held more discretionary spending money than do younger or older people. Prime time—the 8:00 P.M. to 11:00 P.M. block that is generally the most popular viewing period—presents the networks with the best opportunity to reach 18- to 49-year-olds, since most of them are home from work during those hours. Consequently, each network's executives try to create a prime time schedule that will attract the largest possible number of households while they simultaneously try to grab the highest percentage of 18- to 49-year-olds of the three networks.

Programming to Win

Explaining how network executives try to program to win explains to a considerable extent the shape and content of the prime time schedule. For example, with the aim of "winning the night," ABC, CBS, and NBC programmers set up their scheules to maximize audience flow from one show to the next. At 8:00 P.M., the start of prime time, they place programs designed to lure both children and their parents, since children are thought to control the set at that point in the evening. After 9:00 P.M., they schedule shows that are more "adult" in theme, since by that time many children have relinquished set control to parents.

The entire evening schedule, though, will be set up to maintain an overall tone that will encourage audience flow across time periods. So, for example, a network might schedule an evening of situation comedies, starting with a "family-oriented" sitcom at 8:00 P.M. and moving to more adult humor as as the evening progresses.

Because of advertiser interest in 18- to 49-year-olds, the executives choose programs they believe, or determine through research, will attract that group along with others. **Counterprogramming** may occur if a competitor seems stubbornly successful at holding on to one segment of the desired audience. So, for example, when ABC uses a football game on Monday evening to attract a large percentage of 18- to

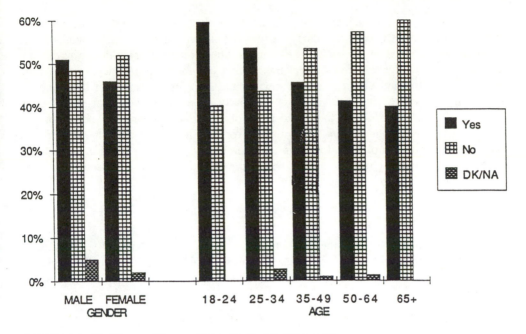

CHART 4.1   Do Viewers Change Channels During Programs?

The rising popularity of the remote control has led to a new term among
marketers: **grazing**. Grazing is the act of flipping across the channels quickly.
People who do it often want to see what is on the tube, particularly when the
station they have been viewing is airing commercials.

Available ratings devices do not detect much of the grazing, since it happens so
quickly. Nevertheless, the activity has drawn the concern of advertisers and
broadcasters because it may mean that people are not really watching individual
shows or commercials.

Note that DK/NA stands for "don't know" or "no answer."

SOURCE: *Channels* 1989 Field Guide, p. 127.

49-year-old males, CBS and NBC sometime counterprogram with "women's" movies
and series to lure 18- to 49-year-old females and advertisers interested in them.

CBS was also involved in a different sort of counterprogramming strategy during
the late 1980s. The network found that it was not competing well for the most
desirable slice of the 18- to 49-year-old segments—those at the younger end. As a
result, instead of trying harder, network strategists began to tout the importance of 45-
to 55-year-olds to advertisers and to skew their program buys in that area.

Madison Avenue was not convinced that the older audience offered as good a
target as the younger one, however, and CBS marketers were unable to change their
minds. CBS found itself suffering monetarily under the weight of relatively low
ratings and an undesirably old audience. In 1990, the network's new entertainment
chief signalled his intention to orient programming toward age groups that would
please more TV advertisers.[26]

The meaning of the example should be clear: Just as important as the material ABC, CBS, and NBC schedule during prime time is the material the networks have learned not to schedule as a response to their client requirements. Programs aimed exclusively at youngsters are unacceptable, as are programs for people over 60. The reason is that the networks can attract much more advertising money at that time of day by trying to lure 18- to 49-year-olds. Similarly, programs that are not upbeat in at least some basic way, or are too provocative or controversial, are frowned upon by network executives. The reason is that most advertisers feel that such programs do not provide the best environment for their commercials. Program production executives have picked up this criterion, as they have the general advertiser-oriented network perspective.

Production Rules

Consequently, over the years the production executives have negotiated specific rules with the networks that make their ideas for shows much more likely to be accepted for the schedule. The guidelines extend to the very structure of the programs. So, for example:

> The plot must be created with natural breaks about every ten minutes so commercials can be inserted.

> The regular characters of a series should reflect (or attract) viewers whom the networks are hoping to draw for advertisers. An 8:00 P.M. situation comedy (the most popular eight o'clock show in recent years) must therefore have at least a couple of children for the youngsters in the house to like, a good-looking male lead for women to ogle, and at least one pretty woman for male encouragement.

> If the sitcom is due to be broadcast on Saturday, the requirements are even more specific. Saturday evening is a period of high VCR use and out-of-home activities among white young adults. An unusually high percentage of network viewers during this period are African-Americans and senior citizens. They tend not to be as mobile or own VCRs in as great a percentage as other groups. In attempting to attract these audiences to their channels, network executives make sure their Saturday evening programs are populated with blacks, older people, or both. As a result, the census of blacks and older people is higher Saturday evening than during any other time of the week.

This sketch can convey only some flavor of the way the producer-client relationship affects the creation of material in network television. Changing circumstances in the industry and in the world may influence the way the relationship gets played out on a daily basis. During the Persian Gulf war, for example, network news producers began to feel pressure from national advertisers to deemphasize their coverage. Sponsors, they said, were afraid their upbeat, consumption-oriented commercials might not look good shown next to images of dead or maimed soldiers. At NBC, the pressure led to decisions by executives to refrain from offering special reports if possible. Even though the network received high ratings, it sold only about 20% of its commercial time, making the specials economically unfeasible for the network. "Commercials need to be seen in the right environment," explained an advertising executive. "A war is not an upbeat environment."[27]

WHEN CLIENTS ARE NOT ADVERTISERS

It is important to point out that this kind of widespread influence is not confined to media in which advertisers are the clients. Take elementary and high school ("el-hi") textbook publishing as an example. The primary clients for el-hi texbook publishers are various state and local school systems around the United States. Often, a central administration will periodically create a list of the only books that educators throughout the area can choose. Teachers will then pick from that list.

Naturally, textbook publishers are eager to get their textbooks on the approved lists in as many places as possible. As a result of the need to get school boards to accept their texts, editors and marketing executives pay close attention to the educational and moral guidelines that school board members voice. They pay attention to the public controversies that swirl around particular issues or titles and the positions of school boards on those controversies. They try to please advocates of change as well as traditionalists. They even pay attention to the way school board members inspect the books.

A popular inspection technique is the "flip test." It involves flipping the pages of a text to note the kinds of activities that are illustrated, as well as the number of whites, African-Americans, Hispanic-Americans, Native Americans, and Asian-Americans who are named or drawn. From this feedback, the editors draw up guidelines about what school systems will accept that they pass along to authors of the texts.

Because publishing firm executives want to remain under consideration by as many school boards as possible, they tend to urge authors toward texts and illustrations that will be acceptable everywhere. The lists of "dos and don'ts" are typically long and specific. Prohibitions include refusal to present such possibly controversial topics as divorce, mixed marriages, and religious observances. Requirements include representation of various minority groups in specific numerical quotas, often so that they will be noticed in a flip test.

The result, say many educators, are homogenized textbooks which are acceptable to everyone but which present material in so predictable and bland a manner that students are not challenged to think about their surroundings; in fact, students often become bored. Authors and illustrators are often exasperated with the process, because they feel this least-common-denominator approach to textbook publishing robs them of any opportunities to be creative. Irene Trivas is one person who stopped accepting assignments to illustrate children's readers in the late 1980s. According to *The New York Times*, she was frustrated with publishers' efforts to "be everything to everybody," as she put it.[28] Here is her account of the instructions she received for one book:

It's etched in acid in my mind. They sent 10 pages of single-spaced specifications. The hero was a Hispanic boy. There were black twins, one boy, one girl; an

---

Talking Point 4.1   Confidential Guidesheet

In order to make their books acceptable to as many school boards as possible, elementary and high school textbook publishers often give their authors confidential lists of "dos and don'ts." Here are just a few policies from a confidential guidesheet that a major textbook publishing firm expected all its authors to follow during the early 1980s. Anecdotal evidence suggests many of these are still in force.

- *Brand names, commercial identification*—Do not use or show.
- *Death*—Do not include except in anthologies and only if well balanced by other materials.
- *Divorce*—Do not include.
- *Evolution*—Avoid, except in science texts where it is a necessary part of the curriculum. Make sure all reference is to theory, not fact. Include statement required by Texas in front matter.
- *Mixed marriages, religious or racial*—Do not show.
- *Religion*—Do not show symbols of. Avoid all references to unless it is the theme of a story of exposition. If it is central to the piece, consider leaving the piece out. Avoid topics considered by some to be antireligious—for example evolution, witchcraft, secular humanism.
- *For materials in preparation this year, represent minorities in the following minimum percentages—whites, 68%, blacks, 15%, Hispanic-Americans, 10%, Asian-Americans, 1%, Native Americans, 1%.*

SOURCE: Confidential.

---

overweight Oriental boy, and an American Indian girl. That leaves the Caucasian. Since we mustn't forget the physically handicapped, she was born with a congenital malformation and only had three fingers on one hand.

One child had to have an Irish setter, and the setter was to be female.

The Hispanic had two parents. The father has a white collar job. The mother is an illustrator and she works at home. At one point, they are seen through the kitchen screen door making dinner, having spaghetti and meatballs and a salad. The editor appended a note that said, "Make sure it's not iceberg; it should be something nice like endive."

They also had a senior citizen, and I had to show her jogging.

I can't do it anymore.[29]

Ms. Trivas and others in and out of the el-hi industry fault textbook publishers for not trying hard enough—or not being brave enough—to use the producer-client relationship to influence school boards toward less formula-ridden approaches. The result, they argue, is that American schoolchildren are being taught with books that make little attempt to acknowledge that youngsters, like adults, want materials that will interest and excite them.

A PROFOUND IMPACT

Neither this el-hi textbook example nor the network TV case—nor any of the illustrations in this chapter—can cover all the implications the producer-client relationship holds for the output of mass media systems. Clearly, though, the relationship's impact is profound. When working in media organizations, reading industry trade magazines, or merely being an aware media consumer, it is useful to try to trace the links between production firms and their clients. Obtaining a wide grasp on their influence on one another can lead to a better understanding of the forces that guide media output.

One key purpose of the producer-client relationship has so far only been hinted at: its role in defining the audience. It may have occurred to you during the discussion of schoolchildren, or while reading any of the other examples in this chapter, that notions of the audience loom large in any producer-client relationship. Yet the concept of audience, and the part the producer-client relationship plays in it, is not as straightforward as it may seem. At the same time, targeting audiences is a major activity of mass media producers and clients. The activity is so important, and so fascinatingly complex, that the entire next chapter will be devoted to it.

NOTES

1. See also Garth Jowett and James Linton, *Movies as Mass Communication* (Beverly Hills, CA: Sage, 1980), pp. 25–64; and Janet Wasko, *Movies and Money* (Norwood, NJ: Ablex, 1982).
2. Telephone conversation with Bruce Snyder, President, Domestic Distribution, 20th Century Fox Film Corporation, June 20, 1991.
3. These figures are from *Advertising Age*, December 26, 1990.
4. These figures are from *Advertising Age*, December 26, 1990.
5. *Advertising Age*, March 29, 1989, p. 82.
6. Quoted in *Advertising Age*, November 24, 1980, p. 68.
7. Howard Aldrich, *Organizations and Environments* (Englewood Cliffs, NJ: Prentice Hall, 1979), p. 267.
8. William Evan, *Organization Theory* (New York: Wiley, 1976), p. 123.
9. Laura Loro, "Philadelphia Papers Appeal to Agencies," *Advertising Age*, January 28, 1991, p. 12.
10. J. W. Click and Russell N. Baird, *Magazine Editing and Production* 2nd ed. (Dubuque, IA: William C. Brown, 1979), p. 4.
11. *Folio* magazine editorial data base.
12. Cited in Leonard Mogel, *The Magazine* (New York: Spectrum Books, 1981), p. 2.
13. Mogel, p. 3.
14. Christopher Sterling and Timothy Haight, *The Mass Media: Aspen Guide to Communication Industry Trends* (New York: Praeger, 1978), p. 372.
15. Click and Baird, p. 2.
16. Click and Baird, p. 24.
17. *Advertising Age*, October 19, 1981, p. S-6.
18. Les Brown, *Television: The Business Behind the Box* (New York: Harcourt Brace Jovanovich, 1972), pp. 49–50.
19. Jowett and Linton, *Movies as Mass Communication*, p. 39.

20. Jennifer Howland, "Ad vs. Edit," *Folio*, December 1989, pp. 92–100. Quote is on p. 94.
21. Click and Baird, p. 33.
22. Howland, p. 92.
23. Click and Baird, p. 263.
24. Howland, p. 95.
25. *Advertising Age*, October 19, 1991, p. 20.
26. Rick Dubrow, "Fall TV Schedules Aim at the Young and the Restless," *Los Angeles Times*, May 30, 1990, p. D1.
27. Bill Carter, "Few Sponsors for TV War News," *The New York Times*, February 7, 1991, p. C1.
28. Susan Chira, "Writing Textbooks for Children: A Juggling Act," *The New York Times*, January 17, 1990, p. B8.
29. Chira, p. B8.

CHAPTER FIVE

Targeting the Audience

All of us use the word *audience* almost every day of our adult lives. We talk about the audience for a TV show, the audience for a movie, the audience for a concert. A movie review we read might discuss the audience's reaction. A parent might tell us about the audience's response to a child during a public performance at school. We ourselves might worry about how the audience will receive a speech we will be giving.

Rarely, though, do people stop to think of the meaning of the word *audience*, or its implications. Simple as it sounds, and as commonly as it is used, *audience* is a complex, often misunderstood term. As it relates to mass communication, the word stands for a variety of activities that profoundly influence the way media creators see society and the way members of society see themselves and the world. The aim of this chapter is to explore the activities that lie behind "the audience" and to tease out their significance. To begin, it will be useful to introduce the most important point about an audience: that it is a concept, a construction of reality.

THE AUDIENCE AS A CONSTRUCTION OF REALITY

To explain what it means to say that the audience is a construction of reality, a nonmedia example might first be helpful.

Imagine a professor's audience in a university lecture course. The professor faces a collection of individuals. Each individual sees himself or herself as embodying certain attributes—friendly, selfish, religious, and the like. Friends, enemies, strangers, and mere acquaintances may think about these individuals in other ways.

The professor, however, looks out at the individuals in the lecture hall and thinks of them not as individuals whom he knows separately and personally in very different ways. Rather, he sees them as a *group of students*. This collection of students is the professor's audience. He thinks of them as students because the university pays him to think of them that way. The professor will not be rewarded—he might even lose his job—if he thinks of the people in front of him as volleyball enthusiasts and invites them out for a game in the gym.

As straightforward as it sounds, this approach to the individuals in his class has major consequences. The professor talks to the people whom he faces in the lecture hall according to his understanding of the way professors are supposed to talk to their students. The categories he thinks about when he creates his lectures are student-related categories—how bright they are, how interested they are, how knowledgeable they are about the subject, and what most students around the country are expected to know about the subject.

His lectures are not likely to be guided primarily by whether people in the class are pregnant or whether they actively practice certain religions. If, however, the professor were facing those same people at an abortion rights rally, categories such as their religious beliefs and whether they are parents would be quite relevant.

The purpose of this example is to help make the following points:

First, although individuals are real, audiences are not. **Audiences are abstractions**. They are ideas about groups of people.

Second, **audiences are constructed**. That is, an audience gets created when certain categories are chosen over other categories to describe a group of people.

Third, the **categories people use to construct their audiences flow out of the reward systems that guide them**. You will recall that the professor defined his audience as students because his employer (the university) expected him to see "students" in that classroom. All audiences are constructed in this way, whether those doing the audience creation know it or not.

Constructing Mass Media Audiences

The generalizations apply to the mass media, as well. In theory, there is an infinite number of ways that executives of mass media production firms can discuss the people who come into contact with the materials the firms release. Audiences can be constructed with categories that range from eye color to religious preference and beyond—and those categories can constantly change.

In practice, though, the executives tend to discuss their firm's audience along much narrower lines that are quite predictable. It is no surprise to someone working in television that commercial network executives talk primarily about the age, gender, and race of their viewers. Nor will it cause a stir within the consumer magazine industry to state that executives emphasize incomes and acquisitive spending in addition to age and gender when building images of their readers. In neither case are such items as their grandparents' countries of origin, their kissing habits, or their religiosity likely to play a part in audience construction.

To understand how the basic categories of audience become established within a media production firm, it is important to remember the producer-client relationship that was discussed in the last chapter. Recall that clients are organizations—advertisers, bookstores, movie distributors—that pay producers for the creation of media products before those products reach the public. As shown in Chapter 4, clients exert powerful influences on the guidelines producers adopt regarding their output. At the same time, production firms often take part in negotiating the demands their clients make of them.

It is through this ongoing interchange between producers and their population of clients that the categories of people the clients want to reach through the producer's media output get established. Production firms get money from their clients for creating materials that attract these audiences. In turn, the producers may lose support—they may even go out of business—if they cannot provide materials that satisfy enough clients to keep the enterprise alive.

The Case of Children's Books and TV

To get concrete about this interorganizational construction of audience, consider the contrasting forces that affect the way an audience called "children" gets constructed in the library market as opposed to the television market. The children's library marketplace is comprised of publishers who sell most of their books to children's libraries. The children's television area is comprised of TV production firms and networks that support programming through selling air time to advertisers (mostly toy, candy, and cereal companies).

The two sets of relationships are drastically different. Children's libraries are run by librarians, who have gone to school to learn about children and their development. They have been taught to view youngsters as esthetically inclined, intellectually developing beings whose interests in a diverse range of experience ought to be cultivated. Categories such as age and gender become starting points for asking what can and should stimulate creativity at different ages. Abstract designs, illustrations that reflect artistic individuality, stories that have emotional tension and that, for older children, display moral difficulties—these are among the traits that librarians feel describe the best children's books.

Practical considerations also enter into the librarians' purchasing approaches. For example, branch librarians typically want to encourage children to borrow many books from the library because when their branch's circulation statistics increase, they get more book-buying money from the library system. The result might be that certain types of books which the librarians dislike but know children and their parents enjoy—Richard Scarry picture books, for example—might be ordered for the shelves as a nod to circulation concerns. In general, though, librarians are convinced that they can and should help to shape what is popular among their borrowers. They learn to point youngsters toward what they feel are fascinating books that also help the children grow esthetically and intellectually.

On the "producer" side of this producer-client relationship, the editors from publishing firms who want librarians to buy their books pay careful attention to the criteria librarians hold about what constitutes a good book. Generalizing from the large population of librarians they know, the editors construct images of children and priorities toward children that are compatible with those of their primary clients. In addition, they choose authors and manuscripts that fit these images and the criteria that go along with them.

They might even try to influence librarians' criteria in directions they feel are useful for their firm. So, for example, the acceptability of adolescent "problem" novels by authors such as Judy Blume might get a boost among librarians through editors' initiatives. A decision such as this will have to be framed within the boundaries the library field has set regarding children's needs and capabilities at certain ages.

Contrast the library market approach to that of commercial network television. Network officials commission programs for children in response to the needs of their clients—advertisers and ad agencies. The cereal companies, toy companies, and candy companies that advertise to children face requirements that lead them to construct their audience very differently from the way librarians do. Their mandate in reaching children is to convince them to buy certain products, or to nag their parents to buy them.

The categories they see children through are therefore related not to broad concerns about youngsters' esthetic and intellectual development but rather to an interest in children as little consumers. Wanting to attract advertisers, network officials select TV programs and construct their children's TV schedules with the same goals in mind. Challenging children's creativity and responding to a variety of individual interests take a far back seat to capturing the greatest number of possible juvenile viewers so as to make it efficient for advertisers to buy time to reach them. Along the same lines, a child's age and gender become not so much indicators of capabilities and broad interest areas (as they are with the publishers) but tags that imply purchasing habits, knowledge of consumer culture, and commercial persuadability.

One upshot is very different guidelines for selecting "children's" material. For example, librarians typically reject TV-based books such as those about the Ghost Busters and Smurf cartoon series that are sold in department stores and supermarkets. They dislike the books' predictable plots, flat illustrations, and their presence as advertisements for the many other Smurf and Ghost Busters products.[1] To advertisers, however, sponsoring programs around these characters—using the same style of plots and illustrations of the books—would not at all be considered drawbacks if they reached enough of their targeted audience. Moreover, the link between the programs and items based on them that children can buy might be considered a benefit to advertisers, since they believe it reinforces in young viewers the idea that commercially driven popular culture is acceptable.

The point here is not to make the library market publishers look good and the network executives and their producers look bad. Rather, the idea is to show how the categories that executives in media production firms use to describe the audience they need to reach serve the interests of the marketplace in which they work and affect their content selection guidelines. In this case, very different constructions of "children" and their needs emerge as a result. So do very different attitudes toward the acceptability of certain kinds of content.

The same process of audience construction takes place in other media situations. It takes on particular day-to-day intensity where producers compete vigorously with one another for advertisers' cash. Looking for market niches that will help them draw the money clients may otherwise spend on competitors, producers often choose to focus on **narrowly specialized attributes** that they feel will appeal to advertisers.

Audience Construction in the Magazine Business

The magazine business is a good example of such **targeting** or **narrowcasting**. Consider, for example, the way *Popular Mechanics* and *Rolling Stone* magazines portray themselves and their audiences in ads to the advertising trade.

Rolling Stone executives often reach out to potential clients who shy away from advertising their products in the magazine because of an image that the audience is made up of holdover hippies from the 1960s who shun material goods and would reject commercialism. The idea that readers of *Rolling Stone* are former hippies who still think on a nonmaterial wavelength is a possibility that *Rolling Stone's* marketing department wants to actively discourage. Its job is to point out that the magazine provides an environment to successfully reach leisure-oriented *consumers*.

An example of their work is a two-page spread in an October 1989 issue of *Advertising Age*. The left page shows the face of a curly-haired young blond woman. It is done in the style of a 1960s "flower child," and her eyes are closed as if she is meditating. The caption above the photo reads: "Perception." On the right side, under a caption that reads "Reality," is the face of a somewhat older woman. No longer flowered, it is impeccably made up, with streaks of suntan lotion on her lower lip and nose. Clearly the eyes are closed not for meditative reasons but so that she might tan in the sun. The paragraph below the photo makes the point clearly:

> When the moon was in the seventh house and Jupiter was aligned with Mars, the readers of *Rolling Stone* were painting their faces to keep out of the establishment. Now, they're painting their faces to keep out of the sun. Last week, *Rolling Stone* readers established themselves as users of sun protection and skin care products more than 62 million times. If you're looking for one of the best markets under the sun, you will find plenty of exposure in the pages of *Rolling Stone*.

In the same *Advertising Age* issue, *Popular Mechanics* constructs a different audience, but with similarly commercial inclinations. The magazine says it is designed to attract "the must-know man," an active, intelligent adult male whose inquisitiveness ignites acquisitiveness in himself and others. *Popular Mechanics* says that it has succeeded in becoming a "must read" for this important advertising target, and it then proceeds to add particulars to the image:

> The Must-Know Man comprises a huge 25% of American males over 18 with a substantial household income. That's 13.3 million Americans. A very special breed of Americans, the doers, the men who make things work.
>
> The Must-Know Man is a very different type of man. He's the man who isn't content to read the news about technology; he must know what it is and how it works.
>
> The Must-Know Man is equipment intensive. He buys power tools, electronics, automobiles, boats, and much more. He is the consumer willing to buy the best, whether it's a computer or a power drill, or a life insurance policy for his family.
>
> The Must-Know Man also influences the purchases of many other men and women. When you reach The Must-Know Man, you're reaching an expert.[2]

Note that both *Popular Mechanics* and *Rolling Stone* back up their visions of the people they try to attract with specific information about buying habits by those people. The information that they present fits hand in glove with the audience visions they are creating. Characteristics that are irrelevant to the audience image that the magazines want to present to advertisers—their church-attending records, for instance—would not be included in the appeal to clients.

In the examples presented, *Rolling Stone* constructs an audience of leisure-oriented consumers of the good life; that image is extended by trumpeting the amount of suntan lotion its readers purchase. *Popular Mechanics* portrays its constituency as

TABLE 5.1. Top Twenty National Publications Among Adults With Household Income of $60,000 or More (1990)

Title	Circulation
National Geographic	9,251
Better Homes & Gardens	8,990
Reader's Digest	8,610
TV Guide	7,426
People	7,281
Time	7,165
Newsweek	5,739
Sports Illustrated	5,480
The Wall Street Journal	5,037
USA Today	4,526
HG	4,166
Money	3,974
U.S. News & World Report	3,824
Smithsonian	3,526
Travel & Leisure	3,411
The New York Times (Sunday)	3,179
House Beautiful	3,015
Country Living	2,910
Bon Appetit	2,873
Architectural Digest	2,783

Relatively wealthy segments of the population attract many marketers. Consequently, many magazines try hard to attract the relatively wealthy.
  Figures are in thousands.

SOURCE: *Advertising Age*, July 9, 1990, p. S1.

confident men whose take-charge style when it comes to equipment extends to buying the very best products to get the job done. The list of products its readers purchase fleshes out this image and becomes a crucial part of it.

The underlying message that these ads present is clear: The magazine firms are acknowledging that to attract advertisers they need to do more than construct an audience image and build an editorial environment to suit it. The producers know they must prove to their potential clients that their media vehicles do actually reach people with those attributes.

This requirement raises three major questions about the construction of audiences in mass media industries.

First, how does a production firm go about trying to prove to its clients that its media output will, in fact, reach people who match desirable characteristics of audience the producer has promised?

Second, to what extent can such a "proof" be considered genuine reflections of the characteristics of the individuals who actually make up the producers' audiences?

Third, what might be some social consequences of labeling certain segments of society according to images created as a result of producer-client relationships?

"KNOWING" THE AUDIENCE

The short answer to the first question, and the beginning of an answer to the others, is that media production firms commission **audience research**. Audience research involves *systematic investigation* to determine if the numbers and kinds of people the producer has decided to reach with certain media materials are attracted to the output.

This answer is only a partial one, though. While many firms do rely on a good deal of audience research, many others find it either too expensive or impossible to accomplish when it is most relevant. Before exploring the variety of projects that come under the audience research heading, then, it will be useful to examine when audience research is conducted and when other ways of "knowing" the audience are used by producers to convince clients that they do, in fact, draw the people they say they draw to their media materials.

Note that the emphasis here is on the role that audience research and other forms of knowing the audience hold for a production firm's interactions with its clients. At its heart, audience research is aimed at *reducing the risk* that those relationships will fail and that the clients will leave. It should not be surprising, however, that audience research carried out for external organizations is also used *within* media production organizations to reduce creators' individual risks of failure and to guide them toward certain types of output. This function of audience knowing will be taken up in Chapters 7 and 8.

Deciding to Conduct Research

To begin examining the way audience knowing works for producers and clients, consider a newspaper firm that is involved in developing ideas for a new weekly section on science. Newspaper executives might commission research to determine if the section will be read by a sufficient number of the individuals who are attractive to the target advertisers—computer, camera, and business equipment stores. The executives realize they are dependent on advertisers and their agencies for support. Before spending large amounts of money, these parties might demand research to back up the newspaper's audience-reaching claims.

In this example, both producers and clients consider audience research a useful way to come to terms with the question of audience—to see if people with the categories the advertisers and producers want to reach will, in fact, say they would read the new section. Yet audience research is not always conducted at the point of creation in every area of the mass media. There is a spectrum of attitudes toward this kind of exploration. Some media producers consider audience research on individual products critical to their success. Others use it sparingly, while still others hardly use it at all.

The trade book segment of the book industry lies on the end of the spectrum where audience research is minimal. **Trade books** are hardbacks directed mostly to bookstores and general libraries. When asked why they refrain from conducting market research on their titles, publishing executives typically point out that every book title is a unique product, not directly related to the other titles they publish. Conducting audience research on simply the idea of the book before it is created will not, they feel, allow for an accurate gauge of consumer response to a particular manuscript.

Publishing executives also do not typically conduct audience research *after* the book is created. Their reason is that the title is not like a bar of soap that the manufacturer wants to sell in standard form for many years to come. It is, rather, merely one of a continual stream of new publications that the publisher hopes will find a place, usually temporary, in the market. Trade executives contend that spending time and money to test every new title when it is ready to be shipped to the stores would be too expensive an activity too late in the process.

Alternatives to Audience Research

The trade book publishers' reluctance to conduct audience research on individual titles does not, however, mean that they ignore considerations of their ultimate consumers. To do that might be deadly, especially from the standpoint of convincing bookstores that their works will sell. Instead, they have developed other methods for supporting the position that the proposed product matches their audience's likes and dislikes.

One is to use sales figures that the publishers hold in their computers. If a manuscript is submitted that is on a topic similar to titles that the firm previously sold an average of, say, 10,000 copies at $19.95, marketing personnel might inform the editorial staff that expected sales will likely be in that ball park. Decisions about the potential book's shape, length, marketing program, price—even sometimes its publishability—will proceed from there.

Also used to make presumptions about the audience are generalizations from sales figures that large bookstore chains such as B. Dalton and Waldenbooks sometimes share with publishers. Conversations between key store executives and publisher representatives may lead the publishers and stores to construct ideas about emerging interests in segments of the audience. That, in turn, might encourage the creation of certain books to fill the clients' perceived need.

Related but nevertheless distinct techniques for claiming knowledge of the audience in the absence of systematic research are **the use of track record talent and the use of track record content**. A **track record** talent is a creator who has a list of proven recent successes and a strong reputation in his or her field. To trade publishing executives and their bookstore clients, an author whose book made *The New York Times* best-seller list last year is a good bet for success this year. The expectation is that somehow the author has a feel for the interests that a considerable number of readers share.

As a result, the manuscript that the creator generates becomes a way to define the concerns of the audience—at least until sales of the next book drop drastically. So, for example, a manuscript about a group of amateurs working toward being on the U.S. Olympic rowing team might not draw the attention of a top trade editor. Submitted by popular author David Halberstam, however, the book's possibilities suddenly seem greater, since Halberstam has shown over time that he attracts a large number of readers. Halberstam also has a better chance than unknown writers to appear on a television talk show or to garner a newspaper writeup of his book. This fact, too, can help sell books and so convince bookstores to carry the title.

Track record content works in ways similar to track record talent to reduce perceptions of risk and crystallize impressions of audience interests. Track record content refers to subjects and approaches that have enjoyed success in media material during the recent past.

If, for example, books about hobbies have been profitable, a publisher might feel that a book in that general area might be attractive to distributors and garner good sales. Of course, there is always the danger that following what many others have been doing will place a production firm on the downward side of a trend. For firms interested in exploiting track record content the trick is to seize upon subjects that have not yet reached the peak of their popularity. Adapting ideas that are making their mark in other media is one strategy to use.

So, for example, an editor who notices an interest in sensational murders among newspapers and broadcast organizations may alert the sales force that it can help convince bookstore agents that an audience exists to support a book on the subject. Tying into topics that are widely popular is also a good way to generate publicity for the books in other media—and this, too, can convince booksellers to allocate store space for the title.

The Case of the Movie Industry

We have noted that executives in book publishing and their clients have become accustomed to using track record considerations as primary ways to predict what the audience will like. The trade publishing people have felt that the individualistic nature of their materials makes it either impossible or too expensive to quantitatively study audience response to a work before it is fully created. This perspective is shared in several publishing areas—for example, scholarly periodicals and children's books. A lot more areas of the mass media, though, place a premium not so much on individual products as on research-based predictability of success with the consumer.

On the spectrum from little to much audience research, the Hollywood movie industry is somewhere in the middle. Hollywood takes an approach to knowing the audience that is both similar to and different from trade book publishers. As in the book industry, producers of theatrical films must justify the selection of individual projects to their clients.

In the moving picture business, the clients are often major movie distributors or banks that lend producers money for individual projects (see Chapter 4). Like trade book editors, movie producers traditionally have contended that they create individual products which are not amenable to proper audience response testing before they are made. They have argued that people cannot judge whether they want to see a film based on a short description of a story; people might respond positively to the description and negatively to the finished product, or vice versa.

Preproduction Research

As a result, audience research has traditionally not been conducted as a prelude to creating a particular film. Instead, the other techniques of "knowing" the audience have come into play. Like trade book publishers, movie producers have used general numerical profiles of their customers (the makeup of moviegoers in terms of age, sex, and race) along with track record talent (successful directors, writers, actors) and track record content (clearly popular themes and subjects) to guide their project choices and convince their clients that the product would succeed.

During the past decade, though, movie executives have become more research-oriented when looking at new projects. Movie studios might test promising plot lines on samples of moviegoers to see which draws the most interest. Even the script might be analyzed quantitatively. A company called Emotional Response Index System (ERIS) claims it can forecast whether a movie will be successful even before it is completed. Based on a sampling of thousands of people, ERIS has concluded that it can analyze scripts to see if they have the qualities wanted in theatrical films.[3]

Preproduction research such as this is still fairly uncommon in the movie industry, but it may increase. Part of the reason is the new generation of executives that arrived when conglomerates took over the major studios during the 1970s and 1980s. The executives are more trained in consumer goods and advertising research than their predecessors. They are used to conducting consumer research on the earliest stages of product development, and they see no reason that movies should be treated differently.

Another part of the reason has to do with the skyrocketing costs of movies. Consider that the cost of generating a typical trade book is not likely to go above a couple of hundred thousand dollars, including marketing expenses.[4] By contrast, the cost of creating an average American film exceeds $23 million, plus almost half as much for marketing expenses.[5]

While the book publishing cost is by no means low, publishers seem to feel that combining track record considerations with numerical figures of popularity from their own records and those of bookstore chains can reduce the risk of failure across their slate. Audience research would increase the cost of the enterprise to a level where the final price of each book would be far above the going rate for books. Moviemakers, however, are dealing with much more money in the entire venture. Spending on research to try to ensure the optimal potential of a title is considered acceptable because it amounts to only a small portion of a film's total cost.

Postproduction Research

After their product is completed, the movie studios' approach to the audience has long been more aggressive and systematic than that of book publishers. Three types of audience research are common: title testing, previewing, and tracking.

Title testing involves conducting interviews with filmgoers in shopping malls and other public places to determine which of a number of possible names for upcoming films is most likely to reflect the nature of those movies in such a way as to draw people to the theaters. The belief is that the first wave of people who choose to see a new film will be attracted by its name and cast.

If that first group likes the film, they will talk favorably to friends about it, a phenomenon that is called strong word of mouth. Executives believe that strong word of mouth is a key to a release's success, often even more so than positive newspaper, TV, and magazine reviews. If, however, the title is boring or draws an audience expecting to see a different kind of picture, it can severely damage the word of mouth and cripple the movie's chances.

As an example, take the movie *Field of Dreams*, a romantic comedy with a baseball backdrop. Originally, the creators proposed naming it *Shoeless Joe*, a reference to a legendary baseball player. Title testing revealed, however, that potential moviegoers thought that a film with that title was a baseball biography or a comedy about a hobo. Producers feared that these perceptions would bring the wrong group of initial moviegoers into the theater, with a resulting poor word of mouth. They changed the title to *Field of Dreams* when they felt it communicated the film's romantic inclinations more clearly.[6]

Previewing takes place after a film is completed but before it is formally released. The studio will show a preliminary (**rough-cut**) version of a movie to an audience of theatergoers. Sometimes, the director and producers will attend the screenings and note reactions at certain points. More often, researchers will give the viewers cards to fill out which ask questions about what they liked or didn't like about the movie.

The reactions might be used to reedit parts of the film. The original sad ending of *Fatal Attraction*, for example, was changed to make it happier after negative audience reactions during previews. Preview audience answers also guide studio marketing departments and ad agencies toward themes that would most likely encourage people to see the movie.

Tracking takes place from about two weeks before the movie is released through the first month of release. Its purpose is to determine the effectiveness of publicity and word of mouth that the producer and distributor have been trying to stir up over the film. Three times during each of those weeks, a company named National Research Group surveys a random sample of Americans by phone. National's operators read a list of current or soon-to-be-released films to people who say they have recently seen theatrical movies. For every film on the list, the people are asked (1) if they are aware of it and (2) if they want to see it.

National Research Group sells the results to the major movie producers and distributors. The findings come too late to do anything to the movie or to change its pattern of release to the theaters. Nevertheless, the film's marketers see this way of knowing the audience as indicating whether revisions to their publicity and advertising plan are needed to help draw optimal ticket sales.

If, for example, people tend to be aware of a new movie but do not want to see it, marketers would conclude that the **weight of publicity** and advertising has been fine but the **creative approach** to informing people about the product has been poor. They may then take steps to correct the problem. In the worst case, marketers feel that a tracking study can help indicate what *not* to do when they try to entice certain groups of consumers to certain films.

FORMAT-DRIVEN AUDIENCE RESEARCH

Recall that it is the individualistic, stand-alone nature of trade books and (to a lesser extent) Hollywood movies that lead producers and their clients to feel reluctant or unable to rely on audience research, especially before the product's release in the marketplace. There are, though, other areas of publishing and moviemaking where there exists little concern with one-shot creations. Think of juvenile adventures such as those based on Nancy Drew and the Hardy Boys; the groups of books about home repair or World War II that Time-Life Books markets; the old Little Rascals movies of the 1930s; the various *Star Trek* films of the 1970s and 1980s. These are just the tip of an iceberg of materials in publishing and moviemaking that rely not on new products every time for their money but on the continuation of previous themes, characters, even plots.

Such a consistent arrangement of symbolic material—the layout, tone, and general approach—across two or more versions of a cultural product is called a **format**. When a succession of products is associated with a particular format, that group of items is called a **series**. The Hardy Boys, Nancy Drew, and James Bond formats are all connected with series—in books, film, and TV. The term *format* can also be used to describe the consistent approach that a specific mass media channel—a particular TV station, magazine, newspaper—takes to its material. It is a format that creates what people think of as the "personalities" of those channels.

Typically, for example, radio stations act out their particular formats through the songs they play and the sounds of the on-air personalities. WMMR-Philadelphia, a radio station with an "album-oriented rock" format, carries a mix of certain kinds of music, news, and features that is designed to lend a character to the station even though the specific songs played change from week to week.

Magazines and newspapers have easily detectable formats, too. *The New York Times* is recognizably *The New York Times* every day, while *People* magazine follows a very different, yet consistent, style.

When it comes to television, the term *format* may apply to both the channel and the series carried by the channel. *Nick at Nite*, a nightly cable service loaded with TV shows and movies chosen to attract people who grew up during the 1950s and 1960s, is but one example of a TV channel that is formatted. *Leave It to Beaver*, one of the several hit 1960s situation comedies *Nick at Nite* sends over the wire, is an example of a series format. Week after week, the program carries the same setting, characters, and approach to plot.

When this kind of long-term approach is intended from the start (and it often is), producers and their clients agree that it makes research on the target audience's reactions a good deal more feasible than with stand-alone creations. One reason is that producers view the cost of research as relating to a stream of future products, not just a single item. Just as important, producers consider that formats make audience research practical from a logistical standpoint. They feel a format provides them with a completed product to test that will be similar to forthcoming products.

ADVERTISERS AND AUDIENCE RESEARCH

It is no accident that virtually all media that are sponsored by advertisers are organized by formats. Advertising executives are rooted in a package goods marketing tradition where quantitative evidence rules. They demand research-based evidence that the media they use will attract individuals with characteristics that match their marketing needs. The creation of media materials as part of formats allows the quantitative research demands of advertisers to be satisfied much more easily than if the material were fully distinct from one another.

From the production firm's standpoint, use of formats allows producers to construct audiences that particular advertisers would like, to create materials that will attract those audiences, and to hold onto them over time. For their part, advertisers accept the idea that if you take a sampling from a format—say, two issues of a magazine or a week of a radio station's broadcasts—you will get material that is representative of the format at other times as well. They also accept the proposition that if a stable format can be shown to attract a certain audience at one point in time, it will likely attract that audience at other points in time. This reasoning makes audience research more economically feasible than if the readers of every issue of the magazine or the viewers of every episode of the TV series had to be studied.

What advertiser-supported media firms sell to their clients, then, is formats that can be used to reach audiences of predictable sizes and types. Just how much audience research a company commissions to prove that predictability varies widely. Magazines that cater to narrow audiences, for example, often cannot afford to conduct the kinds of readership audits, tests, and surveys that large mass market magazines can. That such small media often thrive within their niches indicates that advertisers, too, vary in their insistence that research back up their media buys.

Audience research on advertiser-supported media falls into two broad categories:

Research on the vehicle's format before it is introduced to the marketplace

Research on the format after it is introduced

Concept Testing in Ad-Supported Media

Research on the format before it is introduced often involves trying out ideas on potential audience members, a procedure called concept testing.

As an example of concept testing, consider the way Time Inc. Magazines tried to find out if there was a lucrative market for an entertainment guide that two of its employees had dreamed up. The two were given the money to find out whether the proposed periodical had the potential to draw the number and kind of subscribers who would be attractive to advertisers. An advertising packet was mailed to 500,000 people who had been culled from Time's magazine subscriber lists. The packet described the periodical, included mock-up cover pictures, and asked the individuals receiving the letter if they would like to subscribe.

Enough said yes for Time to set the projected circulation base at 500,000. More important, Time associated the ones who wanted to subscribe with audience characteristics that typically draw strong advertiser interest: main age group 25–45; 72% college educated; about 50:50 male/female; and median income $40,000. In addition, Time learned that 85% of those responding owned VCRs, 51% owned CD players (versus 15% nationwide), and 66% regularly bought hardback books. This suggested strong potential in home electronics, alcohol, automotive, TV programming, and mail-order book, video, and music-club advertising. Impressed, Time's management moved further toward giving the go-ahead for the magazine, which came to be known as *Entertainment Weekly*.[7]

Concept testing is not confined to the magazine industry. A radio station owner toying with a major format change, a television station concerned about the look of its local news hour, and a television network interested in mounting popular series all place figuring out how viable their ideas are with the target audience among the points to discover before they move ahead.

Concept testing typically involves interviews in one or more of the following settings:

Over the phone

In an auditorium

In a focus group

Via a cable television channel

The first three methods are used regularly in the radio industry. **Telephone calling** is a particularly common way of testing and refining radio formats. Members of the radio station staff or personnel from a research firm it hires phone people who match the characteristics of the intended audience. The people may be chosen in a number of ways. They may be drawn from the telephone directory; they may be contacted from a list of known listeners; or they may be chosen through dialing numbers generated by use of a **random numbers table**. The random numbers technique starts with the first three digits of prefixes assigned by the telephone company to the listening area. The last four digits of the telephone number are taken from a list of random numbers found in statistics books or generated by computer.

When they contact individuals over the phone, the radio station representatives first make sure that the person fits the characteristics their firm wants to attract. If, for instance, the target audience is 18- to 35-year-olds, the callers will not care to explore the opinions of someone older or younger who answers the phone. When they reach someone appropriate, the interviewers play short portions of songs the station intends to use as part of its format. They ask the people to rate those songs, and they ask a variety of other questions aimed at getting a picture of their respondents' radio listening habits throughout the day.[8]

Unlike the one-to-one nature of phone interviews, **auditorium** testing takes place in large groups. An example of concept testing in auditoriums can be drawn from commercial network television's testing of series. One-paragraph descriptions of the series formats are read to viewers who, typically, have been invited to the auditoriums—often called "preview" theaters—to evaluate programs and commercials. The viewers are asked if they would watch the series based on the descriptions. If a producer's concept receives high marks from appropriate audiences (i.e., audiences the network and its advertisers are pursuing), the network interested in commissioning the series will pay for the creation of a pilot.

A **pilot** is the first show of a proposed series. It is designed to illustrate the possibilities that its format holds for attracting an audience and holding it through a succession of weekly episodes. **Pilot testing** means showing the pilot to groups of viewers, either on specially rented cable TV channels or in preview theaters. When cable TV is used, the individuals selected are asked to view a movie or series on the channel at a certain time.

After the program has ended, the people are asked questions over the telephone about what they saw. In the theaters, the viewers sometimes sit in chairs equipped with dials that are used to indicate how much audience members like what they see on the screen. These responses, along with written comments the viewers are encouraged to hand in, help network executives decide whether or not to commission the series.

Pilot testing is simply another term for audience research that evaluates a completed version of a format before it is released to the marketplace. This kind of evaluation takes place in a number of media industries, print and electronic. While the auditorium is a popular site for pilot testing by network TV and movie firms, executives in the print area tend to prefer individual interviews with consumers or focus groups.

A **focus group** is a collection of six to twelve people who have been chosen to match the media producers' (and advertisers') preferred audience profile. Lured by cash or free food, the people are encouraged by a specially trained moderator to comment on a variety of topics related to the format and its competiton.

Local television news formats are often the subject of focus groups. Local news is a potentially highly profitable part of a station's operation, but it is also a very expensive area involved in a tight battle for audiences and advertising dollars. Stations often use focus groups to explore how target audiences evaluate aspects of their formats compared with those of the competition.

Moderators encourage the participants to express opinions about the news anchors and reporters on the stations, as well as about the stories the stations cover and the images that the newscasts have. The responses from several focus groups are among the considerations that the station manager and news director take into account when making decisions regarding their station's approach to news.

Persuading Advertisers to Support a Format

Let us assume a format passes concept and pilot testing and has been released into the highly competitive media environment. Now the production firm's challenge is to persuade advertisers that they are reaching the size and type of audience that they desire. That is done through research that zeroes in on four features of the audience: circulation, demographics, lifestyles, and psychographics.

Circulation research involves determining the number of individuals who are consumers of the producer's media output. In the case of newspapers and magazines, the actual number of subscribers and single-copy sales are verified by an independent firm, the Audit Bureau of Circulation (ABC), which is paid by the publishers. Audited circulation is impossible with the three major electronic media that typically carry ads, radio, broadcast TV, and cable TV. The reason is that consumers do not subscribe to specific ad-supported programming channels (as they do subscribe, for example, to the unsponsored Home Box Office pay cable service). Instead, in about 98% of American homes, people have the ability to receive over-the-air material free through their radios and television sets. In well over half of American homes, they also purchase the right to watch any of a broad number of advertiser-supported channels. Auditing the time that everyone who uses these media spends with those media would clearly be unrealistically expensive.

Talking Point 5.1   Mapmaking and Market Research

Most people can readily see that psychology, sociology, computer programming, and statistics can be applied to the targeting of audiences. Cartography—the science of making maps—is not a skill that one is likely to think of when considering the brainpower that firms apply to learning about and reaching potential customers.

Nevertheless, mapmaking is increasingly important for helping marketers, particularly direct marketers (those who advertise via the telephone and mail). They use a variety of maps to organize, and make sense of, the welter of geographic and demographic data that the United States Census Bureau and other huge data bases present to them. In 1990, at least four separate efforts were under way to map out that year's national census for the benefit of those who sell:

- The R.L. Polk market research firm and Geographic Data Technology were developing an address coding guide that would enable marketers to match postal addresses on a map of part of a community with census data. The work takes advantage of the U.S. Census Bureau's file of computer-generated maps of all U.S. roads and addresses. Polk's aim was to sell marketers the ability to zero in flexibly on large or small groups of homes to find out the median household income, median age, percentage of minorities living there, and other data.
- The Strategic Mapping research firm was developing a software package similar to Polk's, but with the ability to allow marketers to combine census data with information in its own proprietary data bases.
- CACI, another research company, was marketing a consumer market segmentation program named Acorn. For a fee, it intended to enable marketers to draw maps of each of 250,000 neighborhoods defined by the census. Through the use of census data, the neighborhoods would be classified into forty-four distinct consumer types, such as "high-income suburban families with young children" and "mainstream Hispanic-Americans."
- Similarly, the firm Claritas was selling a well-known market segmentation system called Prizm, which stands for Potential Rating Index by Zip Markets. Prizm classifies all U.S. neighborhoods into forty basic lifestyle segments, or clusters. Claritas intended to match the 1990 census data, transformed into its clusters, with postal zip codes.

SOURCE: *Advertising Age*, December 10, 1990, p. 46.

Over the years, however, the advertising industry has accepted as standard a number of ways to provide circulation figures for the electronic media. All approaches are based on the proposition that the TV and radio habits of Americans can be estimated quite accurately by contacting a statistically random sample of the United States population. Sizes of the sample are determined by careful mathematical calculation and vary depending on the specific goals of the research. The research methods used to estimate circulation differ in the particular way in which they go about eliciting information from the individuals in the sample. One approach is to use a diary, another is to conduct interviews, and still another is the to use a meter to monitor media use.

A **diary** is simply a notebook in which an individual radio listener or TV viewer is asked to record radio listening or TV viewing information. Typically, the notebook contains a grid that lists stations on one axis and time (by quarter hours or half hours) on the other. **Interviews** try to elicit this information directly, by telephone or in person. The interviewer may draw on the individual's memory (e.g., "Did you listen to the radio yesterday between 6:00 A.M. and 10:00 A.M.? If so, what station?") or may ask about what the person is doing at that time ("Are you listening to the radio now? If so, what station?").

Meters are the major measurement tool in the TV industry. In the United States, the A.C. Nielsen Company, a huge marketing research firm, has a virtual monopoly on its use of meters in a sample designed to reflect national viewer patterns as well as in samples aimed at tracking habits in each of the nation's largest metropolitan areas. For its research on metropolitan areas, Nielsen installs a meter on every television in the several thousand households that are sampled. The meter measures whether a TV is being viewed and it notes the channel (over-the-air, cable, or VCR) that is being viewed.

Since only the sets, not the people, are metered, the results allow the company to generalize about TV use for the household, but not for specific individuals. Nielsen derives generalizations about the habits of individual viewers by comparing its meter data with diary entries from another sample of viewers.

A newer strategy, which Nielsen at this point has only in the approximately 4,000 homes that comprise its national sample, is to use a **People Meter**. This small box, connected to the TV sets of the sample households, holds a preassigned code for every individual in the home, even visitors. The research firm asks each viewer to push his or her button at the start and at the end of viewing. These individual actions, transmitted to Nielsen computers through telephone lines, become the basis for the firm's statements on national television viewing habits.

Whether they gather the media use information by diary, interview, or meter, research firms combine the findings to get a measure of circulation—how many people watched or listened to what programming at what time. Circulation numbers from electronic and print media are the most basic figures used by **media buyers** at advertising agencies. Media buyers are responsible for helping executives at advertising agencies choose the most **efficient** media vehicles for their advertising message.

To a media buyer, the most basic measure of a mass medium's efficiency is **cost per thousand** (cost per mil, or CPM). A medium's cost per mil is the amount of money an advertiser must pay to reach 1,000 people in its audience. With print media, the number is usually based on the price of an entire black-and-white page. So, for example, if a newspaper has a circulation of 100,000 and charges $1,000 for a page, the CPM would be $10 ($1,000/100,000 × 1,000). That would be considered a more efficient media buy than a newspaper in the same area with the same circulation that charges $1,500 per page, since its CPM would be $15.

But CPM based purely on circulation can sometimes be a misleading measure of efficiency. Neither magazine nor newspaper publishers, for example, are content to have advertisers think that their periodicals' readership is limited to the Audit Bureau of Circulation figures. They point out that individual copies are often shared among a number of readers, especially in places such as physicians' offices and beauty parlors.

To support what they say with quantitative data, they commission additional research, often from MediaMark (MRI) or Simmons Market Research Bureau (SMRB), to come up with the average number of people who read an issue of their periodical. This figure, called the **pass-along rate**, is particularly high when a periodical is placed in physicians' offices or beauty parlors. The number is meant to convince media buyers that the actual circulation of the periodical makes it an even better buy than audited circulation indicates.

But pass-along possibilities are not the only limitations that producers and their advertisers find in basic circulation figures. An even more important one has to do with the inability of raw circulation numbers to say anything about the *kinds* of people who use particular print or electronic media.

Imagine that you are a media buyer trying to find the most efficient medium with which to reach physicians in a city with two newspapers. It would be nonsense to suppose that your actual CPM would be $10 and $15 respectively. The reason is that you really have no information about how many physicians read the two papers.

If, for example, 1,000 physicians were among the 100,000 readers, the relevant cost per thousand would really be $1,000 for the first newspaper and $1,500 for the second. These high rates might make you think twice about using the general circulation papers to reach such a narrow audience. You might be inclined, instead, to advertise in a newspaper or magazine that is directed squarely toward physicians in the area. You would reach more of them, and it is likely that the relevant cost per thousand would, by comparison, be quite attractive.

Targeting Narrow Audience Segments

This kind of thinking is not at all unusual. Over the past few decades marketers in the United States have been trying to tailor products to increasingly narrow segments of the audience. "Doctors" may, in fact, be considered too broad a category by many companies. To them, specific kinds of doctors (surgeons, obstetricians, dermatologists) or doctors with specific kinds of hobbies (cars, travel, skiing) might well make up the relevant audiences. Clearly, media firms that cater to advertisers interested in reaching such segments of the population cannot use circulation figures alone to prove their value. Instead, they commission research that aims to bring out the characteristics of their consumers that will attract their advertisers.

The investigations can be divided into three basic forms:

Demographic

Psychographic

Lifestyle

Demographic characteristics are the most common traits that audience researchers gauge. These are basic social features that researchers use to distinguish people from one another. Examples of such categories are age, gender, geographic location, occupation, and race.

Advertising executives are typically interested in reaching segments of the population that have substantial **disposable income**—that is, money for items beyond the bare necessities of life. This interest in disposable income leads them to pursue demographic categories that they feel clearly predict spending ability. As a result, such items as age, gender, occupation, race, and profession typically take importance over favorite color, ability to swim, and height. (Of course, if the latter categories *can* be shown as predictive of buying habits, they will be used as well.)

The past few decades have seen many attempts to construct audiences with characteristics that go beyond demographics. The reason is that fierce competition among marketers has led them to look for other features of the population that they can target to encourage consumption of their products or services. At the same time, fierce competition among media firms for advertisers has led them to claim that although their audiences are small, they possess characteristics that make them especially desirable to particular advertisers.

To do that, media producers have been paying for research on their audiences and storing them in computers. The resulting **computer data bases** allow the producers to sift through large amounts of information that might make the audience attractive to particular advertisers.

An example comes from the newspaper industry. In the early 1990s, newspaper companies began to use data bases as a way to halt their eroding share of the ad market in their communities. Executives believed they could use targeted lists of readers to attract advertisers and discourage them from turning to other media such as catalogs and other direct-mail products. In one case, Cowles Publishing Company's *Spokane-Review*, and *Spokane Chronicle*, both in Spokane, Washington, used contests, questionnaires, and promotions to build small data bases of readers with special interests such as computers and hunting. The company then tried to attract advertisers interested in targeting those kinds of readers.[9]

TABLE 5.2. 1989–1990 Season Average Ratings of Top Ten Shows Among Adults with Household Incomes of $60,000 or More

In decades past, the television networks were unlikely to consider relatively high income as a selling point for some of their programs; the largest numbers was what they counted. In the competitive 1980s and 1990s, though, network salespeople have been targeting and selling increasingly selective parts of U.S. viewers to national advertisers. Below are the top-rated shows in terms of their ability to reach the relatively well-off at the turn of the decade. In this table, a rating of 28.1 means the program reaches 28.1% of adults with households earning over $60,000 that have TV sets.

Program	Rating
Roseanne	28.1
Cheers	27.9
Dear John	24.2
Wonder Years	24.1
NFL Monday Night Football	24.1
L.A. Law	23.4
The Cosby Show	23.4
America's Funniest Home Videos	23.2
60 Minutes	22.9
Chicken Soup	22.7

SOURCE: *Advertising Age*, July 9, 1990, p. S-1.

As this example suggests, marketers and the media producers who try to appeal to them pay particular attention to their personality characteristics and their lifestyles. **Lifestyles** research ties media users to recreational or buying habits. Many times, the activities are quite specific—for example, the number of trips readers take, the number of homes they own. In touting the lifestyles of their audience, media firms often combine them to create a kind of composite personality. *Popular Mechanics'* "Must-Know Man," described earlier in this chapter, is an example of an attempt to combine demographic and lifestyle attributes into a character that would appeal to male-oriented advertisers.

Actual research on the personalities of audience members is called **psychographic research**. The aim is to attach traits such as leadership, sociability, independence, conformity, and compulsiveness to the people who use a magazine, cable channel, newspaper, or other media vehicle.

In the mid-1980s, for example, SRI International used its popular VALS (Values and Lifestyles) survey to argue that people it called "belongers" are heavy commercial TV viewers, while "inner-directed" individuals are the heaviest public TV watchers. Radio stations, TV stations, magazines, newspapers, and other media use these data to persuade advertisers that they reach people who have the temperament to purchase certain kinds of products.

The use of specialized research to segment consumers into specialized audiences is growing. This trend is having an impact on the way advertisers use media. During the past decade, there have been growing complaints by advertisers that their ads are getting lost amidst the barrage of commercial messages hurled at consumers by the most popular media.

Concern about such **commercial clutter** has been strongest in the broadcast media, though it has been voiced about certain print organs, too. Advertisers have also shown growing dilemma in sponsoring print media for the wealthier segments of the population.

Although these busy people may well subscribe to a substantial number of publications, it is not at all clear that they have the time to read much of what is in them, especially the ads.

In Search of New Ad Vehicles

In response to these concerns, a variety of major advertisers have begun to rethink their approaches to media support. Ad-supported cable television channels have been one collective beneficiary of their intention to sometimes look away from over-the-air broadcasters in an attempt to reduce clutter. Nickelodeon, Lifetime, ESPN, and Cable News Network, among the more popular channels, have been quite successful in convincing certain advertisers that, along with reducing clutter, they construct audiences in a way that may well be more effective than certain broadcast TV purchases for some sponsors. Commercials in movie theaters and on videotapes of recent films have also become increasingly popular.

Three other ways to reach consumers that have gained strength among marketers in recent years are:

Promotion

Direct marketing

The use of captive-audience media

Promotion involves payment by a marketer to be associated with an event or individual. Think of Nike's payment of professional basketball players to wear Nike shoes, Virginia Slims cigarettes' sponsorship of tennis matches, and the placement of products from the *Spiegel* catalog on the *Wheel of Fortune* television game show. **Direct marketing** describes the activity of using the mail or the telephone to persuade consumers about products and services. Clothing catalogs, automatic phone dialers (where a machine conveys a message and invites information), and the blizzard of brochures people typically call "junk mail" are but a few of the categories that characterize this arena.

Also growing fast is the **captive-audience** approach to mass media. A mass medium with a captive audience is one in which the people who are exposed to it have nowhere to go when they encounter it and few (if any) alternative media to distract them. POP Radio Corporation, which broadcasts customized music and commercials to supermarkets, is a typical player in this area.[10] Whittle Communications, a firm half-owned by Time Warner, is probably the most well known (and controversial) of firms that target captive audiences.

Whittle's *Special Reports* magazines dominate thousands of doctors' waiting rooms; its *American Style* magazine holds a near-monopoly on readers in thousands of beauty salons; and its Channel 1 television service brings ads with news directly to students in classrooms. By building projects around the long-term sponsorship by a number of "participating advertisers," companies such as POP and Whittle aim to solve advertisers' problem of clutter and their fear that consumers will ignore the media they sponsor.

None of these forms of salesmanship—neither promotion, nor direct marketing, nor attempts to find captive audiences—is new. What is different about their contemporary situation is the upsurge in the amount of money that marketers have been commiting to them. One potential consequence if they continue to grow is that large advertisers will siphon substantial advertising support from traditional broadcast and print media.

Even more likely is that, to remain attractive, traditional newspapers, magazines, and broadcast outlets will bend their editorial materials to fit the interests of major advertisers even more strongly than in the past. This possibility concerns people who worry even now that American media are guided too often by business pressures of which their readers, listeners, or viewers are ignorant.

RELIABILITY, VALIDITY, AND THE CONSTRUCTION OF AUDIENCE

The increasing desire of marketers to target ever more specific audiences in ways and places that most persuade them to buy is being fed by data base companies. These are firms that collect huge amounts of information about individual consumers, through credit card purchases, loan application disclosures, periodical subscriptions, and simi-

CHART 5.1 Leading Ad Spenders on Broadcast Network News, Children's Shows, and Sports

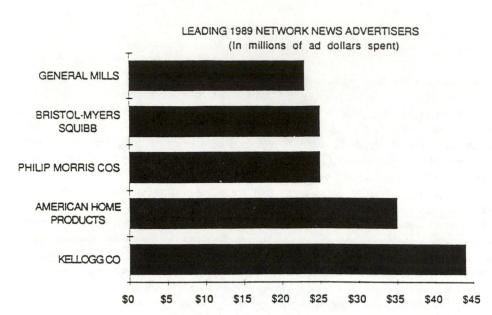

LEADING 1989 NETWORK NEWS ADVERTISERS
(In millions of ad dollars spent)

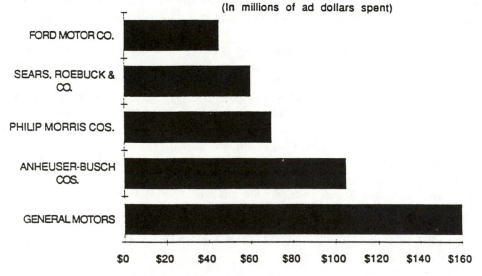

LEADING 1989 NETWORK SPORTS ADVERTISERS
(In millions of ad dollars spent)

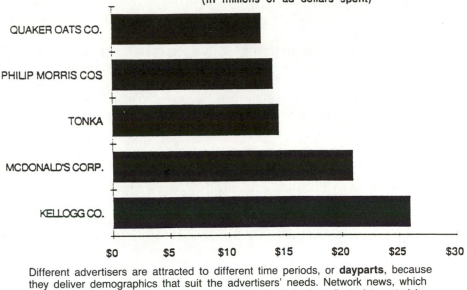

LEADING 1989 NETWORK CHILDREN'S SHOW ADVERTISERS
(In millions of ad dollars spent)

Different advertisers are attracted to different time periods, or **dayparts**, because they deliver demographics that suit the advertisers' needs. Network news, which "skews old," attracts pharmaceutical, bran cereal, and other clients interested in older Americans. Toy and cereal manufacturers go after Saturday morning children's TV, and car and beer firms pursue men through sports programming.

SOURCE: *Advertising Age*, May 26, 1990, pp. 33–45.

lar behaviors. Marketers tend to believe that information about people's previous purchases are important signals of their future consumption activities. As a result, many pay high prices to extract from data bases a wide variety of surprisingly personal information about individual American consumers: how much they get as salary, how much they paid for their house, what cars they own, how old their children are, and a good deal more.

Research and Privacy

The computer data base is an important contributor to direct marketing's swift rate of growth. It has given advertisers the confidence that they can narrow their focus to special consumers, particularly affluent ones.

Direct marketers contend that the cutting edge of merchandising lies in using data bases to target potential customers with information especially dedicated to their interests. The marketers say that they can use demographic and lifestyle categories from data bases to target people who are most likely to purchase certain kinds of products. They argue that because this identification of prospects is so efficient, it pays to pursue them with handsome catalogs, audio cassettes, even video cassettes in addition to (and even instead of) advertising in newspapers, magazines, or on TV.

Sometimes, direct-marketing materials are adjusted to the needs of specific individual consumers with information derived from the data bases. The Volvo auto company can personalize a brochure to John Jones with the year John bought his most recent car, for example.

Access to this kind of information raises many concerns regarding citizens' right to privacy. In fact, as the 1990s move forward, a growing number of voices have been expressing concern about the marketing and use of data bases about Americans. We might also ask whether these information banks are accurate. For that matter, we might ask how accurate are any of the approaches to audience research that have been noted in this chapter.

Research and Accuracy

The question of accuracy in audience research is a complex one. Over the past several decades, certain audience research procedures have come to be accepted as standard in certain areas of the media. This means that both producers and clients in those media consider the procedures to be the best available mix of reliability, validity, and economy.

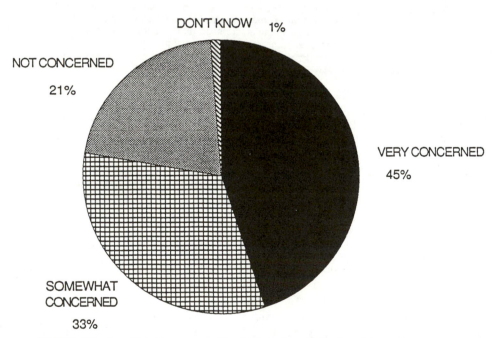

CHART 5.2 Are You Concerned About Marketers Gathering Information About You Without Your Knowledge?

When they are asked, people voice concern about the rush by companies to use data bases in marketing their products to targeted audiences.

SOURCE: Gallup national survey, reported in *Advertising Age*, May 6, 1991, p. 3.

Reliability refers to the ability of two researchers using the same methods to arrive at results that are the same from a statistical standpoint.

Validity means that the results can be understood to be truly representative of what goes on in the population as a whole, outside the survey situation.

Economy points to the need to pay attention to the costs of audience research.

Research that raises to intolerable levels the price producers must charge advertisers or consumers will not be commissioned by either party. It follows that the need to economize on audience research may well introduce problems of reliability and validity. If, for example, a telephone survey based on random digit dialing finds that 25% of those called do not answer, the accepted procedure would be to phone again. Experience has shown that with many repeated attempts it is possible to get an over 90% completion rate on calls.[11] Contacting a number several times is, however, an expensive procedure that most marketers do not want to incur. If the callback procedure is not carried out carefully, though, problems of reliability will result. Yet standardizing enough callbacks to get a 90% completion rate is expensive. Typically, research firms content themselves with only one extra attempt to complete a call. The result is that the validity of the sample of people who are considered to be a statistical representation of "the audience" is suspect.

Enduring Problems with Validity

In many cases validity problems remain even if no cost considerations are involved in determining the research approach. One reason is that the act of drawing a truly representative sample of the users of certain media has proved to be nearly impossible.

In the television ratings business, for example, Nielsen has often had a difficult time drawing a statistically random sample from the nation as a whole. Some families may refuse to allow peoplemeters in their house; others may demand that they be taken out after they have been installed. Nielsen has had a particularly difficult time auditing poor areas of the country, where theft and breakage of the meters are not uncommon. The research firm also finds that to persuade poor people to be part of the sample, it must pay them a good deal more than the token amount it gives to most families in the sample.

In Nielsen's case, and in the case of much audience research, another major problem of validity arises. It is that following people's activities and asking them to say what they do on a daily basis inevitably causes them to speak and act differently than they would if no one were tracking them. It is a common joke in the industry that Nielsen families turn on the TV even when they go out for the evening because they want to help their favorite shows. Similarly, people who fill out radio diaries often put down the station they would have listened to if they had been listening. The same kind of problem obtains with newspapers and magazines. When people are interviewed about the periodicals they read, there is always the difficulty of separating wishful thinking from accurate remembrance.

Many of the inaccuracies become part of the data bases that are sold to advertisers who are deciding what media to sponsor. Magazine-selling companies compound the inaccuracies by, in effect, providing customers with incentives to lie about themselves in order to get lower rates.

So, for example, nonstudents who get "student discounts" to *Time* magazine become part of a student data base group that *Time* uses for its own internal marketing plan as well as to sell to other firms. Small inaccuracies such as these get repeated many times over with respect to a wide variety of demographic and lifestyle categories. The upshot is a multitude of data sets with questionable validity regarding American consumers.

The most sophisticated of audience researchers, advertisers, and media producers are quite aware of the drawbacks that make their work suspect. Their reply is that they do the best they can with what they have. Attempts to correct the most controversial problems often take up the energies and development costs of research firms. Nielsen and a few other firms, for example, have been working on what is called a **passive peoplemeter**. The idea is to have a computer recognize individuals in the television room so that they do not have to push buttons.

No audience research system will ever be totally free of problems, though. From a practical standpoint, the audience research methods that are used typically reflect attempts to achieve results that both sides of the producer-client relationship consider valid and reliable at costs that are acceptable to both advertisers and producers. People in the media business require audience numbers to justify their actions and lower risks. As a result, media executives act as if their research procedures and audience numbers are basically satisfactory, even if a little reflection would show that the problems connected to gathering the numbers make their generalizability highly suspect.

THE LARGER POINT

There is an even larger point to make, however, and it has been the underlying theme of this chapter: Even if all questions of reliability and validity could be brushed aside, it still remains that every media audience is a construction of reality. This realization does not mean that the categories that production and client organizations use to construct audiences have no basis in fact. Audience research is aimed at ensuring that those categories can be related to real individuals "out there."

The point to remember, though, is that the questions asked in audience research are questions designed by the organizations asking the questions for their own purposes. In mass media industries, producers and clients, not consumers, control the basic terms by which audiences are defined. Sometimes this causes problems. Individuals or groups of consumer do not like the way mass media industries are defining them. They want to be thought of differently, so that the media will deliver different mass media materials to them. What that means, and how it works itself out, is the subject of the next chapter.

NOTES

1. See Joseph Turow, *Getting Books to Children: An Exploration of Publisher-Market Relations* (Chicago: American Library Association, 1979).
2. *Advertising Age*, October 23, 1989, p. 21.
3. Joseph R. Dominick, *The Dynamics of Mass Communication* (New York: McGraw-Hill, 1990), pp. 496–498.
4. Edwin McDowell, *The New York Times*, May 8, 1979, p. 6.
5. *Motion Picture Almanac, 1991*. Also, telephone conversation with Bruce Snyder, President, Domestic Distribution, 20th Century Fox Film Corporation, June 20, 1991.
6. Interview with Perry Katz, Universal Pictures marketing, March 6, 1990.
7. Alfred Balk, "The 'Entrepreneurs' Behind *Entertainment Weekly,*" *Folio*, November 1989, pp. 79–83.
8. Joseph Dominick, Barry Sherman, and Gary Copeland, *Broadcasting/Cable and Beyond* (New York: McGraw-Hill, 1990), pp. 342–343.
9. Janet Meyers, "Papers Study Data-base Marketing," *Advertising Age*, November 5, 1990, p. 60.
10. Allison Fahey, "Actmedia Is Ready to Fight Back," *Advertising Age*, March 19, 1990, p. 18.
11. Hugh Malcolm Beville, Jr., *Audience Ratings; Radio, Television, Cable* (Hillsdale, NJ: Lawrence Erlbaum, 1985), p. 96

CHAPTER SIX

The Power of the Public

We can all recall moments when we have been annoyed at a newspaper we have read, a radio station we have heard, a TV station we have watched. Sometimes, for some people, that annoyance turns to anger, and the anger turns to action. One need only to flip through the pages of major newspapers or trade magazines to find cases where the rage people feel about what is presented by certain mass media firms explodes into demands for change. In organized groups or individually, those people insist on a variety of alterations—in images the firms present, in people who are in charge of the media materials, even in government and corporate policies that set the structure of media industries in the first place. Consider a few of the controversies that have received attention in the recent past:

> A group of physicians tried unsuccessfully for years to convince *The New York Times* to ban cigarette ads from the newspaper. The group also demanded that the paper increase coverage of its anti-*Times* viewpoint. That was turned down, too.[1]
>
> In 1989, a Pepsi-Cola television commercial starring rock star Madonna provoked a number of religious organizations to anger. The spot showed Madonna performing her song "Like a Prayer." The religious organizations contended that the music video from which the spot was made was blasphemous. They pointed to the singer's sexual posturing while surrounded by religious symbols such as a cross. They insisted that the commercial be withdrawn. It was.[2]
>
> *Days of Rage: The Young Palestinians*, a documentary about Palestinian–Israeli hostilities from a Palestinian viewpoint, became the center of controversy during 1989. Critics of the program, which was partly funded by the Public Broadcasting Service, argued that not only was the documentary stridently anti-Israel but it also received hidden support from Kuwaiti and other Arab interests. The critics insisted that PBS not air the show. PBS did air it, but added a panel discussion immediately after the telecast about the program's pros and cons.[3]

These incidents represent just the tip of an iceberg of recent attempts by people outside mass media industries to influence those industries by themselves or together with others. Sometimes they succeeded; sometimes they didn't; sometimes there were compromises. The purpose of this chapter is not to catalog these attempts, or even to list the most important ones. The aim, rather, is to create a framework for understanding such incidents as well as to confront a basic question:

Under what circumstances can individuals or organized groups exert influence when they want to change mass media materials?

OUTSIDE PRESSURE ON MEDIA FIRMS

To begin answering this question, it is helpful to build upon ideas that were introduced in previous chapters. One theme that has woven through the pages of this book is that a mass media production firm must rely on its environment for survival. The environment provides the resources—the money, supplies, people, information, permission—that a production organization needs to create and release mass media material to the public.

Previous chapters have also made clear that the resources mass media producers need are not distributed randomly throughout the environment. On the contrary, the chapters have shown that organizations taking on the power roles of authorities, clients, exhibitors, and distributors hold key resources and make important demands on producers in exchange for them.

Recall, too, that production firm executives are not passive when it comes to their environment. Typically, their intention is to avoid becoming too dependent upon specific entities that provide them with money, supplies, people, information, and permission. They keep their independence by hiring specialized boundary personnel to shape the demands that outside groups make on them. So, for example, lobbyists for broadcasters try to ensure that government regulation of radio and TV stations is not burdensome. Similarly, marketing executives from newspaper firms try to shape their clients' perceptions of their papers' ability to deliver desirable audiences.

Media production executives are, in other words, people who respond actively to pressures in their environment. They try to deal with those pressures in ways that benefit them. At the same time, they recognize that in order to take resources from the environment, they must give in to certain demands. Not all demands are equal. For example, if the cash of a particular advertiser is crucial, or if the permission of a government agency is necessary and unchangeable, the executives are more likely to accommodate the needs of these organizations than when the power of those outside organizations is negligible.

Generally speaking, production firm executives are likely to respond to outside pressure with three major considerations in mind:

The **importance** of the resources that particular organizations offer

The **substitutability** of those resources

The **negotiability** of the demands on them

These considerations are evaluated together. The money of an advertiser may be important to a newspaper, but not *that* important if substitutable advertisers can be found. A compromise might be worked out if the advertiser is willing to negotiate. From a producer's standpoint, it may be best if a client can be accommodated while the producer's control over organizational policies are not affected.

The concerns media executives hold about the importance of resources, their substitutability, and the negotiability of demands on them can serve as a useful entry to understanding how they deal with demands for change by individuals or organized groups. The question for this chapter is how seriously the executives evaluate demands by public or public advocacy organizations and how far they are willing to go to negotiate compromises with them that satisfy demands on both sides. As will be seen, the answer has much to do with the relative value of the resources that various constituencies bring to the producer's table.

PRODUCERS AND MEMBERS OF THE PUBLIC

It might be logical to start at the most basic level—the response that production firms have to direct comments or suggestions about mass media material by individual members of the public. Such offerings are certainly not rare. Moreover, for the most prominent media firms the stream of reader, viewer, or listener phone calls, postcards, and letters can be very large indeed.

A staff member in *The New York Times* Letters to the Editor department estimated in 1990 that 70,000 people write to the newspaper each year.[4] Of course, the hope that a letter will be printed on the editorial page might have been a strong incentive for some readers to write. Still, the count appears to be high even when people know they will not see their names in print or on screen. In the late 1970s, Herbert Gans counted 351 letters to NBC television news anchor John Chancellor in one month.[5]

The Influence of Individuals

What influence do those people have on the creation and release of the materials they are calling or writing about? A better way to phrase the question is as follows: What resources can an individual member of the public offer the production firms that the firms cannot get elsewere without giving up as much independence of action to that person? It would seem that the answer will vary depending on the situation. All else being equal, the more production personnel perceive an individual's comments to be in sync with organizational policy, the greater the chance that they will respond positively.

Organizations might actually welcome certain types of comments. As noted in Chapter 5, one consideration that goes into forming organizational policy is ongoing concern about the audience's likes and dislikes. Remember, though, what media executives mean when they talk about audience interests. Chapter 5 stressed that executives in mass media production firms think of audiences through lenses that reflect business needs. That is, they pay particular attention to categories of their target consumers that they and their clients (for example, the advertisers) find useful.

Often based on market research, these categories become a part of media executives' assumptions about the environment that leads them to generate the organization's routines—that is, its daily patterns of activity. Successful routines typically result in output satisfactory to clients and many consumers. Still, even successful production personnel constantly try to improve their performance. They are likely to welcome suggestions for change that fit their basic assumptions about their audience and environment, even if the suggestions seek to change some of the routines that led out of those assumptions. The reason is that acting positively on suggestions that flow with organizational plans involves giving up only a little organizational independence in the service of ideas that might yield profit.

On the other hand, the more an individual's demands require the production firm to depart from basic policies, the less chance that production personnel will respond positively to the individual claimant. Instead, the demands will likely be rejected as irrelevancies, nuisances, or threats. The reason is simply that assumptions, policies, and routines are developed with reference to the resources held by powerful sets of forces in the environment—competitors, clients, distributors, exhibitors, authorities, and the like. Production personnel will likely feel that one person who threatens not to view, attend, or purchase a media product can do little harm compared with the resources an important advertising client or regulatory agency can remove from the production firm.

Precisely how does a media production firm respond to contacts from members of the public? How do members of the organization channel the comments, positive and negative, in ways usable to them? Recall that in order to manage the environment efficiently, production firm executives develop routines for themselves and specialized boundary personnel. In line with this understanding, we would expect any producer regularly receiving comments from individuals outside the organization to develop an organized set of responses that will be used when such comments appear. Organization researchers James March and Herbert Simon have called this kind of routinized response pattern a **performance program**.[6]

Performance Programs

The performance program that a media organization develops for public contacts may be simple, involving a couple of steps and people, or it may be elaborate. An important difference between print and broadcast media in the United States is important to note here. As explained in Chapter 3, print has traditionally been free of prepublication regulation through safeguards dating to the earliest days of the republic. The broadcast industry has not been so lucky. There, regulation mandates an individual's right to usurp air time under certain narrow circumstances.

Specifically, the **Equal Time** provision of the 1934 Federal Communications Act requires broadcasters to allow announced candidates who are qualified for public office "equal opportunities" to state their views at the same rates.[7] Moreover, broadcasters, unlike print firms, operate as public trustees of the airwaves and must renew their licenses every few years. Radio and TV executives therefore have a strong incentive to develop performance programs that protect their money-making routines and at the same time limit the number of citizen complaints to government officials.

The kinds of routines they evolve, then, will probably depend on the kinds of demands members of the public are bringing, the fear executives have of government regulation, and the public relations goals of the company. In the case of letters to *The*

New York Times, it is clear that management does not see this kind of input as a threat to the firm's autonomy or as a problem that can spark government regulation. Instead, the editor of the letters section is expected to turn it to the *Times'* own benefit.

In describing his department's routines for dealing with public input, Kalman Siegel, the letters editor in the early 1970s, makes it clear that his organization keeps total control over the use and disposition of the material it receives. Siegel suggests that the letters section has long served several company goals at the same time— journalistic, marketing, and public relations goals. On the journalistic front, Siegel points out that *Times* management believes that the letters section "is one of the paper's great responsibilities in helping to form public opinion."[8]

He notes happily that marketing is in sync with journalism here: The letters section is popular—usually among the most widely read parts of the paper. Kalman suggests that in addition to journalistic and marketing purposes, the letters section fills a public relations function. He gives the distinct impression that famous people and people in power will have easier access to the letters section than will members of the public without such influence. The reason is obvious. Prestigious letter writers reflect prestige on the paper.

The *Times* policy of controlling the public's access to organizational activities while using public input for the company's benefit can be seen in many media organizations. Consider the way a major market radio station dealt with letters that were not written for public consumption but, rather, to complain about station pro- gramming and urge change. Like many media managers, the station's executives did not consider individual complaints to be representative of the audience; they saw only their market research as tapping into that.

Their goal with complaining letters was therefore to handle the comments quickly without affecting the organization's efficiency. However, because they also were con- cerned with maintaining a good public relations posture and not have problems at license renewal time, they wanted to dispose of the complaints without alienating the correspondent.

The Case of a Radio Station

A study of the station's handling of the letters revealed a clear-cut performance program.[9] While every letter received a personal answer (in that the letter writer's name was mentioned and the subject noted), the reply was patterned after a standard form. The station's editorial director, writing in the name of the station manager, followed a systematic procedure. It answered the letters efficiently while insulating the comments from the station personnel they discussed so as not to upset organiza- tional routines. The responses followed a formula. Sandwiched between a fixed introductory thanks for the writer's comments and a fixed final hope that the writer would continue listening to the station were remarks that attempted to deal with the particulars of the complaint, demand, praise, or question.

The packaged replies to complaints were aimed at defusing threats to the station by associating station policy with basic principles with which the plaintiff was un- likely to argue. As Table 6.1 shows, in reply to a negative opinion of a station personality, the "station manager" said that "thousands of listeners feel different from

TABLE 6.1. Feedback Letter Topics and a Radio Station's Replies

Topics
I. Favorable remark about the station's on-air personality
II. Nonstation related request
III. Opinions and proposals relating to current events
IV. General complaint about a personality's actions
V. Specific complaint about a personality's actions
VI. Complaint about station policy
VII. Complaint about a specific station action

Association of Topics with Replies	
Topic	*Reply*
I.	"Always happy to hear from a satisfied listener."
II.	"Here is some information that may help you . . ."
	"Write to this government agency to get information."
III.	"Why don't you call our talk shows and present your ideas on radio?"
	"Since we feel that your idea is most interesting, why not present it as a rebuttal to our editorial? Contact our editorial director . . ."*
IV.	"Our moderator is among the best informed in the country."
	"Thousands of listeners feel different from you."
V.	"Our moderators often take positions they don't really believe for the sake of stimulating discussion."
	"You may be assured the problem will not be repeated."
VI.	"It is a practical truth of broadcasting that high commercial content is necessary to maintain high quality service to listeners."
VII.	"We have no obligation under Federal Communications Commission regulations to provide equal time . . ."

* This response was evoked by two complaints against the rudeness of a talk show host and by one complaint against the rudeness of a producer.

SOURCE: Joseph Turow, "Another View of Citizen Feedback to the Mass Media," *Public Opinion Quarterly 41* (Winter 1977–78), pp. 535–543.

you." A commitment to intellectual excellence and superior performance was the defense used in the comment that a talk show host is "among the best in the country." A charge of bias or racism on the part of a talk show host was countered by an invocation of the principle of diverse and free-flowing ideas. And a complaint against too many commercials was met by a statement about the need to recognize the connection between good business and good service.

Interestingly, when a feedback letter invoked a rule—the Equal Time rule, for example—the station countered by saying that the writer had misunderstood its meaning and applicability: "Until [one of two men who are both obviously running for public office] announces his candidacy, we have no obligation under Federal Communications Commission regulations to provide equal time to either man."

PRODUCERS AND PUBLIC ADVOCACY ORGANIZATIONS

It is very likely that in the great majority of cases production organizations do not have to go beyond this kind of containment when they deal with critical comments and demands from members of the public. One reason is that it probably works most of the time. In the study just described, analysis of questionnaires that were sent to, and answered by, eighty letter writers indicated that the stations' pattern of replies was quite successful at accomplishing the station manager's objective of not alienating them. Moreover, the little evidence that exists about people's knowledge of media operations suggests that most individuals will not take the time or trouble to find out what further steps they might take toward successfully pursuing their demands.

Strength in Others

When individuals do pursue their complaints and demands, it is often because they have found strength and ammunition in other individuals who share an interest in the issues they raise. They might tap established organizations with broad-ranging activities—for example the NAACP, the American Civil Liberties Union, the Ku Klux Klan. They might seek organizations that pursue specific interests or deal with specific media—for example, Morality in Media, the National Citizens Committee for Broadcasting. Or they might start their own organization.

In any of these cases, the media-related complaints may be part of a larger agenda for society that the group wants to implement. Take an organization interested in combating ethnic and racial prejudice as an example. Its leaders might choose to complain about commercial TV's portrayals of certain ethnic groups because of their broad concern for the medium's power to circulate negative images throughout society. A more politically attuned reason for centering attention on television might be that the medium provides a pool of images that many people already know, can label as negative, and mobilize around. In other words, organizations sometimes choose to pick fights with commercial TV because the medium can easily be used as a rallying point with which to recruit new members and keep old ones.

Production firm executives do not like to discuss their arguments with advocacy groups publicly because they do not want to encourage other complaints. Advocacy group leaders, for their part, sometimes like to sound as if their challenges were more successful than they really were in order to hold on to their followers. Despite the reluctance of the parties to divulge details, some generalizations are possible.

One basic premise is that a large number of organized protesters is in a better situation to encourage change than are individual plaintiffs. The reason is simply that production personnel would likely be more concerned about the strong public relations damage that large protest groups can wreak compared with unknown individuals. This intimidation would be particularly felt in a media organization not used to such protests. Executives there might be uncertain how to preserve their independence of action.

At the same time, we would expect executives in a media organization familiar with protests to have worked out a set of routines for evaluating and handling angry demands. As usual, the goal of such a performance program is likely to be organizational autonomy in the production of messages. That means maintaining the firm's efficient production routines as well as the flow of the resources the organization needs from its environment to continue those activities.

Four considerations will probably enter into the calculations of how to respond to outside demands.

The greater the change the group proposes, the more difficult it will be for the producer to accept it.

The greater the probability that the change will alienate major resource providers, the more difficult it will be to accept it.

The less critical the resources are that the group itself can marshal against the producer, the less likely the producer will listen.

Even if the group's resources are important, the greater the ability of the producer to get those resources (or substitutable ones) elsewhere, the more likely the producer will refuse to give in to the demands.

The Whittle Communications Case

Briefly comparing the outcome of two producer-directed activities will help to illustrate these points. The cases involve different special interest publics—teachers groups and public health advocates. The one involving teachers was a protest against Whittle Communications during the late 1980s and early 1990s. During that period, Whittle Communications embarked upon a program to bring an advertiser-supported TV news channel to junior and senior high schools.[10]

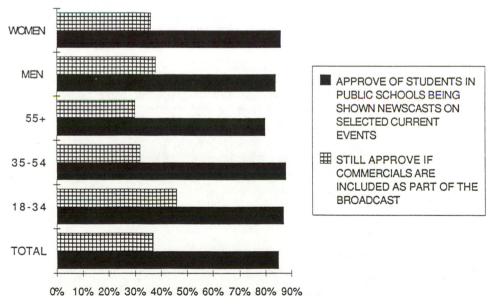

CHART 6.1 Most People Disapprove of In-School Commercials

A national survey by the Gallup organization for *Advertising Age* revealed that most adults did not want TV commercials in school. Despite such evidence and public outcries against Channel One, Whittle Communications went ahead with it. See text.

SOURCE: *Advertising Age*, August 14, 1989, p.4

Whittle's plan was to provide all the equipment needed to receive satellite programming in a large number of classrooms per school. In return for doing that, the schools would agree to show all students in the classrooms a daily twelve-minute news program, with two minutes of commercials. The commercials, paid for by advertisers interested in reaching youngsters, would recompense Whittle for the costs of the technology. Whittle's expectation was that over time Channel One would yield the firm handsome profits.

When Whittle's plan for advertiser-supported TV in schools was announced, it drew angry protests from the American Federation of Teachers, a large teacher's organization, as well as from parent-teacher groups around the country. The protesters argued that forcing students to watch commercials was contradictory to the aim of education. They contended that education involves critical evaluation, which, they complained, does not mesh with the opposite of forced feeding of advertising messages. Whittle should drop the whole idea, they insisted. They got support from the Board of Regents of New York and the Superintendent of Public Instruction in California, which represented all the public schools in those two large states. The hope of the protesters was that with the organizations representing the resources of two large school regions on their side, Whittle would give up.

That did not happen. Whittle's management calculated that a very profitable number of schools around the United States was willing to trade showing Channel One for the merchandise that the company was offering. School budgets were hurting and many principals saw the deal as a way to get technology that could be applied to many useful educational purposes. Just as important, major advertisers still agreed with Whittle that Channel One might be an efficient way to turn a high-spending yet elusive demographic group—American teenagers—into a captive audience.

Whittle clearly saw the public attacks against Channel One as an unacceptable attempt to infringe on its profit-making autonomy. With an adequate number of schools willing to sign on and the resources of major advertisers behind them, the firm was eager to show that the groups militating against it did not even represent the collective opinion of educators. As a result, Whittle formed a board of twelve educators and public figures to provide what it called "advice and direction" for the programming on Channel One. Made up of two university presidents, well-known authors, and a former U.S. secretary of education, among others, the panel was clearly designed to deflate the groups who were claiming that education would be ill-served by Channel One's arrival. The project moved forward.

The Harvard Alcohol Case

Place this episode next to a very different kind of bid to influence production—the attempt by professors at Harvard University's School of Public Health to insert themes about the perils of drinking and driving into TV programs. Over the years, many activists, researchers, and other members of the public have condemned broadcasters for portraying the drinking of alcohol irresponsibly—as a comfortable, upscale thing to do or as the basis for drunken humor.

Noting that alcohol is one of America's major highway killers, Jay Winsten, director of the Harvard Alcohol Project at the school, began a campaign in 1988 to do something about TV's handling of the issue. His initial meetings were set up with the help of the former heads of NBC and CBS. These contacts led him to connect with many of the industry's writers and producers. Winsten prodded them to be careful about how they portray drinking. He particularly suggested that they mention the "designated driver" in their programs. That is the practice of appointing a person in a group of friends as the nondrinker for the evening so the person can drive the others home.

By the spring of 1990, Winsten had met with more than 160 writers and producers. He claimed that more than 80 series episodes had carried some reference to the dangers of drinking and driving since he began his campaign. Hollywood TV producers confirmed that had made an impact on programming. "They are extremely effective lobbyists," noted a producer from a firm with a number of popular sitcoms. "They have a way of making you feel bad if you don't get involved."[11]

Comparing the Alcohol Project with the Anti-Whittle campaign, it is possible to suggest a number of resource-based reasons for the Alcohol Project's success, and the anti-Whittle activists' failure, in accomplishing their goals. One point that should not be ignored is that the difference in the media involved gave advocacy groups more leverage in the network TV case than in the Channel One case. TV broadcasters operate as public trustees and must renew their licenses with the Federal Communications Commission at regular intervals. Channel One, by contrast, is essentially a closed-circuit satellite-to-cable service that does not fall under the FCC's broadcast station licensing rules.

While the production firms technically do not fall under government regulation, the valuable stations the networks own do, as do the stations of their affiliates. Broadcast station owners are sometimes skittish that FCC regulators might interpret rules and license renewal petitions in ways that reflect tides of public indignation they see directed at broadcasters. Since they are not responsible to a federal agency, Whittle executives may feel less need than their broadcasting counterparts to satisfy large or prestigious segments of the public that are not directly relevant as audiences to their advertisers.

But the different reactions of the network TV producers and Whittle were clearly not based only, or even primarily, on the regulatory sensitivities of the firms involved. As the earlier comment by a sitcom executive implied, the reactions seem mainly to have related to the way the activists approached the thorny issue of organizational autonomy and established routines. The anti-Channel One groups forced Whittle Communications into an uncomfortably public all-or-nothing position in the face of a potentially lucrative program.

The Harvard Alcohol Project, by contrast, was content with limited goals. Its members did not insist, for example, that the TV networks eliminate beer commercials from their airwaves or alcohol from their shows altogether. They ignored critics who said that giving the networks an excuse to justify the presentation of alcohol (by showing a designated driver) was not helpful to the antidrinking cause. Instead, they pragmatically accepted the needs of producers, networks, and advertisers and offered to work with them to create pro-social messages that would fit into established routines and make the creators feel good.

"They are already depicting alcohol use in many instances," Winsten told *The New York Times*, "and we just ask them to use sensitivity in how they portray the issue. They can save lives with a line or two of dialogue." He added his belief that part of his group's success stemmed from its nonconfrontational approach.

"There are advocacy groups that are prepared tactically to bring pressure to bear and then there are efforts to recruit writers and producers voluntarily," he said. "The programs that are successful are those that had at their origin or very quickly developed support from within the industry."[12]

Winsten's comments suggest that all-or-nothing demands are very risky even in the broadcast arena, where sensitivity to public demands may be greater than in other media. It is, in fact, difficult to think of a single program that ABC, CBS, NBC, PBS, and Fox have removed from their schedules as a result of public advocacy group protests. Flareups over TV programs as diverse as *Days of Rage: The Young Palestinians, Beulah Land* (where protesters zeroed in on what they considered to be unfavorable portrayals of blacks), and *Thirtysomething* (where antigay groups objected to an episode with a homosexual love affair) indicate that when pressure to remove a program or an episode becomes public, the networks will refuse, even when it is not clear that the show will lose money. Their fear is that caving in will set a bad precedent and invite an avalanche of similar protests.

That does not mean that all-or-nothing pressure by movements on media organizations is totally futile. The possibility must be considered that a succession of advocacy group protests will cause executives to pause before releasing material that will bring another storm of petitions. They might fear that continual protest by powerful constituencies can ultimately embarrass them publicly, cause advertisers to hesitate in their sponsorship of material, and invite agencies of the federal government to hold regulatory hearings. Still, the refusal of media companies to yield to direct demands causes great frustration among advocacy groups. As a result, they often turn directly to powerful go-betweens for help—legislators, regulatory agencies, courts, and advertisers.

PRESSURING PRODUCERS THROUGH AUTHORITIES

Organizations and individuals have a straightforward purpose for looking to legislatures, regulatory agencies, and courts in bids to reform mass media material. Lacking the leverage to influence producers directly, they hope to convince the authorities to join forces with them and, through the increased leverage they would achieve, carry out their goals of making changes in the media.

Two major assumptions underlie this advocacy activity:

Authorities truly do have substantial leverage with producers.

Public advocacy organizations can enlist the authorities to help them by using that leverage.

An examination of the forces at work in these sorts of situations will show that the two assumptions are not always warranted.

The Range of Pressure Points

The territory this discussion covers is large. Public advocacy groups may be interested in virtually any government decision affecting the *structure* of a mass media industry or the industry's *relation to other industries*. They may voice their arguments at the *federal, state*, and *local* levels. Moreover, at each level they may choose *courts, legislatures*, and *regulatory agencies* as arenas in which to make their arguments.

Advocacy groups often choose the courts to appeal for changes in media when they believe that current laws are unconstitutional or when they feel that the courts' interpretation of existing law will support their interests. When activists decide that lawsuits are not the best vehicle to implement change, they may resort to legislation by elected representatives or rulemaking by regulatory bodies such as the Federal Communications Commission, the Federal Trade Commission, and a city's cable commission. Members of those bodies are typically chosen by the chief executive at the federal, state, or local level (the president, the governor, the mayor) with the approval of the relevant legislature (Congress, the state assembly, the city council).

Mark Nadel, in his general study of "the politics of consumer protection," notes that a public advocacy group's success is based on its ability to make politicians believe that it has a major **constituency**—that is, a large following among the voters. The successful advocacy organization, he says, "takes phenomena defined as problems and lifts them to the point where they become political issues—a larger public becomes aware of the problems, and governmental participants feel pressure to take action on the problem."[13]

Nadel points out that "the public's knowledge of government hearings and records come from the media." Mass media are therefore important in expanding the constituencies of all sorts of pressure groups, whether their targets are media firms or other areas of life.[14]

Ironically, though, the difficulties of reaching potential members are compounded for an advocacy group when mass media industries themselves are the group's target. Two areas of difficulty stand out. One is that media executives might oppose the aims of the activists and therefore hinder their use of media to get public support. The second problem is that attempts to change media through the government are often stifled as a result of the First Amendment to the United States Constitution. It guarantees freedom of speech and the press from government control. As such, it strongly limits the ability of government representatives to join with advocacy group members in forcing media organizations to create certain types of content.

These difficulties, together with the constituency-expansion challenges that all types of public advocacy organizations face, mean that any influences on mass media materials through government pressure will typically be complex and limited. Room does not permit examination of the many paths that lead out of this subject. The following sections will sketch some consequences of the two most intentional sorts of attempts by activists to shape content:

Pressuring authorities to provide *access* to a production firm's mass medium

Pressuring authorities to *eliminate* certain materials created by mass media firms.

PRESSURING AUTHORITIES TO PROVIDE ACCESS

A. J. Liebling, the writer and journalism critic, once quipped that in America there is freedom of the press for the person who owns one. It is true that people who own media vehicles have tremendous freedom to decide who and what gets represented on them. As noted earlier, the First Amendment protects the rights of most producers of mass media material to say no to people who want to use a medium to express views contrary to who controls it.

When speaking about this kind of access, though, an important distinction must be made between the regulated and unregulated media. Broadcast television, radio, and cable television are regulated. Newspapers, magazines, books, audio recordings, and video recordings fall into the unregulated category.

With respect to unregulated media, the United States Supreme Court implied strongly that governments have no right to force the insertion of content. In the Tornillo case of 1974, the Court declared that laws requiring newspapers to allow individuals they attack to reply are unconstitutional. Writing for the Court, Chief Justice Warren Burger's position was uncompromising: "A responsible press is undoubtedly a desirable goal, but press responsibility is not mandated by the Constitution and like many other virtues cannot be legislated."[15]

It is this perspective that gives *New York Times* editors the belief that they hold a legal right to refuse space to the anticigarette activists mentioned at the start of this chapter. Legal observers have generally interpreted the Court's discussion of the press to include all unregulated media. When it comes to regulated media, however, the government has reserved a greater right to intervene in favor of citizens desiring a direct voice. A major U.S. Supreme Court decision in Red Lion Broadcasting vs. the FCC (1969) justified the difference. The Court allowed that the distinction between broadcasting and most other media hinges on the idea that broadcast frequencies comprise a "scarce resource."[16]

While there is no law of nature that prevents anyone from starting a newspaper, the justices said, there are simply not enough broadcast frequencies to go around. That being the case, it is permissible for the federal government to regulate the use of airwaves by issuing licenses. The airwaves belong to the people, not the licensees, the Court asserted, and "it is the right of the viewers and listeners, not the right of the broadcasters, which is paramount." Consequently, "there is no sanctuary in the First Amendment for unlimited private censorship operating in a medium not open to all."[17]

When it comes to the public's access to broadcasting, federal regulators have claimed the right to intervene in two areas:

The acquisition and use of channels

The right to reply and debate

The Acquisition and Use of Channels

The allocation of rights to use of the electromagnetic spectrum is a federal power that dates to the the Radio Act of 1927 (see Chapter 3). This allocation of frequencies has sparked struggles among companies that want pieces of the lucrative broadcast and cable pies. They have also sparked the interest of advocacy groups who express concern that minorities—mainly blacks and Hispanics—get represented as licensees.

It was not until the 1970s that the FCC felt enough pressure to agree that minority ownership of broadcast stations is important as a way to encourage the airing of minority ideas. So doing, the FCC reserved the right to consider minority applicants one of its priority concerns in awarding new licenses and in allowing the transfer of existing licenses from one broadcast company to another.

Pressure to Reply and Debate

Authorities' claim on the second access area—the right of reply and debate—has centered narrowly on the **rights of candidates for a political election** as well as broadly on the **rights of all individuals or groups to debate controversial issues** over the broadcast media.

As noted earlier in this chapter, the rights of candidates were spelled out in the so-called Equal Time rule of the 1927 Federal Radio Act. The rule has withstood the test of time. The right of members of the public to use broadcast and cable media licensed to others as platforms for debate has had a more stormy history.

The Federal Communications Commission set forth this right through a so-called **Fairness Doctrine** in 1949. It stated that broadcasters had to "afford reasonable opportunity for the discussion of conflicting views on issues of public importance." The FCC later extended the ruling to program originators on cable television systems.

In the landmark 1969 Red Lion Broadcasting case, the Fairness Doctrine was challenged in front of the U.S. Supreme Court. The justices upheld its legality. Invoking the natural scarcity argument outlined above, the Supreme Court ruled that a federal requirement of citizens' access, while not acceptable in print media, can be applied to broadcasting.

Yet while the High Court used the Red Lion decision to validate citizens' rights to demand "fairness," it developed a line of reasoning in later cases that made successful demands for access to the broadcast medium difficult. The justices suggested that notions of "fairness" should not be interpreted too literally. They felt an obligation to protect the commercial nature of the broadcasting system. Supreme Court Justice William O. Douglas expressed the fear that a radio or television station that was constantly forced to disrupt its programming to be a forum for public debate would find it difficult, if not impossible, to create an attractive, predictable environment for advertisers. As such, the station would probably cease to function. Since the purpose of the First Amendment is not to interfere with but to encourage free speech, he said, any such result runs counter to the nation's best interests.[18]

By the late 1980s, support for even a limited Fairness Doctrine had diminished among regulators. An increasingly conservative Federal Communications Commission decided it was in broadcasting's best interest to do away with the rule. It was killed in 1987.[19]

The regulatory history of other attempts to allow citizens more access in broadcast media compared with print media has seen similarly narrow openings. For example, while the FCC has touted its interest in promoting minority ownership of licenses, the actual number of stations transferred to black and Hispanic interests under this program has been very small. Moreover, the commission has cut short the growing trend of **citizen-licensee** agreements to force access. These are pacts with station owners to air certain types of programming under the threat that if they don't air them, the activists will drag the station through an expensive challenge to its license at renewal time.

When the idea of such pacts became popular during the early 1970s, broadcasters voiced alarm over the loss of autonomy and ad revenues such forced programming implied. Still, those targeted for the agreements often felt they had to yield to the pressure for the sake of hassle-free license renewal. In the late 1970s, the FCC came to the industry's rescue. The commission stated that it would sanction no agreement in which a broadcast licensee delegated its programming decisions to people outside its organization.[20] In the 1980s, the FCC made citizen-licensee agreements even more irrelevant. It allowed the renewal for most broadcast outlets to be so predictable and unchallengeable that broadcasters no longer felt much of a need to consider activists.[21]

Cable TV and Access

When it comes to cable TV, the recent regulatory climate has worked against broad citizens' access there as well. It is true that local communities select the cable systems they want. They could, if they chose, give franchises to minority-owned firms as a matter of policy. In the matter of program content, though, the Cable Communications Policy Act of 1984 freed cable operators from most rules covering the programs they carry. Some provisions in the act did call for various kinds of local "access" channels for school, government, and public use. However, even as the act was passed, many argued—correctly, it turned out—that those requirements would be overturned by the courts as running counter to the First Amendment.[22]

Three access requirements in the 1984 Cable Television Act have not been challenged by the cable TV industry, possibly because they seem to pose little threat to industry profits or autonomy. One mandates **leased access**. This is a channel on which individuals or groups willing to pay a set fee can present any programming they wish as long as it is not "indecent." A second demands the same Equal Time considerations to candidates for public office that apply to broadcasting. The third extends the Fairness Doctrine to cable. Interestingly, while it was negated by Congress for broadcasters, it was never dissolved for cablecasters.[23]

Cycles of Regulation

It should be clear by now that regulation of access is a political process, with the desires of the broadcast and cable lobbies making their imprints upon decisions by the FCC, the Congress, even the courts. While activists have never found access rights to the electronic media generous, certain periods have seen regulations that are more forthcoming than others.

In the 1980s, for example, the FCC went quite far in closing off access. It was a time when Republican President Ronald Reagan, his appointees to the Federal Communications Commission, and many members of Congress were convinced that cable television, radio, and over-the-air TV stations were overregulated. They pointed to the growing number of media channels in the United States, and to the many local requirements that cable television operators offer public access channels, as evidence that the public would be well served if broadcasters were allowed to compete in the marketplace according to their own desires.

Following this logic, the FCC responded to the pressures of the cable and broadcast lobbies to allow them more control over their programming operations than ever before. The dissolution of the Fairness Doctrine is a case in point.

Radio and TV station executives had never liked the doctrine, cutting as it did into their decision-making autonomy. In lobbying against the ruling, they claimed that the requirement was leading stations and networks to inject less controversy into their medium than would otherwise be the case. They argued that news producers were avoiding controversy as much as possible so as not to be accused of leaning toward one side and being forced to give up valuable commercial time—and decision-making independence—to contentious individuals.

The increasingly conservative FCC (aided by Reagan administration appointees) agreed. However, commissioners were unsure if the doctrine was simply an FCC rule, which they could then repeal, or a law, which Congress would have to invalidate. They decided to try Congress first.

Twice during the 1980s, the commission asked Congress to abolish the doctrine. Twice, though, a Congress divided on the issue did nothing. Finally, a federal court cleared up the legal ambiguity by ruling that the Fairness Doctrine was not a part of statutory law but simply an FCC regulation. Seeing its chance, the FCC killed the rule.[24]

The political maneuvering did not end with the FCC's 1987 action. Many in the democratically controlled Congress disagreed with the FCC's abandonment of the Fairness Doctrine. Not allowed by law to override a commission decision directly, Congress formulated a version of the doctrine and mustered enough votes to pass it into law. President Reagan vetoed it twice, however, and the FCC's approach stood firm.

Still, as the 1980s turned into the 1990s and the Reagan administration turned into the Bush era, observers were remarking that new FCC appointees as well as the Republicans in Congress were taking new, hard looks at whether the broadcast and cable industries were meeting their public responsibilities. To optimists it seemed that the government might be returning small but important opportunities to public advocacy input at the policy and programming levels.[25]

PRESSURING AUTHORITIES TO ELIMINATE MATERIALS

While United States regulatory authorities have been reluctant to provide public advocacy organizations with access to mass media except in narrow situations, over the years they have been more willing to help certain activist groups try to *eliminate* certain mass media material. Some of this willingness to narrow the boundaries of acceptable content undoubtedly has to do with the emotional and political load of the topics often involved—sex, violence, and misleading advertising. When these issues have come up, the rhetoric on all sides has often been high-pitched, the battles have been rough and tumble. Often, too, pressure through authorities has been carried out in tandem with direct pressures on producers or other organizations in the targeted industry. A good many times their activities have had important consequences. Yet even the most significant results of activists' pressures through authorities to eliminate mass media materials have not always been the ones the activists have expected.

The reasons have to do with a number of factors:

First Amendment concerns

The desire by courts to define terms clearly

The ingenuity of media firms to stick to the letter of restrictions while sabotaging their spirit

The Case of Sexually Explicit Literature

The influence of the first two considerations can be seen quite clearly when looking at the outcome of militancy against sexually explicit literature. That militancy both changed its nature and gained momentum in the nineteenth century. Until that time, antagonism to such works in America was made mainly on religious grounds; people saw the creators as sinners against God. After that, public advocacy group opposition to sexually explicit literature tended increasingly to show up in courtrooms as cases of obscenity, not religion.

The 1821 Massachusetts court decision banning *Memoirs of a Woman of Pleasure (Fanny Hill)* was the first United States judicial case in which sexual content was the sole issue. Court cases were few until the last quarter of the nineteenth century, though. It was during that time that groups of citizens began calling for censorship. They targeted fiction of all types, classics as well as dime novels.[26]

Space does not permit even the briefest sketch of the ways such advocacy organizations as the Watch and Ward Society, the New York Society for the Suppression of Vice, and the National Organization for Decent Literature have tried to use federal and state courts, as well as legislatures and police, to prohibit the publication or sale of sexually explicit material throughout the country. Here the purpose is narrower. It is to point out that while those organizations scored some impressive victories, particularly during the first half of the twentieth century, the lasting product of their labors was quite the opposite of what they expected. Rather than encourage censorship, their work led to the elimination of the threat of being censored as obscene from the great majority of books with sexual themes.[27]

The sequence of events that started the ball rolling in this direction was a series of court challenges between about 1910 and 1930 by antipornography organizations. Their targets were Greek, Roman, and French classics with erotic motifs that were being imported or produced in the United States. It was assumed by most judges (and upheld by the Supreme Court in 1957) that obscene publications are not protected by the First Amendment.

The difficulty, however, was in defining "obscene." Vigorous defenses by publishers and importers of the historic importance and enduring qualities of the classic works targeted for censorship brought various judges to develop specific criteria for obscenity. Those criteria indicated much greater leeway for newer books that at the time were being called obscene. Historian Felice Flanery Lewis captures the point well: "In challenging the classics, censors ironically precipitated the birth, in a very restricted form, of the concept that literature with social value was outside the scope of censorship laws, a concept that would eventually do much to defeat the banning of literature."[28]

Jawboning

Ironies like this also weave through the history of movies and television. There the contested range of topics has been much wider than in the general trade book industry. Sex and sexual innuendo have stirred much controversy, to be sure. But so have violence; racial, gender, and ethnic stereotyping; the quality of material for children; and a number of other issues.

A major difference between battles over obscenity and battles over other aspects of movie and television content has been use of the courts. While lawsuits have been the preferred path to force elimination of obscenity, they have not been nearly as frequent with respect to other areas of content. With a few important exceptions, the most popular advocacy group tactic has been to apply pressure to government regulatory or legislative officials so they, in turn, will try to bully (**jawbone**) producers into making changes.

Politicians so pressured will probably respond along the lines outlined throughout this chapter. They will likely assess the size of the the group, the sophistication of its public relations apparatus, and the ways it can help them gain reelection. Then they might place their perceptions of the group's power against that of the industry they are being urged to attack.

Industry leaders, too, are likely to conduct a formal or informal cost-benefit analysis. In doing that, they will compare the power of the pressure group with the potential revenues the company will realize from the material that has caused the fuss. They will also consider the possibility that key politicians might be persuaded to drop anti-industry positions. Failing that, they will assess what long-term political and economic damage they might bring on themselves if they ignored calls for changes in content.

If they feel harm will be minimal, the producers may do nothing. In certain situations, though, they might well conclude the damage would be great. That may then set into motion performance programs that aim to pacify the legislators and advocacy groups while still keeping control over the production process. Two typical ways to do that are self-regulation and lobbying.

Self-Regulation

As the term suggests, **self-regulation** is an activity through which firms police their own activities in an attempt to discourage government interference in industry affairs. Mass media practitioners generally prefer self-regulation because it allows them more flexibility than government legislation to respond to quick-changing demands of the marketplace while they quiet the anger of various public constituencies.

Recall from Chapter 3 that it was fear of government censorship that led early Hollywood producers down the path of self-regulation. The movie industry's approach became a model for the National Association of Broadcasters (NAB) code when radio (and later TV) executives moved to head off government/advocacy group pressures. The NAB has abandoned its code, but the American Association of Advertising Agencies and the Public Relations Society of America still have codes of ethical practice.

Sometimes, severe threats of government interference lead firms to cave in on particular issues. That happened in the music recording industry during the early 1990s. Loud outcries were issued by a number of conservative groups against rock lyrics they considered harmful to young people. They persuaded legislators in more than two dozen states to consider bills requiring warning labels to parents on albums. Record manufacturers, fearing government regulation, voluntarily complied.[29]

Advertisers have particular reason to fear restrictive legislation or rulings by the Federal Trade Commission (FTC) because they practice what the courts call **commercial speech**—that is, the use of language in the service of commerce. Over the decades, several U.S. Supreme Court decisions have stated that the advertising industry's guarantee of free speech is not equal to the guarantees given to noncommercial materials. While ruling that certain aspects of advertising do come under the protection of the First Amendment, the justices have made it clear that government is free to regulate commercial speech which is "false," "misleading," or "proposes illegal transactions."[30] As might be imagined, advertisers would like to have the ability to control how such terms as *false* and *misleading* are understood. Self-regulation would give them the room to create definitions of false and misleading that would quiet critics but at the same time not be as restrictive as government regulations might be.

Lobbying

Lobbying is often used to justify self-regulation, to argue that it is enough, that legislation is not needed. When the cycle of regulation is on the upswing, a media industry's response is often to beef up lobbying defenses. In the ad industry's case, for example, the upswing in regulatory interest was met by the banding together of several trade groups that typically do not work together—the American Advertising Federation, the Association of National Advertisers, and the American Association of Advertising Agencies—to support coalitions that lobby for particular causes.

In rare instances, none of the lobbying works and laws are passed prohibiting certain media materials. Much more often, the combination of lobbying and self-regulation brings about conclusions that are frustrating to the advocacy groups. Citing the First Amendment or other key philosophical principles, authorities refuse to enact legislation that imposes prior restraint on production firms' creation of media materials.

In those situations, politicians try to appease all sides by negotiating compromises with the producers who are under fire. Politicians may jawbone the producers to bow somewhat to government pressures. That way, the producers appear contrite to members of the general public, and the politicians look tough. At the same time, producers may pursue a self-regulatory course that appears to surrender to their opposition but, on closer inspection, does not—or creates new problems. The reason is that mass media practitioners often believe content elements that activists dislike (sex, violence, cartoons) are basic to their firm's survival in the marketplace.

Talking Point 6.1   Indecency and the FCC

Since obscene or indecent language is not protected by the First Amendment, the Federal Communications Commission has the right to penalize stations that air indecencies. Indecency is defined by the FCC as "language or materials that, in context, depicts or describes, in terms patently offensive as measured by contemporary standards for the broadcast medium, sexual or excretory activities or organs." The difficulty, of course, is knowing what is "patently offensive" by community standards. Therein lie the seeds of battles that typically have ebbed and flowed with the power of conservative political movements in the nation.

Several of those battles were fought during the turn of the 1990s. Responding to complaints by radio listeners from around the country, the Federal Communications Commission began cracking down on "indecency." Those opposing the FCC insisted they were not defending "smut" for the sake of smut. Rather, they argued, government involvement in taking messages off the air was worse than the messages' offense. Battles to protect civil liberties, they insisted, are always fought at the borderlines of good taste, since those borders define the limits of individuals' freedoms.

People who thought the FCC was moving in the wrong direction pointed to "obscenity" cases which, they argued, were not nearly as clear-cut as the FCC judged they were. In October 1989, for example, the commission fined KLUC radio in Las Vegas $2,000 for playing Prince's "Erotic City," and it fined WTZA radio in Miami, $2,000 for playing "Penis Envy" by Uncle Bonzai. Defenders of the first song argued that it contained the phrase "we can *funk* until dawn," not the four-letter *f* word the FCC considers obscene. No listener had complained in four years of radio airplay. May 1988, however, saw someone with a tape recorder hear the song on the air and tracked down the sheet music—which does contain the dreaded word. The person alerted the FCC and the FCC condemned the piece.

"Penis Envy" contains the following line the FCC had trouble with: "If I had a penis, I'd still be a girl/But I'd make much more money and conquer the world." Defenders of the line contended that the song is jokey, and the offending line really is a feminist political point. They lost their case.

SOURCES: Jon Pareles, "Outlaw Rock: More Skirmishes on the Censorship Front," *The New York Times*, December 10, 1989, p. 32; Kevin Zimmerman, "Yo! Rap Zapped by Lyrics Flap," *Variety*, March 7, 1990; Denis Wharton, "Media Groups to FCC: Back off on 'Indecency,'" *Variety*, February 28, 1990, p. 40.

Pressure on the Movies

One example of this ironic turn of events can be presented here. It is a movie case that harks to the early days of the Motion Picture Producers and Directors Association (the MPPDA), Hollywood's self-regulatory arm that began to develop its first movie code in the 1920s. The code muffled many of the organized voices of protests that wanted government regulation of the movies. With state and federal legislators calmed, film executives began to see the MPPDA and its director, Will Hays, as instruments by which they could test—and define and slowly expand—the outer limits of movie respectability. Producers and writers learned quickly that it was easy to get around the spirit of the code's mechanical morality.

Take the MPPDA's requirement of **compensating values** as an example. It asserted that virtue had to be rewarded, and sin punished, in movies, since "if good eventually triumphed and evildoers perished miserably, the laws of God, man, and the drama would be simultaneously satisfied." Movie historian Arthur Knight notes the ironic consequences of this approach:

> The studios were quick to perceive that what this meant, in effect, was that they could present six reels of ticket-selling sinfulness if, in the seventh reel, all the sinners came to a bad end, and they could go through all the motions of vice, if, at the last moment, virtue triumphed. Censors around the country might continue their snipping of occasional scenes, but who could object to movies in which "morality" was so eagerly espoused.[31]

Certainly, public advocacy groups did not expect the Motion Picture Code to lead to such films when they pushed the industry toward self-regulation. Such, however, was the unanticipated consequence of forcing media practitioners to give in to advocates' demands without considering the marketplace demands and routines, which generally get first priority. Similar patterns of response can be cited regarding the many episodes of legislative and FCC jawboning of network officials over the years in response to advocacy group outcries over violence; sexual innuendo; racial, ethnic, and gender stereotyping; and the need to eliminate objectional plot lines and characterizations in children's television.

When violence has been a major issue, the producers have replaced it with sexual innuendo or "action comedy," where the fighting is softened with laughs. When sexual innuendo has raised major legislative eyebrows, TV producers have switched to violence. When advocacy groups have joined with authorities to rail against racial, ethnic, and gender stereotypes, those have been replaced by more subtle stereotypes of the same groups, or by other groups that might evoke similar audience responses. And children's television has incorporated elements that mollify some advocacy groups while not really changing the fundamental plot lines and characterizations that stirred the opposition in the first place.

All this implies that when advocacy groups have been powerful enough to pressure legislators and regulators toward action, production executives have moved to eliminate certain types of content, sometimes greatly. The point to underscore, however, is that what has emerged as a result of the battle has often not been what the advocacy group members or the government officials anticipated. Because the media practitioners have held business imperatives above even government pressures, what has sometimes also emerged has simply been another version of the same problem.

PRESSURING PRODUCERS THROUGH CLIENTS

Advocacy group members who are frustrated with the runaround they get when they appeal directly to producers, and with the maddening snail's pace, hesitation, and unpredictability they find when they try to change material by working through legislatures or courts, have been increasingly turning their energies toward the organizations that sponsor the mass media content. Their reasoning is straightforward. They figure that since the buying patterns of primary client organizations are crucial to mass media producers' survival, successful advocacy pressure on the clients should create powerful leverage to make the desired changes in the producers' material.

In reality, though, the situation is not that straightforward. Like producers and authorities, organizations that take on the client role are continually faced with many competing interests in their environment. That makes their sensitivity to advocacy groups not at all clear-cut.

The probability is that, like their counterparts in production and authority organizations, the leaders of client firms will conduct cost-benefit analyses to decide whether they should give in to advocacy group demands—and, if so, how, when, and to what extent. Of course, media clients can be very different from one another, and it is impossible to make blanket statements about the outcome of such cost-benefit calculations. It does seem that government organizations which act as the clients (as opposed to regulators) of producers may be quite responsive to activist pressure. The reason is that public officials up for reelection are quite aware that in supporting mass media producers they are spending public money and are therefore open to public scrutiny.

An example at the federal level comes from the early 1990s, when the National Endowment for the Arts (NEA) was attacked vigorously by conservative groups for supporting a photographic exhibition with homosexually erotic works. The protesters succeeded in getting U.S. Senator Jesse Helms to push a proviso through Congress that the NEA should not use its funds for purposes that could cause sexual, religious, or ethnic offense. Helms' requirement was watered down substantially a year later. Nevertheless, advocates of government support of the arts argued that the result was a distinct chill in the kinds of materials the NEA took the chance of supporting in museums, in broadcasting, in movies, and in print.[32]

The Case of Textbooks

The power that advocacy groups hold to manipulate government funders of mass media producers, and, by extension, to influence media producers, is seen most commonly at the level of state and local governments. The targets there are elementary and high school textbooks. Since textbook selection is an activity conducted by state and local agencies and controlled by elected officials, it is an activity wide open to many pressures from public advocacy organizations. Moreover, the tradition in the United States is that parents have the right to help guide curriculum development in their children's schools. There also seems to be an undercurrent of concern about the texts that officials choose. Incidents of extreme public unrest regarding the texts chosen by schools seem to go in cycles.

A rash of textbook controversies erupted during the mid-1970s, for example. The chairperson of the American Library Association's Freedom to Read Foundation warned that "a nationwide, persuasive, anti-intellectual movement is developing that can be compared to the McCarthy era."[33] Such advocacy groups as the Citizens for Decent Literature, the Hard Core Parents of Louisiana, the Ku Klux Klan, the John Birch Society, and the National Parents League raised objections to textbook content that created a climate of fear among book selection committees around the country.

A centerpiece of protest was a book selection conflict in Kanawha County, West Virginia, in 1974. The tension was instigated by a single member of the Kanawha School Board, the wife of a fundamentalist minister, who objected to the method of textbook selection. She was joined by thousands of protesters against the board's adoption of 325 books they felt "denounced traditional institutions," paraded the notion of cultural relativism, and in general subscribed to an ideology of secular humanism as a substitute for orthodox conceptions of the rule of God and the Bible.[34] Tempers flared. The antitextbook protesters organized, held marches and rallies, circulated petitions, appealed to elected officials, and boycotted the school system. Violence broke out. Vandals destroyed school property, and a picketing protester was shot. After the majority of a special citizen review committee recommended that all but thirty-five of the books remain in the classrooms (a minority report recommended many more be banned), the Kanawha Board of Education building was bombed and partially destroyed.

By the end of 1974, the protesters initially appeared to win a number of concessions from the county school board. However, the revised guidelines were declared illegal by the state superintendent of schools. In the meantime, many parents had begun to send their children to newly created private Christian schools. This activity siphoned off much of the core of the protest movement, and the situation calmed a bit. Sociologists Ann Page and Donald Clelland, commenting on the situation four years later, noted that "although the vehemence of the protest has subsided, the anger lingers on."[35]

The Kanawha conflict and others like it mobilized teachers and librarians around the country in preparation for further textbook battles. Professional publications such as the *American School Board Journal* and *Library Journal* suggested performance programs that its readers could follow so as to minimize the damage created by the fiery groups. "Don't *you* get scalded," warned one article.[36]

Nevertheless, books in several communities were changed in response to public protests and renewed interest in school board elections. More important, into the 1980s a climate of fear and caution spread over many textbook committees that were not embroiled in controversy and did not want to be. Reflecting on such self-censorship, legal scholar Paul Goldstein contends that "the public's greatest influence [in textbook selection] lies in its silence, and in [school professionals'] decisions to reject materials that will spark controversy and rouse the public from its silence."[37]

Book salespeople and their editors know that, says Goldstein, and they create textbooks that are likely to fit the least controversial common denominator of acceptance among relevant school systems. As one textbook company executive noted, the dominant concern of a supervising editor has become

> to achieve a compromise between the controls necessary for national acceptance and the originality of the author's contribution to education. In the el-hi field, particularly, he must balance skillfully the demands of contradictory curricular material, of "progessive educators" and traditionalists, or exponents of the science-centered culture and the humanists, and above all of the majority and minority pressure groups.[38]

One indication of this influence was the guidesheet a major publisher of elementary school texts gave to its authors in the early 1980s. The stapled pages advised against depicting death, divorce, and games of chance, among other activities. In addition, they cautioned that the authors best "avoid topics considered by some to be antireligious, e.g., evolution, witchcraft, and secular humanism."

Advertisers and Pressure

We move from an example of advocacy group pressures on publicly sponsored client organizations to one relating to private clients, large television advertisers. The biggest threat that advocacy groups seem to hold over TV advertisers is a widespread boycott of their products. Big companies that turn out a multitude of consumer goods are sometimes quite skittish—even more skittish than the producers or networks—about getting on a major advocacy movement's hit list.

One can make a strong argument that it was advertisers' fear of a boycott—a fear reinforced by research reports from giant ad agency J. Walter Thompson—that forced the United States television networks away from several years of violence-oriented action programming in 1977. Similarly, it seems that threats by the Coalition for Better Television and the Moral Majority to finger sponsors that supported sexually and ideologically "immoral" programs in the early 1980s created a climate of fear among advertisers and led network programmers in directions that were sensitive to the activists' complaints.

Of particular significance to their cause was the public endorsement of its aim to "improve" television by the giant consumer goods firm and the then-largest TV advertiser, Procter & Gamble. Word in the trade press was that Procter & Gamble executives had been nervous over reports that the Coalition for Better Television was going to list the firm among companies that sponsored unacceptable prime time programs. Executives were even more worried that the coalition might later move to attack Procter & Gamble's ownership of six sultry daytime soap operas, a huge and important investment for the manufacturer. "P&G was afraid the soaps would be a problem down the line," said a television network executive. "By focusing [the coalition's] attention on prime time, I guess they figured they'd get them off their backs."[39]

This comment reflects an awareness of the intricate strategies sometimes involved when advertisers and advocacy groups meet head-on over commercial TV. On the other side, television distributors and producers generally try to convince advertisers and ad agencies that the particular advocacy organization or movement is unrepresentative of the public at large and that, in any case, product boycotts tend to be ineffective. Moreover, in the 1990s networks, syndicators, and producers have special interests in sometimes pushing programs past conventional TV limits. They feel that in an era where VCR tapes and pay-TV movies cross those limits regularly, conventional TV must take those risks to attract the attention of certain audience segments that advertisers desire. As a result, conventional TV may take the risk of alienating certain advertisers if the audiences it attracts draw other sponsors.

In the early 1990s, this posture was adopted by the Fox Television network, which aggressively targets high-spending young adults, and by Tribune Entertainment, which compete furiously for the lucrative market of women who are at home during the day. The Fox show that particularly drew antiadvertiser fire was *Married With*

Children, a Sunday evening situation comedy series that turned the traditional family sitcom on its head. Far from being amused, a concerned woman from a Detroit suburb managed to convince advertisers that *Married With Children* insulted family life and was filled with immoral conversation and allusions. As her campaign progressed, it became clear that many people around the country agreed with her.

In the Tribune Entertainment's case, opposition arose separately in several areas of the country to *Geraldo*, the popular daytime talk show that Tribune Entertainment distributes. Activists, including local Parent-Teacher Associations, were angry that *Geraldo* was routinely highlighting such subjects as "Women Who Date Married Men," "Girls Who Can't Say No," "Campus Rape," and "Parents of Slain Prostitutes." They insisted to local stations and advertisers that the topics were beyond the pale of good taste, especially when aired in the late afternoon, when children might be watching.

Fox and Tribune handled the cases differently, in tune with their perceptions of the benefits and costs of losing advertisers or forcing the producers to make the changes desired by activists and sponsors. Fox representatives publicly refused to back down from their support of the show. Instead, they tried to turn the publicity about the series to their benefit, denying that *Married With Children* was immoral while playing up its attraction to young, hip audiences. If word was sent to the producers to be more cautious with certain themes in the future, this was certainly not communicated widely.

Tribune executives, on the other hand, expressed public alarm at the stream of large advertisers (General Motors, Coca-Cola, Weight Watchers, Kroger Co.) that were deserting *Geraldo*. They also acknowledged that several TV station program directors, reeling from the controversy and losing some local sponsors, were considering whether they should place the show in less desirable time slots or drop it altogether.

The result was a public admission by *Geraldo* creator and host Geraldo Rivera that he had gone too far. Through interviews with the advertising and electronic media trade press, through direct meeting with TV station executives, as well as a videotaped address sent to station managers around the country, Rivera talked of "walking a tightrope between exploitation and sensible balance." He promised that his program would often deal with issues that were socially responsible, which advertisers could be proud of, and sometimes even tie into. He was, he said, "a reasoned voice, a businessman and a lawyer," who was now seeking a balance of topics that would be more acceptable to all the parties involved.[40]

"I'm my own best salesman," he told *Advertising Age*. "Part of my ethic is that if there is a problem, I want to fix it."[41]

It is doubtful that the changes *Geraldo* planned to institute would satisfy all the program's detractors. As Rivera himself suggested, the purpose of "remixing" the elements of his show was primarily to lower the controversy enough so that advertisers would come back but not so much that a core audience of viewers would stop watching. Ultimately, calming concerns of advertisers, local station managers, and (potentially) regulatory agencies was of greater immediate importance than making the advocacy groups happy.

That should be expected. As this chapter has shown, demands by the public are

---

Talking Point 6.2   Making Parents Angry

In an episode of the NBC-TV series *Thirtysomething* first aired during January 1990, a character, Elliot, described the chance to watch *Geraldo* as one of the best things about being unemployed.

"Today he's doing nude transvestites," he tells his friends Michael and Gary.

Picking up on Elliot's cue, *Advertising Age* compiled a factual list of some of the topics *Geraldo* covered during the month of November 1989. Considering that in many places the program was broadcast after school gets out, the list suggests in near-humorous detail many of the shows (some of which were mentioned earlier in the text) that had made Parent-Teacher Associations livid during that year. Here it is:

Nov. 6—Prison Motherhood

Nov. 7—Lady Lifers: Bad Girls Behind Bars

Nov. 8—The Bad Girls' Business: Teen Prostitutes

Nov. 9—Women Who Date Married Men

Nov. 10—Girls Who Can't Say No!

Nov. 13—Murderers Who Should Never Get Out of Prison

Nov. 14—Campus Rape

Nov. 15—Ilicit, Illegal, Immoral: Selling Forbidden Desires

Nov. 16—Parents of Slain Prostitutes

Nov. 17—Cocaine Cowgirls: Female Drug Smugglers

Nov. 20—Chippendales

Nov. 21—Battered Lesbians

Nov. 22—Contract to Kill: Running from the Mafia

Nov. 23—Victoria Principal as *Blind Witness*

Nov. 27—Men Who Marry Prostitutes

Nov. 28—Transsexual Transformations: Stages of Transition

Nov. 29—Angels of Death

Nov. 30—Secret Lives of Stars

SOURCE: *Advertising Age*, January 15, 1990, p. S-4.

---

constantly transformed within mass media production firms by organizational and interorganizational demands that receive greater priority. The bridge that sometimes connects producers and the public is long and scarred by holes, broken planks, and weird passageways.

NOTES

1. See Loren Ghiglione, "Newspapers Should Stop Cigarette Ads," *The Christian Science Monitor,* October 4, 1989, p. 19; and Alan C. Miller and Myron Levin, "Smoking Critics

Seek Sweeping Restrictions on Ads For Cigarettes," *The Los Angeles Times,* June 15, 1990, p. D1.

2. Richard Yao, "The Other Cola War: A Tale of Two Boycotts," *Business and Society Review,* Winter 1990, pp. 44–47.
3. See Walter Goodman, "How PBS Handles Mideast Viewpoints in Two Documentaries," *The New York Times,* December 5, 1989, p. C19; and Steven Emerson, *"Days of Rage*: Journalism or Propaganda?" *The New York Times,* September 6, 1989, p. A23.
4. Telephone conversation, October 15, 1990.
5. Herbert Gans, "Letters to An Anchorman," *Journal of Communication* 27 (Summer 1977), pp. 86–91.
6. James March and Herbert Simon, *Organizations* (New York: John Wiley, 1978), p. 141.
7. Sidney Head, *Broadcasting in America* (New York: Houghton Mifflin, 1972), pp. 347–350.
8. Kalman Siegel, *Talking Back to* the New York Times (New York: Quadrangle Books, 1974), p. 8.
9. See Joseph Turow, "Another View of Citizen Feedback to the Mass Media," *Public Opinion Quarterly* 41 (Winter 1977–78), pp. 534–543.
10. See, for example, Susan Chira, "Whittle Says Channel One Is On Target," *The New York Times,* February 16, 1991 p. D17; Scott Hume, "Channel One Ads Bug Adults, Survey Shows; News Programs Backed," *Advertising Age,* August 14, 1989, p. 4; and Bill Carter, "Whittle Names a Board to Advise Channel One," *The New York Times,* August 28, 1989, p. C8.
11. Richard Stevenson, "And Now a Message from an Advocacy Group," *The New York Times,* May 27, 1990, Section 2, p. 26. Quote is on page 29.
12. Stevenson, "And Now a Message."
13. Mark Nadel, *The Politics of Consumer Protection* (Indianapolis: Bobbs Merrill, 1971), p. 211.
14. Nadel, p. 213.
15. Quoted in Jethro Lieberman, *Free Speech, Free Press, and the Law* (New York: Lothrop, 1980), p. 123.
16. Christopher H. Sterling, *Stay Tuned: A Concise History of American Broadcasting* (Belmont, CA: Wadsworth, 1990), p. 427.
17. Quoted in Lieberman, p. 126.
18. Oscar G. Chase, "Broadcast Regulation and the First Amendment," in Michael Botein and David M. Rice (eds.), *Network Television and the Public Interest* (Lexington, MA: Lexington Books, 1980), p. 143.
19. Joseph Dominick, Barry Sherman, and Gary Copeland, *Broadcasting/Cable and Beyond* (New York: McGraw-Hill, 1990), p. 411.
20. Ronald Garay, "Access: Evolution of the Citizen Agreement," *Journal of Broadcasting* 22 (Winter 1978), p. 103.
21. Sterling, pp. 523–526.
22. Sterling, p. 530.
23. Dominick et al., p. 412.
24. Dominick et al., p. 411.
25. For an early example of the move for change, see Richard Huff, "N.Y.'s Koch, 18 Other U.S. Mayors Begin Cable Reregulation Campaign," *Variety,* August 2, 1989, p. 4.
26. See also Felice Flanery Lewis, *Literature, Obscenity, and the Law* (Carbondale: Southern Illinois University Press, 1976), p. 7.
27. Lewis, p. 45.
28. Lewis, p. 45.
29. *Variety,* March 14, 1990, p. 47.
30. Don R. Pember, *Mass Media Law* (Dubuque, IA: William C. Brown, 1977), pp. 351–352.

31. Arthur Knight, *The Liveliest Art* (New York: Signet, 1958), p. 112.
32. Allan Parachini, "Senate Defeats Attempts by Helms to Cut Art Funding," *Los Angeles Times,* October 25, 1990, p. A1.
33. "Textbook Battles," *American School Board Journal,* July 1975, p. 21.
34. Ann Page and Donald Clelland, "The Kanawha County Textbook Controversy: A Study of the Politics of Life Style Concern," *Social Forces* 57 (September 1978), p. 268.
35. Page and Clelland, p. 278.
36. *American School Board Journal,* July 1975, p. 21.
37. Paul Goldstein, *The Changing American Textbook* (Lexington, MA: Lexington Books, 1978), p. 38.
38. Goldstein, p. 57.
39. Colby Coates and Bob Marich, "P&G's Rap at TV Laid to Fear of Boycott," *Advertising Age,* June 22, 1981, p. 85.
40. Craig Endicott, "Geraldo Remixes 'Heat, Light,' " *Advertising Age,* January 15, 1990, p. S-2.
41. Endicott, p. S-2.

CHAPTER SEVEN

The Production Process

Americans who pay casual attention to the radio sounds, the television images, and the print materials that surround them daily see and hear a welter of different claims, opposing opinions, arguments. A manufacturer advertises that one product is better than another. A politician quoted by a newspaper opposes a presidential action. Two psychologists on a radio talk show scream at each other about the best way to solve interpersonal problems. A TV movie acts out conflicting views on mercy killing. A hit record revels in the joys of love, while another mourns that "love stinks."

The list could go on and on. To casual observers it may seem that there are no limits to the number of topics mass media can raise, the ways they can raise them, or the people who can state their viewpoints. But casual observers would be wrong to believe that. As the first six chapters of this book have shown, the firms that create mass media materials are limited in what they can do. Clients such as advertisers, authorities such as federal and state governments, distributors such as the TV networks, and other organizations taking on various power roles within a mass media industry make crucial demands on production firms, even to the point of defining the audiences they ought to pursue. These influences lead producers to limit the kinds of arguments and depictions they can generate.

When forces with substantial leverage voice displeasure with a production firm's content, the result can be severe harm to the production firm. Aware of the demands on them, production companies develop courses of action to satisfy their own needs as well as needs of the outside forces. These courses of action, or **policies**, attempt to shift organizational activities in directions that respond to outside demands. Production firms may make changes in the audiences they target, the types of materials they create, and the values they portray in the materials.

What has not been discussed so far in this book is how this process works. Exactly how does power over resources within society at large get channeled into power over what media personnel do and, as a result, into the media images they create? How, for example, do resource-related pressures influence the storytelling approaches that editors and reporters rely on? How do the pressures from outside and inside organizations affect the way magazine columnists, movie producers, and situation comedy writers get their work done while not going crazy? This chapter and the one after it explore these and a bundle of related questions.

RESOURCES, IMAGES, AND LEGITIMACY

To begin the exploration, it is relevant to review a few basic ideas from Chapter 1. Remember that mass media bring cultural models to huge numbers of people through fiction and nonfiction stories or other performances. The cultural models depict conduct, and the consequences of the conduct, by individuals and institutions. Institutions, you will remember, are loosely knit groups of organizations that exert control over key aspects of social life—education, health care, law, the military, business, and more.

The organizations that make up institutions do not always agree on the best way to approach key issues. In the medical institution, for example, major arguments about health care policies have erupted between nursing and medical physician organizations, between medical physician and osteopathic physician groups, and between physician organizations and government departments that control many of health care's purse strings.

The most powerful organizations within an institution make up its **establishment**. These organizations have the primary clout to guide the most common practices in the institution's domain of social life. The American Medical Association, for example, has historically been such a powerful force within the medical institution in representing physicians as to undoubtedly qualify for the "establishment" label.

Mass Media and Institutional Legitimacy

The reason the notion of an institution is important when discussing mass media production firms is that media producers portray institutional practices whenever they depict aspects of society in fiction or nonfiction stories. Many in the audience likely accept the presentations as "common sense" or "the way it is," for others if not for them. But for some people the media images might provoke discontent. The images might lead them to want to place their version of society alongside the others that they see or hear. They might want to call attention to themselves, to gain legitimacy for their cause within the institution and society at large.

Are all versions of reality equally likely to find a place in the most important mass media? Scholars from a variety of backgrounds say the answer is no.[1] What they mean is that the most common versions of reality presented in news, entertainment, and advertising are those that accept the authority of the most powerful organizations in every institution. Another way to say this is to state that the mass media tend to uphold the **legitimacy** of the established economic, political, educational, artistic, religious, and military organizations of the society.

When writers say that mass media uphold the legitimacy of these forces, they mean the media justify the organizations' authority, their right to exist as powerful elements of the society's institutions. Production firms tend to create cultural models that actually portray the right of those organizations and the institutions to which they belong to remain powerful in the society, to control resources and hold leverage. Police shows on television portray the police as rightfully in charge. Situation comedies show going to school as a necessary part of growing up. Discussions of religion in major newspapers affirm the right of major religious denominations to exist. Movies about sickness accept the importance of hospitals in society.

The scholars who make these points do not mean that the mass media are always unquestioning and bland with respect to these organizations. Certainly, in glancing through newspapers and magazines, watching television dramas, or listening to the radio, we often come across arguments that attack the dominant political parties, articles that criticize large corporations, songs that make fun of teachers, stories that demand military reform. Moreover, we note that intellectual fashions change, that social divisions occur, and that these and other tensions find their way into the media. It seems clear, too, that some mass media materials often displease members of an institution's elite (for example, business leaders) as well as other portions of the public.

Recognizing that mass media materials often display social tensions and conflicts does not, however, sweep away the argument that mass media content tends to legitimize the establishment. Despite depictions of social problems, most mass media in a society rarely challenge the nation's dominant institutional forces to the point of raising realistic alternatives. Rarely, for example, do United States television programs seriously portray solving the nation's economic problems by doing away with the capitalist banking system, reducing the nation's armament problems by completely dismantling the military, or reducing a viewer's own monetary difficulties by stealing and then mocking the police. To the contrary, in all but the most unstable societies, the legitimacy of established in stitutional setups and their values is a theme weaving through the bulk of mass media.

Certain kinds of mass media production firms are more likely than others to be concerned about pleasing the establishment. The difference has to do with where the firms get their resources. Production companies that rely on getting a great many of their most important resources (money, authority, personnel, services, and the like) from the mainstream of society (governments, giant advertisers, powerful advocacy organizations such as mainstream religious denominations, necessarily huge and diverse audiences) will likely arrange their activities so as to offend as few of these entities as possible. On the other hand, production firms that can rely on resources from areas of society that are outside the mainstream (nongovernment bodies, specialty distributors and exhibitors, rather small and homogeneous audiences, small advertisers interested in reaching those specific audiences) might not have fears about attacking the mainstream.

The difference is between what can be called **mainstream** and **peripheral** media output. So, for example, in the United States it is possible to produce novels extolling communist ideologies as a solution to social problems; the First Amendment to the United States Constitution prohibits government interference. However, it is doubtful that such peripheral material would be highlighted on network television or considered attractive by major movie studios, such as Paramount, Columbia, and Fox. They hold solidly mainstream approaches to their products.

Legitimacy and the Price of Entry

Fear of advertisers, distributors, exhibitors, and other forces in the production firms' environment is not, however, the only reason mainstream production organizations legitimize the establishment. The price of entering mainstream media business is another factor. Gone are the days when near-indigent entrepreneurs could found daily newspapers or magazines aimed at "the masses" and succeed. The costs of technology and labor for the industrialized production and distribution of messages are such that financing even mid-size media ventures can cost millions of dollars. Those costs can generally be met only by wealthy firms. Because they want to keep their wealth and power, the firms have a vested interest in the society's basic economic and political ways of doing things.

Consider the newspaper industry. Price tags of three newspaper acquisitions in 1987 reflect the wealth needed to manage the descendents of the penny press: The Media News group bought the *Houston Post* for $150 million; Ingersoll Publications acquired *The Daily Record* of Morristown, New Jersey, for $100 million; and, in one of the most expensive newspaper purchases ever, the Hearst Corporation took over *The Houston Chronicle* for $415 million.[2] Such costs tend to limit entry to the daily newspaper industry to the already well heeled, to people and companies with vested interests in the establishment and, by extension, in the established ways of depicting institutional reality.

In other areas, too, entering the mainstream usually presupposes being part of at least the economic establishment. Television and radio licenses regularly trade for hundreds of thousands, even tens of millions, of dollars. Foreigners and convicted criminals are not even allowed to obtain licenses. As for the costs of producing and distributing movies, they can easily shoot into the tens of millions. Buying an ongoing film studio and its diverse holdings requires stratospheric sums; Sony Corporation paid $2 billion for Columbia Pictures Entertainment in 1989.[3]

Even in the magazine business, where technology and labor expenditures need not be astronomical, launching a periodical economically but wisely will cost at least several hundred thousand dollars. The reason is that in the magazine industry, as in the record and book industries, the key to success lies not just in producing material that will attract the public. If that were the case, magazines, records, and books could be produced at very low costs by just about anyone.

The trick, rather, lies in also building distribution and exhibition channels for the product. With a magazine, that means promoting the periodical strongly to advertisers, subscribers, and a viable number of distributors and exhibitors to get them to feel that supporting the product will bring them money. This many-sided promotion can be very expensive, in time as well as money. Previous experience (a "track record") in the business is crucial, since that makes it easier to cultivate the trust of wholesalers, retailers, advertisers, investors, and banks.

Buying an already successful magazine can cost millions. In 1988, for example, McFadden Holdings bought *The National Enquirer* for $412 million.[4] That same year, Dun & Bradstreet sold *The Official Airline Guide* and its related products to Maxwell Communications for $750 million.[5] And, in the biggest magazine publishing deal of the 1980s, Rupert Murdoch paid $3 billion for Walter Annenberg's Triangle Publications. A major factor in Murdoch's interest was that Triangle not only held a valuable lineup of publishing holdings (including *TV Guide, Seventeen*, and *The Racing Form* newspaper), it controlled a powerful magazine distributing operation as well.[6] (Several years later, crippled by debt, he sold all the titles except *TV Guide*.[7])

The point has been made: The costs and connections needed to set up a production firm that has a chance of being successful in the mainstream generally demand that the owners themselves be part of the establishment. But a number of questions arise:

> How do the people who work in firms oriented toward mainstream resources actually learn what it means to create portrayals that legitimize established institutional structures?

> Do production companies that tilt toward the economic and political mainstream develop explicit policies that guide their employees to uphold the establishment?

> If so, how have these policies developed, and how do media personnel learn how to translate them into content?

> If not, how do such portrayals get established? Do news reporters, TV fiction writers, magazine columnists, and radio talk show hosts intend to uphold the establishment when they carry out their work? What happens to them when they disagree with certain ideas they are working with?

> What about media workers who belong to minority groups in the society? To what extent do they get involved in creating output for mainstream organizations? When they do, how much freedom do they have to portray their ethnic identities as separate from the majority? How do they learn acceptable portrayals of society's institutions?

THE IMPORTANCE OF ROUTINES

In searching for answers to these questions, one point becomes especially clear: Many of the people who create mainstream news and entertainment have little daily sense of a duty to reinforce fundamental institutional norms in the materials they create. Their bosses do not emphasize this idea on a daily basis. Nor do the firms' boards of directors exhort employees about the importance of respecting the pillars of society's institutions—the church, the presidency, the law, medicine, capitalism itself.

To the contrary, the people who create mass media materials have much more specific requirements to think about. A congressional reporter for a newspaper, for example, is likely to focus on writing good summaries of the government rivalries she is covering. A songwriter wants to find a combination of lyrics and music that will grab listeners. The writers of a TV situation comedy episode will likely be centrally concerned about getting laughs from the audience. Moreover, many of the people who work in mass media production firms consider themselves intelligent, critically aware individuals. They might be insulted to think that they spend their time trying to "propagandize" for the establishment.

As it turns out, the most powerful engines for supporting established institutional approaches in mass media are the activities people think about least: the standard procedures, or **routines**, that become part of their professional working lives. Routines have much in common with habits. They guide people through procedures they need to carry out without forcing them to think too deeply about them. That helps an organization to get work done quickly. Of course, when the routines employees carry out lead them toward products that fail in the marketplace, they pose a problem. When they are successful, however, routines keep an organization's activities efficient and on track.

But routines do more than help media producers create efficient content. They also are a major force in leading the people who work for mass media production organizations to generate materials that mirror the legitimacy of established institutional power. Without realizing it, creators who use the routines are following guidelines that media practitioners created many years ago to solve very practical problems of getting their work done. At the same time—and probably without realizing it—those people built into the routines ways of portraying the world that harmonize with the establishment.

THE ORGANIZATION OF NEWS ROUTINES

Consider an example from the news business. Ask a journalist what the most important concept that guides reporting is, and he or she is likely to answer "objectivity." Nowadays, the journalist may quickly add that of course there is no such thing as absolute objectivity. Objectivity in journalism, he or she may say, means being as fair as possible.

Ask how one writes an objective story, and the person will probably list a number of criteria. Here are four:

- The piece should proceed according to the **inverted pyramid** form. That is, its first paragraph should note the story's essentials—the who, what, where, when, how, and why of the incident—and then expand on details as the article unfolds.
- The piece should be written in the **third person**; the reporter should not intrude into the article or color it with his or her personal opinion.
- This "objective voice" should be accompanied by **quotes** from the individuals involved as well as from credible observers.
- Care should also be taken to include at least *two* sides to the story.

Newspeople are typically quite careful about writing their stories according to the guidelines of objectivity. They believe that in most cases the approach leads to stories that are free from political preferences. Scholars who write about newswork, however, insist that news very much reflects the preferences of the most powerful groups in society. Gaye Tuchman, for example, has argued that "news both draws upon and reproduces institutional structure."[8] And Phillip Tichenor, George Donahue, and Clarice Olien have observed that "where there is diversity in social power, media tend to reflect the orientations of those segments that are higher up on the power scale."[9]

How can such seemingly neutral approaches to writing a news story perpetuate patterns of seeing the world that mesh with the establishment? To answer this question, some history is necessary.

Origins of News Objectivity

Present-day requirements that news reports be objective trace their origins to the emergence of the penny press in the late 1830s. The papers were responding to major changes taking place in the United States as a new, restless population of urban workers ("artisans" and "mechanics") emerged on the scene. These city laborers became increasingly angry with what they saw as the control that the established merchant class held over American institutions. Their anger was not reflected in the mainstream daily newspapers of the big cities. Those "sixpenny" papers, supported as they were by the dominant political parties and by expensive subscriptions, followed their wealthy readers in looking down on the working class.

By contrast, Benjamin Day of *The New York Sun*, James Gordon Bennett of *The New York Herald*, George Wilkes of *The National Police Gazette* and others positioned their penny products toward "the great masses of the community."[10] They chastised the sixpennies for their alliances with "cliques and parties" and not with the general public's good.[11] The penny paper entrepreneurs claimed to speak for all, worker *and* merchant. A newspaper costing only a penny would give all citizens equal access to knowledge, they argued, and the commonsense reports the paper would present, controlled by no party and no class, would benefit democracy.

In their editorials, the papers managed to blend a concern with traditional American institutional values—individual property rights, the market system, and power of the state—with a concern for the rights of workers to move upward in the society. It was this approach that led to the development of objectivity as the key criterion of good journalism. The reason was quite practical. The newspaper publishers needed to appeal to readers of all political and economic stripes with stories that the readers would believe. Their solution for attracting both workers and owners, both rich and poor, seemed easy: Present them with "the facts"—the objective reality—and let them make up their own minds.

The idea of an objective reality was accepted easily in the United States during that time. People felt that facts represented truths everyone could agree with. Science could discover the absolute truth; photographs would not lie. Today, many people do not accept such notions so easily. They believe that photos *can* "lie"—or, at any rate, they can present one of a number of perspectives on the same scene. But nineteenth-century journalists, like most other people of their day, were sure it was possible to reveal the world impartially, to separate fact from fiction. Publishers, editors, reporters, illustrators, and photographers worked hard to establish routines that would allow them to present factual, objective accounts of events.

Slowly, over years and in response to a variety of technological, economic, and political demands on newspapers, the procedures that represent objective journalism developed.[12] Today, journalists and their audiences take for granted such conventions as the inverted pyramid, the third-person objective voice, the use of quotes from credible sources, and the expectation that more than one side of a story will be told. They usually consider these practices neutral tools that, when used professionally, can reveal "the facts" about situations.

Close examination, however, will show that the routines of objectivity are not the neutral recording instruments journalists like to believe they are. As this historical sketch has suggested, those procedures had a particular view of reality built into them. That view was a middle-of-the-road approach that tried to balance the interests of both merchants and laborers, of rich and middle class, while upholding the traditional institutional structure. On the one hand, the journalists chose stories that showed the workers that the papers could stand with them against unscrupulous wealth. On the other hand, the objective methods of reporting what they found led journalists to uphold the wealthy class even as they exposed the problems of one part of it.

Objectivity and Authority

To see how objectivity works to present an establishment view, consider one guideline: that quoting credible sources is evidence that a report is objective. The common-sense logic of journalism is that the most credible sources are those who hold legitimate positions of authority. These tend to be government leaders, police spokespeople, corporate executives, and keepers of official statistics rather than alleged criminals, admitted nonexperts, or people who have no special knowledge of a complex situation.

As a result, the facts and perspectives of people in authority are dominant in objective news reports. Their presence in stories about corruption within the establishment therefore quietly supports those who claim that the problems are due not to the system but to a few rotten apples.

Sources journalists consider authoritative can also **manage the news** in many instances. That means they can guide reporters to certain topics and not others so as to erase or obscure threats to their powerful positions within the established system.

The requirement to present more than one side of a story is another objectivity guideline that can be seen as legitimizing the establishment. Being "balanced" in this way obliges the journalist to be evenhanded. It also forces the journalist to sound uncommitted, and it allows people in power the opportunity to defend themselves, even if the journalist knows they are being inaccurate and insincere.

This posture of neutrality was purposefully built into the role of the journalist over the past century. Editors did take pride in the adversary relationship that had developed between the newspapers and the government (see Chapter 4), and in the support they offered the laboring classes of Americans. Many news organizations prided themselves, and continue to pride themselves, on uncovering social problems that suggest the need for correcting society.

Yet the key word here is "correcting," not destroying. This **remedial** role of journalists became so clear, in fact, that many writers began to refer to the press as the **fourth branch of government**. The phrase reflects a clear understanding that an "objective" press does not stand in opposition to the established order of things. To the contrary, it exists to participate in the growth of that order.

THE ROUTINES OF FICTION

Many of the same points about the legitimizing role of routines in mainstream U.S. journalism can also be suggested about mainstream mass media activities that are not journalistic. A large number of writers have argued that the most widespread fiction tends to accept the established institutional setup of the society as given. Certainly there are areas of popular culture that have a tradition of expression that stands directly against mainstream values.

The American music industry has always had a side to it that accommodated groups that stood in direct opposition to the establishment. In the early 1990s, the "peripheral" side of the recording industry ignited obscenity trials of music groups such as Dead Kennedys and Two Live-Crew along with widespread indignation that the lyrics of a number of rap groups were racist and sexist. Record stores tended to carry the groups' albums, especially when huge conservative outcries against them made them into money-making celebrities. Radio stations, afraid of alienating advertisers and the Federal Communications Commission, tended to stay away.[13]

Fiction and the Establishment

Writers on mainstream popular culture stress that even mainstream materials sometimes is critical of the establishment. Popular fiction, they note, often exposes tensions between different classes or groups in society and holds certain elite types up for laughter or even scorn. Think of unfavorable images you have seen recently of bankers, bosses, strict parents, government bureaucrats.

Yet, the writers point out, even when these materials focus on problems of the society, whether in comedic or serious ways, the portrayals should not be considered antiestablishment because they tend not to support radical breaks with traditional ways of doing things. Love with one person at a time is still the standard romantic appeal in songs; the nuclear family is considered the most desirable living condition for adults with children; government agencies are regularly depicted as crucial for the functioning of society; jobs, bosses and all, are shown as facts of life that must be endured and that can even be enjoyed; robbing a bank is rarely condoned. The tendency is clear on TV, in the movies, in comic books, in songs played on the radio, and elsewhere in mainstream mass media.

Communication researcher George Gerbner suggests that fiction can portray institutional values and prejudices much more clearly than news can.[14] The reason is that journalists must be guided by "the facts" and so cannot make up endings to their stories. If a gang of drug addicts robs a bank in real life, a reporter who knows nothing about them cannot portray them as mean and ugly and say that they have been caught. A writer concocting a bank robbery for a movie plot can, by contrast, do just that. The producer, director, and casting director can also make sure that the robbers are of an age, sex, ethnicity, and race that will suit the needs of the story and not offend large numbers of people in the audience.

The selection of particular types of people over others for certain roles in mainstream materials often reflects institutionally accepted notions about who belongs in what positions in society. When grade school teachers are portrayed mostly as women and truck drivers mostly as men, it reinforces notions that people have learned to accept as the commonsense values of society. Violence in storytelling also depicts social values. Violent criminals are bad but violent heroes are good, mainly because they use their power to catch criminals, who threaten society. Fiction emphasizes the need for law enforcement to protect society's values, even if the enforcer has to be a special arm of the law (James Bond or Dick Tracy), a vigilante cop (Bruce Willis in *Die-Hard*), a private detective (Mike Hammer), or Batman.

Storytelling Formulas

Writers of fiction, like writers of news, often have no idea that they are legitimizing established institutional practices when they create their works. Like news, however, these ideas are built into the storytelling routines. No one has traced the roots of those routines. Part of the difficulty of this kind of investigation is knowing how far back in time to go.

Storytelling is as old as humankind. Folklore from around the world contains themes of institutional legitimacy and the celebration of social values that foreshadow some of those in mass media material. Even supposedly homegrown American mass media forms have roots in other societies. Research on the Western, for example, indicates its origin in folklore of early colonial settlers, in published memoirs of Indian captivity and movement west, and in the very popular British books of knights in shining armor that Walter Scott turned out in the early nineteenth century. Tracing the historical creation, perpetuation, transformations, and interconnections of a large number of fiction forms in much the same way that people have traced the development of objectivity in American journalism would be a prodigious undertaking.

It seems clear, though, that part of the reason for institutional legitimacy in mainstream fiction lies with routines involving that basic starting point for fiction making in many mass media production firms—the **formula**. A formula consists of widely recognized principles for selecting and organizing material. In fiction, formulas consist of certain types of **settings, characters**, and **plots**.

In a cowboy tale, for example, the setting may be the "wild West" (a frontier on the edge of "civilization"). Typical characters will be the cowboy, the sheriff, the bank robbers, and the female schoolteacher. A typical plot would involve some kind of tension between the three character types.

For example, a number of movies and books adopt the following plot structure: A cowboy who was once a bad guy but has reformed is being blackmailed by the bad guys who want him to return to their side. In the face of a weak sheriff, the bad guys threaten the town. The cowboy (aided by romantic involvement with the schoolteacher) must decide whether to risk exposure as a former criminal or let the town fall to the marauders.[15]

Writers can vary this basic plot structure to come up with a multitude of seemingly different stories. Combining elements from two or more formulas may result in new formulas that may appear more creative and sophisticated than older ones. At the same time, the variations carry with them characters, plot patterns, and even settings that reflect certain ways of looking at the world. The three-way tension noted in the cowboy formula, for example, almost always leads to a plot emphasis on the traditionally American importance of masculine individualism and the correctness of using force to solve certain problems. Pacifism is not a theme that can coexist easily with a cowboy tale.

Formulas and the Rise of the Movie Industry

Popular formulas provide mass media production firms with models for easily manufactured output that seem to have a good chance for success with large numbers of people. At the same time, because mainstream social values are part of their building blocks, creators can use formulas to thwart complaints by the mainstream that their material is institutionally unacceptable.

Movie historian Robert Sklar shows how the use of formulas protected Hollywood production firms in their early years. After World War I, the film industry was assaulted by groups that feared movies were their enemies in a battle they were waging over values in American life. To simplify for the purpose of this brief discussion, their aim was to maintain a conservative, "small town" perspective in the face of an increasingly urban, industrial, and ethnically diverse society. They saw American movies, with their vivid portrayals of crime and salacious behavior, as directly opposing this goal. To those spokespeople for the traditional middle and upper classes, the direction of the movies was particularly worrisome because power over the photoplay rested largely in the hands of foreign-born Jewish producers who, they felt, could not be trusted to promote traditional American values.

The producers' response, Sklar says, was to steer a middle course through the warring factions in American society. The film executives did present new lifestyles on the screen, but in such a way as to "clearly avoid breaking away from the fundamental economic and social mold." A major way they protected themselves was to base their films on time-tested formulas, varied in style and minor detail to fit the period:

> Faced with an audience more divided, more defensive, and yet increasingly avid for visions of alternative styles and behavior, moviemakers not unnaturally sought the subjects and treatments that pleased the most and alienated the fewest. The noisy and well-organized opposition and their own settled beliefs and filmmaking practices kept them from straying too far beyond the remaining stereotypes and formulas of the middle-class order. What they became adept at was reformulating older conventions; only when the need was obvious and overwhelming did they dare to generate a new formula. The results were not so different from traditional culture as reformists and censors sometimes made it appear.[16]

Sklar makes another point about the movie moguls that resonates with what has been said about journalist-entrepreneurs. These men were, despite fears of the defenders of middle-class culture, "deeply committed to the capitalist values, attitudes, and ambitions that were part of the dominant social order."[17] They cared about their businesses and about the society that had let them prosper. And while they may well have wanted to point out its problems and encourage people to solve them, they had no interest in tearing the establishment down.

JOINING THE ORGANIZATION

We have seen, then, that legitimation of established institutions through mainstream mass media materials has deep roots in the history of production activities. We have also seen that the huge costs of engaging in mainstream media production makes it likely that the organizations involved will align themselves with the establishment.

What of the people who work in those organizations? Do *they* accept those values, or do they simply follow formulas and other approaches to content without caring? How, in any event, do they learn what is involved in creating acceptable materials?

Hiring Patterns

Studies of the people who join mainstream United States production firms to help create material suggest that most of them do accept the institutional views that get into their output. That seems particularly true regarding newspeople. Studies of journalists consistently reflect what John W. C. Johnstone, Edward Slawski, and William Bowman have called "the fact that in virtually any society those in charge of mass communication tend to come from the same social strata as those in control of the economic and political systems."[18] During the 1970s, for example, Johnstone and his associates found United States journalists to be overwhelmingly from solidly-middle class or upper-middle-class backgrounds."[19]

Among entertainment performers, this generalization does not hold. A high percentage of the nation's most successful singers and comedians are African-Americans from disadvantaged backgrounds. Sociologists also point out that nonblack entertainers are likely to come from religions—particularly the Jewish and Catholic faiths—that have generally been considered socially disadvantaged. Apart from performers, though, it does appear that hiring throughout both the journalistic and nonjournalistic mass media has tended to reflect patterns of racial, class, and gender dominance in U.S. society as a whole.

Numbers tell only part of the story, but they can be startling. For example, government agencies, women's groups, and labor guilds have presented a good deal of evidence of the low representation of women as directors, producers, and performers for television and the movies. The Screen Actors Guild found that only 19% of all 9,440 parts in theatrical films in which guild members worked during 1989 went to females.[20] Socially disadvantaged men and women of color—red, yellow, black—have found even greater difficulty getting roles. In 1989, for example, fully 82% of all 9,353 parts in theatrical films went to whites.[21]

Economic and political changes in the society at large *have* affected hiring. The prominence and power of blacks as performers in the recording industry during the past few decades, for example, have encouraged firms to hire blacks for the mid-level executive positions with which the performers work. That, in turn, has encouraged other types of minority hiring throughout the industry.

Often, though, changes at the performer level do not radiate very far. Network television provides a case in point. During the 1980s, more black entertainers starred in network TV programming than ever before. A number of factors contributed to this situation. First, the black middle class had grown to become an attractive market for national advertisers. At the same time, ratings companies reported that blacks spend 40% more time with broadcast TV than whites. Moreover, it became clear that shows with certain black personalities (Bill Cosby, Arsenio Hall, Oprah Winfrey) appealed to "crossover audiences" of whites and blacks. In view of these considerations, network

---

Talking Point 7.1   Unequal Access, Unequal Pay for TV Writers

In 1989, the Writers Guild of America, West, released a report detailing the job experiences of its members who are women, members of minority groups, or people over 50 years of age. The findings reflected the continuing difficulty these writers have had in becoming a part of the Hollywood establishment. Here are some highlights of the report:

- In each year from 1982 through 1987, white males have accounted for over three-fourths of the writers employed in film and TV.
- In each year from 1982 through 1987, minorities have accounted for just 2% of the writers employed in film and TV. Although the earnings gap narrowed during this period, it remained substantial. In 1987, employed minority writers earned 63 cents for each dollar earned by white male writers.
- During the 1986–87 prime time season, minorities accounted for less than 1% of the writers for basic and pay cable series and network movies-of-the-week, and only 1.5% of the writers for pilots produced for the networks.
- A slight improvement since 1982 in the employment of women writers in the industry was offset by a decline in their earnings relative to white males. In 1982, women writers earned 73 cents for each dollar earned by white males. By 1987, women writers were earning just 63 cents for each dollar earned by white male writers.
- Among writers employed during the 1986–87 prime time season, female and minority writers were less likely than male writers to be employed as hyphenates—that is, as people having the role of a producer or director as well as writer. Not being employed as a hyphenate—especially as a writer-executive producer—indicates a lack of power within the production firm.
- In each year from 1982 through 1987, writers 40 and under have accounted for over half the writers employed in film and television.
- Between 1982 and 1987, the share of employment going to writers in their fifties and sixties has declined, and earnings patterns have shifted in favor of writers under 50.

Research projects such as this one have helped focus public and industry attention on the need to allow more access for women and minorities in Hollywood. The declining position of older writers, however, has received relatively little attention.

SOURCE: William T. Bielby and Denise D. Bielby, "The 1989 Hollywood Writers' Report: Unequal Access, Unequal Pay" (West Hollywood, CA: Writers Guild of America, West, 1989), p. ii.

---

executives, trying to fight a decline in their general audience numbers, decided to coax black heavy viewers to these shows with the aid of black stars.

The black TV stars did hire some black actors, writers, and administrators to work with them. Still, while the number of key African-American players increased on screen, by 1990 the increase had only a small ripple among TV writers or in the network decision-making suites. According to the Writers Guild of America, West, less than 2% of the Writers Guild members working in television in each year from 1982 through 1987 were black.[22] In network executive suites, the absence of black *men* was particularly noteworthy. Of the eight network vice-presidents or programming directors who were black, only one was a man.[23]

Minorities have been rare in journalism organizations as well. In the early 1980s, only 10% of their employees were nonwhite. When it comes to gender, the insistence by feminist groups during the 1970s that women be given equal occupational opportunities throughout does seem to have had significant impact. Professors David Weaver and Cleveland Wilhoit found that the proportion of women working as journalists in the early 1980s was substantially higher than in the early 1970s (33% as opposed to 20%). It still did not, however, come near the percentage of women in the total full-time work force (43%).[24] In this respect, Weaver and Wihoit comment, journalism was still ten years behind the times.

Hiring Patterns and Media Content

Reflecting on the "mainstream" characteristics of the creators of the society's mainstream news and fiction, some researchers have contended that the reason those mass media perpetuate institutional legitimacy is that the people involved impose their personal values on the content. Johnstone and his associates convey this impression. After sketching the typical background of journalists, they conclude it is "perhaps more than accidental that . . . news in large measure reflects men's rather than women's definitions of newsworthiness . . . and that the establishment groups in the society are virtually always defined as more newsworthy than those of minority or disadvantaged groups."[25]

Political researchers Robert Lichter, Linda Lichter, and Stanley Rothman take this line of thinking to its logical conclusion in their study of the beliefs of journalists who work for newspapers that reach the nation's elites—*The New York Times, The Washington Post*, and *The Wall Street Journal*. They found that the newsworkers in these firms were far more likely than the rest of the U.S. population to describe themselves as politically left of center. The researchers concluded that the liberal tendencies of these newsworkers was the primary reason the newspapers tended to be liberal in their approach to political affairs.[26]

Lichter, Lichter, and Rothman's conclusions can be challenged, however. For one thing, *The New York Times, Washington Post*, and *Wall Street Journal* are not that ideologically different from the rest of U.S. journalism. While they have adopted the historical role of "the fourth estate" more vigorously than many other daily papers, their approach to the world is still fundamentally one of supporting the nation's dominant institutional structures.

Moreover, it can be argued that Lichter, Lichter, and Rothman's logic is backward. Instead of interpreting the findings as meaning that the so-called liberal employees influence the news organizations, it would have been at least as sensible to say that the newspapers' policies led to hiring those types of people. That is, the practice of investigative, relatively challenging journalism attracted, even demanded, people with those interests and characteristics—idealistic people who were interested in working within the system, but not altogether happy with the status quo.

Sociologist Herbert Gans uses this kind of analysis to disagree with the Lichter, Lichter, and Rothman position. He argues that the world of newswork ends up dictating the values of people who can work in it, rather than the other way around. Gans states that neither the personal values nor the upper-middle-class background of most journalists really gets to the heart of why they write what they write on their jobs. Surely, as we will see in the next chapter, personal likes and dislikes influence what appears in print or on the home screen. But, Gans asserts, the "basic shape of news" would not be different if a journalist came, for example, from a working-class or a middle-class home. The reason is that the mainstream perspectives guiding newswork are built into the newswork activities; the work guides the person, not the other way around. Gans suggests that working-class people would have a hard time filling the employment prerequisites for newswork. Even when they could, to act as journalists they "would likely have to shed their working class values and reality judgments."[27]

Having a background that reflects dominant values, then, helps a prospective employee in two ways. First, it makes it easier to obtain a position in a major mass media organization. Second, the background allows the new employee to adapt to media work more easily than a person without that upbringing.

But how does one "adapt" to media work? What is involved in getting recruited to an organization and learning its ways? How does this mesh with the twin acts of getting production work done and legitimizing the establishment? To answer, it is essential to examine the subjects of recruitment and socialization to mass media production organizations.

FORMS OF RECRUITMENT

Mass media firms typically hire some creative personnel as permanent staff members and others for short periods of time. Permanent, or **staff**, recruitment therefore means hiring people to be regular members of the firm. The second approach involves **freelance** work. Management hires creative personnel to carry out specific tasks. They are relied on to do the job according to their best knowledge, and they leave when they finish.

Creative personnel who take on a **selector** role in their organization are quite likely to be recruited on a staff line. Selectors are members of an organization who make decisions about accepting or rejecting certain materials for production. Examples are newspaper editors, movie producers, and advertising account executives.

It is useful to use the term **artist** to describe people who actually generate ideas for the materials selectors they choose. In everyday language, the word *artist* often means that the work performed is of especially high quality. That is not the intention here. The word simply refers to the range of activities that certain types of employees carry out. Writers working on book manuscripts, actors playing movie parts, TV executives creating the schedules for their networks' prime time shows, and journalists creating news stories are all serving as artists.

These examples raise two important points. The first is that selectors sometimes also act as artists. The network TV executives are artists in their creation of the lineups, but they are also selectors in their acts of choosing the shows that will appear in those lineups. Similarly, some book publishers require their editors to write books as well as move them through the production process.

The second point is that while selectors who are also artists typically enter organizations through staff recruitment, artists who are not selectors might be recruited either permanently or freelance, depending on the industry and circumstance. Journalists, for example, are generally recuited for a bureaucratic approach to production, while trade book writers are mostly hired freelance, one book at a time. A newspaper editor, advertising copywriter, and television news anchor typically are recruited in the staff track. By contrast, when a movie studio hires stunt experts to perform in a movie, it is often understood that the company will stop paying them when the filming is over. Screenwriters and novelists are also generally picked up on a freelance basis.

Reasons for Different Hiring Forms

The reasons for the different approaches to hiring vary. Many companies simply cannot support a permanent lineup of highly paid artists. It may be (as in the stuntman's case) that their specialties are infrequently used. It may be (in the case of screenwriters or novelists) that the artists need a long time to complete their work and the firm cannot afford to keep paying them while they are not contributing directly to profits.

There are, on the other hand, movie companies that do keep actors and writers on staff. There are, too, publishing firms that have long-term contracts with writers. Whether a firm hires artists on a continuing basis will depend to a large degree on the financial health of the company, the firm's tradition, and the losses the company might suffer if the artists went to competitors. Sometimes, production executives need artists they can rely on for daily work.

Illustrators in an advertising agency fit this description. So do newspaper reporters. A daily newspaper typically uses its reporters' work every day. At the same time, some papers find it prestigious and ultimately profitable to support a few bureaus and investigative reporting units even if they prepare publishable stories every few weeks or even every few months.

On the other hand, a small scholarly publishing company, a struggling monthly magazine firm, or a new record company might not be able to afford that kind of delayed gratification; some newspapers might not want to. So, circumstances would probably dictate that those firms recruit freelance artists when selectors feel the artists have something specific to contribute, and only for the length of time it takes them to contribute it.

Another condition making it likely that artists will be hired for short periods at a time is an industry where popularity and acclaim are unpredictable from one work to the next. Selectors in areas ranging from scholarly book publishing to network television know that the value of particular artists may rise while the value of certain others may plummet. They realize that in hiring artists for short periods of time they may be forced to pay more money to highly desired recruits than if they locked them into permanent contracts. In many cases, though, this added expense is more than made up by the selectors' ability to choose creators quickly and efficiently so as to meet current fashions and production workloads.

The differences in the ways artistic personnel are brought into the creation of mass media materials suggests that they learn the routines of the organizations they work for in different ways. How does this process take place? Do different learning situations mean that some types of artists are trained in routines that legitimate the established institutions while others are not? Getting an answer means trying to understand how the **socialization** process works in freelance and staff hiring styles.

FREELANCE SOCIALIZATION IN MEDIA INDUSTRIES

Socialization stands for one of the most basic activities of humans in communities of other humans: learning to fit in. It is an active process that takes place through the normal course of daily life, in organizations as well as everywhere else in society. As people move through social situations, they and the people they work with negotiate rules about their interdependent behaviors (their **roles**).

Power—the use of resources to guide someone else's behavior—is a key ingredient in the process. People use resources (knowledge, money, willpower, status) to advance their positions within their organization, and they use their status to garner more resources. Increased power gives them increased control over the organization's activities.

These points apply both to craft and bureaucratic production styles. Socialization does take place differently, however, if an artist is a full-time, long-term member of a particular production firm than if he or she works freelance, getting recruited stop and go by various organizations. For permanently hired artists, much learning to compete for status and resources takes place in the "home" organization, where they work full time. Daily, the continuation of their employment and their promotability are judged primarily by people within that firm. Freelance artists, on the other hand, must not only convince the companies they work for at any point in time to hire them again, but must also develop power bases outside those companies to continue to generate more work in other places.

Doing that effectively generally requires admission to a community of similar artists—of writers, musicians, stunt actors, and the like. It is a community where a complex hierarchy, an elaborate system of contacts, and an often ritually prescribed gauntlet of competition strongly influence the artists' ability to enter production organizations, as well as the artists' market value.

The Case of the Hollywood Musician

Robert Faulkner refers to many of these issues when he writes about the Hollywood studio musician's search for freelance work:

> When he seeks to enter studio work, the unestablished recruit sees his career as contingent upon his ability to develop the proper web of contacts with those who control access to jobs. Sponsorship is the major social mechanism which brings him to their attention, allows him to establish a reputation as a solid and dependable performer, and prepares him to cope with the various pressures of the work itself. From the viewpoint of the sponsors, several important conditions must be attended to: (1) the young musician must be sponsored in such a way that established colleagues are not threatened with loss of power and prestige; (2) contractors and

leaders [who recruit and work, respectively, for the studio] must be convinced that the recruit is competent and can be depended upon; (3) the appropriate timing and pacing of the candidate's introduction into the division of studio labor must be determined and implemented; and (4) the candidate must learn the subtle etiquette of the referral system and, most importantly, that sponsorship is a process of reciprocal exchange.[28]

While Faulkner uses the pronoun *he* in describing the importance of sponsorship in craft socialization, the remarks apply equally to women. In fact, however, his comments reflect the fact that women have not broken into studio musicianship as easily as men. Part of the reason undoubtedly has to do with their difficulty in making the connections that Faulkner stressed are so important. Women and members of minority groups have long pointed out that in mass media industries, as in other areas of business, their inability to join the circles that provide connections and sponsorships have hindered them from being considered for attractive freelance jobs.

The reasons for not making contacts may have to do with activities that seem irrelevant to the talents required. Playing baseball or golf, drinking in bars, and gambling in card games have little to do with musicianship or any other artistic talents. Yet these friendly diversions serve to increase the chances of networking and cement professional relationships. People who cannot get in on them may well be left out of the sponsorship process.

A Delicate Power Struggle

Memoirs of artists from a variety of mass media industries confirm this view. The accounts agree that a delicate power struggle takes place over the recruitment of unknown freelance artists. The struggle involves people in a variety of roles. Chief among them are the neophyte artists themselves. They must learn to convince the right people of their talents. Among the most important of these people are artists and talent agents who already belong to an "inner circle." They decide whether to introduce particular artists or their agents to key selectors within production organizations. Those selectors—the people who do the hiring—themselves often expend great efforts to get to know new talent and help the best of it along. What constitutes "the best" of the new talent becomes part of the complex negotiations that go on within artistic circles.

The frequent pressure freelance artists feel to meet one another in order to get hired typically makes it hard for them to tell social occasions from business meetings. The sense of community then takes on overtones of both comradeship and social control. Ideas are shared, stolen, exchanged. Rules are formulated, changed, reformulated. Expensive deals are initiated by the shake of a hand.

Through it all, there is a strong awareness that at the end what counts is satisfying executives in the particular production firms who hire them for particular jobs. Musicians who will work at Fox have a keen idea what the person hiring there expects. That may be different from the approach the person hiring them at Universal takes. Thoughts of the audience—the people "out there"—fade in daily importance for the artists as the desires of production firm selectors become more immediately crucial.

TABLE 7.1. Top Films By Black Directors 1970–1989

In 1990 and 1991, more films with blacks as directors were released than during the entire previous decade. Low-budget (under $10 million) movies made by Spike Lee (*Do the Right Thing*), Reggie Hudlin (*House Party*), and Mario Van Peebles (*New Jack City*) turned handsome profits in domestic theaters, abroad, and in video.

The trend was not without controversy. Some critics were angry at the relegation of the black directors to the low-budget areas, while some exhibitors were frightened of violence that attended one of the films, Melvin Van Peebles' *New Jack City* in 1991. Nevertheless, after decades of being outside Hollywood's establishment, black filmmakers were beginning to move into it.

Below are the top films by black directors up to the watershed changes of the early 1990s, as defined by their *domestic* box office rentals. The meanings of abbreviations for the film distributors are as follows: Col, Columbia; Par, Paramount; U, Universal; WB, Warner Bros.; UA, United Artists; AA, Avco Embassy; and Fox, 20th Century Fox.

Title (Distrib, Year)	Director	Domestic Film Rentals
Stir Crazy (Col, '80)	Sidney Poitier	$58,364,420
Harlem Nights (Par, '89)	Eddie Murphy	31,500,000
Raw (Par, '87)	Robert Townsend	24,800,000
Bustin' Loose (U, '81)	Oz Scott	15,417,626
Do The Right Thing (U, 89)	Spike Lee	13,420,630
House Party (New Line, '90)	Reggie Hudlin	12,000,000
Let's Do It Again (WB, '75)	Sidney Poitier	11,800,000
The Last Dragon (Tri-Star, '85)	Michael Schultz	11,500,000
Sgt. Pepper's (U, '78)	Michael Schultz	11,414,534
Ghost Dad (U, '90)	Sidney Poitier	11,338,373
Which Way Is Up? (U, '77)	Michael Schultz	8,888,367
Car Wash (U, '76)	Michael Schultz	8,534,564
Jo Jo Dancer (Col, '86)	Richard Pryor	8,015,000
Mo' Better Blues (U, '90)	Spike Lee	7,877,926
Greased Lightning (WB, '77)	Michael Schultz	7,600,000
Beat Street (Orion, '84)	Stan Lathan	7,552,776
Uptown Sat. Night (NGP/WB, '74)	Sidney Poitier	7,400,000
Richard Pryor—Here And Now (Col, '83)	Richard Pryor	7,190,000
Shaft (MGM, '71)	Gordon Parks	7,067,825
Mahogany (Par, '75)	Berry Gordy	6,917,776
A Piece of the Action (WB, '77)	Sidney Poitier	6,700,000
Superfly (WB, '72)	Gordon Parks Jr.	6,400,000
School Daze (Col, '88)	Spike Lee	6,105,250
Under the Cherry Moon (WB, '86)	Prince	5,800,000
I'm Gonna Git You Sucka (UA, '88)	Keenen I. Wayans	5,345,000
Cotton Comes to Harlem (UA, '70)	Ossie Davis	5,145,072
Hanky Panky (Col, '82)	Sidney Poitier	5,120,000
Krush Groove (WB, '85)	Michael Schultz	5,100,000
Disorderlies (WB, '87)	Michael Schultz	4,400,000
Carbon Copy (Avemb, '81)	Michael Schultz	4,208,403
Sweet Sweetback's Baaadasssss Song (Cinemation, '70)	Melvin van Peebles	4,100,000
Penitentiary (Jerry Gross Org., '80)	Jamaa Fanaka	4,000,000
Scavenger Hunt (Fox, '79)	Michael Schultz	3,800,000
Shaft's Big Score (MGM, '72)	Gordon Parks Jr.	3,675,000
Three the Hard Way (AA, '74)	Gordon Parks Jr.	3,500,000
Buck and the Preacher (Col, '72)	Sidney Poitier	3,100,000
She's Gotta Have It (Island, '86)	Spike Lee	3,100,000

SOURCE: *Variety*, March 18, 1991, p. 108.

The extent to which selectors are willing to take chances on new artists varies. The editor of a "little magazine" might be willing to publish a writer who has not appeared in print before, but the editor of a large-circulation magazine will probably not. Established artists and agents learn these preferences and approach new artists with them in mind. In general, these inner-circle members are likely to feel ambivalent about suggesting new names. On the one hand, they know that selectors want to learn about good new faces and are likely to be grateful to artists who can help in this search. On the other hand, sponsoring an artist who fails can be worse than not suggesting someone at all. It must also be acknowledged that established artists sometimes see newcomers as threats to the current generation of talent.

Dues and Track Records

Fear of competition combines with awareness of the needs that selectors face in their production organizations. As a result of these conflicting tendencies, sponsorship systems tend to be conservative. The people involved take few chances on relatively few people. Artistic circles promote the idea that members should not suggest artists for important jobs unless they have **paid their dues** in related work and begun to establish **track records**. Someone establishing a track record is someone who, in paying dues by creating perhaps less widespread or expensive material, has shown that he or she is reliable, talented, and ready for more responsibility.

This emphasis on paying dues and accumulating a track record ensures that a relatively small number of newcomers will move through the recruitment gauntlet. That ensures that most members of the inner circles will continue to find jobs. The approach also tends to weed out artists who might disrupt a production organization's routine activities and profits. Word gets out among freelance artists as to what different companies expect.

The freelancers learn quickly that they will be rehired only if their talent comes without disruption in organizational routines and profitability. Selectors may reject even geniuses if they develop reputations for being inefficient. As a member of the Hollywood television community said in the late 1960s, "A script by a genius may contain a scene twenty-five minutes long that can't be edited." So, to avoid this trouble, a producer or story editor who recruits writers will look not for geniuses but for people "who can meet their deadlines and give him material that he can shoot in six and a half days, within his budget, and without any trouble [from network censors]."[29]

Proving oneself to an artistic community usually means becoming part of the community's establishment. When that establishment is involved in producing mainstream mass media materials, this system of craft socialization tends to act as yet another insurance that portrayals will not challenge the legitimacy of institutional structures. The legitimation operates even when the artists are members of a socially disadvantaged minority group, who might be expected to have some very different views from those who typically create content.

The Case of Minority Writers

A good way to illustrate this is to sketch the position that Hispanic, black, Native American, and Asian-American writers find themselves in when they want to work on those most mainstream of mass media materials, network television programs. The first point to note is that TV writers with these backgrounds are quite scarce. According to several industry sources, a large number of minority writers are interested in applying their skills to this lucrative field, but their efforts have been stymied.

In 1988 only 68 of 6,178 members of the Writers Guild, West, who found TV work in the previous year were members of above-mentioned minority groups. Another startling statistic is that in 1988 only 180 certified members of the Writers Guild, West, were minorities.[30] Putting the two findings together yields the conclusion that at least 112 supposedly qualified minority writers had not worked in TV for two years.

Undoubtedly, some of this exclusion of minorities comes from out-and-out bigotry on the part of people doing the hiring. However, as Len Riley found out when he investigated the subject of black writers for *Emmy* magazine in 1980, an important contributor to this situation is the craft system of recruitment with its key requirements of connections, paying dues, and track record.

These points are closely interwoven. As Riley notes, television producers must create new product each week. They can relieve the pressures caused by this tight time requirement by choosing experienced people they trust. A new writer's lack of experience might cause costly rewrite time. That makes it difficult for all writers to break into the business. However, the situation is more difficult for black writers, since they are very likely to find it harder to develop trusting contacts in the overwhelmingly white TV community. As Riley notes, the doors to employment may be declared open to minorities, but "the buddy system transforms them into revolving doors."[31]

Riley makes it clear that the few writers who do make it through the doors to write for TV pose no threat to the United States economic or political system, or its time-tested formulas. Comparing black and white writers, he found that "the two groups have similar educations, speak the same language with the same idioms, swing in the same economic and social mainstream. . . [and are] all products of the television generation."[32] Still, even those people cannot get the widespread work they want because they are associated with writing only about the African-American experience.

Having paid their dues in that area and developed track records for writing about blacks, the writers are then pigeonholed by artist-sponsors, talent agents, and production firm selectors. As literary agent Rick Ray put it, "They gain their reputation and credit getting the only assignments available [on shows about blacks]. Then an agent's told those writers are too ethnic for a project that doesn't require that background."

Ray's solution is a straightforward one:

> A dramatic writer's a dramatic writer, and it doesn't matter if he's green. If I were to encourage a new black writer, I'd say, "Sit down and write a good script that doesn't have a single black man in the damn thing. Make it a totally noncolor-oriented experience."[33]

It turns out that in the 1980s and 1990s several organizations within the television and movie industries were moving slowly to initiate minority writer training programs. The Writers Guild had one in which a minority writer was given a chance to work with an established writer who had been recommended by a producer "as someone in tune with that producer's series." According to a Writers Guild executive, the program allowed an inexperienced writer to be "shepherded through the system— from initial story conference through finished script—while deriving inside knowledge about a particular show."[34]

A somewhat different approach was taken by Walt Disney Studios, whose record of employment of women and members of minority groups in creative positions was one of the worst in Hollywood through the 1980s. Intent on changing that, a new Disney management started a fellowship program for African-American, Latino, Asian, and female writers. During 1990, 27 writers selected to take part in the program were culled from more than 2,000 applicants from around the country. Each was to be paid $30,000 over the course of the year. "We're trying to develop these writers into first-rate commercial screenwriters," said a Disney executive. She added that "each writer will be assigned to work with [an established] creative team."[35]

These people are given the opportunity of a lifetime. They are escorted into the inner circles and operations of an artistic community that they would find difficult, if not impossible, to enter under normal circumstances. With the opportunity comes a catch, however. While the recruitment programs open up the writing field to a broader area of society, they also ensure that the newcomers will fit into the TV's established approaches to reality. The writers are primarily encouraged to fit in. The programs are not designed to encourage new perspectives on life for the home tube or big screen.

Rather, it seems clear that they are set up to help the writers shed from the work ethnic identifications that might hinder them from working with fundamental formulas and activities that people in the industry share as standard. Certainly, this kind of educational system ends up ensuring the usefulness of those writers to production organizations in the way agent Rick Ray suggested. It also makes it quite unlikely that the writers will generate stories that expose unexposable tensions in society and seriously challenge the legitimacy of established institutional structures.

Staff Socialization in Media Industries

The same statement could be made about writers recruited to staff work, even though the process by which their socialization takes place is likely to be different from the one freelance writers follow.

A key difference between freelance and staff artists is the place they compete with other artists for privilege and prestige. Freelance artists fight for privilege and prestige both as full-time members of artistic circles trying to get jobs and as temporary members of production organizations. Permanently employed artists, on the other hand, need to direct much clearer attention to one source, the production organization that hires them on a long-term basis. A magazine writer working full time will probably direct less attention to cultivating job-related contacts outside his or her firm than will a freelance writer who is continually looking.

Still, it should be clear that the differences between the two types can be exaggerated. Staff magazine writers, public relations practitioners, advertising copy-writers, and journalists are by no means hermits confined to firms. They do get involved with members of their fields outside their organizations. These involvements contribute to their socialization in ways that parallel the influences that communities of freelance artists exert on their members.

Learning Outside the Organization

We can identify five particularly important avenues of involvement outside their current firm by bureaucratically employed artists:

School training

Job mobility

On-the-job contacts

Participation in professional associations

Subscriptions to professional media.

Not every avenue holds equal importance in every mass media industry. Specialized school training is important in cinematography, but not in casting. Moreover, the formal requirements for particular occupations may change over time.

Take United States journalists as an example. For them, college training has been gaining in importance. While journalists who started their careers before World War II tended not to go to college, by the early 1980s most working journalists were college-educated. Still, being college-educated did not necessarily mean choosing journalism as a major. In the early 1980s, a bit fewer than one of three working journalists actually majored in journalism.[36]

TABLE 7.2. From Whom Do Reporters Regularly Receive Comments About Their Work?

Source of Comment	Medium						
	Dailies	*Weeklies*	*News Magazines*	*Wires*	*Radio*	*TV*	*All Combined*
Superiors	29%	28%	41%	42%	49%	42%	35%
Peer	38%	41%	20%	42%	46%	45%	40%
Journalists outside own organization	15%	16%	17%	33%	17%	16%	17%
News sources	48%	32%	33%	21%	33%	36%	39%
Audience	48%	56%	40%	13%	50%	55%	49%
	N=254	N=118	N=30	N=24	N=90	N=288	N=589

Even people who work full time for mass media firms, as reporters typically do, discuss their work with people outside their organizations. Outside colleagues and news sources, in addition to audiences, may play a role in how a newsworker approaches his or her work.

The data in this table come from a nationwide study of journalists conducted during 1982–83. The percentages do not add up to 100 because respondents mentioned more than one source of comments.

SOURCE: David Weaver and G. Cleveland Wilhoit, *The American Journalist* (Bloomington; Indiana University Press, 1986), p. 79. Reproduced by permission.

Another mechanism for sharing journalistic values and routines outside their current news organizations is undoubtedly job switching. In their sample of 1,001 journalists of all kinds throughout the United States, David Weaver and G. Cleveland Wilhoit found that 75% reported working previously for one or more different news organizations. We might suspect that newspeople who work in different organizations tend to carry some of the practices and perspectives of their previous employment to their new situations.[37]

Another study found that journalists tend to conform to general trends of the labor force at large in terms of the timing of their job switches. That is, they more commonly change jobs during early rather than late stages of their careers. Therefore, as a journalist grows older, he or she is likely to be involved with counterparts from other organizations less through job switches and more through on-the-job contacts and participation in professional associations.

On-the-job contacts are very common among working reporters. Journalists from different papers meet one another often in the course of assignments. They file similar stories after viewing the same events, speaking to the same sources, reading the same press releases, and sharing ideas about it all.

The phenomenon has been called **pack journalism**, and it has been cited as a key reason for the similar subjects and angles that reporters covering the same event tend to use. Often, too, reporters get ideas of what is important by reading the same newspapers (*The New York Times, The Washington Post*) and tuning to the same wire services. Journalist Robert MacNeil made this point through an anecdote from his years working for NBC news:

In 1963, when Governor George Wallace tried to prevent the integration of Alabama's schools with his "stand in the schoolhouse door," NBC correspondent Tom Pettit, covering the story there, phoned a producer in New York, who started telling Pettit how to handle the story.
"There's a good story in *The New York Times* this morning," he said.
"We don't get *The New York Times* down here," Pettit said.
"Well, the night lead of the AP says—"
"We don't have the AP."
"Never mind. The UP's got a pretty good angle on it—"
"We don't have the UP either," Pettit said.
The producer said, "You don't have the UP?"
"No."
"You don't have the AP?"
"No."
"You don't have *The New York Times*?"
"No."
"Then how do you guys know what's going on down there?"[38]

Professional associations (such as the American Newspaper Association and the Association for Education in Journalism) and professional media (such as *Editor and Publisher,* the *Columbia Journalism Review,* the *Washington Journalism Review*) also tend to bring journalistic heads together on both large and small issues—from gossip about people in the field to canons of journalistic ethics to the proper way to cover certain types of events. Doing so, they provide umbrellas of public precedent to protect journalists who might feel forced by their organizations to carry out activities they consider unprofessional.

The trade magazines also reinforce the principles of objective journalism among the corps of journalists in mainstream news organizations throughout the country. They do it by singling out practices that deviate from journalistic norms ("The Failure of Network News," reveals the *Washington Journalism Review*), by showing how new problems can be corrected through accepted routines ("Sex in the News: Some Guidelines," suggests the *AP Log*), and by celebrating the accomplishments of those designated the best and brightest (through, for example, the Pulitzer Prizes).[39]

In-House Training

Despite the formal schooling, job mobility, the on-the-job contacts, the professional associations, and trade magazines, the primary training ground for journalists—in fact, the primary training ground for all bureaucratically employed artists—is the organization in which they work.

Learning what to do and how to do it is often the result of explicit instruction,

TABLE 7.3. What Professional Publications Do Journalists Read?

	Frequency of Readership		
Publication	Regularly[c]	Sometimes	Never
Editor and Publisher[a]	29%	34%	37%
Columbia Journalism Review	20	36	44
Quill	18	32	50
Washington Journalism Review	13	30	57
Journalism Quarterly	6	28	66
APME News	7	12	82
ASNE Bulletin	6	13	81
Journal of Broadcasting	6	11	84
Nieman Reports	3	17	81
Editor's Exchange	4	8	89
Wirewatch	4	7	89
ANPA News Research Reports	3	10	87
presstime[b]	3	8	90
Journal of communication	2	7	92
Newspaper Research Journal	2	8	91

[a]Of daily newspaper journalists, 39% regularly read and 40% sometimes read *Editor and Publisher*.
[b]A publication of the American Newspaper Publishers Association, *presstime* was a new journal at the time of interviewing. It is likely the journal is read by a larger audience now.
[c]Regular readership is defined as reading "almost every issue."

The reading of journals and trade publications is one way people who choose careers develop professional identities and keep in touch with what is going on within their field. This table reports the findings from a national sample of print and electronic journalists conducted in 1982–83. The researchers asked them about their use of 15 magazines and journals that are published on subjects having to do with news.

SOURCE: David Weaver and G. Cleveland Wilhoit, *The American Journalist* (Bloomington, Indiana University Press, 1986), p. 110. Reproduced by permission.

learning by example, and learning from mistakes. Organizational resources serve as incentives for the newsworkers. Superiors control resources—permissions, salary increases, special benefits, authority to make decisions independently—which they can release to artists carrying out "good" work.

Colleagues also control resources. They are likely to be more friendly and helpful to artists who do good work than to those who do not. Like every mass media artist, a journalist learns that good work means activities that fit nicely with superiors' policy regarding what the organizations should create and how it should create it. As noted, the norms that make up the basic policy of a mass media production firm have built into them perspectives on the the meaning of legitimate social power, authority, and justice, as well as on the limits to questioning them. By extension, then, a mainstream journalist who does good work legitimates the dominant institutional values of the society while doing it.

VALUE CONFLICTS

In his classic study of the way journalists learn their organization's policy, Warren Breed described many of the learning avenues just mentioned. He called what takes place "social control in the newsroom." By invoking the notion of social control, Breed raised another idea, the possibility of clashes between creators' personal values and the values of the organization as expressed in the firm's journalistic policy.[40]

Note that Breed's approach to the idea of journalistic policy is very different from the one used so far in this chapter. The two approaches do not contradict each other. They simply get at two different aspects of an organization's policy. One aspect, the one this chapter has dealt with until now, is the organization's **core policy**. Core policy represents the fundamental perspective that an organization follows regarding the legitimacy of dominant institutions in the society. The second aspect, the one Breed deals with, is the organization's **general policy**. General policy is built on top of core policy. It represents perspectives that the organization follows in portraying areas of life about which executives set guidelines.

An example might be in order. Take two newspaper firms that conduct their creative activities so as to legitimate society's institutions. They can be said to have common core policies. But, at the same time, say, one paper reflects a Democratic point of view, the other a Republican viewpoint. Also, one encourages investigative reporting, and the other does not.

Beyond their core policies, then, the news organizations diverge in their general policies through which they represent the world. As noted in Chapter 2, such variation among mass media production firms is typical. It stems from differences in the firms' environments and from differences in executives' perceptions of the environments. On the other hand, this chapter has shown that many firms are likely to share the same core policies even when they draw on, as different resources. One reason is that different as the resources are, they still come from mainstream sectors of society. A related reason is that in using the resources, the organizations often follow similar production routines—for example, routines that carry out the ideas of objectivity and formula.

The Commonness of Conflicts

Not much is known about the nature of value conflicts among creators in mass media organizations. It is probably safe to suggest, though, that most conflicts that occur relate to general policy, not to core policy. That conclusion seems logical in view of the high degree of selectivity that goes into the recruitment of creative personnel in any area of the mass media, whether mainstream or peripheral. The selectivity ensures that creators who are admitted to responsible positions have paid their dues, carved out track records, and plugged themselves into social circles that make acceptance of their production firms' core values simply part of their lives.

Herbert Gans was reflecting this idea when he wrote about the middle-class core values of the mainstream news organizations he studied. Gans noted that "relatively few journalists came from working-class homes, and those who did lost touch with their origins long ago."[41]

The same holds outside the mainstream. When William Bowman interviewed journalists from antiestablishment publications during the social upheavals of the early 1970s, he found that they shared negative opinions about the legitimacy of the dominant institutions. They welcomed radical change in the society at large. They viewed mainstream news media as "centralized managers of public consciousness . . . devoted to the preservation of the public order." And, consequently, they saw their role as "opposition to the status quo, with a readiness to question the legitimacy of any social institution and a commitment to involvement rather than detachment as journalists."[42]

Dealing with Conflicts

Regarding the value conflicts that seem to be more common—those involving a production organization's general policy—there is also little known across the broad range of media. In the news business, studies of journalists that ask their opinions about the news process are fairly common. Similar surveys of other industries are rare. Nevertheless, virtually every interview with a creator and every investigation of a mass media organization uncovers at least some clash between what a person thinks the production organization should be creating and what it actually is creating.

Warren Breed's concise summary of the options an artist has for reducing this value conflict is worth quoting.

> At the extremes, the pure conformist can deny the conflict, the confirmed deviate can quit. . . . Otherwise, the adaptations seem to run this way: (1) Keep on the job but blunt the corners of policy when possible ("If I wasn't here the next guy would let *all* that crap get through . . ."); (2) Attempt to repress the conflict morally and anti-intellectually ("What the hell, it's only a job; take your pay and forget it. . ."); (3) Attempt to compensate, by "taking it out" in other contexts: drinking, writing "the truth" for liberal publications, working with action programs, the Guild, and otherwise.[43]

What is most relevant here are the implications Breed's options hold for the mass media materials that firms create. It would seem that option 2 would lead to a near-apathetic approach to work. Consider a TV writer disenchanted with the refusal by series producers to accept scripts about psychological conflicts of the characters; all the producers want is "action." Working according to option 2, the writer may give up on that unusual theme and simply pitch ideas that he knows fit time-tested action-adventure or situation comedy formulas. That, he might say, is his meal ticket, the way to pay his mortgage. If he followed option 3, he would also generally follow the path of least resistance. At times, though, he might also contribute work to organizations holding policies more consistent with his values. So, for example, while proposing traditional plots to most producers, the writer might also try to persuade a prestige-oriented TV production firm that the network would be attracted to a special based on his "special" notion. Failing that, he might get a movie, novel, or magazine short story out of his idea.

Only option 1 would seem to encourage attempts to get around the expressed policy of a production organization. If he followed that line, the disenchanted TV writer would propose plots according to accepted formulas. However, in the scripts he might include one or two scenes where characters reflect the issues he really wanted to highlight. Of course, if he failed consistently to get scenes like that accepted, the frustration that comes from frequent failure might lead the writer to fall back on options 2 or 3.

One option Breed's list ignores is head-on confrontation on an issue with the help of other members of the organization. Written as they were during the 1950s, his "adaptations" do not take into account the increased tolerance for argumentation over policy that has taken place among executives of many mass media organizations since the 1960s. The rise of women's rights, gay rights, Hispanic rights, black rights, and other civil rights movements has led to the hiring of members of previously excluded groups by mainstream mass media firms. While those employees typically accept the core values of those organizations, they may quarrel at times with particular policies relating to the groups they most care about. Groups of similarly inclined employees may come together around those kinds of issues and complain to top management when they perceive a problem in the content produced.

University of Minnesota professor Leola Johnson has been studying such "coalitions" of black journalists in major newspapers around the United States. These loosely formed groups do not do much on a day-to-day basis, but spring into action when one of the members learns something about an impending management or editorial decision that might run counter to the interests of the group. Then, using the news firm's electronic mail system as well as the usual forms of talk, the members may plan ways to stop the actions they oppose. Johnson finds that the coalitions are often not terribly powerful within their organizations. In fact, members whom the top brass sees as too opposed to general policy are not promoted or given good salary increases—indications that they should, perhaps, leave. Still, she concludes that the coalitions do have an important role to play in sensitizing the editorial and business sides of mainstream newspapers, which are typically white and male, to black concerns.[44]

Power and Policy

In general, we can suggest that the more powerful a creator is within an organization, the greater will be that creator's ability to get around general policy—and to mobilize others around it. Bill Cosby's status as the executive producer and star of the most highly rated network TV show of the 1980s allowed him a lot of clout in network executive suites. Similarly, the huge worldwide profits that Sylvester Stallone's *Rocky* movies reaped gave him a lot of power to dictate changes on the set or in the script.

There *are* limits to how far these talents can deviate. Clearly, network executives would allow no one, not even Cosby, to embark on a series so expensive and obviously insulting to traditional tastes as to put the network's ability to turn a profit at risk. Moreover, executives in TV and the movies often peg the success of their creators directly to the formulas they have worked with, and no further. Stallone, for example, found it very difficult to convince studios and banks to invest in movies that allow him to depart significantly from his macho, Rocky-like image.[45] These kinds of roadblocks lead to much tension as creators try to convince the organizations in which they work to allow them to exceed normal boundaries of general policy.

Still, the possibility of getting around policy should alert us to the idea that executives in production firms do sometimes allow, even encourage, changes in the guidelines for creating mass media materials. *Twin Peaks, The Simpsons*, and *Living Color* are recent network television series that reflected alterations of this sort. This chapter has mapped the forces that discourage *basic* changes. Particularly in the case of mainstream material, those forces are powerful and deeply rooted. Moreover, they generally ensure that creators will select and shape output that legitimizes the ways institutions do things in the society. Within boundaries set by those forces, however, many modifications do occur, and they sometimes represent important shifts in the way mass media portray the world. Those changes, and the pressures that encourage and discourage them, are the subject for the next chapter.

NOTES

1. The literature on this topic is broad and deep. It ranges from writings on political economy and sociology of the mass media to linguistic and literary analyses of media text. For accessible summaries of key issues, see Michael Gurevitch, Tony Bennet, and Janet Woollacott (eds.), *Culture, Society, and the Media* (London: Methuen, 1982); John Fisk and John Hartley, *Reading Television* (London: Methuen, 1978); and Raymond Williams, *Marxism and Literature* (New York: Oxford University Press, 1977).
2. Jennifer Lawrence, "Newspapers: Hot Properties in a Cool Economy," *Advertising Age*, January 25, 1988, p. S14; and *The New York Times*, August 7, 1987, p. D3.
3. "Sony-Columbia Deal," *The New York Times*, November 8, 1989, p. C18.
4. Andrea Rothman, "Peter Callahan: An Acquiring Mind," *Business Week*, May 15, 1989, pp. 139–140.
5. Laurie P. Cohen, "Maxwell to Buy For $750 Million Dun & Bradstreet Airline Guides," *The Wall Street Journal*, October 31, 1988, p. B4.
6. David Lieberman, "Murdoch Adds a Few Megatons to His Arsenal," *Business Week*, August 22, 1988, p. 39.
7. Lorne Manly, "K-III Set to Close Murdoch Mag Deal," *Mediaweek*, May 20, 1991, p. 5.
8. Gaye Tuchman, *Making News* (New York: Free Press, 1978), p. 210.
9. Phillip Tichenor, George Donahue, and Clarice Olien, *Community Conflict and the Press* (Beverly Hills, CA: Sage Publications, 1980), p. 224.
10. Dan Schiller, *Objectivity and the News: The Public and the Rise of Commercial Journalism* (Philadelphia: University of Pennsylvania Press, 1981), p. 48.

11. Schiller, p. 48.
12. See Michael Schudson, *Discovering the News: A Social History of American Newspapers* (New York: Basic Books, 1978).
13. "Rap Band Members Found Not Guilty in Obscenity Trial," *The New York Times*, Oct. 21, 1990, p. 1.
14. George Gerbner, "Teacher Image in Mass Culture: Symbolic Functions in the 'Hidden Curriculum,' " in David Olsen (ed.), *Media and Symbols, Part 1* (Chicago: National Society for the Study of Education, 1974), p. 474.
15. See John Cawelti, *The Six-Gun Mystique* (Bowling Green, OH: Popular Press, 1975).
16. Robert Sklar, *Movie-Made America* (New York: Random House, 1975), p. 91.
17. Sklar, p. 91.
18. John W. C. Johnstone, Edward Slawski, and William Bowman, *The News People* (Urbana: University of Illinois Press, 1976), p. 26.
19. Johnstone et al., p. 28.
20. Amy Dawes, "SAG: Women Shortshrifted," *Variety*, August 8, 1990, p. 3.
21. Interview with Rodney Mitchell of the Screen Actors Guild, September 7, 1990.
22. William Bielby and Denise Bielby, *The Hollywood Writers' Report: Unequal Access, Unequal Pay* (West Hollywood, CA: Writers Guild of America, West), p. 1.
23. David Kissinger, "Blacks' Gains on TV Aren't Reflected in Networks' Executives Suites," *Variety*, May 30, 1990, p. 1.
24. David H. Weaver and G. Cleveland Wilhoit, *The American Journalist* (Bloomington: Indiana University Press, 1986), p. 54.
25. Johnstone et al., p. 100.
26. Robert S. Lichter, Stanley Rothman, and Linda S. Lichter, *The Media Elite* (Bethesda, MD: Adler and Adler, 1986).
27. Herbert Gans, *Deciding What's News* (New York: Vintage, 1979), p. 213.
28. Robert Faulkner, "Hollywood Studio Musicians: Making It in the Los Angeles Film and Recording Industry," in Charles Nanry (ed.), *American Music: From Storyville to Woodstock* (East Brunswick, NJ: Transaction Books, 1972), pp. 205–206. See also Robert Faulkner, *Music on Demand: Composers and Careers in the Hollywood Film Industry* (New Brunswick, NJ: Transaction Books, 1983). For a sociological discussion of job-seeking by actors in Hollywood, see Ann Peters and Muriel Cantor, "Screen Acting As Work," in J. Ettema and D. C. Whitney (eds.), *Individuals in Mass Media Organizations* (Beverly Hills, CA: Sage Publication, 1982), pp. 53-68.
29. Thomas Baldwin and Colby Lewis, "Violence: The Industry Looks at Itself," in George Comstock and Eli Rubinstein (eds.), *Television and Social Behavior*, vol. 1 (Washington, D.C.: United States Printing Office, 1972), p. 362.
30. Bielby and Bielby, p. 61.
31. Len Riley, "Writing for Television: All White or All-American," *Emmy Magazine* (Spring 1980), p. 39.
32. Riley, p. 34.
33. Quoted in Riley, p. 34.
34. Riley, p. 56.
35. "Disney Picks 27 for Fellowships," *Variety*, August 27, 1990, p. 22.
36. Riley, p. 54.
37. David Weaver and G. Cleveland Wilhoit, *The American Journalist* (Bloomington, Indiana: Indiana University Press, 1966).
38. Robert MacNeil, *The People Machine: The Influence of Television on American Politics* (New York: Harper & Row, 1968), p. 30. A particularly interesting discussion of pack journalism of a specialized sort is found in Sharon Dunwood, "The Science Writing Inner

Club," in G. C. Wilhoit and William De Bok (eds.), *Communication Yearbook* (Beverly Hills, CA: Sage Publications, 1981), pp. 351–360.

39. David Altheide, "The Failure of Network News," *Washington Journalism Review* (May 1981), pp. 28–29; and Lou Boccardi, "Sex in the News: Some Guidelines," *AP Log*, June 28, 1976, p. 1.
40. Warren Breed, "Social Control in the Newsroom," in Wilbur Schramm (ed.), *Mass Communications*, 2nd ed. (Urbana: University of Illinois Press, 1972), pp. 178–194.
41. Gans, p. 210.
42. Johnstone et al., pp. 176–177.
43. Breed, p. 193.
44. Leola Johnson, personal communication, May 1991. A classic study of conflicts that Hollywood TV producers experience in their interactions with network executives is Muriel Cantor, *The Hollywood TV Producer* (New York: Basic Books, 1971).
45. Cameron Smith, "Requiem for a Heavyweight," *American Film* (January 1990), p. 24.

CHAPTER EIGHT

Coping with Risks of Production

In terms of the production process, what is the difference between newspapers and soap? The question may spark some indignation. "How can the two be compared?" you might sneer. "Newspapers are symbolic creations. They tell us about crucial events in the life of humankind. Soap, on the other hand, is, well, simply an object."

Now, soap companies might object that calling one of their creations "simply an object" misses the profound importance that soap has had for civilization, both as a preventer of disease and as a symbol of cleanliness. Be that as it may, put aside any personal feelings you have about the relative social values of newspapers and soap, and you will see that making distinctions between soap and newspapers regarding *the process of production* is not as easy as it may at first seem.

For one thing, the makers of soap and the makers of newspapers are both involved in the business of creating products for a marketplace. Both types of organizations compete for resources with other organizations. And both need the personnel, the equipment, the distribution clout, the retail savvy, and the public acceptance to maintain a successful, growing, share of the audience. With little effort, in fact, the power roles that were laid out in Chapter 2 as a framework for the process of creating mass media materials can be altered to apply to the manufacture of soap or any other products.

In what way, then, *does* the making of soap diverge in concept from the making of newspapers? The answer lies in the need soap companies and newspaper companies have for **product innovation**. Innovation means changing something that exists, creating something new. It is a complicated word, since different people can have wildly different ideas of what "new" is, as later portions of this chapter will show.

Still, comparing soapmaking and newspaper publishing in terms of the frequency with which the firm needs to make changes in the product reveals a striking difference. Over a short period of time, turning out a brand of soap involves no innovation. Once the soap has been designed and the production process set up, the manufacturer will turn out exact copies of the bar day after day. Any changes made in the soap would come rather slowly, as a result of competitive pressures and careful research and development.

A newspaper publisher could not exist that way. Nobody would want to buy exactly the same newspaper day after day. Newspaper dealers and readers expect new stories with each edition. "New" events must be covered, "new" ads displayed, "new" crossword puzzles presented. Research and development might well plan long-term changes for the paper, but they could not take the place of the need the firm would have for a product that is altered daily.

It is this need for continual innovation, then, that sets newspaper publishers—in fact, all mass media producers—apart from the producers of other goods. Still, like their counterparts in other types of business, the leaders of mass media firms want to be able to turn out products that they *know* will be successful. In other words, while the fast-paced need for newness is part of their business, so is the need for predictability. The problem is that no matter how powerful the firm is in its marketplace, it is impossible to predict success with certainty if content has to keep changing. As a result, executives' impulses are often toward copying what was most recently successful, to continue doing what was done. Yet copying something exactly is not acceptable, and it is never clear what kinds of changes will be successful. Clearly, there is a good deal of tension here: the need for change and the desire for continuity often stand in conflict with one another.

The tension regarding continuity and change exists in one form or another among all creative personnel in all media industries. It exists among executives who choose creators as well as among the creators themselves. Newspaper editors and reporters, television producers and TV writers, book editors and authors all understand that they risk some degree of failure as a result of the inevitable balancing act they must maintain between a need to search for novelty and a need to limit that search in the interest of efficiency and success.

This chapter is about how people in mass media production firms perform that balancing act.

> What kinds of risks are mass media production organizations willing to take with their songs, movies, books, newspapers, TV shows?
>
> How do creators find out what degrees of innovation, what kinds of "newness," are acceptable to the mass media organizations in which they work?
>
> When are they and their organizations likely to be most daring, and why?

RISKS AND ROUTINES

One way people control their search for newness so they do not go dangerously off-track is to use routines. **Routines** are patterned activities that people learn to use in carrying out certain tasks.

Routines are connected to every aspect of our lives. We all have routines about the way we get up in the morning, do our bank statements, choose radio stations in our cars. Without routines we would have to think carefully about everything we do, all the time. Because of routines, we can develop solutions to certain problems in life that repeat themselves, and we can respond to those problems quickly, almost reflexively, next time they arise.

The usefulness of routines carries over to work. Individuals in organizations generally try to develop routines in their work. Routines give them predictibility and speed up certain repetitive aspects of the process.

Chapter 7 explored the way routines lead mass media creators to portray the world in a way that harmonizes with the established power structure in society. From that standpoint, routines reinforce institutional continuity; they block change that leaders of the society would consider fundamental. But routines play another role, too. They help creators to deal with the need for change in mass media without causing problems from the standpoint of either institutional acceptability or organizational profits. To understand how this works, it is useful to draw upon an area of sociology that investigates the strategies people in many different occupations use to cope with change.

Sociologist Everett Hughes suggested that the need for routines in work is particularly strong among physicians, fire crews, and other rescue personnel who deal regularly with what we would generally call emergencies. Hughes noted that when several unexpected events happen at the same time, those workers must be prepared to call quickly upon certain routines for getting the job done efficiently and in some order of accepted priorities. For example, the physician plays one emergency off against the other. The reason he can't run up to see Johnny who may have the measles is that a case of the black plague must take priority.[1]

RISKS, ROUTINES, AND NEWSWORK

Gaye Tuchman pointed out the relationship of Hughes' ideas to what she saw while conducting a scholarly examination of newswork. Tuchman observed that newsworkers confront "emergency" situations all the time. Dealing with unexpected events is a large part of their job. Every day journalists are required to go out into the world, confront a wide variety of ongoing activities, pay special attention to some of them, and write stories about them in time for deadlines.[2]

Clearly, there are risks involved in this kind of work. Say the journalist covered a riot. One danger is that the journalist might focus on the "wrong" aspect of the riot. That is, the journalist's editor might not consider that facet of the riot to be interesting news, or the editor might not consider it news at all. Another potential difficulty is that the editor might not not like the perspective the journalist used in writing about the disturbance. A third risk is that the journalist might write about someone taking part in the riot in a way that might place the newspaper in jeopardy of being sued for libel.

Yet another risk is that the journalist might be so worried about these and other problems of depicting the riot that he or she might not get the story completed in time to be placed in the next day's paper. That would mean one less story possibility for the editor, and one day of wasted salary from the standpoint of the organization's management. Multiply one reporter's problem by similar risks confronting all the journalists in the organization and it is clear the difficulty of getting a handle on what should be reported could have a paralyzing effect on a news organization.

Tuchman points out that journalists have solved the problem by shaping their work according to routines. The routines guide them toward dealing with the world quickly and acceptably. Take the problem of knowing what events make "interesting" news. Reporters constantly negotiate this point with superiors and colleagues within their news organizations. As a result, when they decide to cover something, they usually have a good idea that either (1) the people they work with would have done so too or (2) they can persuade those colleagues and superiors that they would have done it. So, for example, an argument between the President and the chair of Congress's Ways and Means Committee about a new tax bill would likely be recognized as news by everyone in the newsroom. Whether the event deserves to be highlighted on the front page might be a subject of argument among selectors in the newsroom.

The News Net

For efficiency's sake, newsworkers set up a news "net" to make sure reporters are monitoring areas of society that are likely to yield interesting or important news. These areas with the most potential (such as the White House and the Congress) will get the most coverage. Other areas will have sparser coverage, sometimes only with a "stringer" hired when something newsworthy does happen. And many areas will simply not be covered at all.

Laying out the news net means placing "news gathering" equipment and personnel in certain areas of the nation and the world and not in other areas. The way news organizations allocate resources reflects a complicated series of assessments that their executives make about news and society. For example, countries that the executives feel are most relevant to the political and economic concerns of Americans will get the bulk of attention. Ability to gain access to these countries is also crucial for coverage. American politicians' interests in discussing the issue is also a factor. The resulting picture will necessarily ignore large parts of the world while accentuating others. One result is a media "politics of death." Twenty Palestinians who are killed as the result of riots in occupied territories grab several days of coverage on TV and in newspapers, while the forced starvation of hundreds of thousands of people in the Sudan hardly makes it into the news net at all.

Inside the News Net

The creation of news nets is not, however, the only way journalists make the handling of changing events in their world more predictable. Once the news nets are established, newsworkers approach the events that take place inside them in patterned ways, too. They generate expectations of the way news events happen that allow them to decide immediately what human and technical resources to allocate to such events, and what difficulties they will face in doing so. Tuchman calls these expectations **typifications** and shows how they affect the way events get reported.

Take an event that a reporter typifies as **spot news**—that is, as news that is unscheduled and must be processed quickly. An example is the assassination of a national leader. Designating an event in this manner activates routines that place many other members of the news organization on special alert, call for use of the fastest communication technologies possible, and allow for the immediate reallocation of resources (such as pulling reporters off other stories) if and as necessary.

A contrasting case is when a reporter and her or his newsroom bosses typify a circumstance as **continuing news**. When journalists dub something "continuing news," they mean that it is important enough to be followed as a series of incidents that occurs over a number of days, weeks, or months.

An example is the movement of a specific legislative bill through Congress. Not every bill is defined as continuing news by reporters and editors. Some bills are noted only as they are being passed or defeated. Once a bill is defined as continuing news, though, reporters and editors get certain routines into gear.

For instance, seeing a bill's passage as a chain of events that is prescheduled means that the reporter should plan. That might involve conducting research on topics related to the bill, anticipating problems in covering debates over the measure, and taking corrective action in advance to avoid those difficulties. This sort of planning also ensures editors that acceptable news stories will be available at certain times even if enough interesting spot news stories do not materialize. It also enables editors to plan their use of resources efficiently. As Tuchman points out, "at the very least, it enables a city editor to state 'Joe Smith will not be available to cover spot news stories a week from Tuesday because he will be covering the Bergman trial!'"

Recording News Acceptably

Imagine that a journalist's place on a news net has reduced the problem of being where "interesting" news will happen. Imagine, too, that the reporter and others in the news organization have used typifications to decide their strategies for covering the event as well as the resources in time, people, and equipment they will need. The next problem is how to record that in ways that are acceptable to superiors by deadline.

Gaye Tuchman suggests that what journalists call "objectivity" comprises the most important set of routines journalists have developed to deal with this problem. There are many angles to the idea of telling a story "objectively."[3] As noted in Chapter 7, the most well known are use of the "inverted pyramid," reporting in the third person, not injecting personal opinions into the tale, concentrating on verifiable facts, quoting those who were involved, and presenting more than one side of the story.

Video journalists follow some camera-related objectivity rules that their print counterparts need not consider. For example, an objective way of presenting a person on camera is to place the camera at a level direction at the person, as opposed to a view from above or one made with special effects.

Journalists know very well that there are ways to express their personal biases while using the techniques of objectivity. Nevertheless, a story told in an objective manner carries with it an aura of political neutrality within the mainstream news business and throughout U.S. society. Consequently, a reporter using the objective method can be confident that his or her story will not run the risk of rejection by an editor as biased or libelous. More generally, in following the canons of objectivity, a reporter carries out an invaluable series of routines that help him or her frame events acceptably *and* in time for deadline.

COPING WITH DEGREES OF RISK

Gaye Tuchman's examination of the manner in which journalists cope with the risks of their occupation by using an elaborate set of routines alerts us to the roles that routines and risks play in different kinds of mass media organizations. To best understand the use of routines in several media contexts we must speak of the **degree of risk** that creators face.

Degree of risk refers to the extent to which creators in certain media sectors place themselves in **economic** and **political** jeopardy if they fail. Economic risk refers to the possibility of financial loss, while political risk refers to the possibility of losing government support. The higher the possible loss, the higher the risk. Potential for economic loss can be considered low when the amount of cash needed to generate an individual product is relatively small. The potential political loss is relatively low when the product is not likely to fall under the critical scrutiny of organizations that take on authority or public advocacy roles.

Potential for relatively high economic and political loss—and thus high-risk loss—can be found in situations where product development costs and public concern are high.

Contrasting TV and Books

Contrasting the creation of prime time network television programs with the creation of scholarly books can illustrate these points. A television program is a relatively high-risk venture both for its production company and for the network that orders the show. An hour of prime time typically costs a bit over a million dollars. The fee the network pays the producer for two airings of the program often barely covers expenses. Too, all expenses represent costs that cannot be changed whether the people who ultimately view the program in its first showing number ten million, thirty million, or fifty million. Production and network personnel get nervous when rating figures hover at the lower end of those numbers, since it means advertisers have not reached enough audiences by prime time standards.

Because the charges a network can demand of advertisers are based partly on the ability of the network's past and present shows to draw audiences, a low-rated program can cause network profits (and the production firm's reputation) to suffer. Bad ratings for one program might also have a negative impact on a network's profit picture that goes beyond a single time slot. The reason is that low viewership at one point in a network's evening schedule might reduce the audience flow across all that network's programs that evening.

Coupled to this high economic risk is the high political liability a prime time program can incur. Because of network TV's ability consistently to reach a very large number of U.S. households, including the children in those households, the medium draws the special attention of groups sensitive to what they feel are improper depictions of parts of society. Despite the enormous changes that have multiplied the number of media channels into people's homes, prime time commercial network TV is at the center of United States media in the eyes of government and public advocacy organizations. Consequently, there is a good chance a new prime time show would draw scrutiny by those groups.

While the creation of network TV shows lies at the high end of the spectrum of economic and political risks in mass communication, production of scholarly books, what are called **monographs**, is a low-risk venture on both counts.[4] Manuscript acquisition and book production costs for individual titles typically require thousands of dollars as opposed to tens of thousands, hundreds of thousands, and even millions in other media sectors. Book marketing, aimed mostly at libraries through librarians and academics, can often be carried out through mail-order ad campaigns that are inexpensive by media advertising standards.

Book reviews, which cost the price of mailing review copies, also can help the title along. These rather low economic costs go along with low political liability, since the output of scholarly publishers is generally considered by forces outside the academic world to be beyond the day-to-day concerns of ordinary citizens. Few advocacy groups exert energy against narrowly distributed scholarly tomes.

The degree of risk that creators in mass media production firms confront influences the way they orient their routines to cope with risk. In general, the greater the risk involved, the greater the chance that creators will do two things: (1) move toward creating highly predictable, highly patterned mass media content (**content-based techniques of coping**) and (2) develop routines that involve **administrative techniques of coping**, techniques that are not so obviously reflected in the content itself. When risks are not so great, creators will tend to orient their routines *only* toward administrative techniques of coping.

ADMINISTRATIVE TECHNIQUES OF COPING

Administrative techniques of coping are routines designed to help creators seek out information or personnel that will maximize the chance of a particular product's success. Two broad forms of these techniques stand out—the use of **track record talent** and the use of **market research**.

Track Record Talent

A track record talent is a creator who has a list of proved successes and a strong reputation in his or her field. The term was introduced in Chapter 5 to describe a way production executives try to convince client organizations such as networks (for TV production firms) and libraries (for scholarly books) that the material they have created is in sync with audience interests. Production firms assure their clients that if a creator has succeeded in the past with targeted viewers, listeners, or readers, there is a strong chance the audience will accept him or her once again.

Actually, production executives use track record talent to minimize a *wide variety* of risks they confront when trying to balance continuity and change in their materials. Not only is using the same (previously successful) authors considered by producers a way to be reasonably sure about an audience's reaction to new works, it often means it is a way to make sure the organization will be working with people who can be relied upon to complete the work within a particular time frame, in a way that will not cause the production firm unexpected financial or political grief. Celebrities who are difficult to work with may be hired despite the grief they create because of the cash they bring in. Even in these situations, however, familiarity with the "misbehavior" of needed artists will allow the company to arrange its activities to anticipate such problems and so minimize their costs.

It ought to be pointed out that not all track record talents are celebrities. Sometimes, such a person supports the main artists in one way or another, is known to relatively few among the audience for the product, but still has a reputation within the industry of being crucial to the artistic success of a product. An illustration in the television industry is the team of producer Gary Smith and director Dwight Hemion, known for over two decades for putting together successful musical variety programs. In the record industry, producers often develop reputations for eking out the greatest possible chance for success in a group's work through careful selecting, arranging, and editing of material. At different times, John Hammond, Leiber and Stoller, Shadow Morton, Phil Spector, George Martin, Hugh Padham, and Quincy Jones were considered among the ablest and most important record producers in the business.

A variation on this kind of behind-the-scenes use of track record talent is the employment of stars to search out and champion people with the potential for success. It happens all the time in scholarly book publishing. Academic publishing firms continually rely on well-known professors to point them toward new manuscripts. Sometimes, these **academic brokers** give their advice free. Sometimes the publishing company pays them for evaluating manuscripts, searching for potential authors, even serving as editors of series of books they feel warrant attention.

The executives' expectation is that a reputable scholar in search of manuscripts can plug into the various **artistic networks** discussed in Chapter 7 better than can company editors, who generally hold fewer long-term ties to the academic community. Publishers hope the result will be discovery of manuscripts that hold great chance for success. Too, they expect the academic brokers reputations' will rub off on the authors they back.

Market Research

Market research, the second administrative technique for coping, involves a very different approach to the problem of risk. While the search for track record talent looks to past success as an indicator of future profits, market research aims to probe the firm's contemporary environment for ways to reduce a product's chance of failure.

We can speak of two kinds of market research: (1) the kind that searches out ideas for new products, and (2) the kind that evaluates products that already exist or are under development. Both approaches were discussed in Chapter 5 in relation to a particular kind of market analysis, audience research. Audience research searches out attributes of the final consumers that can be targeted. By contrast, other types of market research survey the organizations that help bring the products to the consumers. That might involve checking with representatives from advertisers, exhibitors, or distributors about the kinds of material they would like to but cannot find.

In the trade book business such advice is often solicited by marketing personnel, who are constantly on the lookout for trends they can report to their editors. Particularly helpful is advice from major clients such as the B.Dalton and Waldenbooks chains. Their computerized sales lists often provide management with notions of book-buying trends that can lead to suggesting that book producers emphasize certain kinds of titles over others.

At times, trade publishing executives even ask the store executives' opinions about titles that are under consideration. Sometimes publishers' representatives show buyers from important store chains manuscripts of forthcoming books even before they are set in type. Most of this kind of activity is directed not toward changing the content of a book but toward judging its marketability and honing in on the number of copies to print. In certain special cases, however, a book publisher will contact some of its major clients to ask whether they would be interested in purchasing a title or **line** (a group of titles with a similar format) that is still only on the drawing board.

Marketing executives in Random House did that when they created their highly successful line of children's paperback picture books in the mid-1970s.[5] They wanted to release a line of colorful books based on characters that would be familiar to both children and their parents (for example, the Berenstain Bears and the *Sesame Street* cast), and at the same time far less expensive than most children's books sold in bookstores. Random House executives were concerned that bookstore chains might consider the books too inexpensive to warrant carrying them, since their profit margins would be so low. They also worried that bookstores would resist allowing Random House to install the freestanding racks that marketing executives had determined would be necessary to draw attention to the books. So, before proceeding with production, the executives showed some prototypes to executives of major bookstore chains. Only when they received enthusiastic reception and even a commitment by the chain to stock the books did the new "pictureback" line get the full go-ahead.

This cautious checking of development ideas that production personnel carry out with members of powerful organizations in their firm's environment goes on in virtually every sector of every mass media industry. The checking will probably not take place with respect to all products—for example, every issue of a magazine, every book title, every TV episode. It is likely to take place when new ventures demand long-term organizational commitment.

So, for example, when planning the introduction of a new monthly magazine, it is standard that executives contact major advertising agencies to gauge their interest in supporting the periodical. The same is true for college texts aimed at introductory courses. Because such products cost a lot to produce and must sell in large quantity to be profitable, research on the environment becomes crucial. Accordingly, write three observers of the industry,

> Major text houses know which texts have leading positions in the market and which lag behind: that X has 6 percent of the relevant market, and that Y has only 2 percent. Close analysis of the successful texts and the laggards alerts the publishers to the topics and styles currently in or out of fashion. Then instructors are polled about any changes they would like to see in a particular text. These data are supplemented by information gathered by college travelers. The final result is a text

that is usually bland and "safe" but profitable, since it has been tailored to the demands of the market.[6]

Note that here assessing "demands of the market" does not include polling the ultimate audience, the students. In text publishing, as in other areas of the mass media, production personnel understand that the all-important first step toward success is getting the material in front of the audience through organizational intermediaries. The college instructor serves as an agent for the bookstore. He or she decides on the titles students should buy and then presents the list to the store's purchasing manager. Students typically hold only a very indirect influence on the decision to change the required book in a course. If they find a text really boring or difficult to understand, classroom feedback might sway the instructor from assigning that book. Generally, the students have no choice but to read what is required.

CONTENT-BASED TECHNIQUES OF COPING

Sometimes, as in the case of certain introductory texts, market research results in the creation of material that is considered acceptable but not innovative by any of the parties involved. The same can be said for the use of track record talent. Still, these administrative techniques of coping also allow for situations in which a production firm's environment demands materials that are clearly considered different from what came before.

An example is scholarly book publishing. Academics place great emphasis on ideas that extend or challenge previous writings in interesting ways. Another example is works of individual fiction. Newspaper and magazine book reviewers often judge such works according to criteria that emphasize arresting style, a distinctive "voice," or fresh thinking about life.

The problem for production firm selectors who work in these areas of mass media is that while they must constantly look for materials that are substantially different from previous output, they still would like to reduce the risks involved in doing that. Administrative techniques help them. So, for example, fiction editors can contract with a John Updike, Norman Mailer, or Joyce Carol Oates to write novels, fully expecting that the book will get substantial serious critical attention in addition to earning money in advance of release through sale of the paperback rights.

There are, however, areas of the mass media where creators do not expect that forces in the environment require them to speak through an individual voice or emphasize unusual approaches to the world. In many areas of the mass media, too, creators perceive their responsibility as to simply make money and not at all to advance the cause of art. High-risk products such as network television programs and Hollywood movies tend to fit this description. Yet there do exist some areas of the mass media where product costs are low and individual artistry is still not emphasized. Paperback romances, pornographic novels, and pornographic films fit this category.

The point is that in most high-risk situations and in some low-risk ones, creators try to generate highly patterned mass media material that itself has a record of success. In these situations, administrative techniques of coping become only first steps in trying to reduce the risks of production. Risk reduction through previously tested **formulas** and **stereotypes** plays an important part as well.

FORMULAS AS TECHNIQUES OF COPING

Recall from Chapter 7 that formulas represent widely recognized principles for selecting and organizing material. There the concept of a formula was linked to the routines that make creators' work efficient and, at the same time, reflect the continuing legitimacy of the most powerful elements in the society. Here it is relevant to point out that formulas not only encourage broad boundaries of institutional **continuity** but also help creators efficiently come up with ways to change content within the boundaries. In this sense, formulas are risk-reducing approaches to content. They provide creators with patterned approaches to content that many parties within a mass media industry can agree contain the elements of success.

One of the tasks that creators in many media organizations set for themselves is to recognize the principles of particular formulas and the ways in which they can be varied profitably. Often, their understanding of formulas comes from immersing themselves in lots of mass media materials. Often, it comes from being part of an artistic community, listening to colleagues and competitors talk about the way they created certain movies, books, TV programs, magazine articles, or whatever.

It does not take much brilliance to uncover some of the basic components of a formula and ways in which it can be varied. Take, for example, a list of "the best" and "the worst" of just about anything that one can see just about anywhere. Such lists reflect a popular formula that magazine and book editors have been scrambling to copy and vary. *TV Guide's* J. Fred Muggs Awards and *Esquire* magazine's Dubious Achievement Awards are just two of the many lists that media organizations release.

A nonfiction formula is characterized by subject, point of view, and the sequence in which the argument is developed. Using these categories for orientation, we find that the basic concoction for nonfiction lists seems straightforward: Find a subject that many people confront every day—restaurants, the thought of moving to another city, the need for trivia in conversation, places to live—and find items to represent the best and/or the worst examples of that subject. Quantify the results if possible; a numerical index for the best and worst American cities, for example, is preferable to a simple listing. Stir well with a point of view that bespeaks absolute certainty and, often, urbane cynicism regarding the matter at hand. Bruce Felton and Mark Fowler describe the tone of many of these works when, in their introduction to *Felton and Fowler's Best, Worst, and Most Unusual*, they admit that

> The judgments offered in this book are both subjective and objective, rational and hysterical, serious and sardonic. In assessing their validity, you should bear in mind the words of Leonardo da Vinci: "I take no more notice of the wind that comes out of the mouths of critics than of the wind expelled from their backsides."[7]

This same "knowing" cynicism and sarcasm seemed to be the standard point of view writers took up in magazine discussions of political and social trends during the 1980s and early 1990s. The approach did not apply to nonfiction formulas that reflected more personal aspects of the target audience's life. How-to articles on cooking, building, repairing, and gardening, and articles on coping with divorce, unemployment, sex, parenting, and dating seemed to require a more empathic tone.

A still different tone seemed to belong in another formula, the Hollywood star's autobiography (often written with someone else). Whether such works carried insight or just vanity, it seemed de rigueur for them to fit the following mold. Start with a key incident from the height of the star's career. Slowly ease back toward stories of birth and upbringing. Then move the story along through tragedies and disasters to triumph or, at least, to a better world today.

Formulas exist in fiction as well. Fiction formulas can be characterized in terms of setting, character types, and patterns of action. In Chapter 7 the Western was discussed as an example of a storytelling form that has built into it enduring American values, such as the importance of masculine individualism and the correctness of using force to solve problems. Here it is relevant to stress that the Western—as well as the detective, superhero, family situation comedy, and other formulas, for that matter—is useful to production personnel because it helps reduce the risk of change. Popular formulas provide creators with comfortable molds that suggest how stories can be altered while the essence of characterization, setting, and even patterns of action remain the same.

The Western Formula

John Cawelti, who has studied the Western formula, provides a good example of this standardized approach to change. The plot of a Western, Cawelti says, comes from having three central character types bump up against one another within a predictable setting.

That setting is some kind of frontier, some "meeting point between civilization and savagery."[8] The central character types are townspeople, who are the agents of civilization; the savages or outlaws, who threaten this first group; and the heroes (often cowboys), who are above all "men in the middle." That is, they possess many qualities and skills of the savages but are fundamentally committed to the townspeople. Cawelti notes that this three-way tension that is built into the Western points the way toward concocting a variety of plots.

> For example, the simplest version of all has the hero protecting the townspeople from the savages, using his own savage skills against the denizens of the wilderness.
>
> A second, more complex, variation shows the hero initially indifferent to the plight of the townspeople and more inclined to identify himself with the savages. However, in the course of the story his position changes and he becomes the ally of the townspeople.
>
> This variation can generate a number of different plots. There is the revenge Western: hero seeks revenge against an outlaw or Indian who has wronged him. In order to accomplish his vengeance, he rejects the pacifistic ideals of the townspeople, but in the end he discovers that he is really committed to their way of life (John Ford's *The Searchers*). Another plot based on this variation of the character relations

is that of the hero who initially seeks his own selfish material gain, using his savage skills as a means to this end; but, as the story progresses, he discovers his moral involvement with the townspeople and becomes their champion (cf. Anthony Mann's film *The Far Country*).

It is also possible, while maintaining this system of relationships, to reverse the conclusion of the plot as in those stories where the townspeople come to accept the hero's savage mode of action (cf. John Ford's *Stagecoach* or, to a certain extent, Wister's *The Virginian*). A third variation of the basic scheme of relationships has the hero caught in the middle between the townspeople's need for his savage skills and their rejection of his way of life. This third variation, common in recent Westerns, often ends in the destruction of the hero (cf. the films *The Gunfighter* or *Invitation to a Gunfighter*) or his voluntary exile (*Shane, High Noon, Two Rode Together*).[9]

Formulas in Pornography

Clearly, combining the three elements of the Western formula in different ways can yield a multitude of "new" stories. Cawelti points out that the people producing the Western in any mass medium are quite conscious of the formula. In some mass media organizations, though, selectors are not content to rely on their artists to pick up the most effective approaches to certain kinds of material. Here, from the mid-1970s, are notes by a writer of pornographic novels on the approach his publisher expected him to take:

> It [the pornography] is aimed at the male market and is written to formula. There are seven basic story categories: incest (the single most popular genre), lesbianism,

---

TABLE 8.1. Milestones in the Evolution of TV's Doctor Show Formula

---

A popular culture formula is dynamic. That is, its setting, characters, and patterns of action change over time.

Below is one analyst's list of the TV series that marked significant changes in the doctor show formula. For a look at the forces behind the changes in the formula, see Joseph Turow, *Playing Doctor: Television, Storytelling, and Medical Power* (New York: Oxford University Press, 1989).

- *Medic*: NBC, 1954–56; starred Richard Boone
- *Doctor Kildare*: NBC, 1961–66; starred Richard Chamberlain, Raymond Massey
- *Ben Casey*: ABC, 1961–66; starred Vince Edwards and Sam Jaffe
- *The New Doctors* (segment of *The Bold Ones*): NBC, 1969–76; starred E. G. Marshall and David Hartman
- *Marcus Welby, M.D.*: ABC, 1969–76; starred Robert Young and James Brolin
- *Medical Center*: CBS, 1969–76; starred Chad Everett and James Daly
- *Emergency*: NBC, 1972–77; starred Robert Fuller and Bobby Troup
- *Medical Story*: NBC, 1975–76; anthology series (no continuing star)
- *Quincy, M.E.*: NBC, 1976–83; starred Jack Klugman
- *Lifeline*: NBC, 1978; documentary (no stars)
- *Trapper John, M.D.*: CBS, 1979–85; starred Pernell Roberts and Gregory Harrison
- *St. Elsewhere*: NBC, 1982–89; starred an ensemble cast of numerous actors.

SOURCE: Robert S. Alley, "Medical Melodrama," in Brian G. Rose (ed.), *TV Genres: A Handbook and Reference Guide* (Westport, CT: Greenwood Press, 1985), pp. 73–90.

Lolita plots, domination, older woman/younger man, career girl plots, and straying from the marriage.

The publisher's style sheet advises: "The plots of our stories should involve a sexual problem of some sort . . . the *dénouement*, a solution. How the characters get there is what it's all about. . . . What this means is that we don't want detective stories with a lot of sex [or] Westerns with a lot of sex. . . . We want explicitly written, highly erotic novels of real people's experiences. . . . We CANNOT consider the following themes: male homosexuality, child molestation, bestiality, excretion, violent sadomasochism, or murder as part of the sex act. ALL CHARACTERS INVOLVED SEXUALLY MUST BE AT LEAST FIFTEEN YEARS OF AGE.[10]

Formulas in Music

The discussion of fiction formulas has revolved around books and movies until now. But the use of formulas has long been a standard way to reduce risk in many areas of the mass media. American music publishers in the 1860s and 1870s, for example, tended to divide the types of songs they accepted into eight categories: love, family, reform or moral, religious, comedy, minstrel, tragedy, and topical. By helping them evaluate ups and downs in the sales of particular categories of sheet music (the major way songs were sold back then), the classification provided publishers with a way to choose songs and songwriters who matched the trends of the day.

Since that time, the mainstream music world has become much more stratified. Some areas, such as parts of the progressive rock scene, place greater emphasis than others on ideosyncratic artistry and unusual approaches to the world. We would expect that in such areas producers would turn primarily toward administrative routines (in particular, the consideration of track record), not formulas, to cope with risk. There are, however, many areas of the music industry where selectors and artists try to spring toward success with minor variations on tried-and-true approaches to words and music.

This is particularly the case with respect to singles. Singles are typically songs that recording companies release with the hope they will get aired on radio stations with formats that play hits. Video versions of singles are directed toward the MTV cable music video channel and its broadcast TV imitators. Because of the importance of singles for album sales in many cases, and because of the high risk of failure in getting airplay (most releases do not get significant exposure on radio), singles will often be the most formularized of all cuts on an album.

Record producers are well aware that program directors and music hit predictors receive an enormous number of songs to sample. As a result, they sometimes listen to only the first three seconds of a song to decide whether they should select it as "hit bound." Formulas are considered crucial; the artistry is in creative variation of the formula so it appears different and compelling. Here is part of the way Clive Davis, a powerful executive at CBS and then Arista records from the 1960s into the 1990s, has described the general singles formula:

A hit single is a question of musical ingredients—they've all got to complement each other. You start with the "hook," a basic repetitive melody or lyric line that grabs hold of the listener. In lyrics, the safest theme, naturally, is love or lost love. . . . Ideally, the lyric *and* melody combine within the hook to make this line something nearly impossible to forget. But hooks come in all sorts of rhythmic, melodic, and lyrical shapes and sizes. . . . When I hear a song, my mind works like a computer. The "hit" ingredients register in it, and they are shunted off to various preprogrammed compartments for analysis. Voice is terribly important. Certain kinds of voices *don't* lend themselves to Top Forty play.[11]

Formulas in Series and Serials

Two ideas that creators generally recognize as related to the formula are the **series** and the **serial**. A series is a collection of individual products (books, magazines, movies, TV shows) that have the same key characters moving through separate adventures in each product. A bit different is the serial, wherein the same key characters move through continuing episodes of adventures across the products; the serial is a kind of chapter play.

We see series and serials all the time. The *Peanuts* newspaper comic strip is a series, while the *Doonesbury* strip is a serial. TV's *Star Trek: The Next Generation* is a series, while the *Star Wars* odyssey is a serial. Interestingly, during the past decade, the concepts of series and serials have been intermixed in television. *L.A. Law* provides an example. It can be called a series, since most of what happens in each episode begins and ends with the episode. Typically, however, one subplot continues across a number of episodes. Writers and producers call this serialized part of a series an **arc**.

It is easy to understand why creators in high-risk media industries consider series and serials useful to their work. For one thing, start-up costs of episodes in an ongoing series or serial are lower than those in a new project. Continually thinking up new heroes, villains, and ways to inject life into old formulas is more time-consuming than tinkering with one basic set of characters, setting, and plot pattern. In television, having the same actors, crew, locations, and props for every episode makes production a lot less expensive than producing a new program from scratch every day.

Sometimes, stand-alone products do so well that creators cannot resist the opportunity to turn them into series. In 1950, Universal Pictures' *Francis the Talking Mule*, based on a book by David Stern, was a runaway success. That movie begat *Francis Goes to the Races* (1951), which begat *Francis Goes to West Point* (1952), which begat *Francis Joins the Wac* (1954), which begat *Francis in the Navy* (1955), which begat *Francis in the Haunted House* (1956). The first five films were directed by Arthur Lubin, who went on to create a similar TV series called *Mr. Ed*, about a talking horse.

There is an ironic flip side to the efficiency and risk reduction possibilities in series and serials. When the cost of several episodes must be allocated in advance, failure might involve much greater cost than would any particular product that stood alone. That is the problem television program producers face on a continual basis. When a series "hits," it can be a huge, consistent moneymaker for many years, but when it fails badly, the cash and airtime already committed to it can drain network resources badly. Consequently, the commercial networks have evolved an elaborate chain of strategies to develop, test, and schedule series so as to maximize their chances for success.

When searching for a series idea, production firm executives and their network counterparts typically say they look for material that is "refreshing," "exciting," and "different." At particularly honest moments, many also admit that the best ideas they find will echo material already popular on TV or in other media. This contradictory approach leads them to combine a strong reliance on popular formulas with attempts to find interesting variations on those formulas that will stand up over many episodes.

Consider the cycle of prime time TV situation comedies that worked off the formula of mischievous but basically good kids in a high school. *Head of the Class,* the lone entry of 1987, was joined in 1988 by *A Different World,* which, while it took place in a college, nevertheless used many of the character types and plot patterns of the high school formula. They were joined in the 1990–91 season by *Ferris Beuler* and *Parker Lewis Can't Lose.* The same year, more serious spins on the high school

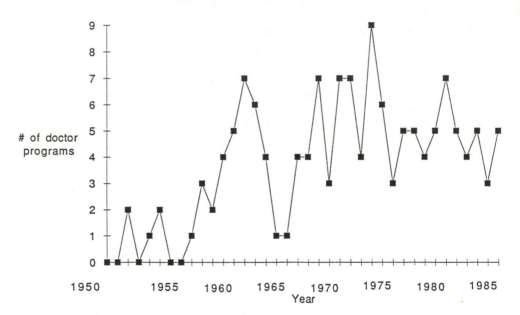

CHART 8.1 The Popularity Cycle of a TV Formula

Like all forms of popular culture, formulas on network TV go through times when they are used often to times when they are used little. The reasons are complex and reflect a variety of considerations relating to the industry as well as audience interest. In any event, TV producers profit most when they work up the "right" formula in the "right" way at the "right" time. The trick, of course, is knowing when and what "right" is.

As an example of a formula's cycle of popularity with network programmers, consider the changing number of doctor series aired from the 1952 through 1989 TV years. A TV year runs from September, when shows debut, to the following September. The 1952 TV year, therefore, spans from September 1952 through August 1953.

SOURCE: Joseph Turow, *Playing Doctor* (New York: Oxford University Press, 1989), pp. 277–279.

setting came in *Hull High* and *Beverly Hills 90210*. Some of these shows did better than the others in the ratings. Being part of a cycle does not guarantee success.

The Formula in History

The search for the right formula-based material with staying power to make a successful series is not new with television or the movies. The series was a clear part of American popular theater from the early 1800s, and it was used extensively in magazines and books of that century.

Here, for example, is a fascinating letter that Ormond Smith, head of the powerful Street and Smith publishing firm, wrote to Gilbert Patten. At the time, the 1890s, Patten was a well-known writer of juvenile dime novels. Smith's purpose was to hire Patten to write a new series (or "library") of juvenile books for the company:

December 16, 1895
Gilbert Patten, Esq.,
Camden, Maine.

Dear Sir:

Replying to your favor of December 13, at hand today, we beg to state that the material of which we wrote you in our last letter is intended for a library which we propose issuing every week; something in the line of the Jack Harkaway, Gay Dashleigh series which we are running in *Good News* and the *Island School* series, all of which are expressed to you under separate cover, the idea being to issue a library containing a series of stories covering this class of incident, in all of which will appear one prominent character surrounded by suitable satellites. It would be an advantage to the series to have introduced the Dutchman, the Negro, the Irishman, and any other dialect you are familiar with. From what we know of your work, we believe you can give us what we require, and would be pleased to have you write one of these stories at once. Upon receipt of it, if satisfactory, we will be prepared to make a contract with you to cover twenty thousand words weekly for this library and a sufficient number of *Good News* stories to keep them running in the columns of *Good News*, if you believe you can turn out this amount of work.

It is important that the main character in the series should have a catchy name, such as Dick Lightheart, Jack Harkaway, Gay Dashleigh, Don Kirk [characters in previous series by Patten], as upon this name will depend the title for the library.

The essential idea of this series is to interest young readers in the career of a young man at a boarding school, preferably a military or a naval academy. The stories should differ from the Jack Harkaways in being American and thoroughly up to date. Our idea is to issue, say, twelve stories, each complete in itself, but like the links in a chain, all dealing with life at the academy. By this time the readers will have become sufficiently well acquainted with the hero and the author will also no doubt have exhausted most of the pranks and escapades that might naturally occur.

After the first twelve numbers, the hero is obliged to leave the academy, or takes it upon himself to leave. It is essential that he should come into a considerable amount of money at this period. When he leaves the academy he takes with him one of the professor's servants, a chum. In fact, any of the characters you have introduced and made prominent in the story. A little love element would not be amiss, though this is not particularly important.

When the hero is once projected on his travels there is an infinite variety of incidents to choose from. In the *Island School* series, published by one of our London connections, you will find scenes of foreign travel, with color. This material you are at liberty to use freely, with our hero as the central character, of course, and up-to-date dialogue.

* * *

This letter will, of course, be held as confidential. After you have fully examined the *Island School* material, kindly return to us.

Yours truly,
Ormond Smith[12]

STEREOTYPES AS TECHNIQUES OF COPING

Smith's reference to "the Dutchman, the Negro, the Irishman" brings up another content-based device creators of mass media material use to cope with risk: the **stereotype**. A stereotype is the portrayal of an identifiable social group in such a way that members of that group are consistently invested with certain personality characteristics and social activities. The Dutchman (actually, *Deutschman*, the German), the Negro, and the Irishman were butts of comedy in many turn-of-the-century novels, magazines, films, and recordings.

Much has been written on the nasty characterizations that racial, ethnic, and other groups in society have suffered in popular culture through the years.[13] Chapter 7 noted that such portrayals picture those groups' position in society from the vantage point of elites who want to retain power. Here the purpose is to point to an important *organizational* reason for the perpetuation of stereotypes. Simply put, stereotypes are vehicles for getting work done quickly, efficiently, and with a lower risk of individual failure than would otherwise be the case.

Not all stereotypes are useful. Today's mass media creators recognize that the clout of various public advocacy organizations, along with social changes, have turned some social types into liabilities. In the commercial television networks, censors routinely review scripts and completed programs to guard against consistently negative portrayals of individuals belonging to certain groups. African Americans, Native Americans, Hispanics, homosexuals, senior citizens, and women have made the censors particularly sensitive to certain injustices during the past several years.

Despite the sensitivity and the pressure, many studies show that stereotypes are alive and kicking on TV and in other mass media. Often the offense is more subtle than was true before the advocacy groups complained. TV creators may, for example, move away from depicting Hispanics as drunk and lazy, but they may still show almost all of them as ignorant and holding low-paying jobs. Or the creators may choose to exclude them totally from the scene, even when the plots take place in Los Angeles, where Hispanics comprise a large percentage of the population.

Exclusion has often been the fate of Mexican Americans, Native Americans, and homosexuals. When a social group does not have a strong advocacy body in its corner—as, for example, in the case of gypsies and, until recently, Arabs—media creators feel no need to be subtle. Using these groups as well as Nazis and extra-

---

Talking Point 8.1   Good Girl/Bad Girl Stereotypes

Stereotypes are sometimes difficult to notice, since they are so much a part of people's thinking about the world; we accept them as "common sense." To get sensitized to stereotypes at work, it sometimes pays to go back in time and look at the way groups in society were portrayed. Strange patterns then jump out at you.

Consider, for example, the following descriptions of women from two Western novels by Zane Gray that were written in the first quarter of the twentieth century. The first, out of *The Lone Star Ranger*, describes the best kind of women. The second, of Ruby the dance hall girl in *The U.P. Trail*, describes a dangerous, bad woman. As historian Russell Nye notes, such descriptions were common in the early 1900s:

> He stood holding her tight, with the feel of her warm, throbbing breast and the clasp of her arms as flesh and blood realities to fight a terrible fear. He felt her, and for the moment the might of it was stronger than all the demons that possessed him . . . , and now, with this woman in his arms, her swelling breast against his, he bent under the storm of passion and joy. . . . Their lips met in their first kiss. The sweetness, the fire of her mouth seemed so new, so strange, so irresistible. . . . She met him half-way, returned kiss for kiss, her face scarlet, her eyes closed, till her passion and strength spent, she fell back upon his shoulder. Presently she recovered, and she only drew the closer, and leaned upon him with her face upturned. He felt her hands on his, and they were soft, clinging, strong, like steel under velvet. He felt the rise and fall, the warmth of her breast. A tremor ran through him.

> Her arms were bare, her dress cut very low. Her face offered vivid contrast to the carmine on her lips. It was a soft, round face, with narrow eyes, dark, seductive, bold. She tilted her head to one side and suddenly smiled at Neale. It startled him. It was a smile with the shock of a bullet. The girl took hold of the lapels of his coat. She looked up. Her eyes were dark with what seemed like red shadows in them. She had white teeth. The carmined lips curled in a smile—a smile impossible to believe, of youth and sweetness, that disclosed a dimple in her cheek. She was pretty. She was holding him, pulling him a little toward her.
>
> "I like you!" she exclaimed.
>
> He felt her, saw her as in a dream. Her face possessed a peculiar fascination. The sleepy seductive eyes; the provoking half-smile, teasing, alluring; the red lips, full and young through the carmine paint. All of her seemed to breathe a different kind of power than he had ever before experienced—unspiritual, elemental, strong as some heady wine. She represented youth, health, beauty, terribly linked with evil wisdom, and a corrupt and irresistible power, possessing a base and mysterious affinity for man. The breath and the charm and the pestilence of her passed over Neale like fire.

SOURCE: Russel Nye, *The Unembarrassed Muse: The Popular Arts in America* (New York: Dial Press, 1970), p. 296.

---

terrestial creatures, producers can dip into a storehouse of unfavorable cultural images—foreign, secretive, alluring, dangerous, deceptive—to evoke certain moods and accomplish certain plot goals.

Stereotyping is not limited to ethnic and racial groups. Certain physical characteristics and occupational labels are quite often associated with personality characteristics and social activities. Overweight people, short people, people with glasses, blue collar workers, private detectives, police, physicians, nurses, high school teachers, college professors—these and other labels often ignite standard characterizations on television, in movies, and in formula-based paperbacks.

In the early 1990s, commercial television's weekday afternoon and weekend cartoons for children were brimming with stereotypes regarding the way characters looked and sounded. People with messy hair and angular, lined faces were almost always bad while people with neat hair and smooth, round faces were almost always good. Glasses implied nurdiness. And deep, raspy voices in men as well as high, shrieky voices in women were often associated with evil.

Casting

The use of stereotypes extends to **casting**, the choosing of actors for shows. The casting of even small parts—roles where actors say little—could be time-consuming if casting directors worked hard with producers, directors, and agents to think about the social and dramatic implications of their choices every time they hired people for an episode. Instead, they have developed shared beliefs about what types of people the audience will find credible in what roles.

They justify these "clichés" (as they call them) by saying they are used both to save time and to help the "look" of the show. Small parts, they stress, should function like moving wallpaper. While these are crucial for populating the program, they should not not call attention to themselves, since that would mislead viewers into believing small parts are relevant to main elements of the plot. Here, for example, are comments by a producer in the late 1970s about the approach people in TV hold toward choosing certain types for small parts:

> You have to recognize what the audience can buy instantaneously. Unless it's a plot point. Because if you have somebody walk in as a police officer, the audience should [snaps fingers] accept him as a police officer. So you look [at the script to find out] where he is walking. I mean, you could have a little more effeteness in a policeman in Beverly Hills than you could in Watts. By a damn sight, you would be far more likely to accept a white or Chicano policeman in Beverly Hills than a black policeman. . . .
>
> Why should I start arguments in a living room or den between husband an wife? I mean, why make a point out of something that's not a point? Carpenters are male. Telephone operators are female. Now, there are a lot of male telephone operators now. But not enough so that when you say "telephone operator," the immediate thought isn't female.[14]

Stereotypes such as these become part of the routines of casting so that the people involved may follow them even when they do not agree they are necessary. Talent agents, for example, know the "rules" of social typing when they scan TV scripts or script summaries called "breakdowns" looking for parts for their clients. They are reluctant to break those rules. The following interview of an agent about age considerations in casting show how adherence to generally perceived rules often discourages nontraditional suggestions.

> AGENT: Oh, they list [age in the script and breakdown] and they sometimes stick to it and sometimes don't. What I do when I make up my list [of actors to be sent to the casting director]—if they say 30, I'll give them anything from 25 to 35.
>
> INTERVIEWER: Do you find most age requests stop at 35?

AGENT: For men, there are a great number of roles over 40. Women over 40—not many, obviously.

INTERVIEWER: Why is that?

AGENT: Well, there's just not that much call for them. Because of the story lines. The story lines are always dealing with heavies, with troubles in situations. It's always men involved. Whether he's a banker, a doctor, or a lawyer, a Mafia chief, whatever.

INTERVIEWER: Under what conditions would you suggest a woman if the breakdown said "banker"?

AGENT: I wouldn't, because it would say "he."

INTERVIEWER: Do you see "he" as necessarily denoting a male?

AGENT: Oh sure; I even look down [the breakdown page] for the "he" or "she" to see which [part] starts with "he or "she." They say "all roles will be considered regardless of ethnic group, sex, et cetera." That's baloney. Well, sometimes you can take a role and if it's not in the script you can turn it from white to black.

INTERVIEWER: Will unusual casting notions affect your standing with casting directors?

AGENT: You don't send them in. What I do, if I have an offbeat idea, to protect myself. You say, "You know, I got an idea; you probably won't even like it. It's really off, far out. . . ." And you protect yourself. If they like it—"terrific!" If they don't, "Yeah, it really was offbeat."[15]

FORMULAS AND ARTISTIC PERSONALITY

Despite recognition of the importance of standard approaches to characters, settings, and plots for managing risks in the creative process, mass media creators often try to establish their own artistic personalities within the formulas' boundaries. Horace Newcomb and Robert Alley point out, for example, that while television producers are "clearly aware of the limitations" the industry imposes on them, they "work within, around, and through them to achieve creative goals.[16]

Creators who become successful members of their artistic communities might develop reputations for working in a particular style or reflecting a particular view of life. In TV, Marcy Carsey, Steven Bochco, Steven J. Cannel, Linda Bloodworth-Thomas, Barney Rosensweig, Donald Bellasario, Fred Silverman, David Lynch, David Wolper, and Herbert Brodkin are just a few examples of executive producers whose programs reflect a particular style or view of life. These are individuals whose approaches resonated with the needs of their industry at the time they worked. Most, such as Silverman (*Matlock, Father Dowling Mysteries, Perry Mason* movies), Bellasario (*Magnum, P.I., Quantum Leap*), Bloodworth-Thomas (*Designing Women, Evening Shade*), Cannel (*The A-Team, Wiseguy, 123 Jump Street, Loose Cannon*), Rosensweig (*Cagney and Lacy, The Trials of Rosie O'Neil*), and Carsey (*The Bill Cosby Show, A Different World, Chicken Soup*) reworked standard formulas slightly in directions designed to match changing times. Others—Bochco (*L.A. Law, Doogie Howser, M.D., Cop Rock*) and Lynch (*Twin Peaks, American Chronicles*) come to mind—sometimes took greater risks than the others by trying to change the tone and direction of established formulas more drastically.

The presence of Wolper and the late Brodkin on the list highlights the fact that production companies exploit different niches in their industry. The heads of the majority of TV production firms choose to compete in the most popular areas of network programming, providing them with bread-and-butter material stamped with their track records and styles. Others choose to be more selective about their activities and contribute "prestige" fare that the networks need once in a while. Brodkin's *Holocaust* and *The Missles of October* and Wolper's *Roots* are famous examples. Whatever their niches, however, all these people are keenly aware of industry demands on them that influence what they can do, how they can do it, and when they can show it.

INTEGRATING CHANGE INTO ROUTINES

The quote above implies that casting ideas that are considered "offbeat" do sometimes get accepted. It is difficult to predict when some unusual recommendations will get picked up by production firms and others will not. One broad way to understand how much change is acceptable is to link it to the executives' perceptions of the political and economic risks involved. A suggestion that selectors consider dangerous politically or a huge monetary gamble will not be tried under ordinary circumstances. Instead, the changes that will take place will be those fitting into the "low" or "mild" risk categories. The creative changes that they allow will typically mesh well with traditional approaches to formulas and stereotypes.

There will, however, be times when executives of some mass media production firms, their distributors, and their exhibitors decide to take what they consider high risks in releasing new products. How they define high risk and when they take it will vary by mass media industry and even by companies within particular industries.

In 1990, the talk in Hollywood was that while much TV programming reflected formula-ridden business as usual, a number of television producers and networks had taken the plunge with drastically "unconventional" spins on formulas.[17] Particularly eyebrow-raising approaches being tried were the casting of a handicapped person as a regular cast member (in *Life Goes On*); the use of hauntingly unusual tone and photography in a dramatic serial (*Twin Peaks*); the merging of two seemingly incompatible formulas, the musical and the gritty cop show, in a series (*Cop Rock*); and the scripting of previously unacceptable, foul, language (in *Against the Law, Uncle Buck*, and a couple of other series).

Reasons Firms Take Risks

What conditions lead executives in a television production firm and a network—or, for that matter, in any mass media industry—to take risks they perceive as unconventional, while others do not? Industrial sociologists suggest that unconventional risk taking is more likely to take place in relatively small organizations within an industry than in its largest companies. The reason is that large organizations with lots of products tend to develop long chains of command to handle the daily business of taking care of business. The resulting bureaucracy tends to mean a rather rigid and

---

Talking Point 8.2   Talking in Codes

When television producers pitch ideas for series to one another and to network program-mers, the language they use is filled with shorthand references to the way their "new" ideas fit into series with formulas that have proven records of success. To get a feel for this code, consider the following excerpt from a piece about the cop series *Hill Street Blues* and its relation to the hospital series *St. Elsewhere*, two shows that appeared on NBC during the 1980s.

Hill Street Blues had germinated . . . when Fred Silverman, then president of NBC television, suggested to Brandon Tartikoff, his chief programmer, and Michael Zinberg, the vice-president for comedy development, that what the network needed was "a cop show in a neighborhood with a heavy ethnic mix." Tartikoff and Zinberg, in turn, approached two producers from MTM, Michael Kozoll and Steven Bochco. The two had worked on police dramas a few years before. Police dramas had been out of style for a while because of an antiviolence swing against TV, but Silverman was convinced the form was coming back. MTM, with a good reputation among the critics as well as a track record for drawing audiences, might smooth the path.

The NBC executives stressed that Silverman wanted a nervy, rough show from the viewpoint of police on a real-world frontier. Paddy Chayevsky's movie *Hospital* was cited for its ragged, frantic style, its near-surrealistic depiction of the horrors of medical life, its mockery of the conventions of medical shows. David Gerber's *Police Story* TV show was cited because its police officers had personal lives. Most of all, to Bochco and Kozoll, the NBC executives mentioned *M*A*S*H* and ABC's sitcom *Barney Miller*. It came down to "a little bit of *M*A*S*H*, a little bit of *Barney Miller*. We'd like you to develop a show that has more to do with cops' personal lives."

. . . Although [*Hill Street's*] early ratings were dismal, Silverman and Tartikoff held on to it as a message from the then number-three network that it would support Hollywood creativity. They were rewarded after the first year when the series, after winning a gaggle of Emmy awards, began to climb sharply in popularity.

According to some insiders, that is when Silverman said, "Now we can do *Hill Street* in a hospital."

SOURCE: Joseph Turow, *Playing Doctor: Television, Storytelling, and Medical Power* (New York: Oxford University Press, 1989), pp. 238–239.

---

time-consuming approach to innovation. Companies with just a few people and few products, on the other hand, often take a "we try harder" approach that makes them quicker and more daring.

Industrial sociologists also point out that a bad profit picture will move even the largest firms to consider previously undreamed-of risks. When revenues coming into the firm are acceptable and outside forces are acting on the firm in predictable ways, company leaders see no reason to take steps that could drastically disrupt the compa-ny's standing if they fail. On the other hand, when unpredicted problems arise outside the firm that diminish profits in a major way, worried executives may decide that established routines are not working and that bold steps are required to get the firm on track again.

The Case of Newspapers

In the U.S. media scene, it is easy to show how circumstances such as the ones described have led executives to change their approaches to their products. The newspaper industry provides one example.

In the 1990s, many city papers continued to lose circulation and advertising revenues as young adults abandoned the major dailies in favor of suburban weeklies and electronic media. Extremely concerned about the situation, executives at some dailies and their parent organizations began to consider bold moves to make their products attractive again to readers and advertisers. Proposed solutions to get readers included drastically shortening stories to make them more quickly digestible and using computers to tailor newspapers to the specific interests of individual readers. Among the advertiser-luring strategies being tested was the selling of space to sponsors for a long period of time in the most read parts of the paper—even the front page![18]

Newspaper conglomerates often tried to reduce the risks of these and other drastic measures to improve newspapers' readership and profitability by testing the changes in a few of their smaller papers, where failure would not be absolutely disastrous for the parent firm. So, for example, the Knight-Ridder newspaper chain used its Boca Raton daily, rather than its *Miami Herald* or *Philadelphia Inquirer*, to test the leasing of advertising space.[19] By contrast, in commercial network television, unconventional attempts to raise audiences and advertising profits took place on a national stage. In television, the stakes appeared even higher than in newspapers. Executives at ABC, CBS, and NBC considered the first half of the 1990s to be years of turmoil as audiences and profits plummeted because of increased competition by other broadcast interests as well as cable and home video.

The Case of Network TV

Part of the networks' problem was Fox Television. A subsidiary of a large media conglomerate, Fox had assembled a lineup of stations that allowed it to compete with the Big Three's prime time lineup a few days a week. Well aware of their underdog status, Fox's programmers had decided to go out on a limb to commission quirky programs such as *The Simpsons, It's Gary Shandling's Show*, and *Married with Children* that turned traditional approaches to their subjects (families, talk shows) on their heads.

When the series aired, reviewers hailed them as brash, innovative fare.[20] More important for Fox, those programs became the leading edge of shows that began to make Fox competitive in the ratings with the networks on nights in which all four broadcast their programs. Also making Fox attractive to advertisers was its large percentage of viewers between 18 and 40 years old. This age group had been deserting Big Three network fare and had become increasingly difficult for advertisers to reach through broadcast TV.

Fox executives' success with unconventionally irreverent programming led their nervous network counterparts to follow suit. They began to accept suggestions from producers that moved formulas in previously unthinkable directions. "Things have changed," said one producer. "*The Simpsons, Twin Peaks, Cop Rock* have pushed back the boundaries of what it is possible to do."[21]

Nevertheless, most observers agreed that most programming on the three networks—as well as on Fox—would not be of the highly unconventional sort. For one thing, many advertisers expressed a nervousness that they did not want to be associated with anything they perceived as "shredding the envelope," in the words of Madison Avenue. And, while a crowd of small, independent producers was lining up at the networks to pitch series ideas with bizarre twists, executives from the largest production firms, their eyes on long-term profits from syndication, were eager to follow more conservative interpretations of formulas. "We're not in the business of producing trendy TV," the head of Paramount TV's network programming division bluntly told *Variety*.[22]

It ought to be noted that the Big Three's acceptance of unconventional ideas was short-lived. *Cop Rock, Against the Law, Twin Peaks*, and other heralded programs fared poorly in the ratings and were yanked off the air by the summer. Network programmers, worried about a close ratings race in the year ahead, retreated almost fully to the tried and true when they chose ideas for next year's programs. They reasoned that experimentation had by and large failed to draw large audiences for them, and felt it was too risky to take chances on the coming season.[23]

Note, too, that the perception by television industry personnel that *The Simpsons, Cop Rock*, and *Twin Peaks* were unconventionally innovative fare has to be understood from the standpoint of the nature of the TV industry at that time. These programs were very clearly tied to enduring television formulas. Moreover, the individuals involved clearly had no interest in questioning the system of programming or its basic value structure. On the contrary, the people who created the shows had already developed at least some track record within the entertainment community. In an unspoken way, they indicated that they understood and were following many of the commonly accepted routines of popular entertainment. All of which suggests a larger generalization—that producers and distributors of mass media materials judge the importance of change in terms of what has been done before in that industry. From the vantage point of people outside the industry—intellectuals who view public TV, for example, or publishers of scholarly books—the change may not be very significant at all.

NOTES

1. Quoted in Gaye Tuchman, "Making News by Doing Work: Routinizing the Unexpected," *American Journal of Sociology* 77 (July 1971), p. 111.
2. Tuchman, "Making News by Doing Work," pp. 110–131.
3. Gaye Tuchman, *Making News: A Study in the Construction of Reality* (New York: Free Press, 1978).
4. See Lewis Coser, Charles Kadushin, and Walter Powell, *Books: The Culture and Commerce of Publishing* (New York: Basic Books, 1982).
5. See Joseph Turow, *Getting Books to Children: An Exploration of Publisher-Market Relations* (Chicago: American Library Association, 1979).
6. Coser, et al., p. 338.
7. Bruce Felton and Mark Fowler, *Felton and Fowler's Best, Worst, and Most Unusual* (New York: Crowell, 1975), p. viii.

8. John Cawelti, *The Six-Gun Mystique* (Bowling Green, OH: Popular Press, 1975), p. 35.

9. Cawelti, pp. 46–47.

10. Harry Steinberg, "The Porn Brokers," *The New York Times Book Review*, November 28, 1976, p. 55.

11. Clive Davis and James Willwerth, *Clive* (New York: Dial Press, 1970), p. 312.

12. Quoted in Quentin Reynolds, *The Fiction Factory* (New York: Random House, 1955), pp. 88–89.

13. As examples, see Gaye Tuchman, Arlene Kaplan Daniels, and James Benet (eds.), *Hearth and Home: Images of Women in the Mass Media* (New York: Oxford University Press, 1978); Robert Berkhofer, *The White Man's Indian* (New York: Vintage, 1979); and Donald Bogel, *Toms, Coons, Mulattoes, Mammies, and Bucks* (New York: Vintage, 1973).

14. Quoted in Joseph Turow, "Casting for Television: The Anatomy of Social Typing," *Journal of Communication* 33 (Spring 1983), p. 19.

15. Turow, pp. 22–23.

16. Horace Newcomb and Robert Alley, "The Producer as Artist: Commercial Television," in J. Ettema and D. C. Whitney (eds.), *Individuals in Mass Media Organizations* (Beverly Hills, CA: Sage, 1983) pp. 91–107.

17. Elizabeth Guider, "Off the Wall Gets You in the Door, If Not on the Air," *Variety*, August 15, 1990, p. 85.

18. Janet Meyers, "Knight Ridder Aims Young," *Advertising Age*, October 8, 1990, p. 38.

19. Meyers, p. 38.

20. Ronald Grover, "The Fourth Network," *Business Week*, September 17, 1990, pp. 114–120; and Cyndee Miller, "Hey Dudes: Fox TV May Have a Cash Cow in Its Licensing Deals," *Marketing News*, June 11, 1990, p. 1.

21. Squire Rushnell, quoted in Guider, p. 85.

22. Guider, p. 85.

23. Joe Mandese, "Big 3 TV Nets Play It Safe," *Advertising Age*, May 27, 1991, p. 1.

CHAPTER NINE

U.S. Mass Media
in a Global Economy

An American of the 1990s who takes a trip to another country might be startled to finds signs of home all around. In most areas of the world, U.S. products such as Coca-Cola and IBM shout their familiar trademarks from billboards and magazines just as they do in the states. Movie theaters everywhere regularly unspool films from Hollywood. Local television stations air a parade of American series, from classics such as *I Love Lucy* and the Western *Bonanza* to more recent fare such as *Miami Vice* and *Dallas*. Local radio stations play a heavy diet of music recorded in Los Angeles, New York, and Nashville. Major hotels in most of Europe and parts of Asia pipe the Cable News Network into guests' rooms. And for those with inclinations to read about the world from an American source, a wide array of periodicals, including *Time, Newsweek, The New York Times, The Wall Street Journal*, and *Business Week,* can be purchased in most capital cities.

A few statistics that suggest this story are startling. In the 1990s, United States mass media materials account for 75% of broadcast and basic cable TV revenues and 85% of pay-TV revenues worldwide. Fully 55% of all theatrical film rentals and 55% of all homevideo billings worldwide are for U.S. products. American records and tapes account for about half of global recording revenues. And the United States commands 35% of the book-sales market.[1]

Side by side with this "Americanization" of international mass media, though, are vocal reactions against it around the world. Sometimes, those opposed to Americanization give broadly "cultural" reasons for disliking it. At other times, they speak with narrow intentions of gaining political power. At still other times, they have an interest in economic gain. Often, all these considerations are at play simultaneously.

What fuels the international Americanization of mass media?

What objections and limitations have people outside the United States placed in the way of American mass media power?

What trends indicate the outcome of this struggle between Americanization and anti-Americanization during the next quarter century?

The following pages will tackle these questions. Guiding the analysis will be the proposition that the global mass media business, like domestic U.S. mass communication, involves competition over symbolic and material resources. Understanding mass media power on an international scale therefore means understanding how companies and governments use resources to struggle over political, economic, and cultural concerns.

The section that follows this introduction presents an influential view from the late 1960s that criticizes American use of resources to this end. It is followed by an overview of some ways in which American power has been challenged during the past twenty years in both wealthy and poor nations. Much opposition has been from governments, the stated reason being to protect cultural values. Of rising importance are challenges from nongovernment bodies, large non-American mass media corporations that have learned to beat U.S. firms at their own game. The chapter ends by considering two areas of the world where the influence of international competition among media firms is only beginning to be felt—the USSR and, ironically, the United States itself.

THE MEDIA ARE AMERICAN

Few people would disagree that Americans have dominated the mass media scene around the world during the second half of the twentieth century. There is quite a bit less consensus on how that has come about and precisely what it means.

The most sweeping, and provocative, approach to this question ties the widespread Americanization of mass media outside the U.S. directly to the political, economic, and military goals of the nation's elite. In the late 1960s, communication researcher Herbert Schiller developed this perspective in an influential book titled *Mass Communication and the American Empire*.[2]

"The American Empire"

The theme of Schiller's work is as follows: An empire is a conglomeration of far-flung nations or territories acting under the direction of a particular nation. The Romans, British, French, Turks, and Germans are just a few of the peoples who exercised authority over large parts of the globe during past centuries. In the twentieth century, much of the world has been dominated by the American Empire. This empire is, however, uniquely different from all those that came before it.

The difference lies in the resources through which the United States exercises its control over nations. Other empires have imposed and maintained their authority mainly through military force, subduing the locals and establishing armed outposts throughout their colonies. By contrast, the American Empire projects its influence primarily not by the sword but through mass communication.

Schiller spends the bulk of his book detailing what he means by the projection of American domination through mass communication. He argues that over the decades, and especially since the end of World War II, the U.S. government has worked hand in hand with large U.S. corporations to provide an appropriate acceptance of American business throughout the world. That has involved much more than making sure trade agreements are in America's best interests. Many parts of the world have social systems that would not accept American business's ways of doing things or would not have needs for the kinds of products American firms produce. As a result, the long-term goal of the political-corporate partnership has been to transform much of the world along American capitalist lines, with an emphasis on the modern consumer marketplace.

In other words, Schiller says, making the world the oyster of American business and dominating it with American products has first meant making sure that as many nations of the world as possible adopt the American way of life. This sort of projection of cultural power is called **cultural colonialism**.

Schiller argues that American cultural colonialism takes place primarily through mass communication. His discussion points to three broad areas through which this spread of power takes place: mass media content, mass media structure, and mass media technology.

On the matter of content, he argues that the easy availability of American movies, music, and television programs subtitled or dubbed in local languages has been drowning the cultural voices of their societies. Local companies, with relatively

TABLE 9.1. Global Television Prices For U.S. Programs (in U.S. dollars)

Region/ Country	Half-Hour Series (per episode)	One-Hour Series (per episode)
Europe		
Germany	3,500–10,000	10,000–40,000
Poland	450–550	920–1,150
Far East		
Japan	4,000–6,000	14,000–16,000
Malaysia	300–500	600–900
Philippines	900–1,100	1,100–3,500
Latin America		
Bolivia, Paraguay	750–850	1,400–1,600
Chile	375–425	750–850
Middle East		
Israel	550–650	950–1,000
Other nations	650–750	1,300–1,500

These countries were chosen from among those listed in *Variety*. African nations were not listed there, principally because of the unreliability of data. Nevertheless, the table allows comparison between prices that wealthy and poor nations pay. In general, the prices of these programs are far lower than the costs of programs of similar technical quality that nations could produce themselves. Critics maintain that the low prices encourage cultural colonialism. See the text for more consideration of this topic.

SOURCE: *Variety*, April 15, 1991, p. M-107.

little money, have often found it impossible to compete with their huge American counterparts on price, technical know-how, or distribution. The resulting Americanization of mass media has brought portrayals of life and enactments of values which, Schiller argues, do not match the needs and traditions of their societies.

For example, airing TV programs that parade urban wealth in an African nation where people are struggling to survive on the land teaches children and adults incorrect lessons of what to strive for in life. Schiller would say that instead of being presented with TV programs that tempt them with capitalist gratifications, the people should be imbued with values that help them use their own traditions in ways that maximize their nation's welfare and deal with its special problems.

Mass Communication and the American Empire also discusses the way mass media structures have been avenues for cultural empire building. **Structure** refers to the way mass media industries are organized in a particular society. Schiller points out that American ways of organizing and funding mass media have been copied around the world.

Consider the use of advertising to support print and broadcast media. Advertising, Schiller contends, is an inappropriate way to support mass media in many societies. Advertising, he suggests, champions materialist values, discourages saving, and, when foreign firms promote the wares, may weaken the economy of a nation by encouraging the purchase of imported products. Yet the United States government and large American mass media corporations have pressured the governments of many countries rich and poor to adopt a media model which allows advertising. For Schiller, the benefits in this strategy for the United States are clear. The ads provide a platform for American goods while they also favorably act out the materialist values that would encourage people to want those goods.

This spread of "the American way" takes on special concern for Schiller when it comes to America's control over the technologies that bring cultural materials to different societies. The technological power today is as one-sided as when Schiller wrote: No country other than the United States is a net exporter of mass media materials. To make Schiller's argument even more contemporary, one needs only point out that using the latest direct broadcast satellites, American programmers and advertisers already have the expertise to transmit their output to any country in the world, to be received by small, relatively inexpensive dishes. The day is at hand when corporations will regularly slide American mass media materials across national boundaries to billions of people without the cultural leaders of the countries being able to do anything about it.

The American Advantage

Schiller's theme, in short, is that American domination of content, structure, and technology of mass media has helped U.S. political and economic "imperialism" by weakening the indigenous values in countries around the world and making them more "American." His thesis was controversial when it appeared, and it fueled an enduring debate among people who care about mass media and culture.

Many intellectuals applaud Schiller for facing up to what they felt were the subtle ways that American capitalism was spreading its influence. Others insist that spreading American news and entertainment values around the world was not all bad, since doing so might help to encourage democratic ideals and concern for the rights of individuals. Still others contend Schiller incorrectly assumes a power of mass media culture that it did not have. They argue that people from other countries do not interpret American programs as Americans do, nor will their values be changed drastically as a result of their viewing, listening, and reading.

Some thinkers who may accept the notion that American culture is being spread around the world nevertheless reject the proposition that lies at the core of Schiller's book, the notion that the United States is creating an empire. Instead, they see the issue in terms of international trade and the **comparative advantage** of nations with respect to certain products. The notion of comparative advantage argues that the collective wealth of all trading partners is maximized if countries specialize in producing what they do best and trade with one another in order to secure the whole range of products produced between them.

By this account, the media dominance that Schiller discusses came about simply because, compared with the rest of the world, Americans have excelled in devising mass media materials and technologies as well as the organizational structures to go with them. Economist Richard Collins argues, for example, that the United States' preeminence in the international television program trade has come about because of certain characteristics of U.S. TV programs and certain realities of TV production in the United States. The most significant of these advantageous factors are:

Language (English is the most commonly known language across nations)

The large size and competitive structure of U.S. domestic markets (it encourages the creation of a lot of product aimed at broad audience tastes)

The availability of a critical mass of competent creative personnel (this allows the United States a predictable flow of product)

The availability of financial services and manufacturers of necessary equipment (which gives U.S. media producers the basic material resources to sustain their output).[3]

America's leadership in these areas, contends Collins, goes a long way toward explaining the country's leadership in international trade.

Helping to flesh out this comparative advantage approach to understanding the flow of TV programming is the notion of a **public good**. A public good is a product or service for which consumption by one person does not reduce the amount available by other individuals. A TV show fits this description because once it is made, it will continue to exist whether it is viewed by 100 people or 3 billion people.

This characteristic explains why American TV production firms find that most, if not all, of the costs of creating the public goods have already been made back in the domestic U.S. market. Compared with what firms in most countries can afford, American TV production budgets are large because of the competitive requirements of the American TV market and because the country's size allows successful shows to recover their high costs from advertisers. As a result, when the Americans come to the international marketplace, most, if not all, of the costs of creating the public goods have already been made back through their domestic sales. They can therefore

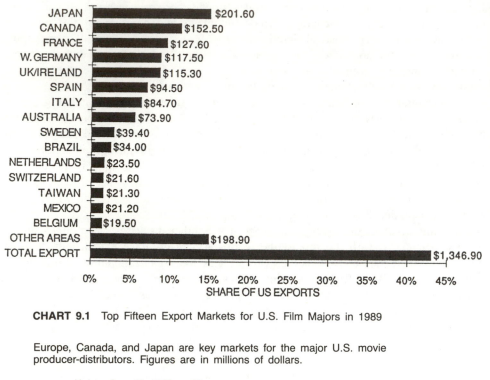

CHART 9.1   Top Fifteen Export Markets for U.S. Film Majors in 1989

Europe, Canada, and Japan are key markets for the major U.S. movie
producer-distributors. Figures are in millions of dollars.

SOURCE: *Variety*, June 13, 1989, p. 10.

offer to countries the most technically lavish programming at prices that are difficult
to refuse.

Although those who advance the comparative advantage approach often use it as
an alternative to the notion that the United States is building an empire, the empire-
building and comparative advantage approaches to mass media need not be seen as
necessarily opposing each other. It is quite possible to see America's comparative
advantage in mass communication as both a contributor to its colonial reach and a
result of its colonial power.

Whatever position one takes on the empire or comparative advantage theses, it is
important to note that since the the late 1960s, when Schiller's book was published,
two major challenges to American dominance have appeared that demand a refocusing
of both approaches to America's international role in mass communication. One is the
entry of huge firms from other countries into the international media scene. The other
is the increased determination by governments around the world to restrict American
mass media products. From the standpoint of American firms, the challenges are
greatest in the nations that have the greatest resources, the countries of the First
World.

THE FIRST WORLD AND AMERICAN MEDIA

When *Mass Communication and the American Empire* was written, American firms did indeed have a corner on the transnational market for news and entertainment. Certainly, American media firms such as Time Warner, Paramount Communications, General Electric, ABC, and Disney still do exert global reach and influence. Yet non-American global media powerhouses now exist as powerful competitors. In the 1990s, more than a few U.S. executives are saying that within the decade the bulk of mainstream mass media production, distribution, and exhibition will be controlled by six or seven firms, not all American. Consider some of the foreign contenders:

> Bertelsmann: A German company that started out in magazine publishing, it has branched out into a variety of mass media throughout the world. In the United States, Bertelsemann owns RCA Records and its record clubs, a chain of bookstores, and a couple of publishing firms.

> News Corp: Owned by Australian-American mogul Rupert Murdoch, News Corp owns strings of highly profitable newspapers and magazines in Australia, England, the United States, and elsewhere. The firm also owns the major movie studio 20th Century Fox along with Fox's various film and TV holdings (including the Fox TV network). Murdoch also has a major stake in the BSB-Sky direct-broadcast satellite venture that is aimed at sending commercial programming directly to the homes of Britons and Europeans.

> Philips: A huge Dutch electronics manufacturer which also owns Polygram Records.

> Sony: The Japanese technology giant owns CBS records and its record clubs as well as Columbia Pictures and TriStar.

> Matsushita: Sony's Japanese electronics rival (the maker of Panasonic products for the United States) bought its own American media conglomerate, MCA, which owns successful theme parks as well as companies that make and distribute theatrical movies, TV shows, records, and videotapes.

Other non-U.S. players in the struggle for international mass media dominance are also noteworthy. They are not as powerful as the firms noted above, but their strategic importance in particular media makes them targets for either takeovers or joint ventures that would expand one of the other conglomerate's reach enormously. Here are a few:

> Hachette: This huge French media conglomerate concentrates mainly on magazines (such as *Elle*) and European broadcasting.

> Fininvest: Controlled by Italian mogul Silvio Burlusconi, its subsidiaries virtually manage Italian commercial broadcasting, have interests in French broadcasting, and place much of the advertising in Italy.

> Springer Group: Owners of the influential newsmagazine *Der Speigel* and

other periodicals, this firm has been expanding into broadcasting, theatrical exhibition, and home video.

Maxwell Communication Corporation: British publisher Robert Maxwell's multibillion-dollar media empire is as varied as the Pergamon Publishing Corporation (based in England), the U.S. book publisher Macmillan, the *Official Airline Guide*, and 40% of a Hungarian newspaper.[4]

The Changes in Western Europe

What caused the rise of Western European and Japanese mass media firms as major competitors to the Americans in the global marketplace over the past two decades? Several factors were involved. In the case of the Western European firms, three long-term developments had the greatest impact.

The general growth of the European economies

The privatization of broadcast media on the continent

The decision by the European Economic Community to eliminate tariffs among its members in 1992

As for general growth of the European economies, it has been steady and widespread. That has resulted in generally healthy advertising revenues for magazine and newspaper businesses across the region. Theatrical film exhibition has also prospered. Some European companies, such as the initially print-oriented Bertelsmann, have used their profits to evolve into large conglomerates with interests in movie exhibition, video cassette distribution, cable TV, and broadcasting, as well as in books and magazines.

The movement of private companies into broadcasting, cable television, and satellite distribution was a great departure from the historical policies of most European countries. Traditionally, the broadcasting structure of Western European nations was founded on the notion of public service. Radio and TV stations were established as public entities, ruled over by bodies established by the government. With few exceptions, the people in charge scorned the United States' approach of giving the airwaves over to private firms that funded their activities through advertising.

That attitude began to change in the mid-1970s. With the appearance of new technologies such as cable television and satellite broadcasting, companies throughout Europe began clamoring for the right to expand the number of channels available to citizens' homes. Bowing to pressure, many European authorities began to allow private firms into the broadcasting, cable, and even satellite realm.

One reason was that the governments did not want to use their own tax dollars to cover the huge amounts of money needed to establish a national presence in those areas. This **privatization**—the introduction of private firms into the broadcast arena—was accompanied by commercialization, the transformation of radio and television into vehicles for marketers. Following the American model, the firms realized that there existed large numbers of advertisers who would pay handsomely to get their commercials into the homes of European consumers. The lure of advertising monies quickly became the engine driving the spread of broadcast and cable channels throughout Western Europe.

Europe 1992

The upward trend in advertising also reflected the keen awareness by international marketers that **Europe 1992** was at hand. Europe 1992 was a shorthand phrase to mean that agreements by the nations of Western Europe through their European Economic Community (EEC) would transform the area into one country from the standpoint of trade beginning in 1992. Previously, tariffs had made it difficult to export goods among neighboring countries of Western Europe. With the EEC eliminating those tariffs, competition across the continent would be encouraged. Experts predicted lower prices throughout the region as a result. They also noted the effects the EEC's decision was having on advertising.

The lure of a tariff-free market of consumers with population size and wealth close to that of the United States was irresistible to marketers from around the world. Traditional advertising vehicles such as magazines, movie theaters, and newspapers, as well as the newly privatized broadcast channels, elicited strong interest from companies that wanted to introduce their products to new parts of Europe or protect their brands in anticipation of the new marketing realities.

The privatization and commercialization of Western European mass media have been accompanied by the rise of powerful advertising conglomerates with international reach. Firms such as Eurocom (French), Saatchi and Saatchi (British), and the WPP Group (British) grew by leaps and bounds during the 1980s as they voraciously bought ad agencies, market research firms, and media buying organizations in Europe, Asia, and the United States.

The growth was often fueled by relatively easy money available through "junk bonds." It was guided by the proposition that multinational marketers expected their advertising agencies to be able to serve their creative, research, and media buying needs across countries and across continents. Perhaps not surprisingly, some executives in these global agencies tended to argue that in many cases it was useful to adopt the same persuasive strategy in every country in which a product is sold. Using the same campaign (with appropriate translation) in different countries of Europe as well as in the United States and Asia for products such as toothpaste and tampons would, they contended, give global marketers the best way to control the appeal and efficiency of their marketing efforts.

A number of major international marketers disagreed that global, or even pan-European, advertising was the way to go. Nevertheless, a number of mass media ventures were designed to cater to advertising across boundaries—for example, MTV-Europe, which aims its ad-supported footprint at more than 16 million cable households in England and on the continent.[5]

The Japanese and Global Media

The rising power of Western European companies in all aspects of the international mass media scene during the 1980s and 1990s was paralleled by the major role that Japanese firms began to play. Sony and Matsushita are clearly their country's most visible representatives. They are not, however, the only ones. Companies such as Fujisankei (a major Japanese movie studio) and Dentsu (the world's largest ad agency)

TABLE 9.2. Top Advertising Agencies Around the World, 1989

Europe

Rank	Agency	'89 European gross income by equity
1	Publicis FCB	$354,773
2	Young & Rubicam	337,494
3	Saatchi & Saatchi Advertising	332,708
4	McCann-Erickson Worldwide	278,082
5	Backer Spielvogel Bates	264,626
6	Ogilvy & Mather Worldwide	260,999
7	Lintas: Worldwide	226,518
8	HDM	222,618
9	J. Walter Thompson Co.	210,725
10	Grey Advertising	197,349

Latin America

Rank	Agency	'89 Lat. Amer. gross income by equity
1	McCann-Erickson Worldwide	$73,464
2	J. Walter Thompson Co.	58,092
3	Ogilvy & Mather Worldwide	42,888
4	Lintas: Worldwide	40,698
5	Duailibi, Petit, Zaragoza	34,616
6	Young & Rubicam	25,887
7	Leo Burnett Co.	24,732
8	Foote, Cone & Belding	17,695
9	BBDO Worldwide	14,533
10	Saatchi & Saatchi Advertising	12,645

Asia/Pacific

Rank	Agency	'89 Asia Pacific gross income by equity
1	Dentsu	$1,314,400
2	Hakuhodo	585,457
3	Dai-Ichi Kikaku	155,795
4	Daiko Advertising	152,064
5	Asatsu	113,879
6	I&S Corp.	94,734
7	Backer Spielvogel Bates Worldwide	93,908
8	McCann-Erickson Worldwide	93,637
9	HDM	88,834
10	J. Walter Thompson Co.	66,562

Note that many of the same names show up in the different regions. That suggests the global nature of the ad business.

SOURCE: *Advertising Age*, June 11, 1990. p. 16.

have involved themselves in the international production realm in one or another major way.

In the early 1990s, there was even a Japanese-founded filmmaking company in Hollywood, Apricot Studios. At the same time, Japanese publishing firms were exhibiting interest in buying minority or controlling ownership in American magazine and book publishing companies.

Unlike the Europeans, almost all of the Japanese involvement in international media production activities have involved not creating new ventures from scratch but financing or purchasing already existing ones. Several considerations motivated the Japanese to join the global mass media bandwagon almost exclusively by purchasing it. One was simply the immense amount of money that many Japanese firms were earning in the world marketplace. The low value of the U.S. dollar and many European currencies in comparison with the yen has made American and European media firms attractive to Japanese firms with media connections. The Japanese could afford to buy the best.

A second, probably more important, factor is that Japanese executives appear to believe that their indigenous production approaches are not well adapted to the international market. Japanese singing stars do not make the hit charts around the world, while U.S., British, and other European stars often do. Japanese TV shows and theatrical films do not travel well, even though Japanese movie studios have tried periodically to concoct product that imitates American action films. Their solution: If you can't beat them, buy them if you have the resources. The Japanese have the cash.

The most spectacular results of this thinking were the multibillion-dollar purchases by Sony and Matsushita of Columbia and MCA, respectively. By all accounts, the two electronic giants were intent on purchasing powerful American record and movie companies that would provide them with the "software" to encourage consumers to purchase new "hardware." Sony officials attributed much of their failure to succeed with their Beta format VCR during the 1970s to an inability to tempt consumers with exclusive movie titles. Their American purchases were aimed at giving them programming clout.

The buys seem also designed to give the manufacturers leverage with the creators of programming. Throughout the 1970s and 1980s, it had become clear to industry observers that fundamental policy splits had developed between production firms and the equipment manufacturers. U.S. record companies, for example, vigorously opposed the Japanese manufacturers' digital audio tape (DAT) recorders on the grounds that it would encourage copyright violations. The Sony and Matsushita acquisitions represented attempts to close those splits by taking control of major forces within the production segments of their industries. It is no coincidence that a compromise on DAT was reached not long after Sony's acquisition of CBS Records.

Continuing the American Connection

Two conclusions emerge from this sketch of the strong European and Japanese presence as international movers and shakers of mass media. The first is that Herbert Schiller's characterization of international mass communication being an almost exclusively American domain needs to be revised at the threshold of the twenty-first century. Rather than an American-dominated activity, global mass communication might best be described as a First World activity. That is, news and entertainment throughout the world are created by companies from several of the richest countries in the world to be shared by the richest nations, the less wealthy, and those that are poor.

The fact that ownership of a substantial segment of transnational media activity is being shared more broadly than in previous decades reflects a decline of U.S. economic clout in the world economy. Yet while companies from other parts of the world are more involved in global mass communication than ever before, the media remain overwhelmingly American in a number of ways.

For one thing, much of the information and entertainment material owned by non-U.S. firms are created by Americans. MCA, 20th-Century Fox, Columbia Pictures, and MGM/UA may strictly not be American companies any more, but Los Angeles is still the base for producing their movies, records, TV shows, and theme parks. Just as important, the dominant model for internationally profitable content in the news, information, and entertainment realm is American, whether it is produced by Americans or not.

When Italian and Japanese producers attempt to create movies for the world market, they consciously try to emulate Hollywood's style—and they sometimes even do it in English. Similarly, when Hong Kong entrepreneurs decide to generate a Chinese language magazine with news about business, the U.S.'s *Forbes* and *Business Week* become relevant models. Atlanta-based Cable News Network has likewise become the standard for an all-news channel in the international cable TV and satellite-to-home business.

The American way does not predominate only in content. Japanese radios, televisions, VCRs, and video disks improve and miniaturize American-generated technologies. Those technologies reflect a long-standing American philosophy of mass communication: that it is a good thing to multiply media channels so that people who can pay can have a variety of news and entertainment options. Much of this privatized, individualized (as opposed to collective, governmentally driven) approach to mass media technologies remains supported by the American model of mass media industries: profit-making production firms supported in the main by advertising. While the persuasive appeals of ads may vary in different countries, the basic American pattern of using mass media as marketing vehicles remains constant.

Canadian Concerns

Not all First World governments support the global, privatized, commercialized, Americanized direction that much of the mass media have taken, and they have marshaled resources against it. Canada provides a particularly interesting example. Politicians in the English-speaking parts of that country have lamented that their people are particularly vulnerable to American influence on all media fronts. Artists, journalists, educators, politicians, and media executives have worried about the continuing flood of news and entertainment products that emanate from their southern neighbor.

One problem Canadians raise is that American films, videos, records, and periodicals dominate their markets for those products. That makes it difficult for local firms to survive. Increasing the American influence are TV and radio stations broadcasting from Buffalo, Detroit, and other U.S. cities close to Canada. They attract a large percentage of the Canadian population, which is concentrated along the long border with the United States.

Alarmed educators and politicians have contended that as a result of American mass media Canadian youngsters know more about current events in the United States than about Canadian concerns. They have urged their government to work against what they see as U.S. cultural domination by encouraging Canadian mass media. Canadian entertainment companies, eager to grow, have supported their activities. Over the past few decades, Ottawa has tried to encourage Canadians to watch Canadian media.

One strategy to help local mass media has been to tax the advertising dollars Canadian firms use when they buy ads in foreign periodicals and broadcasts that reach Canada while not taxing the ad monies they spend on Canadian media. That has helped newsmagazines such as *Maclean's* compete with *Time* and *Newsweek*.[6] Still another tack has been to bolster the movie industry by providing government subsidies to films produced with a certain percentage of major personnel (directors, stars, writers) who are Canadian citizens.[7]

Government grants have also supported production by firms who sell programs to either of the two television networks. The goal of the Canadian Broadcasting Corporation (CBC) is to have more than 90% of its prime time offerings made in Canada. The non-government network, CTV, has a prime time quota of around 60% Canadian content.

To discourage audiences from viewing American programs on U.S. networks (and losing ad monies as a result), the CBC and CTV have sometimes required U.S. production firms to send episodes of TV series across the border before the U.S. networks have aired them. More commonly, the Canadian networks have taken to broadcasting U.S. programs at the same time as their American counterparts. This has benefitted the Canadians because of an advertising arrangement worked out with ABC, CBS, and NBC. As part of the arrangement, the Canadians get a separate feed of the shows, with commercials sold by the CBC or CTV inserted instead of American commercials. Also as part of the deal, Canadian cable systems carrying the American networks show the Canadian commercials, so that the additional audience benefits the Canadian network, not the U.S. affiliate.[8]

Canadian government and industry officials realize that all efforts to "protect and encourage Canadian mass media" are touchy politically. One barrier to simply barring American media from entering Canada is that it would infringe on Canadians' rights to read what they please. Another is that hindrances to U.S. media products displease powerful industry lobbying groups in Washington. Officials argue that Canadian logjams in the face of American media products would simply represent intolerable barriers to fair trade. Canada relies greatly on its commerce with the United States. Canadian officials must therefore tread a fine line between responding to their constituencies at home and not endangering larger U.S.-Canadian trade agreements.

European Tensions

Concerns about external mass media forces are being expressed throughout Western Europe, too. The concerns of some of the smaller countries are not just about

American cultural products. Dutch leaders, for example, have worried publicly that their public TV channels will lose a lot of viewership—and viewer support for funding—as citizens turn to commercial signals in the Dutch language that companies from elsewhere in Europe (especially Luxembourg and Belgium) have thrust across their borders.[9]

Generally, though, the greatest anxiousness has not been voiced about border crossing by European-made products but over materials made in the USA. European intellectuals, media executives, and intellectuals know full well that American adventure movies tend to capture some 70% of their countries' movie seats, that American shows saturate the airwaves on commercial stations.[10] They also know that what they do produce is not in the international league: in a typical year, 90% of European film and TV programs never leave their country of origin.[11] Not always agreeing on what to do about this, European intellectuals have nevertheless been determined to come up with individual as well as collective responses to American mass media power.

Perhaps the most impressive pan-European attempt to encourage entertainment production on the continent was announced at the end of 1990. After a cliff-hanging series of postponements and hesitations, the Council of Ministers at the European Parliament approved a $250-million, five-year funding package for MEDIA, the European Community's attempt to develop its own TV and movie industries that can sell to the world. Boasting twelve programs run out of various European capitals, MEDIA's mandate falls into roughly three areas: distribution, production, and training. Its programs provides seed money for everything in movies and TV production, from scripts and cartoons to feature film coproductions, multinational distribution, and the development of new audiovisual technologies. The goal is to encourage creation of a network of movie and TV professionals of all types so that an internationally competitive European infrastructure in audiovisual industries can emerge.[12]

Actions such as these scare American film and TV executives. They fear that European government initiatives to develop theatrical and small-screen programming will be accompanied by trade regulations that strongly limit mass media products created in the United States. Some countries have already legislated quotas on the numbers of programs that can be aired on individual stations. In France, 60% of prime time programming must be from the European Community.

At the cross-national level, a European Community directive effectively limits United States programming to not more than 50% of air time in member countries. While 50% is still a lot, American executives worry about the precedent of setting such quotas. They reason that with the idea of numerical barriers accepted, 50% today can be lowered to 20% next year.[13]

As a result, lobbyists from U.S. audiovisual industries (representing movie, record, and TV interests) have worked hard in U.S. and European government circles to make sure that their products are well-represented in general fair trade agreements with the United States. Jack Valenti, chairman of the Motion Picture Export Association of America, was among those in the early 1990s advocating that the American government apply substantial material and symbolic resources to ensure that American mass media industries would not be locked out of Europe.

Valenti argued that the central issue was the economic health of the United States in an age of huge trade deficits. He described America's film/video/TV entertainment industry as one of the country's "glittering trade jewels," responsible for a surplus of more than $3 billion annually in balance of trade. And he contended that those in the EEC who were imposing restrictions on U.S. media products were using the "guise" of protecting national cultures as a way to boost their companies' revenues at the expense of American firms.[14]

THE DEVELOPING WORLD AND AMERICAN MEDIA

Strong complaints against the dominant presence of American mass media emanate from the poorest countries of the world as well as from Western Europe. Actually, in many of these so-called Third World countries, the anger is directed as much toward general Western, or First World, media products as toward specifically U.S. mass media materials. Building from a perspective similar to Herbert Schiller's, Third World intellectuals and politicians argue that the Americanized global mass media situation has been harmful to their nations.

The issues they raise are complex and varied. On the subject of imported entertainment, critics argue that broadcasting American and British programs for several hours every day is counterproductive to societies where staying alive and keeping the society going are the main concerns. Rather than spectator-oriented TV, the oppressive social problems demand grass-roots involvement away from the television to have any hope of success.

Western news receives condemnation as well. Third World politicians complain that struggling African, Asian, and Central American countries do not have the resources to compete with American, French, and British news agencies. The major agencies have from fifty to one hundred correspondents abroad and expensive high-speed transmission technology. They dominate the news holes of papers in both the developing and developed worlds. Because Western journalists define foreign news in terms of conflict and tension, people within Third World nations and especially people outside them get views of the developing world as bizarre, corrupt, and war-torn. This picture hinders leaders of poor nations in their attempts to develop tourism and to entice investments by companies from richer nations.

The McBride Commission

Responding to concerns such as these, the United Nations Educational, Scientific, and Cultural Organization (UNESCO) appointed a commission in 1976 to propose solutions. Known as the **McBride Commission** after its chair, Sean McBride, it released a report four years later that instigated a storm of controversy.

At the core of the report was the Commission's insistence that developing countries had the right to place "nation building" as an objective of their media activities, in news as well as entertainment. Comprehensive government communications policies should guide the way to have nation building portrayed in different media. Economic priorities and the development needs of the society should take precedence over freedom of the media. The commission added that journalists as well as other media personnel working in those countries should be expected to cooperate with those goals.

The McBride Report became the takeoff point for even more radical recommendations. Third World advocates proposed nothing less than a true **new world information order** (NWIO). They used that phrase to mean fundamental changes in the access that the rich and poor countries had to the channels of world communication.

U.N. ambassador Mustapha Masmoudi of Tunisia, for example, argued that inequalities of legal and technological resources in global communication had to be corrected if the poorest countries were ever to move ahead economically. The best positions for satellite orbits, for example, should not continue to go only to the countries that could afford them, since that would exclude developing countries from getting good "slots" in the future.[15]

Masmoudi and others from developing nations also helped pass a resolution that UNESCO should sponsor regional news agencies for the nations that had none. Accompanying the resolution were suggestions that those agencies regulate the news coming out of their regions. Some Third World politicians also proposed licensing Western journalists. The aim was to make sure that only those journalists who cooperated with a government's development aims could report from that country.

A number of the NWIO premises, such as licensing and news monopolies, flew in the face of long-held Western ideals of "free speech" and the "free flow of information." Even so, some observers from the West were sympathetic to the notion of a new world information order. They argued that the global situation already prevented true free speech and free information flow from developed to developing nations. Media resources of the former were so much greater than those of the latter that the poor nations could gain control over their destinies only through drastic steps that would release the chains of inequality forcefully.

U.S. Response

Journalists, politicians, and mass media executives in the United States did not buy that argument, though. They countered that the invocation of a new world information order by Third World politicians was, in many cases, just another excuse to solidify dictatorial power over their people through control over the news. They rejected licensing and news monopolies as contrary to the best interests of informed citizens everywhere, and they accused UNESCO of being a bastion of antidemocratic policies. To underscore these points, and to remove from the organization the necessary resources for carrying out its new world information order goals, the United States, along with Great Britain, withdrew from UNESCO in 1984.

The loss of subsidies from the two big powers crippled the organization and derailed implementation of broad changes that would characterize a new world information order. By the late 1980s, the United States and England rejoined a quieter, less insistent UNESCO. The tensions between developed and developing nations over global communication issues have remained, however. They have bubbled to the surface now and then as the activities of Americanized global media operations clash with the objectives of leaders with very different traditions.

In rapidly industrializing Singapore, for example, issues of *The Asian Wall Street*

Journal were removed from circulation after the government passed a new law that required foreign publications to be licensed yearly and post a deposit against legal rulings. An official decree had already reduced the newspaper's circulation in the country from 5,000 to 400 after government officials became angry with material in the publication.[16] Clashes such as these reflect ways of looking at the world that are fundamentally at odds with each other. While not as noisy as the UNESCO debate, they are likely to continue far into the future.

AMERICAN MASS MEDIA AND EASTERN EUROPE

There have, of course, been governments around the world that try to isolate themselves as fully as possible from any First World versions of mass communication. These countries have upheld ideologies that often directly oppose the capitalist-driven engines of news and entertainment that characterize the West. Nations that uphold fundamentalist Islamic beliefs ban public displays of Western entertainment, though the use of American VCR tapes in the home are common. Also in the exclusionary category are communist nations such as North Korea, Albania, and Vietnam. In other communist countries, such as The People's Republic of China, Western media, including advertising, have made some inroads.

From the standpoint of Western media, the Soviet Union and Eastern Europe are probably in the greatest state of uncertainty and change. No one seems to be quite sure what the limits to Westernization will be or who will define them. That is because transformations taking place in what many have called the Soviet Empire have been nothing short of astonishing even to long-time observers of the region. The declaration that the Cold War with the West was over; the dissolution of the Soviet Union's hold on part of Germany; the movement by regions within the USSR such as Latvia and Lithuania to declare themselves independent; the public rejection of communist philosophy among some key leaders within the Soviet Union as well as in its former satellites of Czechoslovakia, Hungary, and Poland—these activities represent merely the tip of a huge iceberg of changes that have been moving Eastern Europe and the Soviet Union through uncharted, and dangerous, waters.

Soviet Media Theory

Mirroring Eastern Europe's remarkable political changes have been the transformations in mass communication. Until just a few years ago, the Eastern Bloc's communication policy reflected beliefs about media, society, and the state that were expressed by the founding fathers of modern communism—Marx, Engels, and Lenin. The approach was called **Soviet media theory** by most observers because it developed its earliest and most detailed exposition in the USSR. It provided the model for media practice and training within the broad Soviet sphere of influence.

Four fundamental premises can be said to have guided traditional Soviet media theory:

Mass media should not be owned by private individuals. Rather, the media should be subject to control by the agencies of the working class—that is, by the various arms of the Communist party.

The press should play a positive role in educating the society toward socialism and should avoid activities that could cause divisiveness.

When reporting events, journalists should present them according to an objectively true—that is, Marxist—interpretation of historical reality.

Flowing from the above ideas, mass media and the personnel who run them are part of the general political and educational structure of the state and so are subject to controls by the state—for example, censorship or punishment—to make them operate properly.[17]

Soviet journalism theorists noted that the creators of news and entertainment were expected to be responsible to the interests of their audience as determined by research and letters. They were also expected to investigate situations in the society that were not conforming to the aims of the government—for example, lazy workers—with the aim of urging things to be made right.

In practice, though, the creators of mass media materials felt intimidated from casting critical eyes on their surroundings. In both the USSR and its satellites, mass media creators often chafed under the pressure of governments that expected to be able to manipulate images directly—often, lie—in the service of their power. The situation seems to have cultivated widespread cynicism of Soviet media theory even among Soviet mass media practitioners.

The Tides of Change

With the rising tides of change in Eastern Europe and the Soviet Union, and especially with the disavowal of communism by many of the countries in the region, what has been called Soviet media theory was thrown out the window in some quarters. Creators in both the print and electronic media responded vigorously to a new openness and self-criticism that reformist leaders encouraged.

In the Soviet Union, newspapers and magazines questioned the value of communism itself, while on TV previously tame prime time information programs turned, at least temporarily, into exciting debates about, and biting satires of, government and society. Advertising became increasingly common on TV and in print as government policies changed to force the mass media and other sectors of the society to respond to market forces in ways that were unknown just a few years before.

In the early 1990s, nothing definitive had emerged to replace the old media system of the USSR, Poland, Czechoslovakia, or Hungary. Some observers insisted that in the Soviet Union, forces that stood a lot to lose by the passing of the old order would push Kremlin leaders back toward control over the press and, especially, the electronic media. In spite of the uncertainty, the Eastern European countries became yet more sites of competition between global mass media firms eager to spread their influence.

As elsewhere in the world during the decade, the players in this region were not only the Americans. While U.S. companies were in the thick of the fray, giants from

Germany, France, and other parts of the First World were also deeply involved. Here are some examples from the early 1990s:

> U.S.-based Time Warner entered into a joint venture with Sovexportfilm to build and operate the first state-of-the-art multiplex movie theaters in the USSR. The theaters were to show American as well as Soviet films. They also announced an intention to develop a "Soviet-American relationship" in motion pictures.[18]
>
> The French Hachette conglomerate's magazine subsidiary created a Russian-language edition of its *Paris Match* that sold 250,000 copies soon after hitting newsstands in Moscow, Kiev, and Leningrad. The edition, which was also sold to Russian émigrés in the United States, was a joint publication by Hachette and *Moscow News*, an independent Soviet weekly. With a color page ad rate of $35,000, which included a page in the Paris edition, the magazine included such advertisers as Yves St. Laurent, BCEN Eurobank, and France Telecom.[19]
>
> The magazine *Movies, USA* began selling in English-language copies at movie theaters in Leningrad, while U.S. publications entering the market with Russian-language editions included *Business Week, PC World, Omni*, and *Scientific American*. Rodale press announced plans to release a Russian-language edition of *The New Farmer*.[20]
>
> MTV Europe, the satellite service then co-owned by U.S.-based Viacom International and the British Maxwell Entertainment Group, began airing a one-hour Friday night broadcast weekly on Soviet network television. For the first month, spots were fully sold to five clients: Benetton, L.A. Gear, Wrangler, Stimorol, and Renault. Managing Director William Roedy noted that the one-year deal was the first step in his ambitious plan to get MTV Europe's twenty-four-hour service into as many Soviet homes as possible.[21] Not long afterward, he negotiated channel carriage to 100,000 cable subscribers in Leningrad. He predicted that further opportunities would come through rooftop community satellite dishes.

A person looking at the empty stores in Moscow and Leningrad in the early 1990s would have to wonder why Western media executives such as Roedy were so excited. In the early 1990s, the Soviet Union still had not altered its laws to allow foreign companies to fully exchange USSR rubles into dollars, deutschmarks, or other currencies. Moreover, the economic distress that marked the nation meant most citizens could not afford the goods advertised.

Even the foreign periodicals that advertised the goods were often out of reach. While the popular Soviet weekly *Ogonyok* cost 72 cents at the official exchange rate in 1990, a copy of the latest edition of *Newsweek* cost $9.22. With an average weekly salary of about $90 and the market price for meat (if it could be found) running $21.60 a pound, the typical person in Moscow or Leningrad was left with little to spend on luxuries such as foreign magazines.

In the increasingly competitive world media marketplace, however, the major players, with resources to invest long-term, are looking toward the future. Major media firms and their advertisers are putting their feet in the door, learning the political and economic layout as it evolves, getting people used to their names. As MTV's Roedy noted, the initial goal was to expose the MTV "brand" to millions of Soviet households. Hachette took a similar view, scheduling its Russian-language *Paris Match* on a twice-a-year basis until the ruble would be convertible or the company could find a way to reinvest in the Soviet market.[23]

The bottom line is that global media conglomerates saw the USSR as a lucrative place to be down the line, and they were using their substantial resources now to jockey for position. Hachette's international advertising director spoke for many when he said that the firm's entry into the USSR was in anticipation of a free-market economy: "We are offering international advertisers a chance to build brand awareness and presence . . . in what will certainly be a huge marketplace."[24] No one was sure whether that free marketplace would evolve, or what it would look like. But, it was clear that, as in other parts of the globe, the mass media conglomerates of several First World nations along with their governments were investing lots of resources in a competition to speed that process along in directions that suited them best.

Were these attempts at cultural colonialism by Western capitalist countries? Or were they just examples of the competitive advantage of nations? Or perhaps they were both.

GLOBAL MEDIA COMPETITION AND THE U.S. MARKET

Many, probably most, American viewers and readers in the mid-1990s have little awareness of such international competition among media firms. It is likely, in fact, that most Americans have little awareness of foreign media products. Traditionally in the United States, foreign-language periodicals and broadcast stations have been considered only temporary outlets for immigrants.

Historically, Germans, Poles, Italians, Scandinavians, Jews, and others coming to the United States from foreign lands continued using their language of origin for one, perhaps two, generations. Newspapers and other mass media in the immigrant tongues typically blossomed to accommodate the needs of the first generation of arrivals and then disappeared or continued in a much-weakened state to serve ever-older audiences.

That is less true with many of the Hispanic groups living in the United States, most notably the Puerto Rican and Mexican communities. Spanish-language materials comprise a large part of the daily media diet for generations of Hispanic-Americans. Although Hispanics comprise the largest and fastest-growing minority in America, advertisers have not been lavish in their support of Hispanic media, probably because most Hispanics do not have the disposable income that advertisers crave. The reluctance on the part of advertisers particularly influences television programming, since it severely limits the amount of money available for indigenous production.

When it comes to Hispanic TV, then, the United States is a large importer of programming. Univision and Telemundo, the two major Hispanic TV networks in the United States, program two-thirds of their materials with Mexican, South American, and Spanish product.[25] A third network, Galavision, directs itself specifically toward Mexican-Americans and uses exclusively material made in Mexico.

TABLE 9.3. Top Ten U.S. Cities in Hispanic Population, 1990

City	Hispanic population
Los Angeles, CA	6,080,304
New York, NY	2,737,098
Houston, TX	1,300,038
Chicago, IL	1,284,147
Miami, FL	1,014,356
San Francisco, CA	1,008,410
San Antonio, TX	987,080
McAllen/Brownsville, TX	815,998
Albuquerque, NM	651,616
El Paso, TX	641,954

Hispanics make up the fastest-growing ethnic group in the United States. Unlike TV programs and movies for most Americans, audiovisual programming aimed at Hispanics tends to come to a large extent from other countries. See the text for more details.

SOURCE: *Advertising Age*, February 4, 1991, p. 30.

U.S. Made

For the great majority of Americans, however, the sound and look of mass media have always been U.S.-made. A middle-aged listener to mainstream American music stations has grown up hearing them broadcast almost no lyrics in a language other than English. For decades, the major American television networks have aired almost no foreign programming.

As for foreign movies, they are alien to the overwhelming number of citizens. Only 16 non-American movies were among the 164 titles the major U.S. film distributors circulated in 1990. Moreover, of the 16, almost half (7) were made in English within the British Commonwealth. Independent distributors did circulate 67 foreign movies.[26] The chance of a large percentage of moviegoers seeing these products was small, however, since the major distributors collectively have a tight grip on the overwelming number of theaters around the country. The fact is that few American cities have theaters that exhibit movies made outside the United States.

To be sure, many Americans knew of Sony's purchase of Columbia Pictures and Matsushita's buyout of MCA in the early 1990s. Yet news stories about those sales —were couched not in considerations of international media but more narrowly in concerns about Japan's increasing ownership of American business. Moreover, the stories emphasized claims by both Sony and Matsushita management that they would be leaving their new American subsidiaries the independence to continue to produce output as in the past. Stock analysts went out of their way to predict that the purchases would have little impact on the movies Hollywood made.

As a result, most Americans probably hold the notion that the U.S.-created, America-centered, English-speaking media world that they and their parents have known will remain intact. Production executives from such countries as France and Italy blame the major U.S. distributors theater owners, who, they say, have purposefully not marketed foreign films properly to the American public so that American movies will get top box office draw. Agreeing is one U.S. independent distributor of French films who finds it difficult to get theatrical, TV, or even homevideo accept-

TABLE 9.4. Foreign Movies Distributed in the United States, 1990

Country	Number of movies	Number of Those Movies Backed by the United States
Algeria	1	1
Argentina	1	—
Australia	6	3
Belgium	1	1
Burkina Faso	1	1
Canada	11	2
Colombia	1	1
Cuba	3	—
Czechoslovakia	1	—
Denmark	1	1
Finland	6	6
France	25	4
Germany	9	1
Greece	1	—
Holland	2	—
Hong Kong	5	1
Hungary	2	—
Iceland	1	1
India	1	1
Iran	3	—
Israel	1	—
Italy	9	3
Japan	9	1
Poland	1	—
Portugal	1	1
Senegal	1	1
Spain	4	—
Sweden	2	—
Switzerland	1	—
Tunisia	1	1
United Kingdom	25	12
USSR	2	—
Yugoslavia	2	1

The nations of the world produce many more films than these. Few of the world's movies make it to American theaters, however.

SOURCE: *Variety*, May 6, 1991, pp. 174–178.

ance. He suggested that the French film industry fight back with its political resources: that it consider harsher quota restrictions on U.S. film and video productions
if U.S. theaters and TV networks are not more open to French product. "If that
would happen," he contended, "I'll promise you, you'd see French films as two-part
miniseries in prime time on NBC."[27]

Of course, as suggested earlier, the American audiovisual industry has been
conducting its own lobbying efforts with the French and U.S. governments to ensure
that such quotas do not get instituted. It is highly improbable that Americans, so long
accustomed to U.S.-made entertainment, will consistently welcome clearly foreign

products with open arms. Nevertheless, it does seem that the content of American mass media will be affected at least to some extent by the struggle over global media resources that has been discussed so far in this chapter. Rather than extending influence through product made primarily for the French or Italian or German market, though, it is likely that in the next quarter century foreign influences will make themselves felt primarily as a result of the increasingly international nature of the production business.

International Products in the American Mainstream

In forthcoming decades, it is likely that a substantial segment of American mass media will be made with a tilt toward the world market. While print media will undoubtedly reflect these changes, they will probably be most apparent in the audio-visual realm—theatrical movies, TV shows, records, home video, and the technologies that follow them.

International Films

This is beginning to happen already. The theatrical movie industry is particularly at the vanguard. It used to be that Hollywood producers saw foreign distribution as a lucrative afterthought, a way to make money after the major dollars were made in the USA. In the 1970s and 1980s, however, Hollywood producers, distributors, and investors began to actually target the international market in the planning stages of movies. Projected foreign theatrical rentals increasingly became an integral part of the financial thinking about whether a movie should be made, and at what budget.

Hollywood producers have long known that certain movies that do decently at U.S. box offices perform stunningly on foreign shores. The James Bond film series, for example, continued to be strong in the international market even as rentals for new episodes decreased in American theaters.[28] It was the foreign popularity of the series, primarily, that kept it going. While major movie studio executives increasingly consider the foreign market as a factor that can tilt a movie that may have only moderate U.S. possibilities, a number of independent producers have actually been tailoring product specifically for the global market.

To do that, they choose a cast of actors from a variety of key countries. Then they select story and production values to minimize the need for talk and emphasize action. In practice, this means a male-centered movie based around war, vigilante activity, or some sort of police action. Think of films with Charles Bronson, Chuck Norris, and Bruce Lee. These types of action films are shot in English, since it has become the international language; dubbing or subtitles are added to match the needs of particular countries. The violence (or "action") makes reading the subtitles almost unnecessary. The films are marketed around the United States, but the producers consider the world market even more lucrative.

Another kind of international film that has been making an increasing presence in American theaters fits what the trade magazine *Variety* calls the Continental English-track category. This type used to be dominated by European products created for their countries of origin. Imported to the United States, with sound tracks dubbed into English, the movies at first hardly made ripples in the American market.

During the past few years, however, the category has begun to be filled with French, Italian, Spanish, German, and Holland productions shot in English for the international market. Until the late 1980s, the major Hollywood distributors tended to steer clear of distributing these hybrid films. As a result, independents circulated such ventures as *The Cook, the Thief, His Wife, and Her Lover* (with Miramax the distributor), *Last Exit to Brooklyn* (Cinecom), and *Santa Sangre* (Expanded Entertainment).

In the early 1990s, however, the majors began to show interest in joining European companies in producing English-language films made on the continent. At the end of 1990, for example, the French pay-television cable service Canal Plus announced that it had entered into a co-production deal with Warner Brothers to produce movies in French.[29] One reason for Warner's involvement was possibly the view that by supporting European filmmaking, the European Economic Community would not threaten to impose tariffs on its imported American-made product. Another reason might be the feeling that Continental English-track films may well make back their investment through combining revenues from French pay-TV and the global market.

International Films in the U.S. Market

The global market includes the U.S. market. These international films will show up on broadcast, in cable, and on home video, if not in theaters. The homevideo market will be an outlet, since many of the American co-production partners have home distribution operations. Local broadcast and cable channels will carry them, because those firms' executives, burdened by small audiences (compared with the audiences of the broadcast networks) and tight budgets, have made it their business to hunt for relatively inexpensive programming sources with sophisticated production values. Increasingly, they will likely decide that, if marketed properly, films such as the ones funded by Canal Plus and Time Warner will attract viewers and cost far less than movies the cable channels can produce themselves.

Even the three major American television networks have begun to see the benefits of international coproductions. In 1990, for example, CBS signed an agreement with British independent broadcaster Granada Television to develop and produce as many as six TV movies over the following three years. CBS also agreed to pay a U.S. firm and a French company to coproduce an action series called *Paris Metal* for its late night (11:30 P.M.–12:30 A.M.) slot. The series would be shot in English in French, and the license fee the network would pay would be 40% of the regular license fee for a U.S. prime time network show of similar technical quality.

Cheaper location costs are not always the reason foreign-made shows can be had for less. Sometimes, the foreign co-production firm is so interested in getting on an American network and sees so much value in international sales that it will accept lower payment and put up the extra money itself. An example from the early 1990s was the CBS late-night adventure series *Dark Justice*, produced by Lorimar in association with Spain's TV3 and shot in Barcelona. According to one source, CBS and Lorimar got off relatively cheaply. However, TV3 put up "an enormous amount of money" that brought the program very close to the budget of a prime time show.[30]

A Break in the Walls?

It is hard to argue that these deals signal a revolutionary break in the cultural walls that have separated mainstream American mass media from voices and images of the rest of the world. Made in English, with characters and plot lines that fit formulas common to U.S. television (*Paris Metal*, for example, deals with a CIA agent), the output actually underscores how powerful American cultural materials have become. They have even become programs of choice outside the United States. The forms are so popular in such wide areas that even non-American companies want to get in on their international production and distribution.

One interpretation of this phenomenon is that television is becoming globally homogenized along American lines. It seems likely, however, that not all signs of a program's origins will always be erased. Even if created in the American style, programming and musical scores generated in foreign countries by foreign personnel will bring something of the other culture with them.

Some of the Canal Plus TV movies, for example, will surely be "truly" French. Over time—and it may take a long time—programs with themes, locales, and sensibilities now absent from American screens may appear with more frequency. An optimist might hope that in a world where Americans are beginning to realize the economic importance of understanding foreign countries, audiences may even begin to welcome TV shows that provide some insight into other cultures. Slowly, the face of American programming may accept some views from foreign lands.

NOTES

1. Carl Bernstein, "The Leisure Empire," *Time*, December 24, 1990, p. 57.
2. Herbert Schiller, *Mass Communication and the American Empire* (New York: Kelley, 1969).
3. Richard Collins, Nicholas Garnham, and Gareth Locksley, *The Economics of Television* (London: Sage, 1988).
4. Holdings change constantly. See Anthony Smith, *The Global Behemoths* (New York: Priority Press, 1991).
5. Don Groves, "MTV Enters USSR," *Variety*, November 12, 1990, p. 58.
6. See Curtis Prendergast (with Geoffrey Colvin), *The World of Time Inc., Volume Three* (New York: Atheneum, 1986), pp. 369–375.
7. See Sid Adilman, "New Canadian Pic Fund," *Variety*, April 15, 1991, p. 56.
8. Karen Murray, "A Hearing Lands CBC in the Middle of a Flap," *Variety*, April 15, 1991, p. M-98; and Sid Adilman, "Indie Producers Seek Independence," *Variety*, April 15, 1991, M-98.
9. "TV Newcomer Grabs a Quarter of the Field," *Variety*, October 29, 1990, p. 40.
10. Carl Bernstein, "The Leisure Empire," *Time*, December 24, 1990, p. 57.
11. Deborah Young, "MEDIA Gets 5-Year Lease on Life in 11th Hour Vote," *Variety*, December 24, 1990, p. 23.
12. Young, p. 23.
13. Young, p. 23; and Morrie Gelman, "Valenti Spurs Pols to Keep U.S. Showbox in GATT Gab," *Variety*, November 12, 1990, p. 12.
14. Gelman, p. 12.

15. See Denis McQuail, *Mass Communication Theory: An Introduction, 2nd ed.* (London: Sage, 1987), pp. 119–121; also S. McBride et al., *Many Voices, One World: Report by the International Commission for the Study of Communication Problems* (Paris: UNESCO, 1980).
16. "Dow Jones Halts Singapore Circulation of the Asian Journal," *Wall Street Journal*, October 15, 1990, p. B7.
17. See McQuail, p. 118.
18. Susan Lewenz, "Joint Ventures in the Soviet Union," *Business America*, March 12, 1990, pp. 2–7.
19. Joel Ostrow and Scott Donaton, "Western Titles Roll into Soviet Union," *Advertising Age*, November 5, 1990, p. 61.
20. Ostrow and Donaton, p. 61.
21. Don Groves, "MTV Enters USSR," *Variety*, November 12, 1990, p. 58.
22. Ostrow and Donaton, p. 61.
23. Ostrow and Donaton, p. 61.
24. Ostrow and Donaton, p. 61.
25. Peter Besas, "Mexicans Ride Again in Hispano TV Sweeps," *Variety*, April 11, 1990, p. 41.
26. Will Tusher, "Nation's Screen Tally Reached a New High in '90," *Variety*, January 28, 1991, p. 3.
27. Gelman, p. 12.
28. Charles Fleming, "Bond Bombshell: 007 Goes on the Block," *Variety*, August 8, 1990, p. 1; and Charles Fleming and Richard Natale, "Sequel Opportunity as Film Franchises Falter," *Variety*, June 29, 1991, p. 52.
29. Bruce Alderman, "Cash-Rich French Firms Invest Francs in Film," *Variety*, December 17, 1990, p. 35.
30. "CBS to Co-produce for Prime Time, Late Night," *Broadcasting International* 3:1 (January 1991), pp. 7–8.

CHAPTER TEN

The Challenge of Synergy

Turn on broadcast children's television in the afternoon, and you are likely to see *Duck Tales*, the hit cartoon adventure series starring Huey, Dewey, and Louey, Donald Duck's nephews, and their other uncle, Scrooge McDuck. Go to a toy store, and you will undoubtedly find *Duck Tales* toys, dolls, coloring books, records, party favors, games, even Play Dough. Want more? A comic book store will yield *Duck Tales* comics, and your local mall's Disney Store might have videos or other *Duck Tales* products to sell. But that is not all. For parents, and many children, too, the *Duck Tales* characters recall Donald Duck. Donald, in turn, ignites interest in Mickey and Minnie and Pluto and the old Disney cartoons. In their original form, they live on in the Disney Channel, Disney's cable TV division, as well as in periodic reruns packaged to independent broadcast stations by Disney's TV syndication division for family viewing during Thanksgiving, Christmas, and other holidays.

Replicas of the characters and playthings based on them also populate Disney Stores as well as toy stores, comic-book stores, and trade bookstores not owned by the Disney Company. They, in turn, promote California's Disneyland, Florida's Disneyland, and the new Disney theme parks in Japan and France—which, in turn, boost the Disney Stores, the Disney Channel, and all the other Disney products. Disney characters on boxes of food and other products around the world make more money for the company while keeping up with children even while they eat. And with Mickey Mouse as the character introducing every Disney Company video, all of Disney's children's products are bound into continual reference to one another.

Through activities such as the ones just described, the Disney Company has been able to achieve a special kind of success. It has been able to make various parts of its business—parts that represent different media—operate so that they help one another. During the 1980s, executives came increasingly to applaud this "synergistic" approach to business. **Synergy** means the coordination of parts of a company so that the whole actually turns out to be worth more than the sum of its parts acting alone, without helping one another. When the TV production division of Disney promotes the company's theme parks and they drum up business for the record and video division, which, in turn, promotes the book division, which, in a circular action, abets the TV division's programming, that is synergy.

The term was so overused that in the 1990s media leaders sometimes have tried to avoid it. Sometimes, they have even played down its importance as a strategy for growth. They have pointed out that many companies have not been as successful as

Disney at cross-divisional activities. Still, the process has continued briskly among the biggest mass media firms. In fact, synergy has become a hub of a series of related strategies that companies have been using to maximize their presence across as many media channels as possible. These strategies have become major building blocks of the mass media system as it moves into the twenty-first century.

The following pages examine that architecture. Bringing together concepts developed through the course of this book, the chapter explores how companies approach synergy and its related strategies. More than the other parts of the book, the chapter uses trends in the present to speculate about concerns that executives and consumers might have about the future. The chapter does so in two ways. It assesses the effects of synergy and related strategies on the structure of the U.S. mass media system. And it considers their implications for the menus of media materials available to different segments of American society.

A basic theme is that media executives' interest in cross-media undertakings built around synergy is a response to a number of key changes that have affected the U.S. media system and others during the past couple of decades. These executives are using synergy and other cross-media activities to face, and shape, their future amid these developments. As such, they are raising important challenges for members of the public as well as for executives of the mass media system.

SYNERGY AND MEDIA FRAGMENTATION

You might remember that in Chapter 1 examples of cross-media ventures similar to Disney's were described as **linking pin activities**. There it was noted that linking pin activities involve the movement of completed material, or of people representing that material, from production firms in one mass media industry to production firms in another mass media industry. From this standpoint, attempts at achieving synergy represent a particular form of linking pin work, one in which the media channels that are used belong mostly to one company. Such a company with many mass media holdings is called a mass media **conglomerate**.

As Chapter 1 suggested, organizations that take on the linking pin power role have always been standard features of mass media systems. Synergy deserves special attention, though. During the past few decades, it has become the strategy of choice of many major media corporations in the United States and elswhere. But synergy's attractiveness to mass media conglomerates has not been limited to the mass media systems of their home countries. To the contrary, firms have used the approach to organize their cross-media activities across national borders. In other words, synergy has become a central strategy shaping the international mass media system.

The Rise of a Fragmented Media World

The increased concern with synergy is the result of a number of developments in the media world that have threatened long-standing ways in which mass media firms have gotten their resources. The most important of these developments is what people who work in the business commonly call the **fragmentation of audiovisual mass media**. The phrase refers to the splintering of channels during the past two decades so as to theoretically make each channel's percentage of the audience pie smaller. The change has been dramatic. To get a picture of it, consider the media menu that faced most Americans in the early 1970s:

Watching television back then meant watching ABC, CBS, or NBC. Public television was available to many communities, but independent commercial broadcast stations were few. Even by 1979, there were only about 100 independent broadcast stations in the United States.

Apart from the relatively new notion of "made for TV" movies, seeing a new film meant going to a theater. The homevideo cassette recorder was not an option. If a person could not see a particular movie in the theater, there was a fair possibility it would show up on one of the TV networks in a few years.

Radio still mostly meant listening to AM. The number and popularity of FM stations was still low in most places.

Besides radio, listening to music via mass media mostly meant playing 33$\frac{1}{3}$ and 45 rpm records. Audio cassettes were just beginning to take off in popularity, with bulky 8-track players competing in home and car with more streamlined dual-track cassette players. CD laser players were not to be found in either place.

Home computers did not exist. Neither did direct broadcast satellite programming.

Cable television was around, but in a form quite different from that of today. Fewer than 8% of the nation's homes had cable in 1970, and they tended to be in rural areas, where people had a hard time getting over-the-air channels.[1] Despite great pronouncements that the medium would create a "wired nation" with a cornucopia of programming choices, cable TV in the early 1970s was essentially a retransmitter of broadcast signals. The cable TV industry generated very little of its revenues through advertising, and pay-TV channels such as HBO were only glimmers on the horizon.

The central elements of the U.S. mass media system in the early 1970s, then, consisted primarily of the traditional publishing enterprises—newspapers, magazines, books, billboards—together with a few audiovisual industries: theatrical movies, vinyl discs and tapes, broadcast TV and radio. At the time, mass media executives undoubtedly considered the number of basic mass media channels to be quite high. Most of them probably had little inkling of the startlingly greater fragmentation than would exist just twenty years later. By 1990 over 300 independent TV stations existed alongside the network affiliates. Cable TV had spread to about 60% of the nation's homes, along with channels carried only by cable. VCRs could be found in about 70% of U.S. families, and personal computers—as well as Nintendo-style game computers—were increasingly common among the middle and upper-middle class.[2]

Threatening Long-standing Approaches

How has this increased fragmentation of media channels threatened long-standing ways in which media firms have gotten resources and used them efficiently? One part of the answer begins with the effect that fragmentation has had on the **size** and **type** of audiences for certain key mass media. The increase in audiovisual channels has tended to *decrease* the audiences for most individual channels. That is because people have taken advantage of their expanded menus.

According to market research, the shift in habits has been substantial. Particularly startling has been the weakening of the most widespread distributors of audiovisual entertainment, the commercial television networks. From the earliest commercial TV days of the late 1940s through the mid-1970s, the combined prime time Nielsen shares of ABC, CBS, and NBC totaled at least 90%. That means that 90% of all those watching television were watching one of the broadcast networks. By the early 1990s, however, the three networks' share had slid to around 65%. The other 35% went to a combination of independent broadcasters and advertiser-supported cable stations, with VCRs also making a showing.

Executives at the major networks contested the Nielsen data angrily in the early 1990s.[3] Major advertisers and their agencies by and large accepted the findings, though. They approached the media system with the aim of finding vehicles with which to reach people they felt were not using broadcast TV as much as before. It also ought to be noted that for many marketers the reported fractionalization of audiences was convenient. It meshed with an increased interest in reaching ever-narrower slices of the population with messages tailored specifically for them.

Some advertisers looked down on traditional broadcast television as aiming at too many types of people at the same time. Rather than "all women, 18–49 years old," for example, they might be interested in reaching upper-middle-class married women 18–25 years old who were working full time and were actively interested in the intellectual growth of their children as well as in purchasing home furnishings. Reflecting the vocabulary of Chapter 5, the marketers were looking for distribution channels that deliver desirable **demographic** and **psychographic** categories. In the evolving U.S. media system, they often concluded that some of the new mass media vehicles, from cable TV channels to home computers, might be better places to find people who fit the profile than at the TV networks, or even at newspapers or radio stations. The marketers began to shift substantial advertising funds away from the networks and toward other forms of media.[4]

This new approach by advertisers caused a ripple effect across the power roles that organizations took on with respect to producers in key industries of the U.S. media system. The situation virtually forced production organizations to design their output with an eye toward moving it across mass media boundaries. The broadcast TV networks were deeply involved in the changes. In their roles of clients for, and distributors of, prime time programs, ABC, CBS, and even leader NBC found that they could not make their money go as far as in decades past.

Firms producing comedies and dramas found network executives more reluctant than ever to pay the full cost of creating series or movies for the privilege of airing each episode or film only a few times. The network people had to insist that since the production firms owned the rights to material, they should cover a fair part of the expenses with the aim of making them up through linking pin activities—in U.S. syndication, on the world market, or in other ways.

New Windows

The new media system was such, however, that even the winners forced producers to move their programs across media boundaries. Ad-supported cable networks were, for example, among the types of firms that were doing better than previously as clients for, and distributors of, programming. Compared with cable networks in the early 1970s, they were flush with cash from advertising revenues as well as from cash that cable systems gave them on the basis of the number of subscribers. That allowed them to make deals with major production firms for series and made-for-TV movies.

Still, those revenues did not always represent the full cost of creating the materials, and producers often had to approach cable deals with the notion that the expenditures would have to be made up elsewhere. The same was true for cable networks supported not by ads but by subscription—for example, HBO and Showtime. Producers within and outside those organizations realized that to justify the cost of creating "network quality" fare for those channels, they would have to find opportunities to make up costs elsewhere.

An executive for the Gannett Corporation put the issue this way as early as 1982: "As audiences become fragmented, the dollars available for programming [on any one channel] will decrease, because everyone's share of the audience will be smaller."[5] The best solution, he said, was not necessarily to make less expensive programming. It was to evaluate the ability of news and entertainment materials to pay for themselves when moved through different channels, or **windows**, of distribution.

That approach was already becoming quite standard in the movie industry. When deciding whether or not a film would make back its cost, planners at the major Hollywood studios were considering more than its ability to pull people into U.S. theaters. They were factoring into their budget estimates of the money the movie would draw across a variety of other windows—foreign theatrical rentals, video cassettes, pay-cable TV, foreign TV, U.S. network TV, local U.S. TV, and basic U.S. cable. The timing of a release from one window to another was planned carefully to maximize the audience at each stage and, by extension, the money the distributor could demand. So, for example, the time gap between the movement of a film from its first theatrical window to video cassette would have to be long enough so that audiences would not stay away from theaters with the notion of waiting to rent it, but short enough for the target audience to still remember the excitement generated about the film in its initial theatrical release.

The increased emphasis on adding distribution windows because of the increased fractionalization of media led many executives to perceive a strong risk. They reasoned that if competitors could control access to major channels, they could refuse to carry the firm's materials or exact an enormous price for doing so. That could harm the profit-making potential of the firm. On the other side of the coin, taking control over those channels themselves could be richly beneficial. For one thing, cable executives could be sure that the material their firm produced would have at least the opportunity to make its costs back in places they considered appropriate. For another, they could accumulate a great deal of power within the mass media system and still not be subject to restrictions on monopolies that authorities might enforce if they tried to control individual mass media industries.

Executives saw the globalization of mass media activities that Chapter 9 discussed as providing yet another incentive for managing many distribution channels. The international reach of marketers and their advertising agencies along with the growth of sponsorship-driven broadcasting in many parts of the world meant to companies with advertisers as clients that opportunities existed for non-U.S. expansion of their product lines. More generally, growth in an era of giant international mass media corporations seemed based on the idea that companies had to have the ability to play off their production materials in a variety of media in a variety of countries. Not having these channels at a firm's disposal meant not being able to accumulate the resources required to grow strongly. That, in turn, seemed to mean not remaining among the top tier of mass media firms in the United States or elsewhere.

Multimedia Acquisitions

Stock brokerage firms, banks, and other firms taking on the investor power role tended to agree. The general merger-and-acquisition fever throughout U.S. business during the 1980s helped fuel public and private enthusiasm for multimedia acquisitions. Some of the biggest deals were Time, Inc's merger with Warner Communications to form Time Warner; the purchase of MGM's library by Ted Turner; and the buyouts by Sony, Matsushita, and News Corp of Columbia Pictures, MCA, and 20th Century Fox, respectively.

Even these huge deals, though, do not give the flavor of the change that was going on. The reason is that the number of holdings alone was not the point. Many large media conglomerates—General Electric, Times-Mirror—had existed long before the 1980s.

The key change during the 1980s was that conglomeration was now seen as a way to link media holdings actively in the interest of greater profits. Power would accrue not just to those that owned vast media holdings but to those who could use them synergistically to play out materials across a gamut of holdings for the most value possible. Consider, for example, the following words from a top executive at Time Inc. Magazines, the magazine division of Time Warner. He describes how planners in his firm saw the requirements for a successful company in the fractionalized, globalized mass media environment in the months leading up to Time, Inc.'s decision to merge with Warner Communications:

> A media company that intended to compete successfully in this environment would have to be big enough to be heard and big enough to hold consumer attention. It would have to propose products and synergies that only a large, versatile organization could offer.
>
> It'd have to be able to move its products throughout the emerging global marketplace and amortize its costs over as many distribution networks as possible. Advertisers would be demanding more speed, responsiveness, flexibility, and teamwork.

Time, Inc. was big and strong and successful, but not big enough or strong enough for the challenges we saw on the fast-approaching horizon.

Long-term, we saw the world accommodating perhaps a half-dozen global media companies. And we intended to be one of them. Bigness for bigness sake didn't interest us very much. We certainly didn't want to get caught up in an old Gulf + Western or ITT type of diversified conglomerate where the core business can get lost along the way.

What we wanted was solid vertical integration so we could offer synergies that would bring together magazines, publishing ventures, studios, cable channels, and other activities into a coherent operation. We wanted to be able to offer more than the Murdochs and Maxwells of the world.[6]

MAKING SYNERGY WORK

This view of the requirements of being a world-class competitor explains why synergy has been the guiding activity among mass media executives. To talk about synergy and praise its possibilities is not, however, to make it work as its strategists want it to work. In the 1990s, executives in huge conglomerates and smaller ones have been realizing that synergy brings with it problems as well as possibilities.

Perhaps the most obvious difficulty is debt. Most of the giant conglomerates had to borrow tremendous amounts of money in order to carry out their multimedia acquisitions. The Time Warner merger, for example, led to an interest bill of $5 million per *day*. That kind of burden might make getting cash to respond to future opportunities quite difficult. And it poses the danger that top managers can become so preoccupied with paying back debt that they lose track of the actual media business of their corporation.

Another problem that synergy brings relates to implementing it. After their broadly optimistic statements about the advantages this approach will bring, even after the careful strategic planning that leads to multiple acquisitions and mergers, executives have found that getting advantages out of their new multimedia enterprise is not as easy as it sounds.

One reason is simply that the people who come from different companies, with different approaches, have no experience working together and thinking about projects that can help other parts of the firm as well. Even more of a problem, perhaps, is the difficulty of knowing how far to go with the strategy. It is not clear that synergy can or should be the core strategy for most firms just because a firm like Disney uses it to great advantage. In tackling their conglomerate's future, executives have to ask basic questions both before and after the acquisition:

Should most of the actions of the firm's divisions be geared to cross-linkages that support the firm as a whole?

Should planners try hard to think up ways in which the firm can create cross-media activities?

Or should cross-media work be carried out only reactively—that is, only when situations in the environment present clear opportunities for synergy?

These basic questions have been faced directly by many mass media corporations as the 1990s have unfolded. The answers have come slowly, as executives have learned to relate their different divisions in the service of activities that mass media firms have been engaged in for a long time. It is through challenges posed by advertising, creative rights, and public relations that approaches to synergy have been evolving.

Advertising, Strategic Partnerships, and Synergy

One obvious way for a mass media firm to use its holdings synergistically is to encourage advertisers to buy ads across them. A corporation that owns several newspapers might induce national sponsors to buy space across most of its dailies. A company with radio networks and billboards might sell time across both media. A firm with several magazine titles and a number of TV stations might offer that cross-title *and* cross-media buy.

Of course, offering these deals is different from getting advertisers to accept them. To be persuaded, sponsors would have to have a good reason to feel that they will get a better deal when working with a multititle or multimedia company than if they approach firms with one individual outlet. One way they might be convinced would be if the price for purchasing the package were lower than the à-la-carte approach. A multichannel offer would also be attractive if the package the media firm put together fit the audience profiles that the marketers were targeting. If a company's radio networks and billboards tended mainly to reach an audience of African-American consumers, for example, that might make the joint offer attractive to certain advertisers.

It was not until the 1980s that many media firms began to try to find or create synergies among their divisions that could be used to pursue increased advertising revenues. Often, competitive pressures in the environment led executives to look in that direction.

The Case of Magazines

Consumer magazines in the 1990s provide a good example. Executives in that industry faced a relatively "soft" advertising market. That was partly a result of a sluggish economy; marketers making less money were placing fewer ads. The magazine ad drop-off was also partly due to a decision by many advertisers to shift substantial portions of their ad funds to other kinds of marketing activities.

The grim situation led magazine executives to try to offer clients more for their money in order to attract a greater share of a shrinking magazine advertising pie. They set up ad packages across different magazines (**cross-title packages**) and across different media (**cross-media packages**) that offered substantial discounts on costs per thousand compared with their own individual title buys as well as those of their competitors.

The action that especially set the course toward package discount was an announcement by the Time Inc. Magazines division of Time Warner that it would be offering to advertisers large discounts if they advertised in a package of the firm's very popular consumer magazines—*Time, Fortune, Life, Sports Illustrated, Money*, and *People*. The move shook up the industry. Hearst Corporation, Murdoch Magazines and The New York Times Company's magazine group were among the largest conglomerates with substantial magazine holdings that announced internal discount programs.[7]

Another result was that executives in firms with only one or two consumer magazines felt quite threatened, especially if their titles competed directly with one or more periodicals in the lineups of the larger competitors. The solution some found was to search out marketing alliances with other, often bigger, firms that could fold the one or two periodicals into a strong package that could offer an attractive discount. *Newsweek*, the only periodical owned by The Washington Post Company and a direct competitor with *Time* for ad dollars, is an example of a magazine that felt a great deal of pressure to look for alliances. The Time Inc. Magazines discount announcement was followed by several weeks of gloom-and-doom talk by ad industry pundits about *Newsweek*'s inability to survive in the wake of its arch rival's discount coup.

Eventually, *Newsweek*'s executives formed a strategic sales partnership with the huge Times-Mirror conglomerate's substantial magazine group to offer discounts to advertisers. The idea seemed to be catching on, within and across mass media. As the trade magazine *Advertising Age* noted, the relationships helped both sides: "While the larger companies have been able to increase the number of ad vehicles for advertisers, smaller companies get a boost in credibility and a surge in audience by linking with bigger players."[8]

Strategic Partnerships

The last two examples highlight an important feature of the cross-media activities that conglomerates have been carrying out. While they have tried to maximize the in-house synergies that can be achieved, they have gone outside the conglomerate to use the channels of other firms if linkups can be profitable. The phenomenon is by no means relegated only to magazines. In 1991, for example, Turner Broadcasting System's Cable News Network (CNN) and Gannett's daily *USA Today* newspaper began offering advertisers sponsorship of a joint Cable News Network–*USA Today* weekly college sports poll. Sponsors would be credited both in the print and TV versions. Around the same time, *U.S. News & World Report* magazine and NBC's Consumer News and Business Channel (CNBC) on cable TV announced a deal that let advertisers buy space in annual guides published by *U.S. News* along with CNBC specials based on the guides.[9]

Executives call such joint ventures **strategic partnerships**. In carrying them out, executives of large conglomerates have often made deals with mid-size and small mass media firms as well as other huge conglomerates. From the standpoint of the giant companies, deals with mid-size and small firms often expand the conglomerate's coverage within particular media industries. As for the smaller firms, they have been shoved toward such linkups to stay alive. Strategic partnerships with the largest firms are often seen by executives as the best ways to stay afloat in a tumultuous environment in which a few large companies are dictating the rules of the game within and across mass media industries. Going it alone against them seems near-suicidal.

"Linking with bigger players," in fact, has seemed to be even more popular across mass media industries than within them. In the case of advertiser-sponsored mass media, a good deal of the encouragement to connect big and small mass media firms across industry boundaries has come from large marketers such as General Motors and Kraft General Foods. They want their advertising agencies and the mass media they use to help them maximize the **efficiency** with which they reach their target consumers. By efficiency, they mean hitting only those people who the marketer has determined are potential buyers for the particular product. Marketers have refined their understanding of such target consumer groups through batteries of market research techniques, including the focus groups and data bases discussed in Chapter 5. The result is that reaching likely consumers has become a process of understanding their life activities and following them through the course of their day as they turn to different sources for news and entertainment. The chief executive of DDB Needham Worldwide, New York, a major advertising agency, noted that this change has been making his firm's media buyers think of mass media in new ways:

> We have 12 major clients on our personal media network, tracking prospects by using syndicated and proprietary research. We are no longer thinking media form or media vehicles until we have tracked the target consumer. We no longer think of print vs. TV vs. radio but rather in terms of how can we combine vehicles to which the consumer is extremely loyal in some sensible consumer pattern and also come out that smaller might be better and more protective.[10]

Clearly, this approach rewards companies that can help marketers send ads to targeted consumers efficiently across several of their own media channels as well as across channels with which they have established strategic advertising partnerships. Picking up on this trend, the Time Magazines, Inc. division of Time Warner pioneered a technique of joining computer data bases about its magazines' suscribers to high-speed printing and binding technologies.

Using the data bases, the company can single out for an advertiser likely targets among the subscribers of *Time, Sports Illustrated, People, Money, Fortune*, and *Life*. It can then individualize the message of an ad to match the subscriber's interests or lifestyle. Finally, it can bind different individualized ads into the regular issue of the different magazines during the regular process of printing and mailing. To both Time Warner and interested advertisers, this activity is a good example of taking advantage of the synergies of different subscriber data bases in the service of advertising efficiency.

SYNERGY BEYOND ADVERTISING

As the 1990s have unfolded, marketers and mass media executives have moved their interest in synergy beyond the realm of advertising. They have contended that setting up vehicles for efficient advertising should be only one factor guiding approaches to synergy in mass media corporations. Just as important, they have said, is the need for mass media firms to guide their divisions toward serving many broad marketing needs of their clients.

The reason behind this broadened approach is a realization by mass media executives that marketers have begun to reevaluate their strategies to encourage sales. Advertising has long been king of the hill when it comes to marketing consumer products. Of secondary note have been various kinds of **promotion** and **direct marketing**.

Direct marketing involves contacting individual prospects by phone, computer, or mailed catalogs. A promotion is a specific act that calls attention to a firm or its products in ways other than advertising. Examples are such tactics as skywriting or underwriting sporting events (activities called **event marketing**), creating contests, giving free gifts (**premiums**), offering discounts, and even giving salespeople cash incentives to persuade stores to push the products on consumers.

Traditionally, companies marketing to the general public treated advertising funds as separate from, and more important than, promotion and direct marketing monies. In recent years, though, marketing executives in many firms have concluded that advertising should not automatically be given higher standing than other ways to reach potential customers.[11] One explanation for the changed attitude is the belief that modern data bases about customers allow implementation of promotion and direct-marketing efforts in ways that are more precise than advertising in traditional mass media.

In addition, some executives support promotion over advertising because they feel promotion holds greater credibility with the consumer. Marketers know that advertising calls attention to the fact that the marketer is trying to manipulate the consumer; people may resent that. Activities such as the support and underwriting of sporting events, on the other hand, may be evaluated favorably by target customers as indicating the firm's sincere interest in their lifestyles. The marketers believe that while promotions are more subtle than advertising, they can sometimes be more effective in creating good feelings about the marketer that may translate into long-term product purchases.

The increased emphasis on promotion and direct marketing, along with the decrease of advertising expenditures in some areas, has been leading executives in mass media conglomerates to work on ways in which they can profit from the trend. They have been asking two questions: How can we find synergies between our media holdings that can meet our firm's needs for promotion and direct marketing? And how can we find synergies between our media holdings that can encourage marketers outside our firm to approach us with their promotion and direct-marketing funds, in addition to their advertising funds? The executives have begun to find answers by exploring synergies that can result from two broad types of marketing activities they carry out: the sale of creative rights and the use of value-added incentives.

Creative Rights and Synergy

Creative rights involve the legal control that organizations exercise over characters, titles, and other original materials their personnel have generated in the course of creating mass media materials. The New Kids on the Block recording group owns the rights to its name and image, for example; anyone using it without permission (**a license**) can be sued. Children's Television Workshop controls the use of Big Bird, the name Sesame Street, and its **logo** (that is, the design that expresses the organization's name). Similarly, The Dow Jones Company owns the rights to news stories that appear in its *Wall Street Journal*, whether printed or carried electronically in computer data bases.

The licensing of creative rights allows a production firm to make money from its creations in forms that go beyond their initial purpose.[12] Executives in firms paying for the right to use the characters, titles, or logos expect a large benefit in return. They hope that the increased costs they incur for adding the images to their products will be more than made up by the instant recognition and interest the mass media images bring with them. The idea is that, for example, some parents would pay more for a pacifier with Big Bird's picture on it than one with designs that are unconnected to any personalities they know.

While the sale of creative rights often takes place with mass media materials that are used by children, adults have by no means been excluded. In the early 1990s, when Cher and Sheena Easton appeared in commercials for Bally's Health and Tennis Clubs, their images from films and records were the assets the advertiser was buying. Such assets can become big business in the adult realm. Think, for example, of publishers that sold film rights to books they published for millions of dollars. Think, too, of the several celebrities who have clothing and perfumes, even spaghetti sauces, named after them.

Despite such occasional bonanzas, creative rights were for decades considered to hold minor interest for the profit-making potential of mass media firms. Their relatively minor importance is reflected in the term by which they were called within media industries: **subsidiary rights**. The word *subsidiary* referred as much to the marginal place of these activities within the production firm as to the monetary value

TABLE 10.1   The Retail Value of Licensed Merchandise

Product Category	1989	1988	1987	1986	1985	1984	1983	1982	1981
Apparel and accessories	35.5%	35.0%	34.5%	34.6%	36.0%	38.0%	38.0%	38.0%	32.0%
Toys and games	12.0	13.0	14.0	15.5	17.0	19.0	20.0	19.0	23.5
Publishing/stationery	10.5	11.0	11.5	11.5	12.0	12.0	15.0	14.0	16.5
Gifts and novelties	10.0	10.0	9.0	9.0	9.0	11.0	13.0	10.0	10.0
Home furnishings/housewares	10.5	9.5	9.0	8.0	8.0	7.0	8.0	9.0	8.0
Sporting goods	3.0	3.0	3.0	3.0	2.0	2.0	3.0	5.0	5.0
Other	0.5	0.5	1.5	2.0	2.0	2.0	3.0	5.0	5.0
Foods and beverages	8.0	8.0	8.0	7.0	7.0	5.0			
Health and beauty aids	5.0	5.0	5.0	5.0	4.5	3.0			
Electronics	5.0	5.0	4.5	4.5	2.5	1.0			
Total dollar value retail (in billions)	**$64.6**	**$59.8**	**$55.9**	**$54.3**	**$50.1**	**$40.1**	**$26.7**	**$20.6**	**$13.7**

Tying into an image that has high mass media visibility is a key aim of licensing, which accounts for more that $60 billion in retail U.S. sales.

SOURCE: *Advertising Age*, Advertising Supplement on Licensing, May 28, 1990, p. L4.

of such rights. Creative rights activities were typically divorced from the larger strategic concerns of the firm. They involved merely arranging agreements with companies that wanted to use certain characters or logos for their own benefit. And they often were handled by a division of low status within the firm.

Times have changed. In an era of mass media conglomerates, companies have increasingly found that their rights to characters, plots, images, logos, and even news can be used synergistically to fuel lucrative activities throughout the entire firm. Product development teams can concentrate on images that are exploitable in different mass media by different divisions within the firm, or through strategic alliances with other companies. Here are some examples:

- Sony Corporation, which owns Sony Music (formerly called CBS Records), Columbia Pictures, and the Columbia House mail-order business, has been finding ways to make the three work together. Creative rights have been an important part of executives' thinking in that area. In 1991, for example, Sony signed recording artist Michael Jackson to a feature film that would be produced and released through Sony's Columbia Pictures. At the time, Jackson was a major moneymaker for Sony's CBS Records division. It undoubtedly made sense to Sony's management to try to maximize the cross-media nature of their relationship with Jackson in the interest of both the record division and the corporation as a whole. Columbia noted that other such crossover projects were in the works.[13]

- Mass media mogul Ted Turner has made linking creative rights from his various holdings a mandatory part of the work of his executives. In 1991, Turner Publishing and Citadel Press co-produced a book called *Kisses* as a St. Valentine's Day gift. The book included 150 pages of black-and-white photos from Turner Entertainment's MGM archive. At the time of its release, Turner's TNT cable channel aired a TV special tied to the book and its subject. The strategy was clear: The firm's film library inspired the book, and the firm's cable channel would help promote it. "Whereas a lot of big corporations talk about synergy," boasted the head of Turner Publishing, "at Turner synergy exists routinely."[14]

- Knight-Ridder, Inc. is best known to many Americans for its twenty-eight daily newspaper holdings, including *The Philadelphia Inquirer, The Detroit Free Press*, and *The Miami Herald*. During the 1980s, however, the firm drew on the information-gathering expertise its news divisions had developed to fuel its growth as a vendor of news-related data bases for businesses. Knight-Ridder's Business Information Services Group includes a variety of divisions that can easily draw on one another and on the firm's news operations. Especially notable are Dialog Information Services, the world's largest on-line and full-text information source; Vu/text, a data base that contains the full text of over fifty newspapers and more than twenty other publications; and Knight-Ridder Financial News, a worldwide, real-time news services delivered via computer to major participants in the financial market-place.[15]

- The Dow Jones Company, owner of *The Wall Street Journal*, the leading national business newspaper, and of *Barron's*, a business weekly, has also used its expertise in creating business news to enter the information marketplace. In 1980, the firm started its Information Services Group to coordinate the computerization and marketing of information that Dow thought it could sell. In 1990, the group merged its electronic libraries with those of Datatimes, a firm owned by Dow Jones and the Oklahoma Publishing Company. As a result, Dow Jones has been selling researchers the right to search electronically through the computerized files of 640 newspapers, magazines, news services, and financial data sources—its own and others.[16]

In all these examples, creative rights from particular divisions typically benefit other divisions within the conglomerate in addition to making profits on their own. A twist in this pattern that is common among entertainment conglomerates is to promote division activities even further through deals with outside marketers. The Disney Company's movement of its characters across a maze of both Disney-owned and non-Disney-owned products is a case in point. As described earlier, Disney's children's book division, video division, store division, and theme park division reinforce one another through extensive crossovers. Yet the company also promotes its own creations by leasing the creative rights for Mickey Mouse, Donald Duck, and other characters to clothing companies, food firms, and other manufacturers. Those companies, in turn, benefit from the cross-media exposures within the Disney conglomerate.

Another tactic that conglomerates such as Disney have been using to attract marketers to their cross-media promotion synergies is called **product placement**. That involves charging manufacturers for the use of their products as parts of the action in movies. In 1991, for instance, Disney was demanding $20,000 for a visual, $40,000 for a brand name mention with a visual, and $60,000 for an actor to use the product in one of its movies, *Mr. Destiny*.[17]

As this example suggests, most product placements are made in movies initially bound for the theaters. Still, manufacturers benefit from a movie conglomerate's synergies with its other divisions, since those movies later move through a number of the conglomerate's divisions, including home video, network television sales, and syndication. Manufacturers that link up with the films in this way often build their own ad campaigns and promotions around their product as it moves through the various media windows. They might even lease creative rights from the media firm to hype their product. Think of the presence of Teenage Mutant Ninja Turtles on Domino's Pizza boxes as a result of the Turtles' eating the food in their first live-action film.

Value-Added Incentives and Synergy

Apart from the exploitation of creative rights, executives in some mass media conglomerates have been moving toward a second broad way to find synergies in their holdings. That tack is called a **value-added incentive**. It means that a mass media outlet (a specific magazine, a particular radio station) promises a marketer extra inducements if it uses the outlet for advertising.

Talking Point 10.1   Licensing Hype

Licensing companies are constantly trying to sell their creative rights to toy manufacturers, clothing companies, sports equipment companies—anyone who will pay to put the licenser's name in a place that will help the image sell even more. The result is that hyperbole comes with the territory.

Imagine a license seller trying to peddle a client's image to a toy maker. Here, according to *Variety*, are licensing's "top ten hypes":

10. The days of just slapping a license on everything that moves are over.
9. They offered it to us first, but we decided to take a pass.
8. It's going to be bigger than *Batman*.
7. We don't want to overplay the merchandise at the expense of the programming.
6. We've turned down over 100 licensees already.
5. We're not just selling a product, we're selling an attitude.
4. It's similar to the Turtles, only better.
3. You don't have to hit a home run every time up. There's nothing wrong with singles and doubles.
2. We're only aligning ourselves with quality vendors.
1. You can fool parents and you can fool Wall Street, but you can't fool a child.

SOURCE: *Variety*, May 30, 1990, p. 41.

The specific kinds of incentives offered have been evolving during the past several years. While long-popular in radio (where DJs would plug products on and off the air), value-added inducements were considered shady and relegated to the margins of many mass media industries. For instance, segments of the business periodical press were known for a value-added practice that was not considered legitimate among most media practitioners. A publisher of a trade newspaper might promise an advertiser that if the firm bought ad space in a forthcoming issue, the newspaper would write a favorable article about the firm in the issue after that. Such activities, though not infrequent, were (and generally still are) considered unethical.

Since the late 1980s, however, the notion of a value-added incentive has taken on strong legitimacy and new meaning as executives in mass media conglomerates attract advertisers to individual outlets by offering benefits of synergies with other parts of the corporation. Much of this activity has been taking place in magazine divisions. A major reason is economic. In the early 1990s, many magazines were hit hard by declining advertising revenues.

One cause was the nation's economic recession, which affected the earnings of companies and lowered the amount they spent on advertising. Another cause was the declining attractiveness to advertisers of several types of periodicals (notably, the major women's magazines) because of declining newsstand sales. A third factor was the movement by advertisers of some funds away from magazines. The cash was used to support other mass media, such as cable TV, as well as promotion and direct-marketing work.

As the problems deepened, both marketing and magazine executives suggested that the companies responding most creatively to this situation were those that were going beyond their roles of selling space to advertisers in the issues of individual titles. They were working with the marketer to create inserts, publicity materials, point-of-purchase tie-ins to the ads, even videos, that would help tell the marketer's story in ways that would extend the advertising.

The activities sometimes encouraged magazine owners to develop mass media expertise beyond their periodicals. Meredith Publications, publisher of *Metropolitan Home*, provides a good example. In an attempt to work out a lucrative advertising deal with Kraft Foods, Meredith personnel suggested to Kraft personnel that they work together to create cookbooks and contests that would extend the message of the ads beyond individual issues. Similarly, in structuring a magazine advertising sale with the Sherwin-Williams paint company, Meredith became closely involved in an extensive promotion campaign for the firm's products. The marketing plan included in-store displays, books, and videos in addition to the magazine ads.[18]

Another example is a deal *Sports Illustrated* magazine announced with Diet Pepsi in 1990. Pepsi agreed to commit to two years of advertising in the magazine. In exchange, the magazine created an elaborate consumer promotion for Pepsi that would be highlighted in two midwinter 1991 issues. Called "Right Ones Fantasy Sports Vacation," it gave winners one of seven "fantasy vacations." Diet Pepsi paid for the trips while *Sports Illustrated*'s event marketing staff took care of all the logistics. As an additional link to the Sports Illustrated image, Pepsi agreed to sponsor a "Super Shape-Up" trilogy of fitness home videos that *Sports Illustrated* was creating for release by its Time Warner parent.[19]

Putting It All Together

Just how "synergistic" such linkups could get in the service of advertising, promotion, and direct marketing can be seen in a Time Warner deal with Chrysler Corporation that was much larger than the *Sports Illustrated*–Pepsi linkup. When it was announced in 1990, everyone in the marketing business seemed sure that the $40–$50 million contract was the largest of its kind to that point. The agreement, which was to extend for over two years, opened the door for the automaker to use all the media firm's divisions.

Creative rights and value-added incentives would be interconnected. The theme for Chrysler's 1992 campaign, "Rediscover America," would be tied subtly to the five-hundredth anniversary of Christopher Columbus's first voyage to the New World. The connection would be drawn through an elaborate cross-media marketing campaign using eleven **advertorials** (long ads with social points of view) inserted in five Time Warner magazines. In addition, the Time Magazines, Inc. division of Time Warner would create special issues of *Fortune, People,* and *Life* in which the automaker would be the only advertiser. Beyond using Time Warner's extensive magazine resources to get its ad messages out in these traditional and nontraditional ways, Chrysler also expected to target customers using the magazine division's selective binding and ink-jet printing technologies.

As incentives and premiums in this marketing effort, Chrysler would be using products from Time Warner's Warner Bros. Records, Time-Life Books, and Time-Life Videos divisions.[20] Going beyond that Columbus theme, Chrysler also said it would be using other Time Warner divisions to help it reach likely customers. Warner Brothers Television and another Time Warner division, Lorimar Productions, would develop TV programming for Chrysler to sponsor. Chrysler would place its cars for publicity purposes in Warner Bros. movies. And, to bring the Time Warner expertise directly to the showroom floor, Chrysler would use Time Warner Direct Marketing to aid in local dealer' sales efforts.

People within the advertising industry heralded the deal as signifying the future. A vice-president for the Ogilvy & Mather Worldwide ad agency argued that "joint marketing efforts with publications are just another type of nontraditional media activity we must get involved in because of the changing media environment, the changing society."[21] His counterpart at the Bozell agency agreed and suggested that mass media firms that took advantage of the synergies possible through cross-media ownerships and strategic partnerships would have distinct advantages. The challenge for mass media executives and marketing executives, he noted, was in finding the most effective synergies. "Integrated communications programs," he concluded, "are going to become much more of a factor in the 1990s and beyond."[22]

CHALLENGES FOR THE PUBLIC

"Integrated communication programs" and other new features of the mass media environment raise an important question for the society as a whole: How will these developments affect the news, information, and entertainment flowing through mainstream media channels as the world moves toward the next century? The answers are not clear yet. Nevertheless, examining the evolving media system with a critical eye on this question is important if members of the public are to understand the forces that are shaping the way they think about the world and act in it.

The final pages of this book are aimed at igniting speculation on this subject. There will be no attempt here to be inclusive, to cover every challenge to the public that mass media synergies may bring. Instead, a few issues will be raised briefly as

TABLE 10.2 Strategic Partnerships in Toyland

A small sampling of toys introduced at the 1991 American International Toy Fair suggests how closely toy makers are aligning themselves with partners in other entertainment media:

Toy Marketer	Product	Partner
Hasbro	*Bucky O'Hare* action figures	Syndicated TV series
	Dark Water action figures	Syndicated TV series
Mattel	*Where's Waldo* game and dolls	CBS-TV Saturday series
	Barbie doll fashions	Benetton, Reebok, McDonald's
Tyco	*National Enquirer* game	*National Enquirer*
	Little Mermaid dolls	Saturday TV series
Playmates	Toxic Crusaders	Saturday TV series

SOURCE: *Advertising Age*, February 18, 1991, p. 3.

examples of the kinds of concerns that ought to be discussed and investigated. Among these are conglomerates' control over the mainstream menus of choice; the changing relationship between marketing, news, and entertainment; and the gap between "knowledge rich" and "knowledge poor."

Conglomerates and Menus of Choice

When fragmentation of mass media due to the spread of cable TV and VCRs began in the 1970s, some observers hoped that the multitude of channels would offer a great number of options for unusual choices that challenge the boundaries of typical news and information offerings. Some optimists still hold out this hope. They now point to the new streams of information, news, and entertainment that fiber-optic, computer, and video disk technologies can bring into the home. And they insist that these technologies will force a diversity of voices to be presented to the great proportion of the population.

The suggestion to be made here is that this seems not to be the case. To the contrary, the way mass media systems have been developing in the United States, Europe, and Japan, it is likely that menus of choice will not be nearly as diverse as might first seem. The reasons are industrial, political, and economic. A counterforce to fragmentation has developed, and it is conglomeration.

Earlier in this chapter, an executive at Time Warner was quoted that his company "saw the world accommodating perhaps a half-dozen global media companies." The executive also noted that "bigness for bigness sake" did not interest Time Warner. Rather, what the firm wanted was "solid vertical integration so [it] could offer synergies that would bring together magazines, publishing ventures, studios, cable channels, and other activities into a coherent operation." Time Warner's aim, he added, was "to offer more than the Murdochs and Maxwells of the world."

Time Warner is not alone in voicing the expectation that six to ten mass media giants will develop by the turn of the century. By many accounts, the mainstream mass media channels in the United States and much of the world will be managed in one way or another by a small number of global firms acting to make the most of the synergies among their holdings.

Exactly what the consequences of this will be remains to be seen. However, by their actions Time Warner and other conglomerates have already indicated a number of probable consequences. One has to do with the range of choices that will be available across the most important TV stations, radio stations, newspapers, cable stations, video stores, and bookstores. Increasingly, these channels are becoming extensions of one another. VCR stores extend the reach of theatrical films; theatrical films extend the reach of books; music videos, on TV or on video cassette, extend the reach of CD and tape recordings—all in the interest of a conglomerate's synergy. The result is to offer not content diversity but **time-shifting capability**—that is, the capability to listen, read, or watch something at one time rather than another.

This does not mean that a few companies will "lock up" and determine *all* the choices that face individuals when they watch TV, read books, go to movies, or watch VCRs. In democratic capitalist societies there will always be room to start up "independent" firms with the aim of being heard. In an age of conglomerates, though, these firms, even while increasing in number, may well be pushed to the margins of their industries even more than before.

The reasons have to do with production costs and distribution clout. The large and mid-size conglomerates will be able to attract investments to create the materials they need to shape the synergies they want across media. Small companies that go with typical flow of content and make deals to link up with the conglomerates will make it into the mainstream as well. On the other hand, firms that steadfastly try to challenge the formulas of mainstream mass media will probably find it increasingly difficult to get anywhere near the busiest public outlets. People may well have to look hard to find their products, if they can find them at all.

Links Between Marketing, News, and Entertainment

Countering the potential diversity possible with channel fragmentation might be only one consequence of conglomerates' push toward synergies. The process seems, in addition, to be encouraging new, potentially problematic, links between marketing, news, and entertainment. Tendencies are at work that may be encouraging practices not acceptable to mass media workers just a few years ago.

As Chapter 4 noted, marketing needs have always shaped the kinds and amounts of news and entertainment available to different publics. If advertisers wanted to sponsor a TV news series, for example, it would be broadcast. If not, the company might not find the resources to air it. Stories have also long circulated about direct influences that marketers have had over the selection and display of particular news items. Powerful advertisers have, for example, occasionally used their power over newspaper publishers to get favorable mention or to exclude items that might harm them. Generally, though, such leverage has been considered disreputable. Over the decades, major mass media companies have made a public point of not allowing direct pressures from clients to influence the presentation of specific stories.

Similarly, journalistic organizations have long touted the creation of newswork as separate and distinct from the creation of entertainment. As noted in Chapter 1, both kinds of mass media work involve telling stories that cast up images of society for society. News executives, however, have always insisted that their creative personnel follow different rules than the creators of entertainment. Newspaper reports, broadcast documentaries, newsmaker interviews, and evening news spots are expected to stick to the facts in ways that fictional presentations do not. One reason news organizations have kept a distance from entertainment has been to assure the public that news holds a credibility regarding "the facts" that neither marketing nor entertainment have.

The rise of synergy-oriented conglomerates that carry both news and entertainment divisions under their umbrellas has raised the strong possibility that the long-standing tradition separating news from marketing and entertainment is in danger of breaking down. The mandate of synergy may be altering the norm that newsworkers separate their stories from the stories their advertisers tell. The cross-media deals that firms such as Time Warner and Meredith have formed with marketers such as Chrysler and Kraft seem to ignore a great number of questions about the relationship between sponsorship and editorial matter that in previous years would have raised powerful doubts in the minds of news professionals of the wisdom of making such connections.

How, for example, would *Time* editors and writers cover a story embarrassing to Chrysler or other automakers during the two years in which Chrysler was becoming identified with the newsmagazine and other Time Warner products? More to the point, what kind of credibility would any type of coverage of this sort have for the magazine when it would be clearly identified with Chrysler? Continuing on the subject of credibility, what is a media observer to think when an entire special issue of *Time* or *Fortune* or *Sports Illustrated* sponsored by one marketer reflects on subjects that are involved intimately with the marketers' products?

Even if no executives from the advertiser or its agency were involved directly with the articles, would not the creators of such custom-made issues tilt their stories to create an environment and perspectives that mesh with the marketer's desired image?

It may well be these questions *were* asked, and satisfactorily answered, by Time Warner and its advertisers. Perhaps they were answered less satisfactorily at Meredith, Hearst, or other magazine firms following the same strategy. At any rate, during this period of profound change within the mass media system, readers should demand public answers to these questions.

They should also ask questions when conglomerates appear to be dropping distinctions between news and entertainment in the interest of synergy. Here, again, Time Warner provides a good example because it has been so blatant in proclaiming its interest in using its various divisions for the good of the larger corporation. Careful observers of the media business noted that the Time merger with Warner had immediate impact on the flagship magazine's coverage: *Time* was highly favorable in its coverage of the controversial merger as it unfolded, and as Paramount Communications tried to derail it. When the merger was finally completed, at a huge debt to the merged corporation and lower profits to shareholders than otherwise might have been the case, the magazine's editors purposefully held back from reporting on it. The magazine's editors knew that word of the merger had leaked to *The Los Angeles Times*. Yet the editor-in-chief, after consulting with the business side of the firm, decided not to cover it. The excuse of *Time*'s editors was that since the word came close to deadline, they would not have been able to put a balanced story together for that week's edition. Others, however, felt that nervousness about reporting about their own company had much to do with the omission.[23]

This consequence of the merger hardly made a ripple in other media. A conflict of interest that did reach the public stage related to the handling of author Scott Turow and his hit books *Presumed Innocent* and *The Burden of Proof*. At the precise moment that Warner Books was releasing *Presumed Innocent* in paperback and a few months before Warner Bros. would release the film version of the narrative, *Time* magazine drew up a cover story on the author that trumpeted both the book and the film.

On the record and off, *Time* magazine executives have denied an interest in using their journalistic media to hype their entertainment products, in this or any other situation.[24] They point to a long tradition in the firm of separating the editorial process ("the church") from business and marketing ("the state"), a tradition that is stronger than that in any other magazine firm. Moreover, they argue that such activities might weaken their journalistic credibility over time.

The last argument might hold up if readers, viewers, and listeners really knew the bewildering maze of ownerships and relations that exist within the mass media system. It is unreasonable to expect that people will keep up on such links. As for the church–state separation blocking attempts on the part of other Time Warner divisions to use the magazines to hype their activities, that tradition may well make such conflicts less likely than in other firms. Nevertheless, conversations with writers and executives at the magazine suggest that the division is getting fuzzier as the Warner Communications entertainment culture begins to take hold.

One *Time* writer, for example, said that while he was sure from personal experience that the Scott Turow case was not orchestrated to help Warner Books and Warner Bros., he was convinced that conniving of this sort was going on. He pointed to a *Time* article about *Scarlett*, a big Warner Books sequel to *Gone With the Wind*. It had appeared far in advance of the book's release to the public. The purpose of the *Time* piece, he suggested, was to generate public interest in the manuscript so that the book company could make a lot of money selling the paperback and movie rights to other firms.

Whether this inference was correct or not, it indicates that even people within the magazine company feel these sorts of "church–state" violations are going on. It also suggests the confusion and concern that are felt even among people in the know, and even at one of the most highly respected journalistic firms. Most of the time, such concerns are not voiced outside the firm. In the Scott Turow incident, public discussion of *Time*'s conflict of interest was sparked by an article in *Time*'s rival, *Newsweek* magazine, that sniped at the act.

Newsweek's vigilance, however, may well have been a one-shot deal, peculiar to that point in time. It seems to have been written, half-jokingly, by a *Newsweek* staffer who had left *Time*. Moreover, it came as the advertising trade press was predicting *Newsweek*'s declining appeal to Madison Avenue. The reason was that the magazine's owner, The Washington Post Company, had nowhere near the cross-media property of *Time*'s parent. Observers speculated that *Newsweek* would not be able to compete with *Time*'s decision to offer deep discounts to clients who purchased advertising on several Time Warner properties at the same time. *Newsweek*'s instigation of the public controversy about *Time* might have been motivated partly by personal jealousy and corporate fear.

A few weeks after the incident, though, *Newsweek* signed a cross-media advertising agreement with the huge Times-Mirror conglomerate. Now it was in the orbit of a firm with major interests in synergies. As a result, *Newsweek* was potentially in a position that would inhibit its executives from making too much of a big deal in print about such things. In fact, as news–entertainment synergies within conglomerates become common, *Newsweek*'s chastisement of *Time* over Scott Turow may be seen as one of the last gasps of old values in an old system. Executives in mainstream mass media organizations may hold little interest in exposing the complex conflicts of interest over news and entertainment, since they might be involved in such activities themselves.

SOME FINAL QUESTIONS

The increasing ability of wealthy corporations to tinker with the mainstream menus of news and entertainment that people meet in their daily lives brings up a clutch of additional questions. For example:

How will the growth of data bases about target audiences affect the way mass media conglomerates create materials? Will the targeting of audiences and the fragmentation of mass media result in separation between the kinds of material that relatively poor and unattractive groups in society have access to compared with relatively well-off and attractive groups? If so, what will this increasing "information gap" mean about the different pictures people from the "preferred" and "unpreferred" parts of society have about each other and the rest of the world?

Will the mandate toward synergies within mass media conglomerates encourage or discourage unconventional thinking by creative personnel? To what extent will creators move freely across divisions, and if they do what will that mean for the materials they create?

How will new relationships between divisions within mass media conglomerates affect the way people are hired and trained by the conglomerates? As noted in Chapter 7, members of minority groups have often tended to be pigeonholed in certain segments of certain industries. In large record companies, for example, African-American executives have tended to be relegated to black music divisions. To what extent will the evolving conglomerates, searching for synergies across divisions, allow greater mobility of all types of employees across divisions? And how will that affect the kinds of mass media materials that the firms produce?

What consequences will the search for synergy have for conglomerates that have holdings in a variety of countries? Will the conglomerates try to link only those divisions that speak the same language? Or will they try to translate the materials that come from one division into the language of another? And if they do push their far-flung holdings toward translation, will that affect the kinds of materials those divisions generate and release to the public?

As for members of the public, how will the domination of mainstream media channels by six, ten, or fifteen huge corporations affect the influence that public advocacy groups have on mainstream media activities? What influence will government agencies have on corporations that often plan their cross-media activities from foreign countries? In general, what should U.S. policy be regarding the ownership of U.S. mass media companies? Federal regulations currently prohibit foreign firms from purchasing only broadcast properties. Should federal regulations also be sensitive to a conglomerate's country of origin when the firm is purchasing "culture-producing" operations in nonbroadcast industries?

Still more questions can be asked about the way the American mass media system is developing, or ought to develop. Other questions can be asked about mass media systems that are developing around the world. The challenges that face mass media executives when they search for the most lucrative synergies for their businesses are more than matched by challenges that members of the public face when they confront the results of these synergies. This book has aimed at providing a framework to see mass media systems in society with informed, wide-open eyes. Asking the right questions, providing the right challenges for yourself and others, is the first step toward making a real difference in the symbolic environment that surrounds us all.

NOTES

1. Christopher H. Sterling and John M. Kittross, *Stay Tuned* (Belmont, CA: 1990), p. 661.
2. "VCR Penetration reaches all-time high," *Variety*, February 28, 1990, p. 90.
3. See Wayne Walley, "Nets Force Nielsen Showdown," *Advertising Age*, September 24, 1990, p. 3.
4. For advertisers' views on TV during this period, see "The Upfront TV Season," a special insert in *Advertising Age*, May 28, 1990.
5. Quoted in "Corporate Planning," *Atari* 2:1 (1982), pp. 2–3.
6. Donald Elliman, Jr., "Trends, Synergy, and the Time Warner Merger." Talk at The Annenberg School for Communication, April 3, 1990, p. 17.
7. Scott Donaton, "Magazines Turn to Buddy System: Books Build Synergy, Ad Pages with Creative Hook-Ups," *Advertising Age*, November 26, 1990, p S-6.
8. Donaton, p. S-6.
9. John McManus and Janet Meyers, "TBS-Gannett Build Ad Package," *Advertising Age*, October 22, 1990, p. 1.
10. Quoted in Ira Teinowitz, "Bigger Not Always Better: Media Execs," *Advertising Age*, November 19, 1990, p. 25.
11. Teinowitz, p. 25.
12. See Larry Carlat, "New Kids Are a Chip off the Old Block," *Variety*, May 30, 1990, p. 42; and Larry Carlat, "How It Really Works," *Variety*, May 30, 1990, p. 41.
13. Richard Gold, "Singers Add Reelin' to Their Rockin'," *Variety*, November 26, 1990, p. 3.
14. William Stevenson, "Turner and Citadel Press Cut a Cuddly Deal With *Kisses*," *Variety*, January 21, 1991, p. 96.
15. Knight-Ridder 1990 Annual Report.
16. "Dow-Datatimes Deal," *New York Times*, July 4, 1990.
17. Marcy Magiera, "Madison Avenue Hits Hollywood," *Advertising Age*, December 10, 1990, p. 24.
18. "Value-added—the New Medium," *Advertising Age*, April 9, 1990, pp. S-36–37.
19. Scott Donaton and Patricia Winters, "Diet Pepsi Teams Up With SI," *Advertising Age*, April 9, 1990, p. 35.
20. Raymond Sarafin, "Chrysler Ups Ad Budget for Time Warner," *Advertising Age*, November 19, 1990, p. 16.
21. Quoted in "Value-added—the New Medium," p. S-36.
22. Quoted in "Value-added—the New Medium," p. S-36.
23. Connie Bruck, "Deal of the Year," *The New Yorker*, January 8, 1990, pp. 82–83.
24. *Time*, July 2, 1990, p. 8, and personal interviews. See also Bruck, p. 81.

Index

Broadcasting (*continued*)
67–69, 79, 111, 116, 127, 133–134, 136–139, 209, 212, 215–217, 221, 227, 228, 235, 237- 238, 253, 257
Brown, Les, 86
Burden of Proof, 254–256
Burger, Warren, 136
Burlusconi, Silvio, 215
Business Week, 227

Cable News Network (CNN), 68, 116, 209, 220, 243
Cable TV, 1, 2, 5, 6, 11, 14, 26–27, 36–38, 39, 40, 45, 68–70, 78–79, 89, 108, 110, 116, 133, 135, 136–139, 206, 209, 216, 217, 220, 227, 232, 235, 237, 238, 239, 241, 247, 249, 252
Cagney and Lacy, 203
Canal Plus, 232, 233
Cartoons, 60, 142, 201, 222, 235
Casting, 160, 174, 202–204
Catalogs, 44, 71, 118
Catholics, 55, 163
Cawelti, John, 194, 195
Caxton, William, 53
CBS, 1, 29, 36, 38, 39, 40, 41, 43, 44, 89, 90–92, 133, 134, 196, 206, 215, 219, 232, 237, 238, 247
Censorship, 66–67, 88, 136, 140–142, 146, 226
Center for Investigative Reporting, 46
Channel One, 118, 132–133
Chicago Tribune, 19–20
Chicken Soup, 203
Chrysler, 112, 250–51
Circulation, 28, 58, 60, 83–85, 99, 109, 111–114, 171, 206, 225
Citadel Press, 247
Citizen- licensee agreements, 138
Citizens for Decent Literature, 145
Clelland, Donald, 146
Click, J.W., 84
Client power role, 29, 47, 48, 55, 72, 74–81, 83–88, 89, 91, 93–95, 98, 101–102, 122, 125, 127, 145, 147, 189
CNBC, 243
Coalition for Better Television, 147
Colliers, 61
Columbia Journalism Review, 175
Columbia Pictures, 1, 155, 215, 220, 229, 240, 247
Comic books, 3, 160, 197, 235
Commercial clutter, 116
Commercial speech, 67, 142
Common carriers, 69
Community Information Project, 46
Compensating values (in movie industry), 144
Compugraphic, 30
Computers, 6, 31, 32 82, 104, 113, 115, 206, 237, 238
Concept testing, 109

Congress, 27–28, 40, 56, 62–63, 65, 70, 135, 138–139, 145, 186, 187
Constitution, 55–56, 72, 135–136, 154
Contact, 14, 43, 82, 191
Cop Rock, 203, 204, 206
Copyright, 28, 56, 63, 67, 219,
Coronet, 83–84
Cost per thousand (CPM), 84, 113–114
Counterprogramming, 90–91
Cowles Publishing, 115
Creative Artists Agency, 47
Creative rights, 241, 245–248
Creator power role, 31–32, 47, 49, 104, 148, 180, 189
Cross-media packages, 242
Cross-title packages, 242
Crossover audiences, 163
Cultural argumentation, 16

Daily Record, 155
Dark Justice, 232
Databases, 7, 115, 119, 121, 244, 246, 247–248
Day, Benjamin, 58–59
Days of Rage: The Young Palestinians, 124, 134
DDB Needham, 244
Del Rey Books, 41
Demographics, 114–116, 119,121, 132, 238
Denisoff, Serge, 44
Dentsu, 217
Denver Post, 155
Department of Commerce, 64
Descartes, 55
Designing Women, 203
Desk-top publishing, 12
Detroit Free Press, 247
Diaries (as marketing tool), 113
Die Hard, 161
Digital audio tape, 7–8, 219
Digital compact cassette, 7
Direct marketing, 43, 71, 116–119, 245, 249, 250–251
Direct response, 78
Directors, 17, 31, 47, 106, 143, 148, 156, 163, 196, 202, 203, 221
Disney, 36, 37, 75, 173, 215, 235–236, 241, 248
Disposable income, 114–115, 228
Distribution, 6, 10–12, 16, 19, 21, 23, 25, 31, 34–44, 64, 75–76, 155, 183, 212, 215–216, 222, 231, 232–233, 238–240, 253
Distributor power role, 29, 48, 107, 229
Donahue, George, 157
Doogie Howser, M.D., 203
Douglas, William O., 137
Dow Jones, 224, 248
Drive-in movie theaters, 41
Duck Tales, 235
Dutch, *see* Holland

Eastern Europe, 70, 225, 226
Editor and Publisher, 175